SHE,
THE
LEADER

SHE, THE LEADER

WOMEN IN INDIAN POLITICS

NIDHI SHARMA

ALEPH

ALEPH BOOK COMPANY
An independent publishing firm
promoted by *Rupa Publications India*

First published in India in 2023
by Aleph Book Company
7/16 Ansari Road, Daryaganj
New Delhi 110 002

ISBN: 978-93-93852-81-6

1 3 5 7 9 10 8 6 4 2

Printed in India.

To my parents,
Chandra Kala Sharma & Lieutenant Colonel K. L. Sharma (Retd.)
Who gave my dreams wings to fly

CONTENTS

INTRODUCTION

6 May 2008 was an eventful day in the Rajya Sabha. The Congress-led United Progressive Alliance (UPA) government, in the final lap of its five-year term, had listed the 108th Constitutional Amendment Bill, better known as the Women's Reservation Bill, for introduction. Presiding over the Rajya Sabha was a seasoned politician, an old Congress hand from Kerala—Deputy Chairman P. J. Kurien.

The government was expecting trouble and thus came prepared. After all, the Women's Reservation Bill had always been an emotive issue. The previous attempts in 1996, 1998, and 1999 to introduce the bill, which sought to reserve 33 per cent of seats in the parliament and state assemblies for women on a rotational basis, had always witnessed high drama in the parliament. Copies of the bill had been torn and tossed in the air and members of parliament (MPs) had made crass statements about 'undeserving' women.

There was a floor strategy in place. Law Minister Hans Raj Bharadwaj had to be physically cut off from all sides, guarded by a ring of women parliamentarians from the Congress, as he introduced the Women's Reservation Bill. The strategy was heavy with symbolism—the most vocal women parliamentarians guarding a male minister and ensuring the bill is introduced. Usually, the minister introducing legislation in parliament is seated in the first row of seats. Bharadwaj sat in the middle row so protesting MPs could not approach him and try to snatch the copies of the bill from him. He sat between two cabinet colleagues—Ambika Soni and Kumari Selja. The approach from the aisle to his seat was guarded by the fiery women along with the minister of women and child development, Renuka Chowdhury, a no-nonsense Jayanthi Natarajan, and the Congress MP from Gujarat, Alka Balram Kshatriya. The strength of this women-led retinue around Bharadwaj was amply tested as he rose to speak.

In a dramatic motion, Samajwadi Party MP Abu Asim Azmi crossed the floor and lunged forward to snatch a copy of the bill from Bharadwaj's hands to tear it. Moving with alacrity, Chowdhury physically blocked him and a scuffle followed soon after. In the commotion, Bharadwaj introduced the bill, which was referred to a parliamentary committee for further examination. Sensing further trouble, Kurien promptly adjourned the house. Congress had scored a moral victory—unlike the previous governments it had introduced the bill in the Rajya Sabha and not the Lok Sabha, so the legislation wouldn't lapse with the end of a Lok Sabha term.

Almost two years later, buoyed by a convincing people's mandate in the 2009 parliamentary elections, UPA-II passed the controversial bill in Rajya Sabha on 9 March 2010 despite opposition from its allies—the Samajwadi Party (SP) and Rashtriya Janata Dal (RJD). Even then, Rajya Sabha Chairman Hamid Ansari bore the brunt of protesting members. Samajwadi Party MP Nand Kishore Yadav tried to climb Ansari's desk. Yadav was deftly prevented by an alert marshal. RJD MP Subhash Yadav attempted to uproot the microphones and pen stands from the shocked chairman's podium. Samajwadi Party MP Kamal Akhtar climbed on to the long reporters' desk in front of the chairman's podium occupied by parliamentary staff taking copious notes and waved his hands in the air. The bill was passed after seven MPs belonging to SP, Janata Dal-United, RJD, and the Lok Janshakti Party were suspended and then physically removed by marshals. The media-shy Congress President Sonia Gandhi gave a rare interview celebrating this occasion in which she expressed surprise that allies like the Mamata Banerjee-led Trinamool Congress had abstained from voting on the bill even when they were excited during a cabinet briefing on the issue before the passage of the bill in Rajya Sabha.

The UPA, however, never found the political will to see the reform through—the bill was not introduced in the Lok Sabha by the UPA. Despite including it in the 2014 and 2019 election manifestos, two successive Bharatiya Janata Party governments led by Narendra Modi have not introduced the bill.

⌣

There are eighty-two women members of parliament in the seventeenth Lok Sabha (2019–24)—the highest ever in independent India. When you break down this statistic further, the fine print is dismal. Women constitute barely 15 per cent of the strength of the Lok Sabha today. In the first general elections held in India in 1952, twenty-four women were elected to the parliament—constituting about 4.4 per cent of the total strength of the first Lok Sabha. An optimist can draw succour from this three-fold increase in women's representation in sixty-seven years of India's parliamentary election history, but the fact remains that India's highest decision-making body is not truly representative of Indian society, where, according to the latest National Family Health Survey, there are 1,020 women for every 1,000 men India[1]. In 1951, merely 2 per cent of the United States of America's House of Representatives and 3 per cent of the United Kingdom's House of Commons was women. In 2022, the representation has gone upto 28.3 per cent in the US and 34.61 per cent in the UK.

The World Economic Forum's Global Gender Gap Index 2022 shows India's poor record on women's representation. India is ranked forty-eighth among 146 countries on the political empowerment sub-index, behind Bangladesh (which is ranked ninth). It is a shade better than the position it occupied on the sub-index in 2021, but compared to previous years, India has fallen from eighteenth in 2020 to fifty-one in 2022.

After the results of the first elections, Jawaharlal Nehru had written to his chief ministers on 18 May 1952:[2]

I have noticed with great regret how few women have been elected. I suppose this is so in the state assemblies and councils also. It is not a matter of showing favour to anyone or even injustice, but rather of doing something which is not conducive to the future growth of the country.

I am quite sure our real growth will only come when women have a full chance to play their part in public life.

Nehru's cabinet in 1952 had one woman leader—Health Minister Rajkumari Amrit Kumar. In 2023, Prime Minister Narendra Modi's cabinet has two women leaders—Finance Minister Nirmala Sitharaman and Women and Child Development Minister Smriti Z. Irani.

Nehru's letter is reflective of how leaders of independent India had expected the natural forces of democracy to throw up women leaders. After all, women had fought shoulder-to-shoulder with men against British rule, sometimes even outpacing the men in spearheading Mahatma Gandhi's call to come out of purdah and give up societal inhibitions. Till then, women had been the object of reforms and not leaders of reforms. The Swadeshi Movement, which called for the boycott of imported British products and use of Indian goods, hinged on the participation of women. Women burnt their saris made from English cloth, refused to wear glass bangles or make-up coming from England, declined to give angrezi-dawa to their sick children, and took to spinning khadi on charkhas at home. Swadeshi Movement became a cradle for women's movement in India pushing ahead educated and emancipated women like Sarojini Naidu, Sarla Devi Chaudharani, Vijaya Lakshmi Pandit, Annie Besant, Swarna Kumari Devi, Tai Ketkar, and Bhikaji Rustom Cama. Most women leaders came from eminent families, which had emphasized on education and had at least one male member closely involved in the freedom struggle. These women leaders became inspiring examples for other women from lower middle-class and middle-class families to shun purdah and come out for small meetings organized against British subjugation.

Mahatma Gandhi felt India's freedom movement could not be driven by one half of the population while ignoring the other half. By involving women, he gave them their rightful place, next to men, as equals—a right they had been denied for centuries by the orthodox Indian society. 'Woman is the companion of man gifted with equal mental capacities. She has the right to participate in the minutest details of the activities of man and she has the same right of freedom and liberty as he.... By sheer force of a vicious custom, even the most ignorant and worthless men have been enjoying a superiority over women which they do not deserve and ought not to have,' Gandhi wrote in *Young India*, on 26 February 1918. When he asked them to embrace khadi, he made charkha a symbol of economic empowerment for the women. 'It is for the women of India, a large number of whom do not get even an anna per day that I am going about the country with my spinning wheel and my begging bowl,' he wrote in an article in *Young India* on 10 February 1927. The Non-cooperation Movement (1920–22) and the Civil Disobedience Movement (1930) saw women responding to the Mahatma's call to actively participate in the movement. The arrest of thousands of women, including Sarojini Naidu, who participated in the twenty-four-day Dandi March, inspired a wave of patriotism amongst women. They came out of their homes, defied set social norms, challenged the British, braved lathicharges, and filled prisons. This laid the foundation of the women's movement in India and spawned several organizations that campaigned for working women's rights and voting rights, and fought against social evils in independent India.

THE WOMEN'S MOVEMENT

The women freedom fighters organized themselves locally and addressed issues such as the welfare of widows, child marriage, purdah, and financial independence at the grassroots level. The earliest pan-India women's organization was the All India Women's Conference (AIWC), founded in 1927 by the Indian-Irish educationist and suffragette Margaret Cousins, which became the largest such organization in pre-independent India. It drew women from across India and brought forth women leaders who went on to shape several movements through their campaigns against social evils. Eminent women such as

Sarojini Naidu, Annie Besant, Kamaladevi Chattopadhyay, Sarla Devi Chaudharani, Anusuya Kale, Hansa Mehta, Aruna Asaf Ali, Muthulakshmi Reddy, Hajra Begum, Perin Ramesh Chandra, and Renu Chakravartty were associated with the AIWC. These women fought for the voting rights of women, the universalization of the law of inheritance, and for fixing the legal marriageable age for girls in pre-independent India. They were instrumental in shaping the politics in the early years of the women's movement in India as they ran schools and campaigned for social change fearlessly.

When India was inadvertently drawn into World War II, women's rights activists led the raksha samitis and mahila sangams that addressed the Bengal Famine and other social problems that emerged after Japanese aggression. Rice production in Bengal was affected after the Japanese bombing of Calcutta in December 1942 and the occupation of Rangoon in March 1942. There was a mass exodus as people from villages and towns fled to safer places. This further affected rice production and Bengal plunged deeper into a food crisis. Women activists organized themselves into the Mahila Atma Raksha Samiti (MARS) in Bengal. Within months, MARS had twenty-six branches across Bengal and was actively carrying out famine relief work. These are some of the earliest examples of organized political activism by women in modern India. Gargi Chakravartty and Supriya Chotani have chronicled the biggest demonstration by women in *Charting a New Path: Early Years of National Federation of Indian Women*:

> One of the biggest demonstrations took place on March 17, 1943, when 5,000 women from the slums and suburbs of Calcutta marched to the Assembly to protest against the rise in prices, demanding more ration shops (only 50 such shops existed in the city then) and an end to violence against women in queues for ration shops... As an immediate response, the chief minister, Fazul Haq, ordered the distribution of 100 bags of rice. Later, eight new shops were opened in Calcutta, of which six were for women.

MARS also organized hunger marches in the districts to the Magistrate office and on most occasions, women were able to secure some concessions from the administration.[3]

MARS brought together women from across ideologies and they contributed to the relief effort in Bengal in several ways—from organizing famine relief work to opening clinics to treating patients of cholera, malaria, and oedema. The emergence of women leaders and women-led organizations in Bengal inspired similar efforts in, what are today, the modern-day states of Andhra Pradesh, Punjab, Manipur, Delhi, Kerala, and Telangana.

India's protracted struggle against the British is embellished with inspiring vignettes of women leaders who fought against colonial oppressions and feudal systems—Bhikaji Cama, who was imprisoned for hoisting the Indian flag on foreign land in 1907; Godavari Parulekar or Godutai, who organized Adivasis in what is known as the Warli Revolt in 1945; Lakshmi Sehgal, who persuaded Subhas Chandra Bose to institute a women's regiment of Indian National Army and then commanded it in 1943; Matangini Hazra or Gandhi Buri, who kept the tricolour aloft as she fell to the bullets of the British crying out 'Vande Mataram' in 1942.

LAYING THE FOUNDATION OF YOUNG INDIA

The idea of equality was engrained in the women of newly-independent India. As the framers of our Constitution debated the need for affirmative action for political empowerment of the socially and economically backward classes, women did not demand any reservation for themselves. It went against their ideals of social and political justice. The Constituent Assembly, which framed the Constitution of India, originally had 15 women out of a total of 389 members. The debates of the Constituent Assembly reflect how its women members vociferously opposed any form of reservation. While discussing inclusion of the principle of equality in the Constitution on 19

December 1946 in the Constituent Assembly, Hansa Mehta said:

> Mahatma Gandhi's name has been invoked on the floor
> of this House. It would be ingratitude on my part if I do
> not acknowledge the great debt of gratitude that Indian
> women owe to Mahatma Gandhi for all that he has done
> for them. In spite of all these, we have never asked for
> privileges. The women's organization to which I have the
> honour to belong has never asked for reserved seats, for
> quotas, or for separate electorates. What we have asked for
> is social justice, economic justice, and political justice. We
> have asked for that equality which can alone be the basis
> of mutual respect and understanding and without which
> real co-operation is not possible between man and woman.
> Women form one half of the population of this country
> and, therefore, men cannot go very far without the co-
> operation of women. This ancient land cannot attain its
> rightful place, its honoured place in this world without the
> co-operation of women....[4]

Dakshayani Velayudan, the only Dalit woman member of the
Constituent Assembly, also opposed reservation while debating
separate electorates for the Scheduled Castes community on 28
August 1947. She said:

> Personally speaking, I am not in favour of any kind of
> reservation in any place whatsoever. Unfortunately, we had
> to accept all these things because the British Imperialism
> has left some marks on us and we are always feeling afraid
> of one another. So, we cannot do away with separate
> electorates. This joint electorate and reservation of seats
> also is a kind of separate electorates. But we have to put up
> with that evil because we think that it is a necessary evil.[5]

The women members stood for equality and did not want any
segregation for themselves. While speaking on the adoption of
national flag in the Constituent Assembly on 11 December 1946,
Sarojini Naidu said:

But if I am speaking here today, it is not on behalf of any community, or any creed or any sex, though women members of this House are very insistent that a woman should speak. I think that the time has come in the onward march of the world-civilization when there should be no longer any sex consciousness or sex separation in the service of the country.[6]

There is only one reference to the reservation of seats for women in the Constituent Assembly debates. Purnima Banerji, a member, said that if a vacancy arises for a seat occupied by a woman in the Constituent Assembly, it should be filled by a woman. Before even making this point, she said she did not stand for the reservation of seats for women. On 11 October 1949, Banerji said:

I wish to make it quite clear that women do not want any reserved seats for themselves, but nevertheless, I suggest to the House that in respect of the number of women who are now occupying seats in the Assembly, if any of them should vacate their seats they should be filled up by women themselves. We have had casual vacancies in this House before this. Three women have retired so far...all these three women have been replaced by men members... Since the entire basis of the State has changed and it is no longer a police state, certain social functions such as education and health now feature among the major items of the State's development. I feel, that not only is the association of women in the field of politics essential but it is indispensable, and therefore I feel that this indispensable section of the people should be amply represented in this House and therefore my amendment proposes that in the casual vacancies which will occur women should at least be returned to the seats which they hold today, if not more....[7]

Over the years, women leaders were elected and accepted in positions of power—Vijaya Lakshmi Pandit joined the

diplomatic services to become independent India's first
ambassador to the Soviet Union, Rajkumari Amrit Kaur was the
first health minister of India and is credited with establishing the
prestigious All India Institute of Medical Sciences, Sarojini Naidu
was the first woman governor in India, Tarkeshwari Sinha was
India's first woman deputy finance minister, Sucheta Kripalani
became India's first woman chief minister, and Indira Gandhi
the first and only woman prime minister. These women leaders,
however, remained aberrations—mere exceptions and not the
rule. Politics remained the preserve of women hailing from
aristocratic or political families.

THE EVOLUTION OF RESERVATION

During the 1970s, women's rights activists changed their stance
on the participation of women in politics. The initial euphoria
after Independence had worn off and a disillusionment with
politics had crept in. Women leaders felt that the political parties
reflected the same biases women experienced in the society. In
1970, the United Nations declared 1975 as the International
Year of Women. It sought a report from all countries on 'The
Status of Women'. The ministry of education and social welfare
constituted a ten-member committee on 22 September 1971.[8] To
date, this report remains the most exhaustive work on the status
of women in India. The report was the first formal document
to acknowledge the need for women's political representation,
especially at the grassroots level. 'There is a general consensus
that political parties have neglected their talk of politically
educating and mobilizing women adequately. They have also
tended to ignore the claims of women in nominating candidates
for elections. This criticism was even voiced by successful women
candidates,' the report observed.[9] 'Majority of the women
candidates come from relatively well-to-do families, with a
sprinkling of members of old princely states. Only one party has
occasionally backed women candidates from Scheduled Castes
or Tribes and Muslims. Majority of the women candidates are

educated, though their levels vary. About 70-80% of the women members of Parliament are, however, relatively better educated,' the report summed up.[10]

During its interactions, the committee received several representations on the need for introduction of reservations in elected bodies. The committee recorded these demands as:

> The difficulties being experienced by women in obtaining adequate representation and spokesmen of their cause in these bodies, and the declining trend in the number of women legislations is the result of the reluctance of political parties to sponsor women candidates. The parties reflect the established values of a male-dominated society, which would be difficult to alter without certain structural changes in the socio-political set up. The parties would continue to pay lip service to the cause of women's progress and the policy of 'tokenism' by having a few women in the legislative and executive wings of government whose minority and dependent status offer serious obstacles of their acting as spokesmen for women's rights and opportunities.... A system of reservation of a proportion of seats for women in these bodies would provide an impetus to both the women as well as to the political parties to give a fairer deal to nearly half the population in the various units of government. [11]

The political parties and elected women legislators, however, felt 'that any system of special representation would be a retrograde step from the equality conferred by the Constitution'. The committee recommended establishment of statutory women's panchayats at the village level to ensure greater participation by women in the political process. 'These bodies are not meant to be parallel organizations to the gram panchayats but should form an integral part of the panchayati raj structure, with autonomy and resources of their own for the management and administration of welfare and development programmes for women and children. At the level of municipalities, the principle of reservation of seats for women is already prevalent in certain states. We therefore recommend that this should be adopted by all states as a transitional measure,' recommended the report. It was submitted on 31 December 1974 to the minister of education and social welfare, S. Nurul Hasan. This was the first recommendation of reservation for women by a government committee. The recommendation was distinctly different from the token measure of nominating women members as was recommended by the B. R. Mehta committee in 1957.[12]

The 1980s brought further clarity on inclusion of women in political machinery and the government's policymaking. In 1983, the Janata government in Karnataka under Ramkrishna Hegde became the first state to introduce 25 per cent reservation for women in panchayati raj institutions. With the support of his Rural Development and Panchayati Raj Minister Nazir Saab, Hegde managed to address all scepticism and roll out the initiative. Retired IAS officer T. R. Raghunandan, who was closely involved in conducting the first elections in Karnataka, says:

> I had the privilege of conducting the first elections in Karnataka in December 1986 under the new Act with reservations in place. I was touched by the remarkable participation in those elections. Later in early 1988, a huge rally of these elected members—there were about 14,000 or so—was organized in Bengaluru. I saw busloads of women coming, particularly tribal women from North Karnataka. They had never probably stepped into a bus in their lives. They were very confident. First of all the myth that not enough women will be found was laid to rest. Secondly, there was a huge demonstrative effect.[13]

The successful experiment in Karnataka paved the way for a national rollout.

The National Perspective Plan for Women (1988–2000) supported a 30 per cent reservation for women—this was the first government document which set the quantum for women's reservation at one-third. It recommended:

Reservation should be made of 30 per cent seats at panchayat to zilla parishad level and local municipal bodies for women. Wherever possible, higher representation of dalits/tribals, women of weaker sections should be ensured. 30 per cent of executive heads of all bodies from village *panchayat* to district level and a certain percentage of chief executives of *panchayati raj* bodies at lower, middle and higher levels must be reserved for women.[14]

In 1988, Prime Minister Rajiv Gandhi decided that Panchayati raj institutions should be constitutionally recognized and women's reservation should be introduced. But there was stiff political opposition to the move. Mani Shankar Aiyar, former rural development minister and a trusted aide of Rajiv Gandhi, recalls a meeting he had with Agriculture Minister Bhajan Lal[15] (at that time rural development was not a separate ministry and came under the agriculture ministry):

> I was joint secretary in Prime Minister's Office when Rajiv Gandhi was Prime Minister. In me, he found a sympathetic proponent of Panchayati Raj and women's reservation. When the constitutional amendment was being drafted, agriculture minister Bhajan Lal came and said to me, 'All this is fine but where will we find such women and so many of them?' This is what most people were wondering then. But I said to him, 'Koshish toh karein (Let's at least try)'. And it worked![16]

Aiyar says his confidence in the local self-government model came from his experience as a foreign diplomat posted in Belgium. 'I was posted for seven years in Belgium. In Brussels, I saw how the nineteen municipalities in the capital with a population of under one million handled governance. Each municipality had its own passport office, its own constabulary. It was not only representative democracy but also participatory democracy,' he says.

Aiyar recounts an incident with then Arunachal Pradesh Chief Minister Gegong Apang, who had insisted that the

Northeastern state be included in panchayati raj system instead
of the traditional tribal councils of a Schedule VI area state.
'But when Apang discovered that there would be 30 per cent
reservation for women (tending towards 33 per cent later), he
met me at my home and thundered—he spoke as if he were
addressing a gathering of thousand people when he was just
addressing just me in the room—he said, "If you force us to have
women's reservation, we will go join China!" This is how stiff
the opposition was,' recounts Aiyar. In 1989, the Constitution
(64th Amendment) Bill was introduced in parliament. Congress
did not have a majority in the Rajya Sabha and suspicious
Opposition parties blocked the bill. This was again introduced
under the V. P. Singh government in 1989 but due to instability
at the centre this attempt was not successful. Finally, the 73rd
and 74th constitutional amendments were passed in 1992 when
a Congress government came to power under P. V. Narasimha
Rao, after the assassination of its chief architect Rajiv Gandhi.

Over 14 lakh women have been elected to Panchayati raj
institutions over the years. There has been a critique of the
system with anecdotal examples of male relatives of the elected
woman representatives usurping the power. But over the years,
it has created a bank of talent for political parties. One would
have expected a natural progression of these women from the
panchayats to the legislative assemblies and parliament, but such
institutions remain male-dominated.

WHAT WOMEN WANT

This brings us to a basic question—why are more women
representatives required in legislative bodies and parliament?
Can't educated modern men represent the interests of women?
Renuka Chowdhury, India's first woman and child development
minister, underlines the intrinsic difference between the decision-
making of men and women. She recalls how, when the men
and women of a village were asked what time they wanted the
bus service to their village to run, women based their decision

over the school timings of their children, whereas men wanted the service to run according to the closing time of the theka (liquor shop) in the nearby village. Women kept the welfare of the family in mind while the men put their personal needs first. In the larger context of a village and probably an assembly constituency, a woman representative may be more inclined to improve education and health parameters. 'Sometimes I have asked the women and men in villages—if you want a road in your village what would you want connected? Almost always, women will want to connect places of worship and schools with their village. Men want cities to be connected. Women think of welfare,' says Chowdhury.[17]

The introduction of women's reservation in Panchayati raj institutions gave a natural fillip to the demand for a similar initiative in the parliament and in legislative assemblies. Chowdhury, an outspoken votary and known for taking on male parliamentarians on their sexist remarks, recalls the scepticism against this move: 'The first attempt to push the Women's Reservation Bill was made in 1996. I remember a delegation of women MPs was going to Lok Sabha Speaker P. A. Sangma to request him to allow the bill at the earliest when an old Haryana MP called out to me, "Chowdhury sab milke kahan ja rahi ho (Chowdhury, where are all you women MPs going together)?" When I told him that we were pushing for bringing the bill ensuring 33 per cent reservation for women, the shocked MP said, "Itni mahila yahan parliament aayengi toh ghar pe roti kaun banaayega (If so many women come here to parliament, who will cook at home)?" I shot back, "Aap subsidy dete hain na Modern Bread ko, kha lena double roti (Don't you subsidize Modern Bread? Then eat bread)." This was the attitude of male MPs towards the bill. They thought that they were giving up something that was rightfully theirs for us,' says Chowdhury.

The United Front government under Prime Minister H. D. Deve Gowda introduced the Constitution (81st Amendment) Bill, 1996, which proposed 33 per cent reservation for women in parliament. The bill could not be passed and was referred to the joint select committee. Since it was introduced in Lok Sabha, the bill lapsed on the dissolution of the Eleventh Lok Sabha in 1998. Later that year, Prime Minister Atal Bihari Vajpayee's government introduced the Constitutional (84th Amendment) Bill, which also lapsed when his government fell in 1999. However, in his third stint in 1999, Vajpayee again made another attempt to pass the bill. The Constitution (84th Amendment) Bill was reintroduced in 1999, but it lapsed once the Lok Sabha term ended in 2004. There was a renewed attempt by the Congress-led United Progressive Alliance (UPA) in 2008 when it introduced the Constitution (108th Amendment) Bill. Chowdhury remembers the intra-party discussions before the introduction of the bill: 'Mrs Gandhi (UPA chairperson Sonia Gandhi) was clear—every time the bill is introduced it lapses with the term of the Lok Sabha. She said the government should introduce it in Rajya Sabha so the bill doesn't lapse with the Lok Sabha term ending. Honestly, the bill was tabled because it had the support of Mrs Gandhi. Right before the introduction, we would sit in Central Hall and hear murmurs of how parties will disrupt the proceedings. A clear strategy was charted before the introduction to physically protect the law minister.' If one sees the political line toed by MPs from different parties during parliamentary debates, there is no overt opposition to the bill. Barring the Janata Dal (United) and Samajwadi Party, none of the parties have expressed any reservations. Political parties from the Hindi heartland have demanded, what is popularly now known as, 'quota within quota'—there should be reservation within this 33 per cent reservation for women from socially and economically backward classes.

WOMEN AS A CONSTITUENCY

Even as India's lawmakers have repeatedly put the legislation on the back-burner, the reality on ground is changing silently but surely. Over the last decade, women have emerged as an electoral force participating more enthusiastically than men. Sanjay Kumar, political analyst and professor at the Centre for the Study of Developing Societies (CSDS) who has been closely tracking this change, says, 'It happened for the first time in the Bihar 2015 assembly elections. We noticed women voter turnout was 3 per cent higher than the men voters. Since then the trend has continued. It travelled to different states. In 2020, Bihar assembly elections, the gender gap in voter turnout increased to 7 per cent in favour of women. Now there are fifteen to sixteen states where women turnout is higher than men turnout. We have noticed this is happening in assembly and Lok Sabha elections.... There are some states where the gender gap in voter turnout is in favour of men, but even in these states, the gap has narrowed down over the last two assembly elections. Gujarat has the widest gap in favour of men voters. Bihar, Himachal Pradesh, Uttarakhand are at the top.'[18]

The studies have reflected another change—women have started taking their voting decisions independently. CSDS, which includes this question in every election survey now, has found that the ground is shifting. 'The proportion of women who take their independent voting decision has increased over the last one and a half decade. By 2004 Lok Sabha we noticed that roughly 30 per cent women used to take their independent voting decision and the remaining used to consult the male members. The male members could be son, husband, or father. Gradually, the proportion of women who have started taking independent decisions has gone up. If I look at 2019 data it is roughly in the range of 55 per cent to 56 per cent. More than half the women are taking their independent voting decision. Now, you may say how do we come to this data? It is a claim by the women voters. We have no way to figure out whether it is really happening. But the women have themselves declared this. This is a big change. The reason for this big change is largely because of the penetration of social media not education. We might think education is playing a big role but not that much. More than education it is exposure to social media. This is what has contributed to higher women voter turnout in various elections,' says Kumar.[19]

Women are now a constituency. This realization has had a direct impact on how political parties shape their campaigns. Kumar says, 'The political parties are realizing that it is a trend and it is not episodic. In every state, women voters are easily 48–49 per cent of the total voters. If a party gets an advantage of 4–5 per cent in this votebank, it can make a huge difference. This trend will not reverse now.' Sanjay Kumar's favourite opening for his lectures is a question thrown at his audience—which state do you think has the most number of women legislators? Almost always, people answer Kerala. Researchers, journalists, students, and sometimes lawmakers themselves make the common mistake of assuming that literacy rates are inherently linked to increased women's representation. Interestingly, it is Bihar that has the most number of women legislators. It is to do with Bihar Chief Minister Nitish Kumar's policy of giving at least 40 per cent tickets to women candidates—a similar initiative has been taken in West Bengal by Chief Minister Mamata Banerjee and in Odisha by Naveen Patnaik. There has been a domino effect. Other political parties like the Congress have also followed. In the Uttar Pradesh assembly elections held in 2022, Congress centered its campaign on 'Ladki Hoon, Lad Sakti Hoon (I am a Girl, I can fight)'. Priyanka Gandhi Vadra, the general secretary of the All India Congress Committee and incharge of Uttar Pradesh, ensured 40 per cent tickets for women in the state elections. But then, as the naysayers point out, the Congress could afford to do this in Uttar Pradesh but not in Punjab (where elections took place at the same time) because the party has no real stakes in the political fight. Women's participation in electoral politics is a double-edged sword—on the one hand it can trigger an attitude change but on the other a defeat can be deciphered as the incompetence of women candidates. The debate on giving more tickets or reserving seats for women comes down to a single word—winnability. Sachin Pilot, the former state unit president of the Congress in Rajasthan, says, 'When we screen candidates, winnability supercedes everything. Once our hands are forced through a legislation, then all parties will have to find candidates. It will be a level playing field. When a seat is reserved for an SC candidate, all parties have to find an SC candidate. It should be the same for women candidates. It is an idea whose time has come.'

⌁

Fighting social inequalities and patriarchal politics, women leaders have managed to create their own brand of politics in the national discourse. This book profiles seventeen women politicians who have been trailblazers in their own right. The book is divided into four parts. The book begins with 'The Pioneers', which focuses on two exemplary women leaders of the twentieth century and their distinctly different political paths— Indira Gandhi and Sucheta Kripalani. Second, 'The Inheritors' reflects on the achievements of the women leaders who inherited their political careers from a male member of the family or a political benefactor. The third section, 'The Lone Warriors', features women who had no political background, chose politics as their vocation and charted their own course without anyone backing them. The final section—'The Future Leaders'—profiles women leaders to watch out for. There is a common thread that runs through all of these profiles—almost all have fought and won popular elections, nurtured constituencies, and have created their own unique political legacy. In choosing these women politicians over others, the parameters have ranged from a fair representation of political parties, regions, and their contributions to governance and policy-making. I have made an attempt to profile them not only as politicians but also as women who face everyday challenges like managing homes, keeping odd hours, and addressing work-related disappointments.

I

The Pioneers

INDIRA GANDHI

The Woman Who Shaped Indian Politics

The five-year-old girl was her grandfather's darling, accompanying him everywhere. She had sat on his lap in a courtroom when he was being tried for an act of civil disobedience during the royal visit of the Prince of Wales in 1921. Today, just about a year later, she was going along to meet her grandfather's friend and colleague Deshbandhu Chittaranjan Das of Bengal, who was visiting Allahabad. Her Dadu had forgotten whether Das's grandchild was a boy or girl and decided to take a doll for the child. Dadu gave it to the little boy who was about two years younger to her. She didn't like it and snatched it away. Within minutes, the two were fighting over the doll. She took the head, the boy was left with one of the legs, and the body disappeared. Her determination to not allow the boy to have the doll was evident. 'It was also indicative of her fierce possessiveness. She would fight like a tigress for what she thought was hers by right,' the boy Siddhartha Shankar Ray would describe the interaction several years later.[1]

Several years later, the spunky girl went on to become India's first and only woman prime minister. About fifty-three years after the two had torn a doll apart, Ray, as the chief minister of West Bengal and a close confidant of Indira, found a constitutional provision to help her preside over the most controversial decision of her political career—proclamation of the draconian Emergency in 1975. Mrs Gandhi suspended civil liberties, clamped down on the media, imprisoned Opposition leaders, and suspended elections for almost two years from June 1975 to March 1977. Her rout in the parliamentary elections post-Emergency saw political pundits writing her epitaph, with little to no clue that she would be back again.

CHILD OF THE REVOLUTION

Indira was born on 19 November 1917 in a prominent Kashmiri Pandit family of Allahabad. Her grandfather, Motilal Nehru, was a prominent advocate and a freedom fighter. She grew up in a joint family where her father Jawaharlal Nehru, mother Kamala, and her aunts Vijaya Lakshmi Pandit and Krishna Hutheesing were deeply involved in the freedom struggle. As a child, Indira was surrounded by conversations on civil disobedience and secret meetings of the Congress Working Committee in the living room of the palatial Anand Bhawan. It was little wonder that her pretend play with her dolls centred around the freedom struggle. She would pretend to be the Rani of Jhansi and Joan of Arc. When she was about eleven years old, her grandfather presented her with a small charkha, on which she learnt to spin. Soon she was organizing a Bal Charkha Sangh where little children learned how to spin and weave. Arrests of family members were common for her, so common that sometimes Indira would be left all alone at home with a governess for company. 'On one occasion, some visitors to Anand Bhawan were met on the doorstep by little Indira who gravely informed them that both her parents had gone out to gaol.'[2] Nehru wrote letters to Indira from jail, which are still considered remarkable for their insight into India's first prime minister, his relationship and worries for his daughter, and the Indian freedom struggle.

In 1930, Mahatma Gandhi gave a call for civil disobedience and chose the simple weapon of salt to give vent to the feeling of anger India felt against Britain. He undertook the historic Dandi March to the village of Dandi in Surat district to defy the authorities and break the law by making salt. Gandhi gave the first call to women to join the freedom struggle in an article in *Navjivan*, a magazine he edited. 'If non-violence is the law of our being, the future is with women,' he wrote.[3] He set before the women two specific tasks—to picket liquor vends and cloth shops to prevent the sale of liquor and foreign fabric. This call from Gandhi stirred women into action. They left the security of their homes, entrusted the household and children to their in-laws and relatives, and ventured out—singing desh bhakti songs and picketing shops. The entire Nehru household got involved— Indira's grandmother Swaroop Rani, mother Kamala, and aunts Vijaya Lakshmi and Krishna Hutheesing came out to picket shops and brave police action. Kamala, who had a weak constitution and was often ill, surprised everyone. 'Kamala astounded Motilal and the household by her energy and her capacity for organized action. In scorching heat she was in the forefront of the defiant crowds. It was as if an invisible power flowed through her. She was everywhere—addressing meetings, picketing, tending the injured knocked down by lathi blows of policemen, organizing voluntary services. From his jail cell, an astonished and proud Jawaharlal began to regard his wife anew.'[4] This was also the time that the household was introduced to Feroze Gandhi, who would later marry Indira.

The Civil Disobedience Movement was Indira's first active brush with India's independence movement. She cut her hair very short and started wearing loose frocks of coarse handspun khadi. All of thirteen years, she formed her very own children's brigade called the Vanar Sena after the mythological army of monkeys that had helped Lord Rama rescue Sita from Ravana, the king of Lanka. 'I did it in a fit of temper. I wanted to be a member of the Congress and the Congress office turned me down and they said you have to be eighteen or twenty-one, whatever it was,' she recalled later. 'I was extremely angry and I said, I will make an organization of my own and that's how it began. My father didn't even know about it till I had done my preliminaries.'[5] Since there were no loudspeakers in India then, Indira would address the meetings through 'human loudspeakers'—she would say a sentence and the child close to her would bellow it out. Indira's Vanar Sena got involved in writing notices, making flags, addressing envelopes, supporting leaders, and carrying messages.

Successive stints in jail had an adverse impact on Motilal Nehru's health, and in 1931 he passed away. This was a hard time for Indira, who was close to her mother, and often faced ridicule from her grandmother and aunts during this time. A casual remark by Vijaya Lakshmi Pandit, calling her 'ugly, stupid', stayed with her for the rest of her life.

It was a tumultuous and nomadic childhood with little room for formal education. By the time she was sixteen years old, Indira had studied in seven different schools, including schools in Switzerland where she had travelled with her ailing mother. Nehru enrolled her in Rabindranath Tagore's Shantiniketan—which became Indira's first real introduction to the world of poetry and fine arts and honed her artistic sensibilities. It was also here that she had her first brush with romance. She met Frank Oberdorf, a thirty-four-year-old German teacher who taught her French. While he expressed his deep love for Indira, she only offered him her friendship. She was called away from Shantiniketan abruptly as her mother's health deteriorated and she travelled to Switzerland with Kamala. It is difficult to ascertain if she would have reciprocated Oberdorf's feelings had she stayed longer at Shantiniketan but she met him and corresponded with him even during later years.

Feroze's devotion to Kamala saw him actively taking care of her during this difficult phase and even spending time in Switzerland before he went to London for higher studies. Kamala passed away in 1936, leaving Indira shattered and for some time struggling to cope with her grief. She left for London to study history at Oxford. During these years, their shared grief over Kamala's death and the time spent together in London brought Indira and Feroze very close. By the time she was twenty-three, Indira had decided to marry Feroze. But it wasn't easy to get married. Despite the opposition from her family and even Mahatma Gandhi, Indira and Feroze married in 1942 in a simple ceremony. A few months later, the couple was jailed for their participation in the Quit India Movement. Indira spent thirteen months in prison and was released in 1943. Her son Rajiv was born in 1944 and Sanjay in 1946. By then, the couple had started having differences. Many say that differences began because of Feroze's roving eye but others believed that Indira moving into Nehru's official residence to play the hostess was the real beginning. Feroze had found his true calling in journalism and moved to Lucknow to take charge of *National Herald*, a newspaper started by Nehru in 1937. 'In Lucknow, separated from Indira, Feroze soon became entangled with a woman from one of Lucknow's prominent Muslim landed families. Rumours of Feroze seeking solace elsewhere reached Indira while she was with her father. She was pregnant and awaiting the arrival of her baby (Sanjay), due in late December.'[6] It was never a happy marriage though the couple tried to co-parent the boys while living separately later.

THE APPRENTICE

After India attained independence in August 1947, Indira was pulled in by Gandhi to help riot victims, especially Muslims, lodged in refugee camps. When Jawaharlal Nehru became the prime minister of independent India, he turned to his daughter to be the hostess at his official residence at 3 Teen Murti Marg. What started as a social assignment of hosting a stream of international dignitaries and unofficial guests soon turned into a political apprenticeship under a prime minister who was trying to make a newly-independent country self-reliant and negotiating a space in the twentieth-century world order.

Indira became an astute observer of world politics as she accompanied Nehru on his official visits to the United States, London, and Geneva. Around the same time, she also became involved in domestic politics. India held its first general election in 1951, which was described as a one-man affair with Nehru as the chief campaigner for the Congress.

> His daughter, while herself refusing to contest, canvassed widely for the party and often filled in for Nehru.... Initially her audiences were small, but her mass appeal steadily increased. Her perseverance, no doubt, had much to do with her success. She recalls with amusement in the Punjab where she insisted on making a pre-dawn election speech: It was a cold and misty January morning with a sharp breeze and at 6 a.m. still quite dark. Not a soul was in sight. All the doors and windows seemed to be tightly secured. However, there was a takhat (platform) and a microphone and some durries (carpets), wet with the heavy dew. Hansrajji (senior Punjab Congressman Raizada Hansraj) felt that we had done our duty by coming and we could now drive on to the regular programme with a clear conscience. However, much to his embarrassment, I insisted on giving a speech whether there was anybody to listen or not. Almost with my first word, windows started banging open and tousled heads appeared. Immediately afterwards the entire vilage poured out from the warmth of their houses, wrapped in blankets and razais (quilts), some with dattun (neem twigs used to brush teeth) sticks and some with tumblers of steaming tea.... Raizadaji remembered this

as the most extraordinary meeting he had witnessed in his long life and spoke of it every time we met thereafter.[7]

In 1952, Feroze Gandhi was elected to the Lok Sabha from Rae Bareilly. Indira's family stayed at Nehru's official residence at Teen Murti House. But very soon, Feroze felt stifled and moved out of the prime minister's residence into his own official house as a member of parliament. Indira's active involvement in politics came at a time when she and Feroze were drifting apart. Gradually, Feroze started targeting Nehru in parliament. His maiden speech in 1954—two years after he was elected to the Lok Sabha—exposed how businessman Ramkrishna Dalmia (as the chairman of a bank and an insurance company) transferred money from publicly owned companies to fund his private takeover of the Bennett & Coleman company. It led to Dalmia's arrest and caught the attention of the prime minister. As Feroze carved out an independent identity for himself as an anti-corruption politician, Indira started climbing the echelons of the party organization. In 1955, she was appointed to the Congress Working Committee—the party's highest decision-making body—with the responsibility of the women wing and youth wing, followed by the Central Parliamentary Board and the Central Election Committee. These roles ensured she was at the core of planning and preparations for the second general election of 1957. Feroze won his second term in the Lok Sabha and exposed what was known as the Mundhra deal[8] and forced the resignation of Finance Minister T. T. Krishnamachari, who was considered close to Nehru. Feroze's next target was Nehru's aide M. O. Matthai. He prepared a dossier on Matthai and released it to a journalist friend. The subsequent news article led to an uproar and called for Matthai's resignation.

Despite the strain, Indira and Feroze ensured they were both closely involved in bringing up their boys. Every day, Feroze had lunch with them at Teen Murti House, and Indira sent Rajiv and Sanjay to his home over the weekends. Many attributed the boys' love for machinery, especially cars, to the time spent with their father who taught them how to take apart and put together toy cars and trains. Visitors to Teen Murti are known to recall how sometimes Feroze would keep sitting at the other end of the table during lunch and would not want to make conversation. The couple rekindled their relationship briefly in 1958 when Feroze suffered a heart attack, and Indira rushed back from a trip to Bhutan to take care of him. She nursed him back to health in Kashmir, and the couple spent almost a month on a houseboat with their sons. However, the tension returned as they came back to Delhi.

The proverbial final straw was to come after Indira became the Congress president in 1959 at the age of forty-two—the third member of the Nehru family and the fourth woman to head the Congress Party. While some close to the family have observed that Nehru had reservations about Indira taking over party leadership when he was the prime minister, many political observers felt that this was a stepping stone carefully crafted by Nehru, who saw in Indira an heir apparent to his political legacy. Durga Das, a prominent political columnist for the *Hindustan Times*, wrote in June 1957: 'If Nehru is consciously building up anyone, he is building up his daughter.'[9] In his memoirs published in London in 1969, Durga Das says, 'He had sensed this when Dhebar (then Congress President U. N. Dhebar) nominated her to the Working Committee two years earlier, and her elevation to the presidency of the party confirmed his suspicions.'[10] However, Nayantara Sahgal differs in her book, 'Nehru did not think it was time for this distinction. His reservations were rooted deep in his respect for the process—personal, political, social, or economic—that lays sound foundations. Work was the crucible of human personality or political strength, and there were no shortcuts to excellence... He was averse to hustle and haste.'[11] She was, in the true sense, an exception. All party presidents between 1951 and 1969 had been state chief ministers but Indira had no such governance experience. 'Her father and grandfather were among the illustrious names in Congress annals who had held the distinction before her.... Her earnestness was looked upon with favour and her inexperience with indulgence.'[12] As party president Indira addressed a press conference in which she said, 'The nation is in a hurry and we can't afford to lose time. My complaint against the Congress is that it is not going as fast as the people are advancing.'[13] The remarks reflected an impatience with the party and an urgency to change things. It was clearly reflected in the role she played in toppling the Left government of E. M. S. Namboodiripad in Kerala. Elected in 1957, the Left government faced protests from wealthy and influential Roman Catholics on the issue of state control of schools and colleges. Indira, as the Congress president, waded into the controversy and proposed President's Rule in the state and fresh elections to gauge whether Namboodiripad had the people's mandate. 'Feroze Gandhi, who counted many Marxists as personal friends, was appalled at the attempts by Indira to topple the communist government in Kerala. Husband and wife had violent arguments where Feroze expressed his anger against what she was attempting to do; but the same strength that she had shown against her father to marry Feroze now came into action and she was defiant with Feroze.'[14] Despite the opposition of Nehru and top party leaders, Indira insisted that this was an opportunity for the Congress to ride back to power. As a result, the Namboodiripad government was dismissed and President's Rule was imposed in Kerala in 1959. In the 1960 assembly elections, the Left party was voted out of power and an alliance of parties led by the Congress won a majority in the state.

The Congress presidents in those days had a two-year term, but Indira occupied the office for eleven months. 'She gave up the presidentship and, without defining her dissatisfaction, made it known she was not being allowed to do as she wished in the party.'[15] The decision came after a patch of bad health. She was operated on for a kidney stone in February 1960. Later, in September 1960, Feroze suffered a second heart attack and did not survive it.

HER FATHER'S DAUGHTER

Jawaharlal Nehru was shocked when China invaded disputed territory along the border in Ladakh and moved swiftly towards Assam in the Northeast. The Sino-Indian War of 1962 left the country battered and Nehru never recovered from the losses India faced in the aftermath of this war. 'To Nehru, now seventy-three, Peking's perfidy was a mortal blow.... Overnight, he had changed into a weary, disillusioned old man. He walked with a stoop, as though in pain, his face was sombre and lined deeply, his elan was irretrievably lost.'[16] As Congress leaders jostled with each other to position themselves as Nehru's political successor, then Congress Party President K. Kamaraj hit upon a novel plan to rejuvenate the political fortunes of a party on the wane. The Kamaraj Plan, as it was called, required central ministers and chief ministers to quit their posts and go back to work and reconnect with people at the grassroots. While Kamaraj looked at the plan in view of the impending 1967 parliamentary elections, Nehru may have had a succession plan for Indira in mind. A few months before his death, in an interview to *Blitz* editor R. K. Karanjia, Nehru spoke of a 'collective leadership' and mentioned the names of K. Kamaraj, Lal Bahadur Shastri, and Gulzarilal Nanda. When Karanjia asked him if he was not ruling out the possibility of Indira playing an important political role, Nehru said, 'Of course, I do not. How can I?.... If the people choose her, or Congressmen select her, then she is welcome to take any post of responsibility so far as I am concerned. I am neither preparing her for anything, nor do I propose to prevent her from taking any responsibilities the country or the people may desire of her.'[17]

In January 1964, Nehru suffered a stroke and was ordered bed rest. Four months later, on 27 May, Nehru suffered another stroke which proved fatal. The party chose the understated and humble Lal Bahadur Shastri to succeed Nehru as prime minister. A Nehru loyalist, Shastri gave Indira her first ministerial assignment with the Information and Broadcasting (I&B) ministry and she was number four in his cabinet. Indira explained her choice of portfolio, 'I really chose it. I mean, I suggested it. It is a fascinating subject. Also I didn't want to take an important ministry, what was then considered important. Though I personally I consider information very important but the public eye doesn't.'[18] What set Indira apart from her predecessors and other cabinet colleagues was her style of functioning. While most ministers were known to sign on files going exactly by the advice of the bureaucrats, Indira was known to pore over official documents and cabinet notes and make her opinion known. She was clearly no puppet. But the differences between Indira and Shastri started showing when she felt slighted at not being made a part of major policy decisions. 'But while being a good man with a genuinely modest demeanour, Shastri was also a tough and wily politician who knew how to safeguard his own interests.... While including Indira he was anxious to see to it that she did not become a rival centre of power. Towards this end, Shastri adopted the policy of showing Indira all surface courtesies but allowing her no share or say in the making of policy. He did not appoint her to the cabinet's major committees.'[19]

The 1965 Indo-Pakistan War was a significant event during Shastri's term—Indira exhibited the same courage which had driven her to relief work after the Partition in riot-hit areas. 'She showed she was a woman of almost limitless courage. While the fighting was at its bitterest, she visited the front line at Haji Pir, a strongpoint in that part of Kashmir the Pakistanis had grabbed in 1947 and had held on to from then, although India is its legal owner. A senior officer of the Indian Air Force forbade her [from] making the trip from Srinagar because it was too dangerous. A helicopter was standing by. Full of resource, she got a member of her staff to engage the officer in conversation. Suddenly, sensing something wrong, the officer swung round and asked: "Where is Mrs Gandhi?" Where indeed was she? Up in the helicopter, on her way to the front.'[20] But this assignment was short-lived. In just twenty-one months, she was called upon by the Congress to serve as prime minister of India.

MADAM PRIME MINISTER

Shastri did not return alive from Tashkent, where he and Field Marshall Ayub Khan had signed the Tashkent Declaration to end the Indo-Pakistan War. In less than twenty months, India had seen the death of two serving prime ministers. Once again, the Syndicate led by the senior leaders of the Congress was faced with the question of succession. The Syndicate comprised K. Kamaraj, S. Nijalingappa, Atulya Ghosh, N. Sanjiva Reddy, and S. K. Patil. When the Syndicate decided to draft Nehru's daughter for the top job, little did they expect that this single mother of two young boys would turn out to be a crafty politician who would eventually split the party in two and become the longest serving prime minister of India. With the parliamentary elections thirteen months away, they thought they would be able to control Indira better than her wily challenger Morarji Desai. Perhaps the Syndicate should have watched her defiance of Shastri more closely.

On 24 January 1966, Indira was sworn-in as the prime minister by President S. Radhakrishnan at the Rashtrapati Bhavan. The job was anything but easy. On the day of her swearing-in ceremony, the day's headlines clearly reflected the challenges before her.

> Trivandrum: All political parties and Trade Unions are planning a one-day 'Kerala Bundh' on January 28 to protest against the meagre rice ration allowed to the people of Kerala.

> Bhopal: Near-starvation conditions are prevailing in the Rewa district on account of successive failure of rains.

> Calcutta: The price of kerosene has shot up in Calcutta to about 12 times what it was a few weeks ago. A 22-ounce bottle of kerosene sold at 25 paise only a few days ago was quoted at ₹3 yesterday.

> Nagpur: The rice distribution scheme is causing widespread agitation...while rice is not available in the open market. It

can be had in any quantity in the Black Market at 2.50 to ₹3 per kilo.

Hyderabad: Andhra Pradesh government employees are threatening 'quit work' if their dearness allowance is not increased.

Yeotmal (Maharashtra): Following the worst drought in this decade, 483 villages in Yeotmal district have been declared scarcity areas.[21]

Two days later, on Republic Day, Indira addressed the nation on All India Radio. She spoke about the food problem caused by drought in several parts of the country and said, 'The coming months bristle with difficulties. We have innumerable problems requiring urgent action. The rains have failed us, causing drought in many parts.... Above all else we must ensure food to our people in this year of scarcity. This is the first duty of the government. We shall give urgent attention to the management and equitable distribution of foodgrains, both imported and procured at home....' Alluding to the Indo-Pakistan War and Tashkent Agreement, Indira said, 'Peace is our aim, but I am keenly aware of the responsibility of the government to preserve the freedom and territorial integrity of the country.... Peace we want because there is another war to fight—the war against poverty, disease and ignorance.'[22] Her first decision as prime minister was to give in to the demand of a Punjabi-speaking state and carve out Punjab and the Hindi-speaking state of Haryana in 1966.

Indian economy was crushed after two wars in three years and an acute food shortage had gripped the nation. Indira, with her limited administrative experience and knowledge of economics, found herself banking on her 'kitchen cabinet', which comprised of Dinesh Singh, C. Subramaniam, Asoka Mehta, and her chief adviser, L. K. Jha, whom she had inherited from Shastri.

During the 1965 Indo-Pakistan War, America had suspended aid to both the countries. Indira looked at American aid to bail

India out of the food crisis. She decided to take a trip to the US
and as she admitted to journalist Inder Malhotra, 'to get both food
and foreign exchange without appearing to be asking for them'.[23]
The International Monetary Fund (IMF) and World Bank insisted
on certain preconditions for the restoration of aid. This included
the controversial decision of devaluing the rupee. Malhotra has
written that Shastri was prepared to accept it before his death
and Indira's kitchen cabinet was 'enthusiastically for devaluation'.
Indira's trip to US was a tremendous success with President
Lyndon Johnson praising 'this proud, able, gracious lady' and
even breaking protocol to stay for a dinner called by the Indian
ambassador, B. K. Nehru. Armed with Johnson's promise of over
3 million tonnes of food and aid of $900 million, Indira returned
home and on 5 June 1966 announced a 35 per cent devaluation
of the rupee. It was her naiveté that she did not foresee the public
and political backlash of the decision. 'An incensed Kamaraj
started blaming himself for having put Indira in power in the first
place, muttering: "A big man's daughter, a small man's mistake."
At his insistence, the Congress Working Committee made history
of sorts by passing a resolution denouncing the government for
its decision on devaluation.'[24] Worse, the promised aid did not
come through—she had devalued the rupee and even mellowed
India's stance on the Vietnam War in a clear departure from
the non-alignment principles of her father. The only reason she
survived an angry Kamaraj's axe, then, was that parliamentary
elections were just a few months away.

In those years, irked party members and an angry Opposition
did not spare her in internal party sessions and in the parliament.
Indira had always been an underconfident public speaker and
her repeated harassment by Opposition members made her even
more tongue-tied inside the parliament. This earned her the
uncharitable sobriquet of 'goongi gudiya'—a dumb doll—from
Ram Manohar Lohia, the eccentric socialist leader and well-
known critic of Nehru. Indira was able to shed this image only
when she spoke directly to the people of India—during her second
term—winning their affections with her bold announcements of

nationalization of banks and abolition of privy purses in 1969 and 1971 respectively.

TAKING ON THE OLD GUARD

The 1967 parliamentary elections sprung a surprise—while the Congress Party retained a majority in the Lok Sabha, the powerful syndicate members lost their election. Patil lost to the firebrand socialist leader George Fernandes, Kamaraj was defeated by a political greenhorn from the newly-floated Dravida Munnetra Kazhagham (DMK), and Atulya Ghosh was defeated in West Bengal. In a way, Indira came into her own in her second term and took the Syndicate head-on. She was quick to realize the importance of a pliant president and denied a second term to incumbent president, S. Radhakrishnan favouring the vice president and renowned educationist Zakir Hussain.

Despite the ignominious loss in the parliamentary elections, the Syndicate did not relent. The sudden death of President Zakir Hussain in April 1969 gave the Syndicate a chance to push their candidate in Rashtrapati Bhavan. They chose N. Sanjiva Reddy as the party nominee, but Indira decided to throw her weight behind V. V. Giri, who filed his papers as an independent candidate. Angry with being pushed over the presidential election, Indira divested Morarji Desai of the finance portfolio and pushed for her planned reform of the nationalization of fourteen banks in July 1969. The move was applauded across the country.

Politically, Indira had declared all-out war against the Syndicate. The presidential election on 20 August 1969 promised to be a close contest so a nervous S. Nijalingappa, then Congress Party president, sought the support of the Jana Sangh and Swatantra Party. This gave Indira the opportunity to take a moral high ground and claim that this act compromised on the Congress's ideals. She called for a conscience vote. Giri won. The split between Indira and the Syndicate was wide open. On 1 November 1969, two meetings of the Congress Working Committee took place—one at the prime minister's residence at Safdarjung Road and the other a few kilometres away at the Congress office on Jantar Mantar Road. After the meeting, Nijalingappa announced Indira's expulsion from the primary membership of the party. She convened a meeting of the Congress Parliamentary Party, which was attended by 310 of 429 Congress members of both houses of parliament. Indira's Congress came to be known as Congress (R) and the Syndicate's faction as Congress (O). With the split, Indira lost majority in both houses of the parliament and reached out to Communist Party of India (CPI), DMK, and other independents to retain power.

In the 1967 parliamentary elections, the Swatantra Party had emerged as a political force with the support of maharajas of the erstwhile princely states, industrialists, and the right-wingers. Indira realized she needed to rein in the Swatantra Party, especially since several princes had fought elections and come to the Lok Sabha. Despite heading a minority government, Indira decided to introduce a constitutional amendment to abolish privy purses, which were privileges enjoyed by the erstwhile rulers. On 2 September 1970, the amendment was passed with two-thirds majority in the Lok Sabha but lost the two-thirds majority by one vote in the Rajya Sabha. Indira, however, was determined and by the same evening, she got a presidential order derecognizing the princes—since they were derecognized as princes they could not claim the privy purses.

Though she had managed to push through her bold decision, Indira realized that it would be difficult to implement her economic reform agenda while presiding over a minority government. In December 1970, she went to President V. V. Giri with the recommendation to dissolve the Lok Sabha and call for mid-term elections in February 1971. The elections were crucial—the Opposition rallied around 'Indira Hatao (Remove Indira)' as the campaign slogan to attack her unilateral and imperious style of functioning. Believing in her vision for a young India, Indira went over the heads of the political class and spoke directly to the people. She famously tackled her critics with the line, 'Woh kehte hain Indira hatao. Hum kehte hain garibi hatao

(They say remove Indira, but we say remove poverty).' Calling
the results unexpected would be an understatement. Indira won
two-thirds majority, cornering 350 of 518 seats in Lok Sabha,
successfully neutralizing all Opposition—the CPI(M), CPI, and
DMK—within the parliament.

On the party front, this phase was marked by a high degree
of centralization. Even in the state legislative assembly elections,
Indira decided which ministers got tickets. It was evident that
the party men needed Indira more than she needed them.
'An atmosphere of fealty, feudal in texture, descended on the
Congress. Her colleagues and associates, with few exceptions,
had no political bases of their own and were dependent on her
for their positions.'[25]

CHANGING THE SUBCONTINENT

At the time when Indira had requested Giri to call for mid-term
elections in December 1970, her Pakistani counterpart President
Yahya Khan had called for free and fair elections in the country.
It was a surprising move since there was growing resentment
in East Pakistan against the repressive regime of West Pakistan.
In the elections, Sheikh Mujibur Rahman's Awami League won
99 per cent of the seats in East Pakistan and won the overall
majority in the national assembly. Working with Zulfikar Ali
Bhutto's Peoples Party of Pakistan (PPP), Yahya Khan stopped
Rahman's Awami League from forming the government. As
Indira assumed power in February 1971, West Pakistani armed
forces descended on East Pakistan and unleashed a reign of
terror. Rahman was arrested in March 1971 and imprisoned in a
jail in West Pakistan. By April, the northeastern states of Tripura,
Manipur, and Assam and West Bengal started reporting a mass
inflow of refugees from East Pakistan. Contingents of the East
Pakistan Army, which had rebelled against the Pakistan Army,
crossed the border into India. The Indian Army started training
them and they organized themselves into Mukti Bahini or the
Liberation Army. By August, Yahya Khan had made it known

that a military trial of Rahman would be initiated. The Mukti Bahini was ready and infiltrated back into East Pakistan and struck at the ports of Chittagong and Jalna to prevent Pakistan from sending more war supplies. Indira started travelling to different world capitals in the hope of getting support for India, and by extension East Pakistan. The conflict, however, pushed a suspicious United States towards China to form a US–China–Pakistan axis. Indira acted swiftly and signed the Indo–Soviet Treaty of Peace, Friendship, and Cooperation, which had been held in abeyance for quite some time.

The seeds of acrimony between Indira and Jayaprakash Narayan or JP, whose call for total revolution proved to be Indira's undoing four years later, may have been sown during this year. JP, a well-known and fiery freedom fighter, travelled to different countries of the world to garner public support against the atrocities perpetrated in East Pakistan. JP organized a world conference in New Delhi to condemn these atrocities. Though this would have helped her in taking military action against Pakistan, Indira did not allow Congress to participate in the conference. Jayaprakash Narayan was livid. "What does Indira think of herself? Does she think she can ignore me? I have seen her as a child in frocks." His outburst reached Indira and it became increasingly difficult for Narayan to get an appointment to see her. Indira did not want a confrontation with him. She was also not prepared to reveal her plans, nor was she willing to give Jayaprakash Narayan the central position as the spokesman for India on Bangladesh.'[26]

By September, about 10 million refugees had reached India to escape the atrocities unleashed by the Pakistan Army. Indira realized that war was inevitable. On 3 December, Yahya Khan ordered aeroplanes to strike at India's main airbases. Indira decided to attack Pakistan and took the Opposition leaders into confidence. She addressed the nation on All India Radio after midnight and apprised them about her decision to march into East Pakistan. Over the next few days, she would breakfast with Chief of Army Staff Sam Manekshaw and take a full briefing.

On 6 December 1971, Indira gave a speech in the parliament where she recognized the independence of East Pakistan, calling it Bangladesh—for this, she was hailed as 'Goddess Durga'. The United States was drawn into the 1971 Indo-Pakistan War even though the global tide of opinion was against Pakistan. US President Richard Nixon saw a devious plan in India's march towards Dhaka—he thought that after liberating East Pakistan, Indian troops would move into Pakistan and upset the geopolitics of the subcontinent. Nixon ordered the US Seventh Fleet, stationed in Japan, to enter the waters of the Indian Ocean. It was thirty-six hours sailing time away from the Bay of Bengal. Indian troops had to finish the war before the Seventh Fleet arrived. On 12 December, with Indian fighter planes hovering overhead to prevent any air strikes by Pakistan Air Force, Indira addressed a public rally at the Ramlila Maidan, Delhi's iconic ground for political rallies. 'We will not retreat. Not by a single step will we move back,' she told the people.[27]

On 16 December 1971 at 4.30 p.m., General A. A. K. Niazi surrendered in Dhaka to Lieutenant General Jagjit Singh Aurora of the Indian Army. By the time the Seventh Fleet had entered Indian waters, the war was over. The winter session of the parliament was on and at 5.30 p.m., Indira addressed the Lok Sabha and told the nation that Bangladesh had been liberated. Pressure mounted on Indira to launch an attack on West Pakistan. But she realized that any such move would draw the two super powers, the USA and Russia, into the Indian subcontinent. On 17 December 1971, she addressed the Lok Sabha and declared ceasefire, 'We should like to fashion our relations with the people of Pakistan on the basis of friendship and understanding. Let them live as masters in their own house and devote their energies to the removal of poverty and inequalities in their country. It is this sincere desire which prompted us last evening to instruct our Army, Navy and Air Force to cease operations...'—at last, Indira had won hearts and a war.

THE DARKEST HOUR

The triumph came with a cost, both personal and political. Indira's closest aides remember how the prime minister changed following the 1971 war. She had never trusted anyone completely, especially after her advisers did not foresee the political cost of her decision to devalue money in her first term as prime minister. But the victory in Bangladesh made Indira believe she was invincible. After all, she had outmanoeuvred a super power, supported 10 million refugees, and shown sagacity in victory.

India could not bear the economic cost of 1971 war. The pressure of feeding refugees for a year had emptied its granaries, and international crude oil prices shot up. Indira thought a good monsoon would solve everything. But the monsoon failed in 1972 and again in 1973. Right after the war, India and Pakistan met in Shimla to sign the historic Shimla Accord in June 1972. Indira acted as the magnanimous victor and ceded diplomatic ground to Pakistan. The monsoon session of the parliament was a stormy affair with the Opposition questioning Indira's intentions over the concessions allowed to Pakistan.

As if being pushed further towards her downfall, Indira distanced herself from her best advisers. Her son Sanjay had applied for a license for a Maruti car factory. The Haryana chief minister, Bansi Lal, helped him get land for his factory, which was near a military base, a prohibited area. The base was shifted to make way for Sanjay's factory. Much to Sanjay's displeasure, Indira's Principal Secretary P. N. Haksar had already warned the prime minister of the unfeasibility of the factory plan on ground. Rather than listening to Haksar's advice with an open mind, Indira gradually started pushing away the man who had ably guided her through the Bangladesh crisis. Interestingly, whatever Haksar had warned Indira about came true—the finance minister, after thorough examination of the company finances and management, directed the governor of the Reserve Bank of India to ask banks not to lend to Sanjay's company. 'The Prime Minister had become very very arrogant. She loved being called

Durga. The Bangladesh victory was the turning point. Sanjay was the only person who had a total hold on her. She had no tolerance for any other person,' commented her former private secretary, N. K. Seshan.[28]

In 1973, JP launched the Bihar Movement against corruption and misrule in the state. Simultaneously, students in Gujarat started the Navnirman Andolan, which accused the Chimanbhai Patel government of corruption. Gradually, the students movement in Gujarat went out of hand and came under the influence of unruly elements—there was utter chaos in Gujarat. Indira did not take any action against this movement as she believed students were her devoted constituency and supported her. But the movement forced Patel to resign and fresh elections were called subsequently. Around the same time, there were growing strikes in the country due to rising prices and labour and wage cuts. In May 1974, George Fernandes, president of the Railway Workers' Union, called for an indefinite strike. This would have meant restricted movement of essential commodities. Indira struck back with vengeance—the army was called in and families of railwaymen were thrown out of government quarters. Though the strike ended, there was a general discontentment in the country. Meanwhile, Indira dared the Western powers by conducting a successful underground nuclear explosion at Pokhran, Rajasthan.

While Indira was battling political and economic crises, a case filed after her landslide victory in 1971 was in the final stages of its hearing in the Allahabad High Court. Her opponent, Raj Narain, an Indian freedom fighter and politician, had accused Indira of electoral malpractice and misusing official machinery to win the election. Nobody had expected anything to come out of the case against the prime minister. On 12 June 1975, the Allahabad High Court found her guilty of electoral malpractice and debarred her from holding office for six years. The judgment shocked Indira and her party and provided the Opposition an effective weapon against the powerful prime minister. Even as Indira prepared to challenge the verdict in Supreme Court, JP called a rally at the Ram Lila Maidan on 25 June.

Former president and an old Congress hand, Pranab
Mukherjee has written in his book, *The Dramatic Decade: The
Indira Gandhi Years*, that the imposition of the Emergency was
really Siddartha Shankar Ray's idea—the chief minister of West
Bengal at the time. Drawing from Ray's deposition before the
Shah Commission, which was set up to enquire the excesses
during the Emergency and led by Justice M. R. Shah, Mukherjee
has written: 'It is believed that Siddartha Shankar Ray played
an important role in the decision to declare the Emergency: it
was his suggestion, and Indira Gandhi acted on it. In fact, Indira
Gandhi told me subsequently that she was not even aware of the
constitutional provisions allowing for the declaration of a state
of Emergency on grounds of internal disturbance, particularly
since a state of Emergency had already been proclaimed as
a consequence of the Indo-Pak conflict in 1971.'[29] Ray was
summoned to Indira's residence at 1 Safdarjung Road on
the morning of 25 June 1975. 'According to Siddartha babu,
Indira Gandhi then read out intelligence reports of Jayaprakash
Narayan's public meeting scheduled for that evening. The reports
indicated that he would call for an all-India agitation to set up
a parallel administration network as well as courts, and appeal
to policemen and those in the armed forces to disobey what
were supposed to be illegal orders. Indira Gandhi, he maintained,
was firm in the understanding that India was drifting towards
chaos and anarchy.' At this juncture, Ray pointed out Article
352 of the Indian Constitution to impose internal emergency to
Indira Gandhi,[30] Indira took Ray with her to Rashtrapati Bhavan
and he was present as she briefed the president, Fakhruddin Ali
Ahmed, who heard her for almost half an hour and then asked
Ray about the exact words in the Constitution.

Later in the day, JP announced the formation of Lok
Sangharsh Samiti with Morarji Desai as its chairman and Nanaji
Deshmukh as the secretary. He appealed to the armed forces and
the police to not obey the orders of the government. JP gave
a call to leaders and the youth to gherao the prime minister's
residence and not allow anyone to enter or leave and to paralyse

the government functioning. By now, Indira was convinced the Opposition was trying to stage a coup and challenge the functioning of a democratically-elected government. She wrote to Ahmed that information has 'reached us which indicates that there is an imminent danger to the security of India.' Indira did not convene a cabinet meeting to approve this decision but promised to call the cabinet meeting the next morning. Overnight, Opposition leaders, including JP and Morarji Desai, were arrested and taken to dak bungalows around Delhi, and electricity supply to most newspapers was cut to prevent them from carrying the news. India's darkest hour had begun.

Ray, however, completely washed his hands off the decision before the Shah Commission. 'Deposing before the Shah Commission, he ran into Indira Gandhi—draped in a crimson sari that day—in the commission hall and tossed a sprightly remark: "You look pretty today". "Despite your efforts," retorted a curt Indira Gandhi.'[31]

Indira's relationship with the media had always been thorny. Unlike Nehru, who was known to have complimented cartoonists and newspaper editors for their honest criticism of his government's policies, Indira made her displeasure known indirectly through her coterie. Nehru met the press corps in the capital once a month but Indira met once in a year. 'Frank Moraes, a leading editor, recalled, "Nehru talked a great deal in an interview. You started him off, and off he went. She is not forthcoming. She's rather like a convent schoolgirl, tongue-tied. Nehru didn't care what the newspapers said about him. With her, if there's an article, editorial or cartoon, she doesn't like, one of her entourage lets her disapproval be known." Her disapproval was generally ignored by the editors and proprietors of leading newspapers, who had a healthy disrespect for authority, but it became noticeable enough after 1969 to be raised in parliament, when Opposition MPs objected to governmental pressure to silence dissent.'[32]

The first indication of what she expected from the journalists came at a meeting of the National Integration Council in June

1968 when she said, 'We have to ensure that our educational processes, the books we read, the radio we hear, the films we see, do not distort the Indian mind but lead it to integration and solidarity.'

'Her remarks were not then construed as a call for reins on the mass media, but they were the first sign that the media must be more pointedly directed by government, the first sign, too, of a policy, contrary to the principle and practice so far, that expression must be free and it was the leadership's duty to safeguard that freedom until it became part of the people's natural expectation.'[33]

But what happened during the Emergency was censorship of a different nature—the newspapers had to submit articles to get a nod from the government. Several journals either shut down or carried blank spaces as a mark of protest against the government's attempt. The foreign press was edged out of India completely. In less than thirty years of Independence a country, whose leaders used to smuggle news through crudely printed booklets to gather support for its struggle for independence overseas had clamped down on free speech. Sanjay and his coterie of friends practically took over the administration. There are several instances cited by authors that clearly show that Rajiv was not in touch with Indira through this period and both he and his wife Sonia disapproved of the Emergency. Indira's close friend Pupul Jayakar has written in Indira's biography that the prime minister had prepared a speech to revoke it in her Independence Day speech on 15 August 1975 but had changed her mind after she got news of the assassination of Sheikh Mujibur Rahman and his family—she feared for her family's safety.

Later, in 1978 in an interview to Lord Chalfont for BBC, Indira was evasive when asked about the exact nature of this danger and said, 'Well, you can't really say anything with great precision.' She alluded to an outside conspiracy to destabilize her government. 'It was supported from outside.... No, the question was had it been only internal with no foreign interference one could have dealt with it in a much easier way.' To the question of whether she concocted a threat to the survival of the state to ensure her own survival, Indira said, 'I am afraid that is a very rude question and it is entirely baseless. There is nothing at all to base it on.' However, she was more forthcoming on media censorship. 'I think censorship was not properly managed. Initially we thought it would be for a very brief period and some code of conduct would be worked out but it was not.' She has justified it and said that even though she declared Emergency she was the one who revoked it. She said that she 'had accepted all responsibility as I happened to be head of the government'.

Sanjay spelt out a five-point programme which included family planning, tree plantation, a ban on dowry, 'Each One Teach One'—aimed at literacy—and the end of casteism. What started as an exercise to control increasing population through camp-based sterilizations became a target-driven programme overzealously implemented by the district administration. 'By the middle of 1976, the family planning drive reached a peak; the targets for sterilization were laid down for every state and district. As the figures of sterilization were reviewed they were continually revised upwards and impossible targets set, with little consideration or concern for the facilities and medical personnel available for such an escalation in numbers.'[34] Whether Indira was aware of the enormity of this exercise is not clear. But in a young country of the 1970s, where physical productivity was equated with virility, the word 'forcible' soon came to be associated with the population control plan. It also started impacting India's vaccination programme as rumours began to spread in villages that all vaccines were really sterilization injections.

By late 1976, something had stirred within Indira. Jayakar attributes this change to Indira's interactions with spiritual guru J. Krishnamurti. On 18 January 1977, Indira announced the release of all the jailed Opposition leaders and set 19 March as the date for parliamentary elections. Despite the advice of the Research and Analysis Wing (R&AW) chief R. N. Kao to release the political prisoners and allow a cooling-off period of six months before calling elections, Indira remained adamant on holding elections in March. The Opposition leaders were confused about Indira's decision—Emergency was partly lifted just as suddenly as it had been implemented. She wouldn't go to elections without being confident of the results, they thought.

THE COMEBACK

As soon as the Janata government came to power under Morarji Desai, it instituted a commission of inquiry under Justice J. C. Shah to enquire into the excesses perpetrated during the Emergency. As the witch hunt began, Congress started bleeding. Even before the parliamentary elections, Indira lost her three trusted leaders—Jagjivan Ram, H. N. Bahuguna, and Nandini Satpathy, who had left to form Congress for Democracy. Cabinet ministers in the Indira government, her own chief ministers, and Sanjay's Youth Congress leaders deposed before the Shah Commission and completely put the blame at Indira's doorstep. Overnight Indira became a pariah with the government even giving feelers to foreign missions against extending invites to her.

But she was a natural leader who was alive to people's problems. In May 1977, eleven lower-caste men were killed in a caste massacre in Belchi village, a remote village 70 kilometres from Patna, Bihar. Torrential rains had hit Patna, making access to Belchi impossible. Indira famously rode an elephant through a flooded river and slush to reach Belchi and meet the grief-stricken villagers. Congress had not won a single seat in Bihar in the just-concluded 1977 general elections, but with her visit to Belchi, Indira had won hearts. She crossed back the river the same night and was welcomed with garlands and a warm meal by village women. With this visit, Indira had regained her confidence and started her mass contact programmes across India. She was arrested by the Central Bureau of Investigation (CBI) on 3 October, making her a martyr in the eyes of the people—a sixty-year-old woman standing alone with a determined government baying for her blood.

In December 1977, there were clear signs that Indira would

chart her own course. She resigned from the Congress Working Committee. A few days later, her supporters declared that they would hold a rival Congress session on 31 December. This was the same as when there was a rift between Indira and the Syndicate. Congress President Brahmananda Reddy expelled Indira from Congress. On 3 January 1978, Indira formed Congress (I) and took the symbol of the open palm, which remains the party symbol of the Indian National Congress till date. Within days, she appeared before Shah Commission absolutely defiant and unwilling to budge from her stated position that she had done nothing wrong. Justice Shah asked her to take the witness stand on two occasions, and Indira maintained that she was not legally bound to make a statement under oath (as that would have gone against the oath of secrecy she had taken as the prime minister of India). Within a month of floating her own party, Indira won assembly elections in Andhra Pradesh and Karnataka. She then sought a re-election to the Lok Sabha from Chikmaglur in Karnataka in November 1978, won, and entered the parliament riding on an overwhelming majority. But her political opponents were not willing to let go of the hurt of the Emergency days. Even before she had won the by-election from Chikmaglur, a privilege motion had been moved against her in Lok Sabha for allegedly harassing government officers investigating Sanjay's automobile company. This was referred to the Privileges Committee of the Lok Sabha, which found her guilty. Prime Minister Morarji Desai moved a motion in the house seeking to imprison her and strip her off her seat. The motion was passed with 279 members voting for it and 138 against it.[35] Indira was imprisoned in Tihar Central Jail in the capital. She used this time in the prison to devise a plan to dismember the Janata Party. By January, she had opened back channel talks with Chaudhary Charan Singh and H. N. Bahuguna and deputed Sanjay to reach out to Raj Narain, who had caused her political debacle and was now a minister in Desai's government. In the monsoon session of the parliament in July 1979, a no-confidence motion was introduced against Desai's government. The prime minister was shocked to learn that no minister was willing to defend his government, and he was forced to resign. Indira promised support to Charan Singh on the condition that she be consulted on major issues. However, she withdrew support within a month and Charan Singh recommended fresh parliamentary elections. Indira won a convincing 351 of 529 Lok Sabha constituencies paving the way for her return to power.

A PERSONAL LOSS

Within six months of Indira returning to power, tragedy struck— her younger son and political successor Sanjay was killed in plane crash just a few kilometres from the prime minister's residence. Indira was shattered and turned to her older son Rajiv, who had intentionally remained aloof and distant from his mother's politics. Her dependence on Rajiv and his family created differences between Indira and Sanjay's widow Maneka, who had presumed that her mother-in-law would be more supportive after the heart-rending loss. Within two years, Maneka walked out of Indira's home with her infant son Feroze Varun.

In her fourth term as prime minister, Indira faced a number of internal security issues. With Sanjay's death, she may have lost her instinctive edge of a natural leader. She faced electoral debacles in Andhra Pradesh and Karnataka in 1983 and her insistence on holding elections in the deeply-divided state of Assam contributed to the gruesome Nellie massacre. By 1983, fissiparous pressures had been building in Punjab. Congress, which had seen the rise of Akali Dal as a political threat, created a new power centre in Jarnail Singh Bhindranwale, who was misleadingly called a 'Sant'—a spiritual leader. 'Bhindranwale's emergence on the political landscape of Punjab can be traced back to 1977 when the Akali Dal–Janata Party government came to power after defeating the Congress in the assembly elections. Zail Singh, the defeated chief minister who later became president of India, was most unhappy, not only because he had lost power, but also because the Gurdial Singh Commission, appointed to look into his conduct as chief minister, had found him guilty of misuse of power. It was Sanjay Gandhi, known for his extra-constitutional methods, who suggested that some 'Sant' should be put up to challenge the Akali government.... Zail Singh and Darbara Singh, who was a Congress Working Committee member and later became chief minister, selected two persons for Sanjay's evaluation. As Sanjay's friend, Kamal Nath, recalled: 'The first one we interviewed did not look a "courageous type". Bhindranwale, strong in tone and tenor, seemed to fit the bill. We would give him money off and on, but we never thought he would turn into a terrorist.' Little did they realize at that time that they were creating a Frankenstein.[36]

Gradually, he surrounded himself with a gun-toting Sikh militia and made the Golden Temple in Amritsar his base for all terrorist activities. After Sanjay's death, Bhindranwale freed himself of the Congress's hold and demanded a separate Khalistan. He unleashed mindless violence to press for secession. There was no dearth of funds as help was pouring in from Sikhs in the US, Canada, Germany, and the United Kingdom. The violence spread rapidly, and Indira looked inept and hesitant in controlling the terror. By mid-1984, a number of bodies were discovered in the drains outside the Golden Temple making it evident that Bhindranwale would continue to unleash violence in the state of Punjab. Indira decided to call the army on 1 June, a tough decision as it meant bearing the responsibility of desecrating the Golden Temple, the holiest shrine of the Sikhs. In a twenty-four-hour gun battle, now known as Operation Blue Star, Bhindranwale was killed and the militants flushed out. There were several civilian casualties as pilgrims had gathered to participate in the celebrations on the martyrdom day of Guru Arjan Dev. Though the Opposition supported Indira in this, Operation Blue Star left permanent emotional scars on the Sikh community.

Senior officials of the intelligence agencies recommended that all Sikh guards from the prime minister's security detail should be removed. Indira, with her innate belief in the secular

fabric of India, brushed it aside and said this would only add
to the feeling of hurt the community felt. After this operation,
biographers have described Indira as being paranoid about the
safety of her family. An oft-cited incident relates to the escort
jeep travelling with Rahul and Priyanka to school meeting with
an accident on 30 October; Indira was convinced that it was an
attempt to kidnap the children. The next day, around 9 a.m.,
Indira used a small picket gate to cross from her residence to
the office when Sub-Inspector Beant Singh, her Sikh security
guard of nine years, used his service revolver and shot her in the
abdomen from close range. Constable Satwant Singh joined him
and fired twenty-five rounds from his sten-gun. Indira was dead.

What followed was mayhem—massive rioting spread in the
capital with mobs of Congressmen looting, raping, tonsuring,
and then killing Sikhs. Indira's assassination also pushed her
reluctant heir Rajiv to the prime minister's chair. Rajiv lacked
the intuition, instinct, and ruthlessness of his mother. He dithered
and the pogram tore through north India. Indira's death had
cost the nation dear.

Indira remains India's only woman prime minister.
Interestingly, she espoused the cause of women's emancipation
but did not approve of Mahatma Gandhi's approach of putting
women on a pedestal. 'In India, in spite of the fact that the
emancipation of women has released powerful social forces, non-
acceptance of equality of women on the part of men is a great
hurdle. Another hurdle is the old ideal of a silently suffering Sita
which remains at the back of the mind of even a liberated Indian
woman,' she said in her speech on 'Tasks before Indian Women'
at the golden jubilee celebrations of the Nathibai Damodar
Thackersey University for Women in June 1963.[37] 'Women in
India have, in theory at least, always occupied an honoured
position.... We have thought—our society has thought—that if
you call a woman a goddess you have done everything necessary,
even if she is suppressed and has no rights. Gandhiji wanted to
keep women on a pedestal, but he tried to lift the reality up to
that pedestal or ideal, so that the Indian woman could perhaps

be able to get some of the attributes of a goddess. I would like our women to be treated like human beings. They do not want to be goddesses, but they must have every opportunity to develop their talent, their capabilities, and to use those talents and capabilities in the service of the community, in the service of the nation,' she said.

But did she exercise the choice of exploring her own talent herself? Did she want to be a politician or lead a quiet life of a housewife settled into complacent domesticity? K. A. Abbas had posed this question to her: what would she have liked to be, if she had a freedom of choice? 'The question seemed to amuse, even fascinate, her. Quite seriously she discussed several possibilities which indicate her variegated interests. "I would have liked to be a writer," she said, then added, "I would have liked to do research in History or, perhaps, in Anthropology for that interests me even more than History. I have always been greatly...." But Anthropology did not exhaust the range of possibilities of an alternative to her political career. "If I wanted to have an easy life, I could have become an interior decorator—I am really interested in the subject." One has only to look round her present house, or to recall how she furnished the Teen Murti House for her father, to believe in her good taste and her talent for interior decoration. Then she gave me the surprise of the evening. "I could even have become a dancer—I learnt Manipuri in Shantiniketan, and Gurudev wanted me to join the dance troupe that he was going to take on tour round the country."[38] But the Iron Lady of India went on to shape the politics of the nation for decades.

SUCHETA KRIPALANI

The Fiery Revolutionary

14 August 1947, 11 p.m.:

The Central Hall of Parliament was decorated with flowers. The visitors' gallery was packed. The president of the Constituent Assembly, Dr Rajendra Prasad, had taken his seat as the presiding officer on the high podium. Two men holding the national flag flanked him. Prasad turned to the thirty-nine-year-old freedom fighter Sucheta Kripalani to initiate India's first steps towards Independence. The entire house stood up. Sucheta, an elected member of the Constituent Assembly from the United Provinces (now Uttar Pradesh), rendered the first verse of Bankim Chandra Chattopadhyay's 'Vande Mataram' in her melodious voice. Prasad's address was followed by Jawaharlal Nehru's iconic 'Tryst with Destiny' speech.

Several kilometres away, the architect of India's Independence was sleeping on a thin mattress at Haideri Manzil in Beliaghata, Kolkata, a Muslim-dominated locality which had been witnessing Hindu–Muslim clashes. Mahatma Gandhi had successfully pacified a mob of rioters and wanted to proceed to Noakhali, a riot-torn area in East Pakistan (present-day Bangladesh). His trusted lieutenant Sucheta had tirelessly worked for months in Noakhali and given a report to him on how the Hindu families had been targeted in orchestrated killings. She had ventured where no leader, leave alone a woman, had gone. She and her group of volunteers had braved mobs to work in the area. Many years later, Sucheta would admit to her husband, the politician Jivatram Bhagwandas Kripalani, that she carried arsenic, acquired from a doctor friend in Delhi, as she was prepared to die rather than fall into the hands of a violent mob.

EARLY LIFE

Sucheta was born in 1908 and brought up in a strict Brahmo Samaj family. Her grandfather Dinanath, born in an affluent zamindar family of Bengal, had adopted the faith after being moved by the social reformer Keshav Chandra Sen's speeches. Dinanath was deputed to work in Bihar and later travelled across Punjab and Sind. Sucheta's father, Surendra Nath Mazumdar, matriculated from Patna and joined Lahore Medical College. He joined the medical service in Punjab and Sucheta and her eight siblings were born and brought up in Punjab. There was a lot of emphasis on education and Sucheta and her older sister Sulekha were sent to boarding schools run by missionaries for their education. Sucheta grew up in a politically-conscious and highly patriotic family. The Jallianwala Bagh massacre of 1919 had fuelled nationalist sentiments across India, and Sucheta's home did not remain unaffected. In *Sucheta: An Unfinished Autobiography*, she recounts this time and how many relatives from Punjab would come and stay at their home waiting 'till things quietened down'. She recalls how a 'wave of indignation and wrath' had swept their house when the relatives recounted the horror to them. A year later, as a schoolgirl, Sucheta staged her own small protest of sorts. She writes, 'Towards the end of 1920, the Prince of Wales was visiting Delhi. The girls from our school were taken to stand near the Kudsia Garden on the Alipur Road in his honour. Since the Jallianwala Bagh massacre, my family had become extra-patriotic, though Father did not give up his service. We took a good deal of interest in the political movement. Sulekha and myself were, therefore, outraged at the idea of going out to honour the Prince of Wales but we did not pick up sufficient courage to refuse to do so. After reaching the garden, in the confusion we two made ourselves scarce and sat behind a bush till the whole thing was over and then joined the girls to walk back to the school. But this did not absolve our conscience of a feeling of shame. We both felt very small because of our own cowardice.'[1]

Sucheta was an excellent student, topping her class and winning scholarships during her school and college days. She completed her BA from Lahore College for Women and then her Master's in History from St Stephen's College in Delhi. She topped the university in History at St Stephen's College even when she had taken her final examinations right after her father's death. She worked as a teacher at a newly-instituted school in Lahore to support her big family. However, she wanted to be a college lecturer and got offers to either join her old college or the Banaras Hindu University, which had become a cradle for the volunteers of the Indian freedom struggle in the 1930s. Though Sucheta wanted to join the freedom movement, she was held back by her responsibility to support her mother and younger siblings who were still studying. She decided to join Banaras Hindu University as a lecturer in history in 1931. 'I joined the university during the height of the freedom movement. The university was very much in the mainstream of the struggle. We had frequent strikes and political demonstrations. Though the staff was in full sympathy with the strikers, they had to make an effort to hold our classes. The girls would, of course, join the strike, but they were in those days not bold enough to go out and take part in the demonstrations staged by the boys. I told my students that, whenever there was a hartal or strike. I would not take regular classes but give them a talk on the significance of our freedom struggle. This succeeded admirably; not only my own students but girls from the other classes flocked to these classes. We used to have lively discussions and the students got a lesson in events of current history,' she writes.[2]

Sucheta's first experience in social service came after a severe earthquake that shook northern India in January 1934. Bihar was the worst affected and the British government struggled to provide relief, so much so that it had to release Rajendra Prasad from jail to organize relief operations. Sucheta took leave from the university and went to Bihar to participate in the relief work. She went from village to village to help in relief and rehabilitation work and witnessed rural Bihar's poverty closely. Interestingly, it was J. B. Kripalani who had encouraged Sucheta to follow her calling and actively participate in the relief work.

TWO SOLDIERS

Sucheta had come in contact with J. B. Kripalani during her time at Banaras Hindu University. He was a soldier of the Indian freedom movement—Mahatma Gandhi called him 'his right arm'. Kripalani lived frugally with few belongings, travelling through India carrying the message of Mahatma Gandhi, and exhorting people to join the movement. In his forties, he was a bachelor, many erroneously even said that he had taken a vow of brahmacharya (bachelorhood). Despite an age difference of over twenty years, the two found each other's company interesting. Over the years, Sucheta and J. B. Kripalani started exchanging letters and developed a bond. 'There was much in common in our ideas and outlook. This gradually developed into strong attachment. We decided to marry, but the impediments were

many. There was a good deal of difference of age, and he led a
life of extreme austerity and even hardship. Mother was opposed
to our marriage, since she wanted a life of ease and comfort
for me, the life of a normal housewife. On Kripalani's side, his
only sister Kikibehn reacted very strongly against the idea of
her 'Sadhu' brother marrying at an advanced age (he was in his
forties at that time). She thought it would impair his reputation
and all his life's work will be destroyed. She was a well-known
and respected Congress worker and leader in Sind. She wrote to
Gandhi ji,' writes Sucheta.[3]

Mahatma Gandhi was opposed to Sucheta and Kripalani
marrying. He was, in general, opposed to the soldiers of freedom
movement marrying as he felt that family responsibilities would
divert their attention from the primary objective—freedom. He
sent for Sucheta and talked to her hoping to dissuade the couple
from marrying. 'If you marry him, you will break my right
arm,' he said to Sucheta. Kripalani felt that loose talk about a
relationship will be detrimental to Sucheta's well-being as there
was already a lot of talk about the couple. The two remained
steadfast on their decision. Even then there was a delay in the
marriage as Jawaharlal Nehru, who was Kripalani's very close
friend, was in jail. The couple waited for two more years, and in
April 1936 finally married according to Brahmo rituals in Benares.
But this was only after Jamnalal Bajaj had persuaded Mahatma
Gandhi to give up his opposition, and he finally relented and
said that though he would not give the couple his blessings, he
would pray for them.

Soon, Sucheta won the respect and affection of Gandhi
and Kripalani's family. J. B. Kripalani writes in a section of
Sucheta's autobiography, 'Gandhi ji, as I have said, was against
our marriage, but he soon came to have a high opinion of her
ability. He appointed her the general secretary of the Kasturba
National Memorial Trust for the service of the women and
children in the villages. The members of my family, my sister
and others, who were against our marriage, soon shed their
prejudice and began to like her. She would carry for them

presents, when she went to Bombay, where they lived; or send them presents on every suitable occasion. They reciprocated. She considered my nephew Girdhari, who was greatly attached to me, as her own brother. Often the two would hatch up plans to purchase a costly thing for my comfort which they thought I would like owing to its high price. They would tell me only half of its price. I am rather miserly so far as my personal needs are concerned.'[4] With her marriage to J. B. Kripalani, Sucheta was formally initiated into politics. Kripalani had been appointed as general secretary of the All India Congress Committee (AICC) in 1934—the same year as the earthquake that plundered Bihar. He set up a proper office at Swaraj Bhawan in Allahabad for the AICC to function—this was the first formal office for the party because till then the AICC office moved to the home town of the incumbent president. With Kripalani at the helm, the AICC got its foreign affairs cell, which was later manned by Dr Ram Manohar Lohia and gradually evolved as the country's window to the world formulating literature on India's freedom struggle.

Sucheta did not quit her job as a lecturer for another two years, and the couple visited each other over weekends and during holidays. This continued till April 1938 when Sucheta resigned from the university in 1939. In Allahabad, Sucheta began working at the lowest rung of the party, as a worker of the local ward Congress committees. Since she did not find the work challenging, she started working at the fledgling foreign affairs department. When Dr Lohia took up the foreign affairs cell, Sucheta was entrusted with the responsibility of organizing a women's department at the AICC and at the provincial level. This involved extensive travelling across India. In an exhaustive interview to Uma Shanker in June 1974, Sucheta said, 'Thousands of women have participated in the various struggles of the Congress, but women had not been properly organized so far and there was no women's organization parallel to, or as part of, the Congress organization. Therefore, they wanted an all India women's department. This work was very difficult because women very easily come over and take part in jail-going programmes, when their husbands, fathers, brothers, or sons are arrested, but it is difficult to get them for day-to-day political work leaving their domestic responsibilities. Therefore, it was a fairly uphill work. I had to go from state to state, meet the Provincial Congress Committee (PCC) leaders, meet all the women workers and set up little women's units in each state. The second difficulty in organizing the women was money. The PCC were always short of money and were very reluctant to set apart some money for the women's work and without money women's work could not be organized as many of them needed some assistance for coming to the office, touring, etc. But, however, in spite of all the difficulties, we were able to organize a fairly well-knit women's department, sending them programmes, sending them literature from the AICC office, sending leaders to go and meet them. Thus, we were able to bring about a better, more coherent, women's organization for the peace-time working of the Congress.'[5]

Sucheta carried on this work for a year till 1940. By this time World War II had already begun and the viceroy had committed India to it without holding any consultations with the leaders. The Congress was opposed to this move and the Ramgarh session of the party in March 1940 decided to launch satyagraha. Since Mahatma Gandhi did not want to challenge the British during World War II, he drew up a list of volunteers or satyagrahis to offer individual satyagraha. The satyagrahis addressed public meetings, denounced the war, and asserted their right to freedom of speech. Vinoba Bhave was chosen by Gandhi as the first satyagrahi. Sucheta's name was sent in the list from Faizabad district in Uttar Pradesh since she had worked tirelessly in the rural areas of Faizabad. She was the eighth satyagrahi. Sucheta describes herself as having an 'inferiority complex' of sorts for not having gone to jail till then and that is why was keen to go to jail 'as soon as possible'.[6]

In the wee hours of the day, Sucheta had to address a public meeting and offer satyagraha when she was arrested and lodged in Faizabad Jail and then transferred to Lucknow Central Jail where most women political prisoners were lodged. She was

awarded one year's imprisonment and a fine of ₹200. Sucheta
was released from prison in January 1942—a very important
year for negotiations between Gandhi and the British government.
On 8 August 1942, Gandhi launched the Quit India Movement
at the Bombay session of All India Congress Committee (AICC).

GOING UNDERGROUND

Both Sucheta and J. B. Kripalani attended the session. They
were staying at Sardar Vallabhbhai Patel's home in Bombay.
They returned home from the session around midnight and by
4 a.m., policemen were knocking on their door. Sardar Patel
and Kripalani were arrested. Within a few hours, Sucheta and
other Congressmen realized that these were mass arrests by the
police to thwart any organized attempt to challenge the British
government. At the time of his arrest, Kripalani had advised
Sucheta against returning to Allahabad, their home base, where
she could have been arrested as warrants were out for Congress
workers in their home districts.

Sucheta later recalled the day of mass arrests and spoke
about the chaos. 'Sometime in the day, I recollect, that we met—
some twenty-five to thirty of us—and decided to carry on an
underground movement. Who were there at the meeting I cannot
recall but Dayabhai Patel, Sardar's son, was certainly there. He
was my host. Dayabhai agreed to raise as much money as he
could and we decided to carry on the movement.'[7]

Sucheta, alongwith the AICC office secretary, Sadiq Ali,
decided to run the underground AICC office as all the prominent
leaders had been arrested. '…because with the arrest of all the
leaders nobody would accept any instruction or directive as
genuine unless it carried some known name. So, they thought, I
being Acharya Kripalani's wife, my name would carry conviction.
So overnight I was thrown into a larger role (than) I had ever
played.'[8] Sucheta and her team faced the challenge of keeping this
small set-up running without raising suspicion of the police. The
office did not function out of one premise but was spread out

over several places. Gandhi's call to 'Do or Die' found supporters across India with young men and women organizing themselves in spontaneous groups and taking to the streets to protest or bring out books to speak against British rule. The Congress workers felt the need to disseminate more information through an accessible medium. Dr Lohia struck upon the idea of an underground radio and with the help of a young woman, Usha Mehta and her brother set up a station. Sucheta has described the way the underground radio functioned, 'This radio had to be shifted almost every day from place to place as the police was out to catch it. I used to prepare the daily bulletins that were read over this radio. We were very proud of this achievement.... Miss Usha Mehta is a very brave young girl and when we knew that we were about to be discovered I told Lohia that we should stop it. But Lohia was very firm. He said, "No. Whatever happens we have to carry on." I said, "But you are not going to jail. It is poor Usha who will go to jail who announced." He said, "Doesn't matter, whoever may go to jail but we have to carry on." So, ultimately Usha was arrested while she was announcing. Her house was raided and she had a very tough time after that in jail.'[9] Being the driving force of the underground movement, Sucheta had several exciting experiences and near brushes with the police. She once spent the entire night outside her home in Bombay after she saw plainclothes policemen on every floor of her building which later turned out to be a raid on a home on another floor. Sucheta averted arrest once while travelling in a train after she tricked the police and disembarked at a station wearing a brightly-coloured silk sari and not her usual handspun white khadi sari. Once Sucheta and three other wanted leaders, including Aruna Asaf Ali and Dr Lohia, spent a night posing as patients at a doctor's clinic as they couldn't go home at the late hour after a surreptitious meeting without being spotted by the police. Sucheta finally got arrested in Patna and was lodged in the Patna Jail for a week and later shifted to Lucknow Jail. The underground movement was driven by young foot soldiers, but by 1944 it dissipated as the workers could not evade arrests and were picked up by the police. After her release from jail eighteen months later, Sucheta went to see Mahatma Gandhi. During this time, Kasturba Gandhi had passed away and a huge amount of monetary donations had been made in her name. Gandhi entrusted the work of the Kasturba Gandhi Memorial trust to Sucheta, and as organizing secretary she travelled extensively across India and worked with women in villages. However, this work came to an end as communal riots broke out in Noakhali in East Bengal in October 1946, and Sucheta became involved in relief and rehabilitation work. She is remembered not only for her fearlessness in going to a riot-affected area within ten days of the first incident of rioting but also for her thoroughness and hard work in bringing relief to the families.

WORK WITH REFUGEES

Sucheta had packed her suitcase to spend two days in Noakhali. After all, she was only accompanying her husband J. B. Kripalani, who had just been elected the Congress president and deputed by Gandhi following reports of communal violence in Noakhali. Sucheta had feared for her husband's life and wanted to accompany him. It took a lot of persuasion for Gandhi to allow her to go to Noakhali. She was sent as she was a Bengali, and Gandhi thought her presence would help J. B. Kripalani in understanding the locals better. Little did anyone know that she would stay back long after Kripalani leaves and steer the relief work in the riot-torn areas of Bengal for seven months.

In her autobiography, Sucheta recalls how there were no reliable accounts of the communal riots in Noakhali as no one had been able to reach Noakhali. 'Some Congress leaders in Bengal had tried to go but they had come back injured, so what actually was happening there was not known and Gandhiji was very worried. You will remember that Noakhali came after Calcutta Day.... This was a well organized incident. The Muslim League as well as the Muslim leaders (in East Bengal) had been wanting to take the revenge for the Great Calcutta killing and they were gradually working among the maulanas, some of whom were MLAs.... They had organized volunteers who were going from place to place for some weeks terrorizing the people. And then, on a particular day, on a signal they went and attacked the people, burnt the Hindu houses, killed people, took away the girls (and) looted them. All the bazars and everything was destroyed. But we knew nobody had any authentic or correct news.'[10] It took two attempts by J. B. Kripalani and Sucheta to reach Noakhali as railway lines had been uprooted and hundreds of boats burnt. They first used a plane from Calcutta Flying Club and then rode a boat to reach the first village.

On ground, they found villages that had been burnt down, Hindus who had been forced to eat beef, and stories of abductions and forcible marriages of girls and women. The villages wore a deserted look, and if there were any Hindu families left, there was a general atmosphere of fear amongst them. Sucheta hit an instant chord with the people, whom she persuaded to share their stories. While J. B. Kripalani left for Delhi, Sucheta stayed on and worked to establish small camps in villages, rescue Hindu families, bring them to safety, and rehabilitate them. This was no easy task as she and her team would walk 27 to 28 kilometres every day and had little food and money available to keep up the rescue work. After Sucheta spent three weeks in Noakhali, Gandhi arrived by rail to see for himself the ground situation and how the rehabilitation work could progress. As a mark of penance, Gandhi decided to walk barefoot through Noakhali. 'As soon as Gandhiji arrived, he made a radical change in our method of work. He said we should not try to take out the people and gather them in camps. Our workers singly or in small units should spread out all over the affected area and work among the Muslims and Hindus to bring about amity between the two communities. After all, the Hindus would have to live there with their Muslim neighbours. We have, therefore, to work for the unity of the two communities.'[11] Sucheta carried on her relief work and also persuaded the government to pay ex gratia to Hindu families so they could start their life afresh. Sucheta worked in Noakhali from October 1946 till April 1947. She returned to Delhi for a short while when she received disturbing news of communal riots in the North West Frontier Province and West Punjab. The Congress leaders could sense that Independence was near and J. B. Kripalani was deputed to hold talks with the maharaja of Kashmir, Hari Singh, and Sheikh Abdullah to bring about a settlement. Sucheta accompanied him, and they travelled to Lahore and Rawalpindi to reach Kashmir. Both the cities wore signs of massive plundering, arson, and communal tension. On their way back, Sucheta stayed on in Rawalpindi and went from village to village to gauge the extent of communal disharmony in the area. 'I went from village to village. There were places where there was nobody to tell us what had happened. Sometimes we would find one Sikh hiding somewhere who would be afraid to tell us but somehow or other we would cross-examine him and get some information.... There was mass killing on (such) a scale which I did not even see in Noakhali. When I saw the things that had happened in Punjab I was absolutely shattered.'[12]

By June 1947, Delhi started receiving a stream of refugees from Pakistan. As communal riots broke out at the time of Partition in August 1947, Sucheta and J. B. Kripalani formed a Central Relief and Rehabilitation Committee so that Sucheta could formally initiate relief work for refugees in an organized manner. Sucheta grouped together volunteers and waded into the intensive work of setting up camps at New Delhi Railway Station, Kingsway Camp, Kalkaji, and other locations in Delhi, appealing to people to provide food and dry ration for refugees and sourcing basic requirements such as tents as Delhi got inundated with trains arriving with thousands of displaced people from Pakistan. Gradually, the committee's work spread to other states including Tamil Nadu, Rajasthan, Punjab, and Karnataka. By now, Sucheta came to be recognized as a leader espousing the cause of refugees and fighting for their right to compensation. Over the next decade, she fought for them inside the newly-formed parliament, sometimes chairing special committees and shaping policies.

REPRESENTING THE PEOPLE

Sucheta was one of the fifteen women members elected to the Constituent Assembly. From 1942 to 1952, she was a member of the Constituent Assembly and the Uttar Pradesh legislative assembly shuttling between Lucknow and Delhi. In 1951, both Sucheta and husband J. B. Kripalani left the Congress as they felt that the newly-formed government no longer adhered to Gandhian principles and programmes. They formed a new party, Kisan Mazdoor Praja Party, which did not fare well in the first general election. Later, the party merged with Socialist Party of India to form the Praja Socialist Party (PSP) in 1952. Sucheta fought the first general election of independent India from New Delhi and not Uttar Pradesh on a PSP ticket. Her following among the refugees was evident in this election. She was returning to New Delhi after campaigning for her party's candidates in Himachal Pradesh when her car met with a major accident and fell into a river. She suffered spinal injuries and was bedridden during the crucial campaign phase. Her entire election was managed by friends, and her victory provided the proof of her popularity in New Delhi. Though she entered India's first Lok Sabha, Kripalani lost from Uttar Pradesh. She was chosen the leader of the party in the lower house of the parliament and worked in close collaboration with other Opposition leaders like Syama Prasad Mukherjee of the Hindu Mahasabha and Hiren Mukherjee and Renu Chakravarty of the Communist Party to force the government to address refugee problems. She passed the baton to J. B. Kripalani after he entered Lok Sabha following a by-election victory.

In 1956, Sucheta was persuaded by then Congress President U. N. Dhebar to rejoin the party and she won the next general election in 1957 on a Congress ticket. In 1955, Dr Lohia and his supporters broke from the PSP and formed a separate Socialist Party. However, Kripalani stayed with the PSP. J. B. Kripalani has described how the couple received flak for being in two different parties: 'It was an awkward situation, because our people had not learnt that in public life, wife and husband may differ enjoying a separate vote in the legislature, each in her and his own right. The result of our belonging to separate political parties was that whenever she stood for election, her rival always said, "her husband does not agree with her". When I stood for election, my rival said, "even his wife does not agree with him". This attitude was adopted even by ministers when they replied to my criticism of their policies. One day in parliament, some minister in answer to my criticism said, "even his wife does not agree with him". I retorted, "I did not marry a highly educated wife to work in the kitchen and breed children." This was a telling reply for the minister. The minister afterwards apologized for what he had said. We talk of modernism but beneath our skin we think and behave in the old ways! We were criticized both ways as was politically advantageous to our opponents. It was the old mentality that the wife was the appendage of the husband in spite of universal franchise.'[13]

It was a chance suggestion by J. B. Kripalani to the senior Congress leader C. B. Gupta, from Uttar Pradesh, that saw Sucheta take on her first ministerial responsibility after playing organizational roles. Gupta was trying to unseat Uttar Pradesh chief minister at the time, Sampurnanand. While meeting Sucheta and J. B. Kripalani during their Lucknow visit, Gupta was angry and turned to Sucheta and suggested that she return to Uttar Pradesh to serve it. 'Jocularly, Kripalani ji said, "Alright you become the chief minister; then she will come and help you." The whole thing was said as a joke. We never thought that he was going to throw out Sampurnanand... When he did so, he started putting through his trunk calls pressing me to come and join him,' Sucheta recalls in an interview.[14] Sucheta was sworn-in as the minister of labour, community development, and industries in December 1960. She travelled extensively to gain knowledge about the workings of the district administration and encouraged people, especially workers, to directly approach her to represent their grievances. In 1963, Tamil Nadu Chief Minister K. Kamaraj suggested to Prime Minister Jawaharlal

Nehru that senior leaders of the party should be roped in for organizational work. As part of what came to be known as the Kamaraj Plan, several chief ministers, including C. B. Gupta, resigned and went back to work at the grassroots to galvanize the party.

INDIA'S FIRST WOMAN CHIEF MINISTER

After Gupta resigned, he threw his weight behind Sucheta and she was sworn in as the first woman chief minister of a state in India. Her term as the chief minister of Uttar Pradesh, India's largest state is marked by several administrative changes that she brought about. As a minister, Sucheta had taken a firm stand against outside interference in running her departments and she continued with the same intolerance towards interference as a chief minister. She found the bureaucracy bogged down by considerations of caste and religion. The initial part of her first year was spent in streamlining the appointments and freeing them of such pressures for a more efficient administration. She appointed a new chief secretary and promoted efficient junior officers to positions of responsibility to implement her vision for the state.

Sucheta is credited with laying the foundation of the Green Revolution in Uttar Pradesh. She set up a separate agency to reinvigorate a large number of defunct tubewells, which were causing losses to the tune of ₹5 to ₹6 crore per year. She also streamlined the directorate of industries and incentivized new businesses in different parts of the state. Sucheta realized that Uttar Pradesh did not have adequate power infrastructure to support the setting up of big industries. She organized three focal points apart from Kanpur—Mirzapur, Haridwar, and Allahabad—and set up big industries. Working on the Gandhian principle of self-reliance through small and cottage industries, she also eased the processes required to provide loans for raw materials.

She witnessed the first major test in 1964 when her government was pitted against the judiciary in an unprecedented constitutional crisis. A Socialist Party worker, Keshab Singh, threw a bundle of handbills from the visitors' gallery on the floor of the legislative assembly while the house was in session. This was considered a breach of privilege and Keshab Singh was sentenced to seven days' imprisonment. He moved a petition in the Allahabad High Court, which in turn released him on bail and issued a show-cause notice to the speaker and Sucheta, as she was the chief minister and leader of the house. Angling for a confrontation, the speaker and the members passed a resolution directing that a warrant be taken out to arrest the two judges who had issued the show-cause notice. The judges filed a petition in high court challenging this resolution, and it was heard by more than twenty judges constituting the entire high court. The judges stayed the arrest of the two judges and issued another show-cause notice to the speaker and the chief minister. Amid this unending conflict, Sucheta sought the central government's intervention and asked the government to seek advice from the Supreme Court. The opinion of the apex court said that the courts could question an act of legislature in a limited nature. The conflict was resolved when the Allahabad High Court dismissed Keshab Singh's petition.

Sucheta had started having differences with C. B. Gupta almost as soon as she took over as chief minister—Gupta did not approve of her changing the way bureaucracy was functioning. By 1966, the rift between the two deepened. Sucheta was at the centre of a tussle between two camps to claim chief ministership. 'By this time, because of my independent way of functioning, Gupta ji was also angry with me,' Sucheta told Uma Shanker in her interview. 'Kamalapatiji (Tripathi) was already opposed. Kamlapatiji had joined my ministry for a short while. Then he had resigned along with his group. And there were two methods by which chief ministers are thrown out in UP. One, by University trouble and the other by a strike in the Secretariat.'[15] Around this time, Uttar Pradesh government officers at the Lucknow secretariat went on strike—this was curious especially since it came after Sucheta had appointed a pay commission and accepted its recommendation for a pay hike. It was evident that the reasons were more political.

J. B. Kripalani has given a detailed account of the last few months of Sucheta's chief ministership in her autobiography. 'A minister at Nainital had been fresh with a European lady, married to an Indian. She complained to the Governor and to Sucheta.... Sucheta called the minister. She told him that the government had nothing to do with his private conduct. But he had created a scandal about himself.... He must, therefore, resign. Reluctantly, he did so. But afterwards he, supported by other Congressmen, who were against Sucheta's continuing as the chief minister, commenced a smear campaign against her.'[16] This coupled with the secretariat staff's strike and students' trouble in Lucknow University upset Sucheta and she sent her resignation to Congress president K. Kamaraj. On 28 August 1966, she wrote to Kamaraj expressing her disappointment over the two factions fighting over the post of chief minister and the party high command not clarifying that the chief minister would not be changed. 'It is not pleasant to read both in the local and Delhi papers day after day that the unity talks have again continued and that the parties are coming nearer and then the next day to read that the talks have broken down for want of common aim, to be resumed again. This does credit neither to the Congress organization nor to the government. It is also a fact that if the officers feel that I am holding the office pending the unity between the two contending leaders and if they have further the idea that talks for the unity after many failures, are still continuing, they cannot give me loyal service. If the high command does not make it clear that there will be no change in the government till the next general elections...it is not worthwhile for me to continue in my present position,' she wrote.[17] The Congress leadership decided in February 1967 that there would be no change in chief minister. However, within a month she was called by Prime Minister Indira Gandhi, who asked her to resign as chief minister and accept governorship of a state. 'Sucheta was surprised and reminded her of the statement that Kamaraj had made about her resignation a month earlier with her (Smt. Gandhi's) approval. Smt. Gandhi told her that she thought that her resignation would facilitate the Congress election campaign in UP. Sucheta told her that she was not unfamiliar with organizing elections.... Smt. Indira Gandhi said that she had no doubt about her capacity to organize the election campaign but elections required large funds which she (Sucheta) may not herself be able to raise.'[18] Indira had told Sucheta that when asked about collecting funds, Gupta had said that he could do it only if he were made the chief minister. Sucheta refused to resign on this account and also declined the offer of governorship. As the two factions against her joined hands, she was forced to send in her resignation in February 1967. The governor told her to discharge her duties till the general elections. Sucheta successfully contested a parliament seat from Gonda in Uttar Pradesh and left state matters to Gupta.

Sucheta remained a vociferous champion of women's rights all through her active political life. She could foresee the need for a better support system if women were to join the workforce. 'If modern India has accepted the social phenomenon of the increasing number of working women, there should be suitable facilities provided for them. For instance, good hostels for young working girls is a crying need. Even in New Delhi, the facilities provided are totally inadequate. Girls working in the rural areas, most often alone, need not only suitable accommodation, but, above all, protection. It is a difficult problem, but it must be tackled by developing a greater sense of social responsibility among the people. The government must be actively vigilant in this regard. With a large number of women working, many social problems will arise, which the government and society must jointly tackle. Finally, no woman should claim to get a job because she is a woman. Let her take her place strictly on merit and ability. But she must be provided with suitable facilities to enable her to fulfil her obligations and to take her rightful place in society,' she wrote in 1974.[19] Even then she spoke against the traditional division of labour between men and women and emphasized the need for the husband to shoulder equal family responsibilities. 'What is the future of women in India? I am sure their progress on the present lines is bound to continue. It is inconceivable that they can ever again be confined within their narrow domestic walls. Most women will certainly be preoccupied with their home and family responsibilities—but the advancement of education as well as economic compulsions will bring out more and more women to seek jobs and careers. With more working mothers, the problems of care of children and running the home will loom large. In a joint family, these problems need not necessarily arise. But in a husband–wife family unit, with both of them working, care of children will be a serious problem. This will require sufficient numbers of creches, day-schools, etc, conducted by society to relieve the working mothers.'[20]

Two years after she entered parliament, the Congress split in 1969 and Sucheta left the party with Morarji Desai's faction. She lost the subsequent election in 1971 and retired from politics. Years of nurturing Uttar Pradesh had taken a toll on Sucheta's health and she had developed diabetes. In 1974, she suffered a heart attack and passed away.

II

The Inheritors

SONIA GANDHI

The Great Unifier

'Friends. Throughout these past six years that I have been in politics, one thing has been clear to me. And that is, as I have often stated, that the post of Prime Minister is not my aim. I was always certain that if I ever found myself in the position that I am in today, I would follow my own inner voice. Today, that voice tells me that I must humbly decline this post,' Sonia Gandhi said in an address to the newly-elected MPs of the Congress Party on 18 May 2004. Cries of 'No, no' filled the Central Hall of Parliament as the grand old party of India grappled with the shock of this announcement. Who refuses the top job in the largest democracy of the world?

Undeterred, Gandhi went on, 'You have unanimously elected

me your leader; in doing so you have reposed your faith in me. It is this faith that has placed me under tremendous pressure to reconsider my decision. Yet, I must abide by the principles which have guided me all along.' Shocked Congress MPs interrupted her again and again. The Congress-led United Progressive Alliance (UPA) had just defeated the incumbent government led by the Bharatiya Janata Party (BJP) veteran Atal Bihari Vajpayee. Through a carefully-crafted strategy of bringing out the failings of India's first stable non-Congress government and stitching together a rainbow seat-sharing alliance with regional parties, Gandhi had delivered a convincing victory. But after a pleasant surprise, she delivered a harsh blow to the Congress. She refused to lead the government. 'Power for itself has never attracted me, nor has position been my goal. My aim has always been to defend the secular foundation of our nation and the poor of our country—the creed sacred to Indiraji and Rajivji. We have moved forward a significant step towards this goal. We have waged a successful battle. But we have not won the war. That is a long and arduous struggle, and I will continue it with full determination. But I appeal to you to understand the force of my conviction. I request you to accept my decision and to recognise that I will not reverse it,' said Gandhi as she read out the message in both English and Hindi. In between, MPs interrupted her and she patiently but firmly said, "Bolne dijiye (allow me to speak).'

Over the next three hours, MP after MP took the microphone imploring her to lead the government. After all, they had sought votes in her name. Mani Shankar Aiyar, a trusted lieutenant of Gandhi's slain husband Rajiv, pleaded with her to listen to the inner voice of the people. 'The inner voice of people says you should become the PM. Please don't leave us. Please continue to lead us. None in this hall other than you deserve to occupy the prime ministership,' he said. Former Madhya Pradesh chief minister Arjun Singh said, 'Forces of darkness exist today as they did in 1948 when Mahatma Gandhi was assassinated...the nation is at the crossroads of history and an opportunity had come for defeating Fascist forces once and for all.'

Gandhi was unmoved. She had begun the meeting with a plea but ended it with telling her partymen to trust her to take her own decisions. On that hot Tuesday evening she had done the unthinkable and with it silenced her critics who had, for decades, painted Gandhi as a megalomaniac foreign bahu (daughter-in-law) of the powerful Nehru–Gandhi family who had undeservedly inherited the political legacy. First taken aback by this decision, Congressmen applauded Gandhi's sacrifice.

Gandhi's decision came after at least three meetings with son Rahul and daughter Priyanka. What went on inside the meetings will never, be known but if party seniors are to be believed, Rahul feared for his mother's life, which became the primary concern guiding her final decision. Later, in a rare interview to the senior journalist Vir Sanghvi, Gandhi said that she had decided in 1999, when the Vajpayee government had been voted out and the Congress was on the verge of forming the government at the centre, that Dr Manmohan Singh would be the prime minister. Gandhi had gone to see President K. R. Narayanan twice—once by herself and the second time with Singh. Gandhi had told Narayanan that if Congress were to form the government, Singh would be the prime minister. 'I let Manmohan Singh know in 1999 that he, not I, would be prime minister,' she said.[1] The impression given by family loyalists has been that Gandhi knew all along that she will never accept the prime ministership, but it was impossible to win the elections in 2004 with this information out in the public.

K. Natwar Singh, a diplomat-politician and one-time trusted aide of the Gandhi family, provides a different reasoning for this episode. 'The Gandhi family, however, was a house divided. Rahul was vehemently opposed to his mother becoming prime minister, fearing that she would lose her life, much like his grandmother and his father. Matters reached a climax after Rahul said that he was prepared to take any possible step to prevent his mother from taking up the prime ministership. Rahul is a strong-willed person; this was no ordinary threat. He gave Sonia twenty-four hours to decide. Manmohan Singh, Suman Dubey, Priyanka, and I were present at that moment. Sonia was visibly agonized and in tears. As a mother, it was impossible for her to ignore Rahul. He had his way. That was the reason for her not becoming prime minister. Only Manmohan Singh and I were aware of Sonia's decision. Later, she called a meeting in which she announced that she was offering the post of PM to Manmohan Singh.'[2]

Irrespective of what you believe, Gandhi's life from the dusty industrial town of Orbassano in Italy to the corridors of power in New Delhi is nothing short of a modern-day coming-of-age story.

THE FAIRYTALE

Sonia Gandhi was born on 9 December 1946 as Sonia Maino to Paola and Stefano Maino, a contractor with his own construction business. The second of three sisters, Gandhi's school teachers remember her as 'vivacious, but not particularly exuberant or effervescent. She studied just enough to get by. What mattered was, above all, having a good time.'[3] After she finished school, it was decided that she would go to England and study at the School of Languages at Cambridge and it was felt that 'Sonia's language skills could help the family in her capacity as an interpreter.'[4] She arrived in Cambridge in 1965, three years after Rajiv and Sanjay—Jawaharlal Nehru's grandsons. 'The homesick Sonia pining for Italian home food discovered that the nearest thing to it was the Greek restaurant called 'Varsity'. There, amidst the noisy and boisterous undergraduates, she had noticed Rajiv who stood out.'[5] It was love at first sight for both of them. The courtship spanned from February 1965 till July 1966. By then Indira Gandhi had taken over as the prime minister of India and met her future daughter-in-law in London. In November 1966, Rajiv travelled to Italy to meet the Maino family. As her father had reservations about his daughter marrying a foreigner and adjusting to a life in a new country and culture, he asked the couple to wait for a year till Sonia was twenty-one. Even Indira felt that a year of separation would help the young couple realize the depth of their feelings. After a year, Sonia arrived in Delhi on 13 January 1968 to marry Rajiv. They got married on 25 February 1968 at the prime minister's residence at 1 Safdarjung Road. Years later, when asked about how she adjusted to life in India, she said, 'Frankly I came here because I was madly in love with my husband and he with me. Nothing else mattered. It didn't matter what I had to face.'[6] Thus began years of marital bliss. The Gandhi family was a traditional Indian joint family and the newlyweds moved in with Indira. Gandhi had a son, Rahul, in June 1970 and a daughter, Priyanka, in January 1972. However, the household changed once Sanjay married the seventeen-year-old Maneka Anand in 1974. There were several breakdowns—one of which involves Maneka flinging her wedding ring at Sanjay and upsetting Indira as it was her mother Kamala Nehru's ring. Gandhi is believed to have picked up the ring and kept it for her daughter Priyanka.

These were tumultuous years for Indira and Sonia managed the household and saw her mother-in-law managing the Indo-Pakistan War of 1971, the unprecedented refugee inflow from Bangladesh, the imposition of the Emergency in 1975, and her subsequent ouster from power. She remained in the shadows then and became a trusted aide of Indira at home. Maneka, on the other hand, was politically inclined. She started a magazine called *Surya* which was used extensively during the Emergency and post-Emergency years to embarrass Janata Party leaders. 'According to an interview with Vir Sanghvi in *Imprint* in June 1984, a disillusioned Khushwant Singh said that *Surya* had been Sanjay's idea because during the Emergency he had approached Khushwant Singh and said of Maneka, "Please put her to some job! Get her out of my hair!".... She was very brash and she never really measured her words before she spoke. And he was getting a little tired and fed up.'[7]

Tragedy struck the Gandhi family in June 1980 when Sanjay crashed his two-seater aircraft and died instantly. The household was numb with grief. Indira had lost her favourite son and trusted political heir. Despite Gandhi's opposition, Rajiv had to

fill his brother's shoes. Speaking to the managing director of
India Today, Aroon Purie, at the India Today Conclave in 2018,
Gandhi explained, 'There were reasons for me for not wanting
my husband to join politics. You see when you are in politics
and if you are a genuine person and you genuinely care then
everything comes second. So with Rajivji he had a few flights
and it was more of leisure time. We had small children and
we were a very happy family. I felt if he joined politics then it
would be the end of that.' Despite her opposition, Gandhi knew
Rajiv would stand by his mother. With Indira as prime minister
and her husband in politics, Gandhi finally renounced her Italian
citizenship in 1983. Even then, she was never heard. She was
shy, introverted, and almost unsmiling in public. She has herself
explained it as her innate fear of an attack on her husband.

In 1984, tragedy struck again. Following Operation Blue Star,
for which army had been ordered to enter the Sikh shrine of the
Golden Temple in Amritsar and flush out supporters of Khalistan,
there was a massive backlash against Indira. On 31 October
1984, her two Sikh bodyguards, Satwant Singh and Beant Singh,
shot her dead at her 1 Safdarjung Road residence as Indira was
walking to her office at 1 Akbar Road for an interview. Gandhi
was taking a bath when she heard gunshots and screamed from
inside. She and Indira's private secretary, R. K. Dhawan, rushed
Indira to All India Institute of Medical Sciences (AIIMS). The
prime minister was declared brought dead. As reality sunk in,
Rajiv told a teary-eyed Gandhi that the party wanted him to
be sworn in as prime minister. On her reservations about Rajiv
taking over his mother's place, Gandhi told veteran journalist
Shekhar Gupta, 'After my mother-in-law was killed, I knew he
too would be killed. All of us, my children and I, knew that it
was just a question of when.'[8]

When Rajiv took over as prime minister, it was the first time
after Lal Bahadur Shastri that the person occupying the high office
had a spouse. Coupled with the natural curiosity the world had
in the family, the Gandhis became like the Kennedys of United
States. Between 1984 and 1989, Gandhi remained the demure

wife who had a ceremonial role in the administration. 'Those who met the Gandhis were surprised to find Sonia standing behind husband never saying a word. "If Rajiv kept standing for hours, even though we could have the same discussion sitting on the chairs in the room, she would also keep standing behind him and would not even utter a word to suggest that we sit down," said some political associates.'[9] The Bofors controversy and the Opposition's campaign 'Gali gali mein shor hai, Rajiv Gandhi chor hai (the people on the streets know that Rajiv Gandhi is stealing)' stuck. Though the Congress emerged as the single largest party in the 1989 general elections, Rajiv could not form the government and sat in the Opposition. India saw two prime ministers—V. P. Singh and Chandra Shekhar—within sixteen months. Finally, mid-term elections were announced for May 1991. Though Rajiv was the star campaigner, Gandhi and Priyanka toured extensively, handling the Amethi campaign. 'Conducting Rajiv's campaign by proxy, mother and daughter "did" as many as fifteen villages a day. The people of Amethi did not mind Rajiv's absence saying, "He has to look after the entire country, while Sonia bahuji is here with us, isn't she?".... Gandhi's speeches were short and to the point. She said, "My husband has worked the hardest for your happiness and prosperity and I am working for my husband. Only the Congress can give you good government. So strengthen my husband's hands." She then folded her own hands and moved on to the next campaign venue, frequently stepping out to talk to the women....'[10] Her life changed on 20 May 1990, when an LTTE suicide bomber bent down to touch Rajiv's feet and triggered a blast at a rally in Sriperumbudur in Tamil Nadu. The world watched Gandhi, who in her hour of intense grief noticed the flowerless coffin of her husband's bodyguard Pradeep and dutifully placed some flowers on it.

When you hold high office it comes with an unimaginable amount of responsibility. Rajiv may have passed away but there was the bigger responsibility of leading India's oldest political party. Within two days of his death, the Congress Working

Committee, the party's highest decision-making body had met and unanimously elected Sonia Gandhi as Congress president. On 23 May 1991, Gandhi declined the presidentship. 'I am deeply touched by the trust placed on me by the Congress Working Committee. However, the tragedy that has befallen on my children and myself does not make it possible for me to accept the presidentship of the party,' she wrote in a letter. Gandhi refused to give in to the demands of the Congressmen and decided to remain in the shadows. It would be political naiveté, however, to conclude that she remained aloof to the party affairs after this. Over the next few years, Gandhi continued to wield power and influence party decisions without holding any post. In fact, when she did not take over as the Congress president after Rajiv's assassination, she chose his successor. In his autobiography, K. Natwar Singh says, 'After the funeral, there was intense political activity. The aspirants to the post of Congress president included Arjun Singh, N. D. Tiwari, Sharad Pawar, and Madhavrao Scindia. Sonia Gandhi herself refused to be the president when it was suggested to her. I told her that the time had come for her to indicate her preference for the role; whoever she chose would naturally become PM. For so momentous a decision, I suggested she ask P. N. Haksar for advice.'[11] On Haksar's advice, Gandhi's emissaries approached the vice-president of India, Shankar Dayal Sharma,[12] and then P. V. Narasimha Rao. Rao was pulled out of retirement to become India's ninth prime minister and the first from outside the Gandhi family to head a minority government and complete a full term in office.

Her impression that the Congress government under Rao was dragging its feet over a probe into Rajiv's assassination defined her relationship with the prime minister. Her first full-length speech in Hindi was in her family's constituency of Amethi in 1995 'deploring the dilatory tactics regarding the inquiry and regretting that the policies of Nehru, Indira, and Rajiv were being given a go-by.'[13] The mistrust between Rao and Gandhi grew. Congressmen aggrieved by the prime minister found audience with Gandhi even though she never expressed her opinion in those meetings. She was careful about appearances. 'When senior cabinet ministers such as N. D. Tiwari, Arjun Singh, and several others were forming a separate party named Congress (T), they were sure of Sonia's tacit support. But when they beseeched her to "grace its inaugural session even for five minutes", she flatly refused.'[14] Her wariness of Rao became so entrenched in her psyche that the prime minister's initiatives have never been acknowledged within the Congress circles or lauded in party literature and his portrait is still given a miss at party functions.

Towards the end of September 1996, Rao relinquished the post of Congress president and the seasoned Bihar Congress leader Sitaram Kesri was elected the party president. India saw three prime ministers—Atal Bihari Vajpayee, H. D. Deve Gowda, and Inder Kumar Gujral—between 1996 and 1998.

LEADING THE CONGRESS

It took Sonia Gandhi six years to show any inclination towards an active role in politics. During these years, the Congress Party lost successive elections. Gandhi used the intervening period to educate herself.

She took primary membership of the party at the 80th Plenary Session of the Congress in Kolkata in August 1997. Former president and Congress veteran Pranab Mukherjee writes in his book *The Coalition Years: 1996-2012*, 'Sitaram Kesri was slowly losing support. He was not popular amongst senior CWC leaders even though they had gone along with P. V.'s proposal to appoint him president. That, coupled with the disenchantment of the Congress MPs in the Lok Sabha with the actions of the party under Kesri's leadership, affected his already receding support base.' The Jain Commission, set up to investigate Rajiv's assassination, submitted its interim report which suggested that the DMK, a part of the United Front government under Gujral, was involved in encouraging LTTE militants. Congress demanded Gujral sack the DMK ministers who held important portfolios. When the prime minister refused, the Congress withdrew support and mid-term elections were announced for February–March 1998. Prominent Congress leaders kept urging Gandhi to take charge of the party. 'Fed up with Kesri's antics, manipulations, and unpredictable nature, leaders like K. Karunakaran, Arjun Singh, A. K. Antony, Jitendra Prasada, Vijay Bhaskar Reddy, V. N. Gadgil, and Madhav Sinh Solanki kept exercising pressure on Sonia to intervene. Singh and Prasada, who had masterminded the collapse of the I. K. Gujral government on the basis of the Jain Commission report, gently reminded her of the need to reciprocate the feelings of the Congress workers who could not tolerate the presence of two DMK ministers in a government supported by the Congress.'[15] On 28 December 1997, on the 112th Foundation Day of the Indian National Congress, Gandhi announced she would campaign for the party in the parliamentary elections. On 11 January 1998, Gandhi kicked off the nationwide campaign from the city of Sriperumbudur—where Rajiv had been assassinated seven years ago. Hours before her arrival, a bomb explosion in central Chennai (then Madras) injured three persons and shattered the glass panes of the United States consular office. The symbolism wasn't lost on anyone. Accompanied by daughter Priyanka said 'she had decided to campaign because unity was under threat, not because she wanted political office herself.'[16]

Years later, she spoke about her decision to enter politics and said, 'The Congress party was going through some problems and many senior leaders came and asked me to help the Congress, to come and participate in Congress activities because they felt that it would help the party to a certain extent. I thought hard about it. There was a conflict within me because I was not ever keen to join politics. In fact, I didn't even want my husband to join politics because I had seen my mother-in-law's life struggle, being rejected, all sorts of calumnies being hurled at her. She led a life of service and a very difficult life and then she was killed. I felt at that time with my husband that possibly the same would happen to him.... Anyways, it wasn't my fear of being killed. It was a difficult decision to take. It was a difficult phase. But I have in my office photographs of my husband and mother-in-law.

Each time I walked past those photographs I felt that I wasn't responding to my duty to this family and to the country.'[17] Once again, Gandhi showed immense political shrewdness as she took charge of the Congress campaign without holding any political office—in a way it was like taking on a job without any moral responsibility. She addressed 130-odd public meetings in the run-up to the 1998 elections drawing massive crowds. The cheering crowds at her rallies, however, did not translate into votes. The Congress added a single seat to its tally but its voteshare plunged by 3 per cent. But the blame was Kesri's to take as Gandhi was above reproach. It is a different matter that for the first time a party president had been kept out of campaigning for elections. The clamour for Kesri's removal increased post elections, and he quit as party president in what is popularly termed as a bloodless coup in March 1998.

Gandhi was formally elected as Congress president on 6 April 1998 at Siri Fort Auditorium in New Delhi. In her opening remarks she spoke of the need to revive the party, 'I am no saviour, as some of you might want to believe. We must be realistic in our expectations. The revival of our party is going to be a long drawn process, involving sincere hardwork, from each and everyone of us. But I do have an abiding faith in the path shown to us by our leaders in the past. It is the only path that will lead us to our goal. And I believe we can attain it if we act together and hold together. In practical terms, our task is to give the people of India an organization that stands for them, that fights for their rights and is anchored to the principles on which our nationhood is founded.....' Gandhi's biggest challenge was a lack of oratorial skills. Though she was fluent in English and knew Hindi well, she was almost wooden in her delivery—a fact she has herself acknowledged. 'Public speaking is not my forte as you all know and in Hindi it is even more stressful for me,' she has said.[18] Her Hindi speeches were typed in over thirty font size in Roman script with only a few lines occupying each page.

As Vajpayee formed a coalition government at the centre, Gandhi got busy putting the Congress in order, calling a party conclave at Pachmarhi and underlining the need to bring back Congress supremacy. Gandhi drafted in Ambika Soni, a long-time family loyalist and an articulate and intelligent politician, as her political adviser.[19] Though Gandhi went for continuity, retaining Kesri's team, the Congress president's office changed drastically. Archana Dalmia, who worked closely with Gandhi as the secretary of the All India Congress Committee (AICC) attached to her office, says, 'Soon after Soniaji took over as the Congress president, we regularly sent her a list of people from all over the country who wanted to meet her. "How can we solve so many problems?" she asked. My answer was, "Half the people who come to see you take a photograph with you [and] go back happy feeling they got an audience with you. Every morning she would meet 400–500 people and leave the petitions to us to handle." "Don't call it darshan," she rebuked us. "It is not a darshan. Call it jan sampark. That is much more appropriate."' A grievance redressal cell was resurrected by Gandhi and all the petitions came here. 'Senior women leaders like Margaret Alva, Ambika Soni, and Saroj Kharpade were made a part of this cell. Every morning we took turns to man the office and listen to the grievances of the people who had begun coming in hordes,' says Dalmia.

Gandhi's first political test came when Jayalalithaa's AIADMK pulled out of Vajpayee's government and the thirteen-month-old government lost the vote of confidence by a single vote in April 1999. Gandhi staked claim to form the government. This is where she metamorphosed from a reluctant politician out to save the Congress to the power-hungry Italian in the minds of the electorate. On the steps of the Rashtrapati Bhavan she famously proclaimed, 'How much do they say they have: 270? Well, we have 272 and we hope to get many more.' She had calculated the numbers opposing the Vajpayee government on the floor of the parliament as numbers willing to support the Congress in its bid to form the government. That was not to be, and Gandhi flunked her first political test. Once again, she did not take the blame—after all she was new to politics and had been misled by off-the-mark calculations of her inner coterie.

As the party prepared to take on the BJP in the 1999 elections, there was internal rebellion against Gandhi's Italian origins. At a CWC meeting, party seniors Sharad Pawar, Tariq Anwar, and P. A. Sangma pointed out that the BJP's campaign against Gandhi's foreign origins was finding favour with the electorate. Then came the unkindest cut. 'We know very little about you, about your parents,' Sangma told her. Those present claim that Sonia was shocked by Sangma's bluntness.[20] Though Gandhi resigned, the party did not accept it and the trio left the Congress to form the Nationalist Congress Party (NCP). Gandhi led the Congress in the 1999 elections and made her electoral foray.

EMERGING AS A LEADER

In the 1999 parliamentary elections, Gandhi filed her nominations from two constituencies—Amethi in Uttar Pradesh and Bellary in Karnataka—both Congress bastions and chosen carefully to convey the impression of a pan-Indian leader contesting from the north and south of India. The BJP, under Vajpayee, had forged an alliance—the National Democratic Alliance (NDA)—of about twenty parties and won a majority, becoming the first such experiment since 1984 and ending years of political instability in India. The Congress sat in the Opposition under Gandhi. The five years as a first-time Lok Sabha MP and leader of the Opposition, pitted against a fiery orator and a clever politician like Vajpayee, were difficult. But Gandhi worked hard to shake off her inhibitions and lead a crumbling Congress in the parliament. 'Having acquired the status of leader of the Opposition, Sonia was expected to interact with her political adversaries like Mulayam Singh Yadav, Chandra Shekhar, Sharad Pawar, Mayawati, P. A. Sangma, and others. As she was shy and reluctant to approach them directly, there was a lack of coordination and functional relationship within the Opposition ranks. Samajwadi Party leaders Mulayam Singh Yadav and Amar Singh began openly discrediting her over her failure to take the Opposition along.'[21]

Initially, she frittered away several opportunities that the NDA government found itself embroiled in—including the Tehelka expose[22], Unit Trust of India scandal[23], and a failed summit between Vajpayee and Pakistan's president, Pervez Musharraf, in Agra.[24] However, she learnt the ropes quickly and the NDA's term was marked by sharp exchanges between a belligerent Gandhi and a sharp-witted Vajpayee. The foundation of the frigid relationship between the two leaders was laid by Gandhi in the run-up to the 1999 parliamentary elections. At a rally in Ujjain, Madhya Pradesh, Gandhi had lashed out at the Vajpayee government for buying sugar from Pakistan at the height of the Kargil conflict. She had used the term gaddar (traitor) and said the traitors had helped the enemy in procuring arms with that money.[25] The Congress later clarified that Gandhi had not named the prime minister, but the BJP ignored it. Narendra Modi, who was the party general secretary and spokesperson then, said, 'That Mrs Sonia Gandhi should call the prime minister of India a gaddar, that she should call a leader of Atalji's stature and record of public service a gaddar, is a new low in perversity—even by the standards of the Congress.'[26]

The exchanges between the two leaders only got more vicious. Addressing the BJP national executive in Goa on 12 April 2002, Vajpayee had said, 'I read somewhere in a newspaper that the Congress party has decided not to topple my government. Should I thank them for this or should I say that the grapes are sour? How would the government fall? They toppled it once, but could not form it themselves. Again people voted and again we were given a chance to serve.'[27] Gandhi took on Vajpayee immediately at the ongoing Congress chief ministers' conclave in Guwahati. Though Vajpayee made a general remark, Gandhi got personal. 'Whenever he loses his mansik santulan (mental balance), he speaks like this,' she said at a press conference at the end of the conclave.[28]

In September 2003, Gandhi snubbed Vajpayee's overture to reach out to the Opposition. He had suggested a 'harmonious tuning of relationship' at a function in New Delhi. However, this was the aftermath of the Godhra carnage in 2002, and Gandhi said, 'Our tunes can never match with those who are attempting to destroy the country's secular fabric by spreading hatred and endangering national unity and security.'[29] In the run-up to the 2004 elections, their relations hit another low. At a roadshow in Solapur, which was supposed to be significant as it saw Gandhi and Pawar sharing the dais for the first time since he walked out of the Congress in 1999, Gandhi again took on Vajpayee without naming him. By now, she had realized that naming him only brought on her the BJP's wrath and did not go down well with the electorate. She referred to him as a mukhota (mask) for the communal forces in the country. 'But a mask will always only be a mask. It does not take much time for the real face beneath that mask to be exposed. It has been ripped off over and over again and the real face has been amply exposed by now. And we must all get together to defeat the communal forces in this country,' she said.[30] It took Gandhi decades to acknowledge that Vajpayee was adept at taking everybody along. Almost fifteen years later, she compared Prime Minister Narendra Modi and Vajpayee and said, 'Vajpayee had great respect for parliamentary procedure.' At the *India Today* conclave in 2018, Gandhi said that democracy should allow for dissent and debate and not monologues. 'The present situation is such that there is no accommodative spirit.... It is our right, it is right of Opposition. We worked very well when Prime Minister Vajpayee was there,' she said, in response to a question.[31]

During these five years in the Opposition, Gandhi concentrated on building a grassroots-level organization and bringing the Congress back to power in the states. She brought a system of various committees in the party. After she took over as party president, the Congress formed governments in Arunachal Pradesh, Assam, Chhattisgarh, Delhi, Maharashtra, Madhya Pradesh, Manipur, Punjab, Puducherry, Rajasthan, and Uttarakhand. However, by 2003, the party ceded ground in the Hindi heartland and lost Chhattisgarh, Rajasthan, and Madhya

Pradesh. It could retain power in Delhi and wrest back Himachal Pradesh from the BJP. Pramod Mahajan, BJP's crisis manager, advised Vajpayee to cash in on this success and advance the Lok Sabha elections by six months from October 2004 to April 2004. By early January, Gandhi had drafted her son Rahul. The election is remembered for BJP's 'India Shining' campaign where the ruling party showcased its national highway project. The opinion polls predicted a BJP victory. Congress crafted a well-designed campaign of 'Aam aadmi ko kya mila? (What did the common man get?)'. In the five years, Gandhi had seen the BJP's coalition government working well. The Congress had realized that coalition politics was a reality. From its Panchmarhi Conclave in 1998, when it declared 'coalitions will be considered where absolutely necessary,' to the Shimla conclave in 2003 where is described coalitions as necessary, the Congress said 'it would be prepared to enter into appropriate electoral coalition arrangements with secular parties.' Congress strategists went state-by-state and entered into alliances with regional parties. The BJP did not realize that the 'India Shining' narrative was restricted to urban centres with increasing forex reserves and upswing in markets, but rural India was struggling with unemployment, increasing debt, rising prices, and a lack of educational opportunities. The Congress successfully tapped into this sentiment and worked on poll arithmetic through its alliances. The result was a shocking defeat for the BJP-led NDA in May 2004—the Congress had pulled off a surprise victory after accepting the reality of coalition politics. The party brought its nineteen alliance partners together under the umbrella of the United Progressive Alliance (UPA) to form the government at the centre.

THE POWER BEHIND THE THRONE

After the victory, Gandhi shocked everyone with her decision to give up prime ministership. Congress veteran Anand Sharma says, 'I know she wasn't keen on taking over as prime minister. All efforts were made to persuade her but she refused to be persuaded. She wasn't yearning for power and did not want the BJP to take advantage of this false narrative they had created. She wanted a prime minister who could deliver equitable development and implement the Congress' reforms-based agenda.' Sharma remembers how the Congress Party constitution was changed as Gandhi passed the baton to Dr Manmohan Singh. By convention, the Congress president is also the Congress Parliamentary Party (CPP) leader, who in turn is invited by the president to form the government. 'The party constitution had to be changed for Dr Manmohan Singh to take charge as prime minister and Sonia Gandhi to continue as chief of the Congress Parliamentary Party. It was a race against time. Pranab da (Pranab Mukherjee), Arjun Singh, and I sat together at the Congress Parliamentary party office. In between Kapil (Sibal) was called and a formulation was worked out which enabled the two to continue in the roles decided for them by the party,' says Sharma. The post of the CPP chairperson was created for Gandhi through one of the amendments. Though Gandhi gave the reins to Dr Manmohan Singh, she became the power behind the throne. Apart from Congress president, she also became the chairperson of the alliance—Gandhi was the binding factor of this alliance for a decade. To date, her phone call to her former UPA allies for convening a meeting on an issue is considered significant with her presence giving heft to a political meeting.

The National Advisory Council (NAC) was constituted with Gandhi as the chairperson within a month of the UPA assuming power. The stated objective was to advise the prime minister, but the NAC soon became the fountainhead of key bills that marked the first term of the UPA. NAC comprised subject experts and social rights activist including Aruna Roy, Jean Drèze, Dr N. C. Saxena, and A. K. Shiva Kumar.[32] The NAC, under Gandhi, was responsible for drafting flagship bills like the Right to Information, Right to Education, Food Security Bill and the National Rural Employment Guarantee Act. During this time Gandhi influenced the government's policy-making through her letters to Dr Singh and the chief ministers of Congress-ruled states. The letters ranged from foreign direct investment (FDI) in retail to austerity measures in government functioning. Both NAC and Gandhi incurred the BJP's wrath, which termed the council as an extra-constitutional body.

In 2006, Gandhi was drawn into a political controversy of her own party's making. Though it was construed as a family feud between the once-close Gandhis and Bachchans, it really was not orchestrated by Gandhi as was widely misunderstood. A Congressman from Uttar Pradesh complained to the Election Commission that Rajya Sabha MP Jaya Bachchan was holding an office of profit as she was the chairperson of Uttar Pradesh Film Development Council. An office of profit is defined as a public position that brings financial gain or benefit to the person. As Jaya Bachchan was disqualified, the BJP and Samajwadi Party started a campaign attacking Sonia Gandhi. The UPA government brought an ordinance to redefine an 'office of profit' and gave a list of positions that would be out of the purview of 'office of profit'. Once again, Gandhi took the moral high ground and resigned from the parliament and the NAC. Just like her act of giving up the prime ministership, this took the wind out of the Opposition's campaign to paint the Gandhi family as power usurpers. The fallout of this controversy was that without its chairperson, the NAC lost its prominence. It would be back in its second avatar during UPA's second term.

The first UPA term was fraught with challenges and saw a falling out between Gandhi and K. Natwar Singh, a trusted diplomat-politician who was close to Indira, Rajiv, and Sonia. He was responsible for shaping Gandhi's foreign policy outlook, several political decisions, and even her speeches when she had taken over as the Congress president. Natwar Singh had a disgraceful exit when the Paul Volcker report in 2005[33] named Bhim Singh of the Jammu and Kashmir National Panthers Party and some corporate houses as 'non-contractual beneficiaries' of the Oil-For-Food programme. It was alleged that Natwar helped son Jagat and his friend Andaleeb Sehgal to get four million oil barrels from Iraq which were then illegally sold to a Swiss company.

The biggest political challenge, however, was posed by the India–US Nuclear Deal which threatened the stability of the UPA government in 2008. Prime Minister Manmohan Singh had pushed for a nuclear deal with the US to end, what he termed as, India's 'nuclear apartheid'. Under the treaty, India agreed to put its civil nuclear facilities under the International Atomic Energy Agency safeguards and the US agreed to provide more civil nuclear cooperation. The deal was three years in the making, from 2005–2008, and faced bitter opposition from the Left allies who were opposed to any proximity with the US. It came at the cost of almost destabilizing the UPA-I government when the Left Front withdrew support, and Dr Singh chose to go for a floor test to save the government in July 2008.

Gandhi showed immense political sagacity in handling the crisis. Though she was often criticized for yielding excessive power and Singh for being servile, spineless, and a pushover, the truth was that the nuclear deal was Dr Singh's project—he was the driving force behind it, and he clinched it. In the run-up to the floor test, Gandhi was obviously worried about the stability of the government but never showed a lack of faith in Dr Singh or questioned his judgement of risking the government for the deal a year before the elections. In fact, she instructed her party leaders to take a complex issue like the nuclear deal to the people and explain why it was important for India. Congress's able troubleshooters Ahmed Patel and Pranab Mukherjee managed to find a new ally in the Samajwadi Party and the government tided over what was a dramatic confidence vote. Within a year, the Congress-led UPA faced elections in 2009 and the campaign saw, for the first time, a political party successfully tom-tomming a complex international issue. Gandhi, once again, showed immense trust in Dr Singh. In the run-up to the elections she clearly stated that Dr Singh was the party's prime ministerial candidate. This came at a time when her son Rahul was finding his feet in the party, and there was a clamour for him to take over as prime minister. But Gandhi clearly stated that there was no vacancy for the top post. The 2009 elections saw the Congress tally going up to 206 seats. The UPA had decisively won a second term under Dr Singh.

THE WOMEN'S CHAMPION

Gandhi has always been a champion of women's rights. Her views on increasing women's participation in politics is reflected in her first speech at the Siri Fort Auditorium in 1998 when she took over as the Congress president. In her opening remarks at the Siri Fort auditorium, Gandhi said, 'Ours must also be the party which gives real responsibility to women. Tokenism will not do and is, indeed, offensive. Women must not find themselves shelved and marginalized into just their frontal organization. It is my purpose to bring them to the party's mainstream. At the grassroots, reservations for women in the panchayats have opened vast opportunities for their political empowerment and active participation in governance. We must, however, give much higher priority than we have done to identifying and readying women candidates for election to the panchayats and nagarpalikas at all levels. In the state assemblies and parliament, we will be unflinching and resolutely committed to reservations for women in our legislatures. We must so comport ourselves that the women of India identify with the Congress as their party of preference. We have not made sufficient efforts to engage community leaders in serious dialogue or win them over to our way of thinking.' She made a beginning towards this end by introducing 33 per cent reservation for women at all levels of the party leadership. There were obvious difficulties in finding women at the block and zila level but the party showed its intention by appointing women leaders as general secretaries and secretaries in the AICC.

This facet of Gandhi's personality came to the fore even when she wasn't active in politics. Mani Shankar Aiyar says Gandhi was opposed to her husband Rajiv's move to pass the Muslim

Women (Protection on Divorce) Act 1986, which is popularly known as the law that overturned the Supreme Court verdict in Shah Bano Case[34] and allowed maintenance to a divorced Muslim woman only during the iddat period or till ninety days after the divorce. 'I know Rajiv consulted her (Sonia) on many issues. In fact, I remember he was quite disturbed by her disapproval of the Muslim Women (Protection on Divorce) Act 1986. But then Rajiv also knew that she (Gandhi) was reacting to it as so many others in India. He told me that I am being called an opportunist but what electoral advantage do I get? He added, "According to my critics, no Muslim woman will vote for me. No modern Muslim man will vote for me. No non-Muslim will vote for me. Only a few orthodox Muslims will vote for me. So, what electoral advantage will I get? No, this is to reassure the minorities that we are a secular country which respects the personal laws of different communities,"' Aiyar said.[35]

Sources close to Gandhi say it is her innate belief that women's empowerment can only come with financial independence and political participation. As the leader of the Opposition, Gandhi had raised the issue of the Women's Reservation Bill in parliament. Speaking in the Lok Sabha on 18 August 2003 on the no-confidence motion against the Vajpayee government, Gandhi said, 'As far as Women's Reservation Bill is concerned, it is now more than clear, more than ever before that the government has no intention whatsoever in getting the Women's Reservation Bill passed. If it had been the intention of the government, as the prime minister had promised us again and again, he could have done so with the help of the Congress party and of the Left. We would have passed the Bill. This government has wilfully destroyed the national consensus in every other area, but suddenly discovers the virtues of consensus on the Women's Reservation Bill. Now, this is simply a pretext for inaction. All of us women are aware of this. All of us know this.'[36]

It was little surprise that when Congress-led UPA came to power she pushed the Women's Reservation Bill. Party seniors openly say that there was little support for this move within the party. Of the forty-five cabinet ministers and ministers of state with independent charge in UPA-I, there were only three women ministers. Then Child and Development Minister Renuka Chowdhury says, 'Only Mrs Gandhi supported the bill. There was a lot of resistance within the cabinet against it. But since she was pushing the bill, there was nothing the male ministers could do.' Gandhi garnered support from even the Opposition parties including the BJP and the Left Front. However, the government did not push it beyond introduction in the Rajya Sabha in May 2008.

Gandhi's belief in increasing women's representation in elected bodies has been inherited by both her children, Rahul and Priyanka. A year before the 2014 parliamentary elections, Rahul, as the Congress vice-president, underlined the need for 50 per cent women's reservation in party positions. Though a noble thought, he could not make it work with Ambika Soni remaining the only general secretary in the AICC during this time. The 2022 Uttar Pradesh assembly elections saw Priyanka, as the general secretary in-charge of the state, reserving 40 per cent tickets for women. It was easier to implement such a change in Uttar Pradesh as the Congress has no real stakes in the election.

A SECOND CHANCE

Though the alliance had won the trust of the electorate a second time, it faced several challenges, including increasing naxalism and internal security threats, inflation, agricultural distress leading to farmers' suicides, the 2G scam, allegations of corruption in the Commonwealth Games 2010, and the Adarsh Group housing row. In the middle of its term, the UPA seemed cornered. Then came the shock. In 2011, Gandhi was diagnosed with cancer at Sir Ganga Ram hospital. Like all politicians, Gandhi was secretive about the illness. The only time the party issued a health update about her illness was when Gandhi underwent a successful abdominal surgery in August 2011 in the US. Since she was the Congress president, her travel necessitated that party affairs should be formally handed over to another person. In this case, she assigned the task to a group of four— son Rahul, her political secretary Ahmed Patel, and party seniors A. K. Antony and Janardan Dwivedi. Rahul had to step in to fill in for Gandhi. As he got more involved in the day-to-day functioning of the party, the angst against Rahul's leadership, especially among the older leaders, pitted years of experience against youthful optimism within the Congress. His experiments in restructuring the party or drafting younger leaders did not sit well with senior leaders. While Gandhi lent a sympathetic ear to grievances, she gave Rahul a free hand.

Despite advice from veterans like Mukherjee, Antony, Dwivedi, Soni, Mohsina Kidwai, and Oscar Fernandes, Gandhi could never succeed in making Rahul a part of the government and gain governance experience. Before every cabinet reshuffle there would be rumours of Rahul joining the cabinet and journalists would assign portfolios like education (then human resource development) or youth affairs and sports, but these remained only in newspapers. Rahul could never shed his inhibition and get his hands dirty doing real administrative work in the government. Gandhi remained fiercely protective of Rahul, to the extent of almost monitoring what statements he was giving. It could probably be a natural reaction after having lived in the shadow of death and losing loved ones to acts of violence. In October 2012, Dr Singh had shuffled his cabinet and Rahul had once again refused to join the government. At the swearing-in ceremony of the new ministers at Rashtrapati Bhavan, journalists cornered Rahul about his reluctance to take up a ministerial responsibility. As journalists surrounded him, the author felt a tap on the shoulder which was conveniently shrugged off. But the tap was persistent. It was Sonia Gandhi smiling, 'I also want to hear what he is saying.' Gandhi's interactions with the media are planned in advance and are closed-door meetings. She doesn't randomly comment, and her every word is measured. Once she joined in, the line of questioning changed and she took over. The impression one got was of a watchful mother, often referred in modern parenting jargon as a helicopter mom who does not want her toddler to get out of her sight.

Gandhi's close aides do not find this surprising. The matriarch, who is known to put leaders in their place with just one steely glance and silence rebellions with an unflinching cold face, often frets if the Karva Chauth moon takes time in rising as her daughter Priyanka observes the fast. There is a gentle and tender side to Gandhi. 'There is an old banyan tree outside her office. She was once on the rounds meeting people. Nobody had noticed but a baby squirrel had fallen off the tree. At that time, she stopped and asked for the baby squirrel to be attended to, "Don't touch it. The moment you touch it, the mother won't accept her back," she said. A towel was brought and the staff used it to put the squirrel back on the tree,' remembers Dalmia, a long-time aide. But then this is the same Gandhi who is firm in her refusal to meet chief ministers for months once she hears corruption charges against them or their close aides.

A year before the 2014 elections, Rahul formally took over as the Congress vice-president at a party conclave in Jaipur in January 2013. He gave an inspiring speech which gave the audience an insight into Gandhi's fear for the family's safety. 'Last night each one of you congratulated me. My mother came to my room and she sat with me and she cried...because she understands that [the] power so many people seek is actually a poison,' he said.[37] In a way it was win-win for Rahul—with Gandhi as Congress president, the family retained control over the party and failures were conveniently laid at the prime minister and the UPA government's door. When social rights activists like Arvind Kejriwal, Aruna Roy, and Nikhil Dey initiated the India Against Corruption Campaign under the Gandhian Anna Hazare, Rahul embarrassed his own party's government by opposing an ordinance which made convicted leaders eligible to contest elections pending appeals in court. By the end of 2013, the Opposition's campaign over scandals on issues such as the coal block allocation and 2G spectrum had reaffirmed the belief that the UPA was a corrupt political alliance being arm-twisted by its regional allies. The alliance was routed by a strong Modi wave in 2014. Once again, Dr Singh's government took the blame and Rahul's uninspiring leadership remained blemish-free. The BJP, under Narendra Modi, won 282 seats with Rahul leading the party to its most humiliating tally ever of forty-four seats.

IN THE WILDERNESS

The loss in 2014 initiated a frustrating period for the Congress. Nothing the Congress did or promised could win back the voters who were enthused by a new model of Hindutva politics. Rahul, who had remained a constant bystander reluctant to wade into the deep sea of politics, took over as the Congress president from Gandhi in 2017. It was a clear signal that Gandhi's health would not permit her from taking part in active politics. But the 2019 elections also showed that the allies were unwilling to do business with Rahul, and Gandhi was what kept the UPA together. The 2019 general elections saw Priyanka taking on a political role as the general secretary in-charge of Uttar Pradesh (East). Though Priyanka had been working in the background for years, advising her brother and taking care of crucial political meetings for Gandhi, this was her first formal political assignment. This further gave credence to Modi's campaign against the politics of dynasty. The BJP under Modi won a second term—a mandate bigger than his 2014 victory. A sulking Rahul resigned as the Congress president, taking moral responsibility for the defeat but also lashing out at his party for not supporting him. Priyanka was even more scathing in her remarks inside a CWC meeting as she blamed party seniors for not supporting Rahul wholeheartedly. Moreover, Rahul refused to take back his resignation. With a sense of drift in the party, Gandhi was once again forced to take over as interim president in August 2019—she is the longest serving Congress president in the history, having been at the helm for over twenty-two years.

In a year's time, the party began getting restless with the leadership—something that the Gandhi family has never experienced. The family is known to attract crowds and inspire party leaders to campaign tirelessly and win elections. Be it Rajiv or Rahul and Priyanka, voters have been so charmed by the family that they like to shake hands or hug them during campaigns—something that has often left the family members with swollen palms and bruised forearms. The August 2020 rebellion was a shock to them. A group of twenty-three party leaders wrote to Gandhi calling for a 'full time and effective leadership' which is both 'visible' and 'active' in the field; elections to the Congress Working Committee (CWC) and the urgent establishment of an 'institutional leadership mechanism' to 'collectively' guide the party's revival. 'Arguing that the revival of the Congress is "a national imperative" fundamental to the health of democracy, the letter, underlines how the party's steady decline comes when the country faces its "gravest political, social and economic challenges since Independence...." Their letter calls for a sweeping range of reforms, decentralization of power, empowerment of state units, elections to the Congress organization at all levels, from the block to the CWC, and the urgent constitution of a central parliamentary board.'[38] No real systemic changes came out of this rebellion except that the Gandhis became more mindful of these dissenters. There was a conspiracy theory which was peddled that the G-23, which included staunch loyalists like Ghulam Nabi Azad, Anand Sharma, Bhupinder Singh Hooda, Prithviraj Chavan, and Manish Tewari were looking for a renomination to the Rajya Sabha.

Sonia Gandhi finally stepped down as Congress president in October 2022, passing on the baton to seasoned Congressman from Karnataka, Mallikarjun Kharge. This is the first time in twenty-four years that a non-Gandhi has been elected president of the party, which has largely been a family preserve. Despite ceding control to Kharge, Gandhi remains a power centre and a unifying force for the Congress Party.

J. JAYALALITHAA

The Autocratic Amma

Who was J. Jayalalithaa? Was she the wronged woman deceived in love by much older and devious suitors who had promised marriage? Or was she the caring politician who called a young journalist when she saw her burst into tears after being molested by a guard in the chief minister's security detail? Was she the teary-eyed MLA with the dishevelled hair and torn sari who stood outside the Tamil Nadu assembly in March 1989 and took a Draupadi-like vow to never step inside till it was a safe place for women? Or the dishonest politician with numerous corruption cases against her? Or who fuelled a cult of violence against political adversaries, journalists, and bureaucrats? Was she the convent-educated Tamil movie star who was never seen on film sets without a book? Or the shrewd politician who convinced the court to translate all the case papers in Tamil because she could not understand English? Was she the young girl always pining for her mother's love and attention? Or the imperious chief minister who liked when partymen prostrated themselves before her in deference and fear? Was she the fading movie star who penned stories on incest in Tamil journals? Or the autocratic Amma whose name became synonymous with welfare and life-size cut-outs in Tamil Nadu?

The life story of J. Jayalalithaa, the four-term Tamil Nadu chief minister, is all this and more. It is full of twists and turns, mirroring the dramatic lives of characters she portrayed on screen or later created in stories penned by her.

THE UNENTHUSIASTIC STAR

Jayalalithaa was born on 24 February 1948 to Vedavalli and Jayaram in what was then Mysore state. Her father passed away when she was only two years old and her mother single-handedly raised Jayalalithaa and her brother Pappu. Vedavalli took up acting in films and adopted the screen name Sandhya. The family moved to Chennai, which was then considered the mecca of the south Indian film industry. Ammu, as Jayalalithaa was fondly called at home, enrolled in the prestigious Church Park Convent School and was a very good student. In her incomplete memoirs published in Tamil journal *Kumudam* in 1978, Jayalalithaa describes how her childhood was spent pining for her mother and sometimes even waiting for days to meet her. 'I'd tie my mother's sari around my hand while sleeping. While leaving she would undrape the sari and ask her sister to wear it and lie next to me. When I'd wake to see her gone, I'd feel shattered,' she wrote in her serialized memoirs.[1] Jayalalithaa's attachment to her mother is also reflected in her decision to name her Poes Garden home 'Veda Nilayam' after her mother. Since Veda was away from home and children due to hectic film shoots, she surrounded them with books and inculcated a love

for the written word in both her children. Reading became a
lifelong habit for Ammu and later, as a politician, Jayalalithaa
often surprised interviewers and published leaders when
she quoted from their works and held long discussions on it.
Ammu's outstanding grades and impeccable manners endeared
her to school teachers and earned her the 'Best Outgoing Student
Award' from Church Park School in 1964. She hated the thought
of becoming a movie star and wanted to study further to
become either an IAS officer or a doctor. However, much to her
disappointment, Ammu found herself following in her mother's
footsteps into the film world because of the family's financial
situation. 1964, soon after completing her matriculation
examination, she was cast in a Kannada film by producer
B. R. Panthulu. Within a year, Panthulu, who was looking for
a fresh face for his next Tamil venture, cast her opposite M. G.
Ramachandran, a superstar and matinee idol of Tamil cinema,
in *Aayiraththil Oruvan*. Ammu was a sixteen-year-old young
schoolgirl, and he was three decades older at forty-seven years.
The movie was a runaway success, and Tamil cinema got its hit
pair in Jayalalithaa and MGR, who went on to star together
in twenty-eight films over the next decade. Interestingly, it was
MGR's wife Janaki who had spotted the young Ammu in a film
and had egged on her husband to take her as the leading lady.
Little did Janaki know that she would have to fight a vicious
battle with her over her husband's political legacy.

It is no secret that as they starred together in movies, MGR
and Jayalalithaa started a relationship. In the much-older MGR,
the young girl found a mentor who looked out for her and
insisted that directors cast only Jayalalithaa opposite him. MGR's
affection towards Jayalalithaa bordered on obsession. He cut out
film directors who did not approve of the influence Jayalalithaa
wielded on him, provided her extra security, protected her
from overbearing relatives, and gradually started controlling
her finances and what clothes she wore. In 1972, MGR had a
falling out with his friend and the Dravida Munnetra Kazhagham
(DMK) supremo M. Karunanidhi and floated his own party, the

All India Anna Dravida Munnetra Kazhagham (AIADMK)—a move many blamed Jayalalithaa for. Around this time, MGR and Jayalalithaa also parted ways and she started starring in movies with other actors. She found love in another married co-star Shoban Babu, who was younger than MGR. The relationship was serious and the two wanted to marry each other. Author Vaasanthi quotes Jayalalithaa's friend Srimathi in her book *Amma* (2016), 'According to her friend Srimathi, "She knew that Shoban Babu was already married and had a teenaged son. But he charmed her.... She did want to marry him in the traditional Iyengar fashion. Probably like Vijayanthimala, who married Dr Bali, a married man. She asked for my help to make an Iyengar thaali—mangalya sutra. She asked me to attend her quiet wedding that would take place in her house. She said she had already purchased saris from Nalli. On that day, early morning at six, she called me and said the wedding was cancelled and hung up."'[2] Some say Shoban Babu's wife objected and some blame MGR for ensuring the relationship broke up. But this was the first relationship she admitted to openly. With her film career nosediving, she tried to cultivate an image of an intellectual and well-read woman and started writing for Tamil weeklies including *Tughlaq, Kumudam*, and *Kalki*. She started telling her life story and wrote about her relationship with Shoban Babu in *Kumudam*. 'The magazine advertised the news over the radio. The commercial over the radio was exciting: Jayalalithaa's own voice was on the air; "I am neither a Sita nor a Savithri. I have done some mistakes in my life and I want to tell you all about it. Read it for yourself and then be my judge.... Her writing began during the lean period of her life and it continues still, with her story appearing in the AIADMK's magazine called *Thai*. She had first begun to write for Cho's *Tughlaq* on a variety of subjects ranging from women's life to mercy killing,' says the cover story 'She Writes to Conquer' of January 1984 issue of *The Week* magazine.[3] However, Jayalalithaa's memoirs remained incomplete as she rekindled her relationship with MGR and never delivered on her tell-all promise.

THE DEBUTANTE

MGR felt his party needed a crowd puller and hoped to find one in the once-popular, fair-skinned actor Jayalalithaa. She, on the other hand, was planning to get a break in politics but was aware it worked differently from the now-familiar film world. In June 1982, Jayalalithaa joined the AIADMK at a party conference organized in Cuddalore. MGR created the special post of propaganda secretary for her. 'The AIADMK party conference was organized on a big scale at Cuddalore, south of Pondicherry, and the whole town thronged to hear the star speaker who was to give her maiden political speech, which she had written herself. They mainly came to see a pretty face, and were instead treated to an impressive, fiery oration.... At Cuddalore she was taken round the streets in a carnival-type procession which the DMK described in its party paper as the "Cuddalore cabaret".'[4] She changed her attire and underwent another image makeover—she gave up her heavy saris with coloured blouses, switched to plain white saris with contrasting two-line borders, and wore minimalistic earrings. Author Vaasanthi says, 'As propaganda secretary, she came in close contact with party cadres at the ground level. She may have been arrogant to her political peers but she was really kind to the common people and the cadres. They just adored her.' Her popularity grew within no time and her proximity to MGR ensured she cultivated her own set of loyalists within the party. But at the same time, senior party colleagues worried about her meteoric rise within the party ranks and started a vicious campaign against her. They watched hawk-eyed, waiting for her to take one misstep. In March 1984, MGR nominated Jayalalithaa to the Rajya Sabha. She gave her maiden Rajya Sabha speech on 23 April 1984 during a discussion on the workings of the ministry of energy and emphatically put across the electricity crisis in Tamil Nadu. Citing statistics, letters addressed by MGR to the then Prime Minister Indira Gandhi, and new power projects established in different states,

Jayalalithaa made a strong case for allocating the entire power output from the first unit of the Kalpakkam plant to Tamil Nadu. With her clear diction, choice of words, and command over English language, the thirty-six-year-old debutante impressed Indira and other senior cabinet ministers. She soon became the face of the AIADMK and MGR's emissary in Delhi's power circles. But MGR realized that Jayalalithaa's ascent was alienating the party's old guard and removed her from the post of propaganda secretary to clip her wings.

In October 1984, MGR suffered a stroke and lost his speech. He was rushed to Apollo Hospital in Chennai and later taken to the US for treatment. Without her benefactor, Jayalalithaa bore the brunt of a campaign to throw her out of the party. She was vulnerable as she did not hold any post within the AIADMK and drew her power from MGR's affection towards her. But she was not one to go down without a fight—she gave it as hard as she got. She openly spoke against the AIADMK party seniors and went to the extent of lashing out at MGR's wife Janaki. During these months, Jayalalithaa found herself cornered, but she did not show any emotions to the world. She found an unlikely confidante in V. K. Sasikala, a lady who ran a videotape shop near her Poes Garden home. Sasikala won Jayalalithaa's trust, and during this difficult phase gained entry into the bungalow. With this began a relationship that spanned decades, fuelled gossip about Jayalalithaa's sexual orientation, embroiled her in various corruption cases, and in her later years distanced her from the electorate which worshipped her like a Goddess.

THE POLITICS OF INHERITANCE

On 24 December 1987, MGR passed away without choosing his political heir. The family ensured Jayalalithaa got no news of where his body was kept. She ran around frantically holding onto bits of information and finally tracked where the body had been kept to pay last respects. A shocked Jayalalithaa stood guard over MGR's lifeless body for two days. 'She did not shed a tear. She did not wail. She stunned the onlookers and mourners by standing vigil by MGR's body for two days.... But the mental and physical torture came from other sources. Several women supporters of Janaki's stood near her and began stamping on her feet, driving their nails into her skin and pinching her to drive her away. But she stood undaunted, swallowing her humiliation and her pride, obstinately remaining where she had taken position.'[5] She was assaulted and thrown off the carriage when the body was being taken for last rites. This won her the sympathy of the people and partymen who now thronged her Poes Garden bungalow. A majority of the elected MLAs, however, threw their weight behind Janaki, and she was sworn in as the new chief minister. However, when Janaki had to prove her majority on the floor of the assembly, there was pandemonium in the house. 'Soon, it became a free-for-all as legislators of the Janaki group and the Congress (I) threw paper weights, slippers, microphones, and even chairs. The speaker's chair was hurled down and his table was pushed in to the well of the House. An MLA backing Janaki rolled up his dhoti, got on to the desk, and challenged his Congress (I) rivals to a trial of strength. Things soon got worse. Outsiders, mostly hooligans, burst into the House and the violence escalated. One thing led to another. As the assembly's Watch and Ward looked on, the city police came in and 15 Congress (I) MLAs were injured in the lathi charge inside the assembly. Six of them suffered severe injuries. Several Jayalalithaa supporters were also hit.'[6]

Jayalalithaa was quick to smell an opportunity and met the governor to demand a dismissal of the government. The governor recommended President's Rule and fresh elections were called in 1989. Both Janaki and Jayalalithaa fought the elections on different symbols. Though DMK won the election, it was Jayalalithaa whose faction won the most seats and was elected the leader of the Opposition. Janaki lost on MGR's home turf and even her deposit. It was during this time that Janaki reached a practical arrangement and decided to give up her claim to the party. Jayalalithaa was formally accepted as MGR's political

heir and inherited his legacy. The development was ironical—a
Tamil Brahmin leader went onto head a Dravidian party which
stood for the anti-caste and anti-Brahmin politics of the atheist
C. N. Annadurai.

Her initiation into real politics as the head of the AIADMK
was dramatic and harsh. The first budget session of the newly-
elected DMK government in March 1989 laid the foundation
of a bitter rivalry between Karunanidhi and Jayalalithaa. On 25
March 1989, Chief Minister Karunanidhi, who held the finance
portfolio, stood up to present the budget, but a ruckus silenced
him. When Jayalalithaa spoke against the chief minister, he passed
an unparliamentary remark, which was expunged. An AIADMK
member lunged forward, snatched the budget, and tore it to
pieces. Karunanidhi lost his balance and his spectacles broke.
All hell broke loose as mikes and slippers flew from both sides.
As Jayalalithaa tried to leave the assembly, a DMK MLA pulled
at her sari and another her hair. The AIADMK members came
to rescue their leader and a visibly shaken Jayalalithaa stood
and swore never to return to the assembly until it was safe for
women. Jayalalithaa campaigned throughout the state on the
plank of a wronged woman seeking justice from people. 'She
played the victim card. She would go before the people and
spread her pallu and say, "I am your sister and I have come
to beg for alms before you. I have been humiliated in the land
of Kauravas." The people were moved by this,' says Vaasanthi.
Jayalalithaa returned to the assembly after two years as the chief
minister of Tamil Nadu after successfully ousting Karunanidhi.
The victory was truly empowering—she had finally come out
of the shadow of her mentor and carved her own identity as a
vote catcher. Jayalalithaa's partymen also realized that they owed
their political existence to her. After being sworn in as the chief
minister for the first time, Jayalalithaa was leaving the University
of Madras when the AIADMK MLA K. A. Sengottaiyan suddenly
prostrated himself at her feet. This show of deference started
a trend—even as the chief ministerial cavalcade passed by or
her helicopter hovered overhead, MLAs would prostrate in her

presence, unmindful of their sparkling white veshtis.

Jayalalithaa's first term from 1991–96 is marked with a certain brashness which was reflected in her dictatorial and devil-may-care attitude. Author A. R. Venkatachalapathy writes in his book *Tamil Characters*, 'In less than a year the process of squandering popular goodwill began its inexorable roll.... During these years all dissent was curbed, political opponents humiliated, and the media hounded. Jayalalithaa's megalomania and hubris apparently knew no limits.' Jayalalithaa always looked at the media with suspicion and disdain. Vaasanthi remembers how when she was the editor of the Tamil edition of *India Today* she sent the chief minister a fax seeking an interview every day for ten years without eliciting even an acknowledgement from her. 'I don't know whether she got those faxes. I don't know whether even her PA saw those faxes because there was never any way of knowing. There was an iron curtain there—journalists could not penetrate it,' she says contrasting it with Karunanidhi's easy style of sometimes answering the phone himself.

In January 2017 cover story 'Jayalalithaa's Legacy' for *Frontline* magazine, T. S. Subramanian writes, 'The Jayalalithaa regime of 1991–96 also used brutal physical violence against the state governor, its political opponents, advocates, an IAS officer, a vice chancellor, the then chief election commissioner, and its own legislators. The AIADMK's cult of violence first came into the open on 14 August 1991, within three months of its coming to power, when armed men stormed the office of *Tharasu*, a Tamil magazine, and stabbed two of its employees to death. The next day, during an Independence Day party, even as Governor Bhishma Narain Singh and Jayalalithaa were chatting on the lawns of Raj Bhavan, women AIADMK MLAs gheraoed the then union minister of state for commerce, P. Chidambaram, to protest against the union government's decision to refer the Cauvery dispute to the Supreme Court. The next day, on 16 August, an AIADMK mob led by four MLAs attacked Chidambaram's car with stones, sticks, and iron rods as he drove out of the Tiruchi airport. The minister was injured on his leg. But Jayalalithaa had the audacity to claim that Chidambaram and others had damaged their cars themselves. Acid was thrown on the IAS officer V. S. Chandralekha on 19 May 1992, when she was the commissioner of the Tamil Nadu Archives and Historical Research. She received severe burns on her face, neck, and hands. On 21 July 1994, as Advocate K. M. Vijayan stepped out of his house to go to the airport, four men beat him up with clubs. Vijayan suffered multiple fractures on his legs. He was attacked for filing a petition in the Supreme Court against the 69 per cent reservation in Tamil Nadu. On 13 July 1994, goondas, brandishing knives, threatened the Anna University vice chancellor for his stand that the university would stick to 50 per cent reservation as per the Supreme Court's orders instead of the 69 per cent reservation ordered by the Jayalalithaa government. AIADMK men blocked the road leading from the airport when the Chief Election Commissioner T. N. Seshan arrived in Chennai on 27 November 1994, because Seshan had made some allegations against the late chief minister and DMK's founder C. N. Annadurai.[7] It was evident that Jayalalithaa encouraged this behaviour in her party members. But the most jarring event of the term was the 1995 wedding of Sasikala's son V. N. Sudhakaran, who was termed as Jayalalithaa's foster son.

In its 30 September 1995 issue, *India Today* termed it as the mother of all weddings. 'A two-kilometre-long, illuminated baraat route, ten dining halls, each seating a modest 25,000 persons, more diamonds than Elizabeth Taylor has seen, a 75,000 square feet pandal, saris worth more than what most people will earn this year, and an entire state machinery on wedding alert.... Tons of plywood, plaster of Paris, and paint were lavished on erecting Jayalalithaa cut-outs, arches and elaborate facades of palaces and gateways and several hundred papier mâché statues. The wedding pandal was no less commanding. It covered an area of over 70,000 square feet, the thatched roof camouflaged by a false ceiling and decorated by the art director Thotta Tharani. The Madras Municipal Corporation deployed hundreds of its staff to level the wedding site, widen approaches, and blacktop roads on the VIP route. The Tamil Nadu Electricity Board (TNEB) installed transformers to supply power to the site; Metrowater diverted water tankers to supply seven lakh litres of water; and government vehicles were employed to transport the cut-outs.'[8] Sasikala and Jayalalithaa wore matching kanjeevarams. By then, it was evident that her popularity had waned considerably. Karunanidhi was voted back to power in the 1996 elections on the anti-corruption plank and soon Jayalalithaa found herself battling a number of court cases. The first was a disproportionate assets case filed by the Janata Party chief Subramanian Swamy, which later proved to be Jayalalithaa's undoing. Swamy alleged that during her tenure as chief minister from 1991–96 Jayalalithaa amassed properties worth ₹66.65 crore disproportionate to her known sources of income. She was arrested on 7 December 1996—a favour Jayalalithaa returned very quickly once she came to power in 2001 and ordered the arrest of Karunanidhi in the middle of the night.

The comeback in the state was spurred by a spectacular result in the 1998 Lok Sabha elections when the AIADMK won 18 of 39 parliamentary seats and provided crucial support to the Atal Bihari Vajpayee-led National Democratic Alliance (NDA) government at the centre. Though the DMK was in power in Tamil Nadu, the Coimbatore communal riots in 1997 and serial blasts targeting the senior BJP leader L. K. Advani in 1998 saw the party performing poorly in the Lok Sabha elections. Jayalalithaa proved to be an unreliable ally, bringing down the Vajpayee government within thirteen months when he did not give in to her demands of dismissing the Karunanidhi government in the state. These impulsive machinations, however, did not dent her electoral prospects in the assembly elections of 2001. Jayalalithaa aligned with the Congress, Pattali Makkal Katchi (PMK), Tamil Maanila Congress, the Communist Party of India (CPI), Communist Party of India (Marxist), Republican Party of India, All India Forward Bloc, and the Indian National League. Since Jayalalithaa had withdrawn support at the centre, the BJP fought the election in alliance with DMK, which found itself

alienated from its other Left allies like the CPI and CPI(M).
More than a vote against the DMK-led government, it was simple
electoral arithmetic. Karunanidhi could not prevent the exit of
its allies like the PMK, which was welcomed into the alliance
by Jayalalithaa. Her nominations from four constituencies were
rejected, which garnered more sympathy for her. During the
election campaign, Jayalalithaa alleged that Karunanidhi had
engineered the rejection of her nominations—a narrative that
people caught on quickly. After the election results, Karunanidhi
said, 'The verdict is the result of the sympathy generated by
the false propaganda that we were responsible for the rejection
of Jayalalithaa's nominations although the rejections were done
legally and as per the Election Commission's order. Even after
(Chief Election Commissioner M. S.) Gill said that the rejections
were legally valid, it is the false propaganda (by Jayalalithaa)
that gained her victory.'[9]

The second term ended abruptly when the Supreme Court
struck down her appointment as she was convicted in the Tamil
Nadu Small Industries Corporation (TANSI) case in October
2000. She appointed O. Panneerselvam as the chief minister in
her absence. But once the TANSI verdict was overturned, she
was back in the saddle. This alternating of power continued and
Jayalalithaa's AIADMK lost in the 2006 assembly elections but
won again in 2011. The disproportionate assets case came to
haunt her again after eighteen years in September 2014, when
she was convicted and spent twenty-eight days in prison till she
was released on bail.[10]

AMMA = WELFARE

When she had taken over the reins of the party in the late
1980s after MGR's death, she was courting an electorate that
worshipped its cinestars and was under the strong influence
of Tamil cinema. But gradually, with changing times and
exposure to television and social media, the polity changed and
the electorate's asks from the political masters became more

aspirational. Jayalalithaa was quick to adapt and evolve into a benevolent ruler. In her third term in 2011, she became Amma—the mother who provided for everything. Amma became the brand name of welfare.

Jayalalithaa's multiple terms as the Tamil Nadu chief minister saw her unveiling a slew of welfare schemes. She introduced schemes that addressed hunger and urban poverty. It showed her eye for detail as an administrator. The first welfare scheme launched as soon as she came to power in 1991 was the Cradle Baby Scheme. Under this, anyone could anonymously give up their newborn babies in the state-run nurseries for adoption. The scheme was introduced when Tamil Nadu was witnessing gender-based abortions and the sex ratio had declined from 977:1000 in 1981 to 974:1000 in 1991. With the state taking responsibility for abandoned babies, Jayalalithaa had hoped to lower female infanticide incidents and improve the sex ratio. By 2001, the sex ratio had improved to 986:1000.

In 2011, her schemes started bearing the name Amma. She introduced the scheme, Thalikku Thangam Thittam or Gold for Marriage. The scheme was named after the popular social reformer Moovalur Ramamirtham and offered 4 grams of gold and cash of upto ₹50,000 to financially backward women for marriage. The government announced free table fans, mixer and grinders, cows, and goats to poor women, and free laptops to all the students studying in state-run higher secondary schools or colleges. Her government earmarked ₹2,353 crore in the first one year of implementation to cover 1.85 crore families that drew rice from the public distribution system (PDS). 'These schemes were launched with an aim to help the poor stand on their own legs and become economically independent. Hence no one should demean such schemes,' Jayalalithaa said.[11] In 2012, she introduced Amma Mediclaim where each family was guaranteed ₹1 lakh per annum for a period of four years. This was followed by opening Amma Pharmacies which sold all kinds of medicines—generic and branded—lower than the market rates.

In 2013, Jayalalithaa introduced Amma Unavagam or Amma

Canteens—a pathbreaking initiative to address hunger, which was later introduced by other state governments including Rajasthan. All the canteens were maintained by women self-help groups and offered food at ₹1. 'The popularity of the scheme can be assessed by the fact that these canteens daily prepare about 4.5 million idlis and 1.2 million plates of pongal for breakfast, 2.5 million plates of sambar rice and 1.1 million plates of curd rice for lunch. The scheme attracted the attention of other states in the country. Even the teams from other countries have visited Tamil Nadu to study the scheme. Amma Canteen Scheme made a frontal attack on urban hunger and malnutrition, as food is served at a highly subsidized price. Further, food is prepared and served in a hygienic environment.'[12] The scheme was altered during the Covid-19 pandemic. 'The scheme never allowed parcel system to avoid misuse. The state made an exception during the second wave as it was not possible to serve food at the canteens. People were permitted to buy breakfast or lunch not only for themselves but also for up to five members of their family. The breakfast, one idli for one rupee and one plate of pongal for ₹5 are available. For lunch, a 350gm plate of sambar rice, lemon rice, and tomato rice were available at ₹5. In Chennai, the food items are packed (free of cost) and given to the customer. In other places, the customers have to get their own tiffin box. Volume of sales, on an average, increased from 600 plates to 800 plates during lunch time. Increase of similar magnitude was witnessed in case of items served during breakfast.'[13] In a way, Amma has lived on through this initiative even after her death.

Jayalalithaa followed these with Amma Kudineer (or Amma Water) in September 2013 which was the cheapest packaged drinking water in the state[14], Amma Salt in June 2014 which provided three variations of double fortified salt, low sodium salt, and refined salt priced at ₹25, ₹21, and ₹14 at government-run PDS outlet, and Amma baby care kits in September 2015 where every mother who gave birth in a government hospital got sixteen types of products worth ₹1,000 free. There were other initiatives targeted towards women like opening breastfeeding rooms at bus stations to give privacy to mothers and bicycles to girl students to reach their schools. Through these schemes, Jayalalithaa had reached every household in the state. But what was truly intriguing was that Amma had become casteless. It didn't matter to the electorate that even as she was the head of a Dravidian party; she openly declared she was a believer and visited temples. The electorate was so besotted with Amma that even the 2014 conviction in the disproportionate assets case did not affect her popularity. Amma, in a way, could do no wrong. It was almost as if they were vindicated when the Karnataka High Court overturned the conviction in 2015, a year ahead of the assembly elections in Tamil Nadu.

The 2016 polls were historic—Jayalalithaa won a decisive mandate on her own. The electorate had learnt to look beyond the corruption charges. This was the first time after 1984 that a government in Tamil Nadu had successfully fought anti-incumbency and was voted back to power. But within months she was hospitalized with dehydration and fever.

THE EXTRA CONSTITUTIONAL AUTHORITY

Jayalalithaa's years in power had the overbearing shadow of Sasikala. She had become Amma's confidante and a powerful gatekeeper. In a rare interview to *The Week* magazine in July 2021, Sasikala opened up about her proximity. She described in detail how she did not step out of the Poes Garden bungalow without Jayalalithaa's permission and also chose her trademark green saris. During her thirty-three-year stay at Poes Garden, Sasikala had never stepped out without Jayalalithaa's knowledge. 'If I was missing at home, she would immediately call me and ask about my whereabouts,' she says. The only place she used to visit without Jayalalithaa was the Milan Jyothi showroom in Chennai to purchase the former chief minister's favourite Garden Vareli saris. 'She loves green, that too dark green. She felt it was her lucky colour,' says Sasikala. Sasikala would buy the sari material in rolls. Two Muslim tailors would then embroider the sari border. 'It would be done as a small patch. I would buy the matching colour thread for the embroidery,' says Sasikala. She would get a sample patch done, get it approved by Jayalalithaa and pass it on to the tailors. 'She was never for expensive jewellery. She always preferred to be simple,' says Sasikala. Every time though, Sasikala would pick a pair of identical saris. 'Whenever she wore a new sari, she would insist that I also wear the same colour and design,' says Sasikala. She recounts how during an income tax raid in 2018 at Poes Garden while she was in jail, a lady officer was flummoxed to see two rows of saris in the same design and colour in the wardrobe.[15] On actor and TV host Simi Garewal's show *Rendezvous with Simi Garewal*, one of the rare interviews where Jayalalithaa opened up, she described Sasikala as 'her mother'.

The thirty-three-year-old friendship had its own ups and downs. There were times when Sasikala and her family members were banished from Poes Garden, but every time Sasikala clawed her way back in. Though AIADMK old-timers say that Jayalalithaa always forgave her because Sasikala knew too much, Sasikala herself says expulsion from party and home were just for outsiders and nothing came between the two friends. Sasikala's interview in *The Week* magazine explains her side. Sasikala's and Jayalalithaa's friendship did hit a rough patch. Sasikala was twice expelled from the party. Between June 1996 and April 1997, Sasikala was in jail in a Foreign Exchange Regulation Act case, which is still pending in a magistrate's court. Jayalalithaa, too, was arrested, but was released on bail forty-five days later. In a press conference, she blamed Sasikala's family and vowed to banish them from Poes Garden. 'Akka has never been without me for even a minute. It [the expulsion] was only for the outside world, but we were talking with each other' reveals Sasikala. 'When I [fell sick in jail] and was taken to the government hospital, the news shook her and she rushed to the hospital. She was on her toes, impatiently inquiring with the doctors about my condition.' Sasikala was banished from Poes Garden again in December 2011. Exactly after a hundred days, in March 2012, she returned to the residence after issuing a public apology to Jayalalithaa.[16]

Sasikala's influence can be gauged from the fact that she was right beside Jayalalithaa when she was shut out by MGR's family after his death, and she and her husband had gone to MGR's widow Janaki to persuade her to give up the claim to the AIADMK after the 1989 elections. Sasikala managed the household and even advised Jayalalithaa on political decisions. Speaking about Jayalalithaa's decision to pull out of the thirteen-month-old Atal Bihari Vajpayee government and bring about another parliamentary election, Sasikala said later that she had advised Jayalalithaa against it. Sasikala says that Jayalalithaa announced her plans to withdraw support when they left Chennai for Delhi. 'I got into the [Chennai] airport through a different gate, while she came in through another one where the media asked for her comments,' she says. 'She was categorical that she withdrew the support. I did not know this. We reached Delhi. And as I switched on the TV, [I saw] Akka's comments. I was shattered. I pleaded with her. I argued, even fought. But she did not relent. The government fell.'[17]

THE FINAL ACT

On 22 September 2016, Sasikala was chatting with Jayalalithaa in the bedroom. The chief minister went inside the bathroom, came out feeling disoriented and suddenly fell into Sasikala's arms. She was rushed to the hospita, and this was the last time people saw Amma. Sasikala and her family guarded her. Information about her health was sketchy in the medical bulletins issued by the Apollo Hospital, and the administration remained paralysed. On 5 December 2016, Jayalalithaa breathed her last, leaving the inheritance question unanswered with a faction-ridden AIADMK. The state government instituted an inquiry commission under Justice Arumughasamy in 2017. The commission submitted its report to Tamil Nadu Chief Minister M. K. Stalin on 27 August 2022. The report, which was tabled in the Tamil Nadu assembly, found Sasikala, former Tamil Nadu health minister C. Vijayabaskar and then health secretary J. Radhakrishnan 'at fault'.[18]

Sasikala's dream of inheriting her Akka's mantle were shattered with her conviction in the disproportionate assets case. The AIADMK suffered a split, but then the two factions merged again following Jayalalithaa's death.The internal wranglings within the AIADMK have continued with two factions—one led by Panneerselvam and the other by Edapaddi K. Palaniswami—fighting over the party headquarters and the claim to be representative of the real AIADMK.

Jayalalithaa ground to dust all set norms and made it in a male-dominated political arena without a so-called pedigree to flaunt. She did not cultivate a second line of command—she was the benevolent autocrat who had no real support base when she started in politics but endeared herself to the electorate to become the people's Amma.

VASUNDHARA RAJE

The Royal Inheritance

'I will take the class today,' said Vasundhara Raje. It was a hot afternoon in August 2014 and the Rajasthan chief minister had made a surprise stop at a primary school in the Bhadsoda municipality of the tribal-dominated Chittorgarh district. She asked a student in class four to read from his Hindi textbook. As the child fumbled and could not read the sentence, a visibly angry Raje asked the teacher how many students he had in the school and what his monthly salary was. Ram Lal was drawing over ₹40,000 salary per month and had sixteen students under his tutelage. Raje directed the district collector to take action against the teacher. As the chief minister took her programme of Sarkar Aapke Dwar (Government at your

Doorstep) and camped in all the seven divisions with ministers and top bureaucrats of the desert state, she came across schools with no teachers, schools with teachers and no students, non-functional computer labs in schools with computers packed in cartons, class six students who do not know the table of four, a primary school student who did not know the alphabet, and yet another who could not spell his name. Shocked with the state of education in Rajasthan, Raje embarked on a politically perilous journey of rationalizing schools and putting in place a computerized management information system.

The administration found 28,000 primary schools with less than thirty students and 50 per cent of teaching posts vacant. Raje suggested the unthinkable—close down schools where there were fewer students, transfer teachers as per the requirement of schools, and manage this through a computerized system. Her trusted bureaucrats warned her that she would be upsetting the apple cart. So far, schools were opened at the whims of the political bosses and not after a detailed study of human resources or local educational requirements. She was proposing to shut down schools when there was an overall emphasis of increasing school enrolment by the union government led by her party, the BJP. But Raje was convinced and spent the next three years rationalizing the education system. Of the 82,000 schools in Rajasthan, 18,000 were shut down and the state had 64,000 schools by the end of 2017. Every school mandatorily had boards with the photograph, address, and phone numbers of the teachers assigned to teach there. A mirror was put in the main corridor of schools so that children could see how they had turned up to school. Separate toilets for girls and boys with running water were constructed.

The rationalization of schools came under a lot of flak from civil society and the Opposition political parties in Rajasthan. The assembly elections in 2018 saw the state following its decades-old political trend of voting out the incumbent government every five years and faithfully alternating between the BJP and the Congress. Raje lost and Congress's Ashok Gehlot formed the government.

There are, however, no regrets. Raje cites the Annual Status of Education Report 2018, an independent survey document, which showed student attendance improved by 3 per cent over 2016 levels, percentage of schools with playgrounds increased from 51.7 per cent in 2010 to 70.3 per cent in 2018, schools with usable girls toilets increased from 50.3 per cent to 80.9 per cent, and schools with computer facility rose from 15.7 per cent to 38.6 per cent in the same time period.

Raje is the only woman chief minister the state of Rajasthan has seen. Serving two terms as a chief minister and commanding a loyal following of partymen and constituents in a feudal state like Rajasthan is a feat in itself. But then Raje has learnt at the footsteps of a veteran—her mother Vijayaraje Scindia, the matriarch of the royal family of Gwalior, who was a founder member of the BJP and is known to have sold off her jewels to arrange for party funds. From a princess in a royal household to an able administrator of a state, Raje's political journey is a case study of grit, conviction, and vision.

INHERITING POLITICS

Born on 8 March 1953 in the powerful Scindia royal family of Gwalior, theirs was a traditional big family with Raje's brother Madhavrao and sisters Padma Raje, Usha Raje, and Yashodhara. All five were brought up in palaces amidst all luxuries fathomable. The children had watched their mother's numerous election campaigns very closely. Her daughters Vasundhara and Yashodhara started campaigning for her when they were barely ten years old. Vaasu, as she is known to her family and close friends, accompanied her mother to parliament sessions in New Delhi.

As she grew up, on her own insistence, Vijayaraje sent her to the Presentation Convent in Kodaikanal. She completed her schooling from the Scindia Kanya Vidyalaya, a school founded by Vijayaraje in Gwalior. Later, she graduated in economics and political science from Sophia College for Women in Mumbai in

1972. When she turned eighteen, Vijayaraje fixed her marriage with Hemant Singh, the young prince of Dholpur in Rajasthan. Within a year, Raje gave birth to son Dushyant and separated from her husband. There were years of litigation as Raje claimed maintenance, and later Vijayaraje filed a case for Dushyant's right to ancestral property. There are several salacious stories about affairs being responsible for the young couple parting ways, but they have remained uncorroborated over the years.

Vijayaraje's memoirs reveal that she harboured guilt for Raje's failed marriage and may have initiated her daughter into politics out of concern. Rasheed Kidwai writes about this in his book *The House of Scindias: A Saga of Power, Politics and Intrigue*, '...but as a sympathetic mother who blamed herself for the failed marriage of her daughter, the Rajmata, throughout the latter part of the 1970s, kept trying to take responsibility for Vasundhara's life by introducing her to politics. It was at this very time that the Rajmata's differences with son Madhavrao became more and more public and increasingly bitter.' The Emergency years were a tumultuous time for the royal family. Like most adversaries of then Prime Minister Indira Gandhi, Vijayaraje was imprisoned. However, Raje's brother Madhavrao escaped to Nepal and asked his sisters to join him. The young Raje and Yashodhara struggled during this time as they bore the brunt of income tax raids, borrowed money from influential friends to pay staff salaries as their bank accounts were frozen, and held on to bits of information trickling in about their mother's well-being in prison. Raje got a brief introduction to the sleazy side of politics when a senior minister in the Indira government invited her to his luxurious hotel suite and asked her what 'sacrifices will you be prepared to make to have your mother set free?'[1] Raje has always maintained a dignified silence about the incident and the identity of the minister. She gave him the royal snub but found out from him that Vijayaraje was lodged in Delhi's Tihar Jail.

After the Emergency was lifted and Vijayaraje released from jail, Vasundhara found a place as a member of the Rajasthan

Social Welfare Board in 1978. Vijayaraje's close associate Bhairon
Singh Shekhawat had formed the Janata Party government in
Rajasthan and was quick to accommodate the young princess
in the board. This was her first assignment in Rajasthan—a
state she would later win and nurture as the chief minister.
However, a more formal role came after the BJP was formed
in 1980 and Vijayaraje was appointed as the vice-president of
the BJP's national unit. In 1984, Raje became a member of the
BJP's national executive and waded into electoral politics. The
BJP gave her a ticket in the 1984 assembly elections, from the
Bhind constituency in Madhya Pradesh. Raje lost to Congress's
Udayabhan Singh—the first and only electoral defeat she has ever
witnessed in her political career spanning over four decades. The
next year, Bhairon Singh Shekhawat suggested that she fight an
election from Dholpur—her marital home. Even though she had
no support from her estranged husband's family, people saw her
as their maharani and she won against the Congress heavyweight
Banwari Lal by 23,000 votes. The foundation of what would
turn into a formidable presence in Rajasthan politics had been
laid. She had graduated from being the princess of Gwalior
to the maharani of Dholpur. Politically, her caste arithmetic is
perfect for Rajasthan, where such considerations matter greatly.
She is a Rajput by birth and married into a Jat royal family—the
two most numerically strong and dominant castes of the highly
feudal and orthodox state of Rajasthan.

Even before her term ended, Shekhawat felt that she should
fight the parliamentary elections from the Jhalawar parliamentary
seat, which is in the parched Hadoti region of Rajasthan bordering
Madhya Pradesh and was a part of the old Scindia estate. The BJP
was hoping to cash in on the Rajasthan electorate's fascination
with royalty. Six-term Rajasthan MLA Pratap Singh Singhvi,
whose seat was close to Raje's in the 1985 Rajasthan state
assembly, told this author about Raje's first meeting in his village
following the decision to field her from Jhalawar. 'I remember the
first time she visited my village Chhipabarod in Baran right after
the decision to field her from Jhalawar. She had to reach there

late evening but could reach only at 2 a.m. My old muneemji
(accountant), who was 84–85 years old, stayed up and came to
see her. I was shocked at the way people had turned up just to
catch a glimpse of her. I asked him what he was doing there in
the middle of the night? He was sheepish and didn't say that
he had come to see her but simply said, "Aise hee aa gaya tha
(I came just like that)." The curiosity to see the maharani was
immense,' says Singhvi. Raje polled over 50 per cent of the votes
and won the seat. She went on to win Jhalawar (later named
Jhalarapatan) in the 1991, 1996, 1998, and 1999 Lok Sabha
elections till she moved to state politics.

CREATING HISTORY IN RAJASTHAN

It was 11 September 2002, her son Dushyant's birthday, and
Raje was in Jaipur to attend a Rajasthan BJP state unit meeting.
The top brass of the party—then Prime Minister Atal Bihari
Vajpayee, Deputy Prime Minister L. K. Advani, the BJP national
general secretary, Pramod Mahajan, and Rajnath Singh—were
present in the crucial meeting. As the meeting ended Raje was
walking out, eager to fly back to New Delhi to spend whatever
was left of the day with Dushyant when a party worker ran up
to her and said she had been asked to stay back by Mahajan.
Wondering what the matter could be, she went back only to be
told that the party wanted her to head the state unit. Raje was
stumped—the party was ridden with factions, the elections were
due in exactly a year, she was an outsider who had lived most
of her political life in Lutyens' Delhi, and no woman had ever
headed the Rajasthan BJP. It was a carefully thought-out decision
by the saffron party. Bhairon Singh Shekhawat had become the
vice-president of India and there was a leadership vacuum. The
state unit was dominated by Brahmin leaders including Bhanwar
Lal Sharma and Lalit Kishore Chaturvedi, but with her royal
allure and the right caste arithmetic, Raje stood out. Shekhawat
threw his weight behind Raje and the decision was taken.

By the time Raje was sent to Rajasthan, she had already

proved her prowess in governance. In the thirteen-months-old Vajpayee government in 1998, she served as the minister of state for external affairs at a time when several countries had imposed sanctions against India following nuclear tests held in Pokhran in May 1998. Raje efficiently worked with the international community to put forward India's point of view. Her hard work was rewarded when mid-term elections were called and Vajpayee formed a coalition government in 1999. She was given independent charge of small scale industries and as a junior minister to Vajpayee, she handled departments of personnel and training, atomic energy, and space.

Rajasthan was no cakewalk. Raje was pitted against incumbent chief minister, Ashok Gehlot, who had cultivated a careful image of being a humble man from the grassroots. Gehlot, who was seen as representing the so-called lower castes in Rajasthan, had worked at the grassroots to effectively steer Rajasthan through a dreadful drought in 2000, and the people remembered it. The BJP was a divided house, and Mahajan sensed it in time. As the local BJP leaders started supporting rebel candidates, Mahajan flew down party workers from his home state of Maharashtra. Raje employed young professionals to give her a demographic profile of all constituencies. Mahajan had sensed the anti-incumbency and worked hard on Raje's image of a maharani far-removed from the reality and travails of commoners. Then Raje started campaigning—she ate at the homes of locals, stopped to have water and speak to people, waded into the crowds, women hugged her, and she warmly embraced them. Former BJP MLA and a known Muslim face in Rajasthan, Younus Khan, who had worked for Raje's first campaign, says, 'The connect she had with women had never been seen before. She went to villages and said, "Sirf do jaatiyaan hoti hain—purush aur mahila. Main yahan aaj mahilaayon ki pairavi karne aayi hoon. (There are only two castes—man and woman. I am here to vouch for women today)." For the first time women thought they had a voice.' Riding high on women vote, Raje won big, cornering 120 of the 200 constituencies in the state.

The first woman chief minister of Rajasthan got down to business from the word go. Bureaucrats remember her first meeting with the department heads. She came armed with a detailed presentation on the problems plaguing the state and what needed to be done. She threw a question at her officers—why doesn't Rajasthan have industries? This kept rankling her. She had identified it as a major concern. A few months later, she met the captains of Indian industries at the *India Today* conclave in March 2004 and posed the same question to them. A senior bureaucrat in the chief minister's office, who did not wish to be identified, told this author how Raje pursued this doggedly. 'She met Azim Premji and Narayana Murthy in Bangalore and asked them to invest in Rajasthan. She sent teams of officers to Bangalore, Hyderabad, and Mumbai. She got vital inputs from the industrialists who told her that they do not get skilled manpower fluent in English and there is hardly an optical fibre network in Rajasthan,' said the officer. English as a language was reintroduced in Rajasthan's government schools and Raje worked closely with the centre to get 5,000 kilometres of optical fibre network and video-conferencing set-ups in all divisional headquarters. She set up the Economic Policy and Reforms Council which acted as a think tank on key economic matters, increasing private sector participation and creating resources and capabilities.[2] Raje included business leaders like Rajendra S. Pawar, Kiran Mazumdar-Shaw, Nachiket Mor, and R. K. Pachauri in this advisory group.

Raje emphasized the on the creation of IT infrastructure in the state and IT education for the youth. She introduced freshly-prepared mid day meals in government schools and anganwadis. All officers touring districts had to taste the mid day meals. 'She herself would stop by at schools during visits and sit on the floor with the children to taste the food. Children would admit sheepishly that the menu had been changed because the school had heard of her visit in the district. Her instructions to the officers were clear—if you cannot eat the food, how will a six-year-old find it palatable? A majority of the children from the economically weaker sections of society were coming to schools for these meals. With a little emphasis, she felt, they could remain in school and the enrolment would rise,' says the officer quoted above.

In the last year of her first term, a brainstorming session with the district collectors brought forth a scheme which is considered Raje's signature scheme. In December 2007, at the annual collectors' conference, Raje asked the officers why bank accounts for people below poverty line (BPL) were not being opened. The collectors pointed out that banks were not interested in opening accounts for people from the lower economic strata. 'She asked the collectors to speak to banks and ensure that accounts are opened. Then she came up with a new idea—open the accounts in the name of the lady of the household. When collectors pointed out that there could be a problem of minimum amount required to put in the account, she suggested that the government should put in the small amount and coordinate with the bank to issue cards,' says the officer. This scheme was later formally launched as the Bhamashah Yojana during Raje's second term between 2013–18 and made the woman head of the household with all the benefits of government schemes being directly transferred in her bank account.

COURTING CONTROVERSY

Even as Raje was credited with bringing investors to Rajasthan, she was criticized for fostering a coterie of businessmen who influenced administration and meddled in policymaking, cornering plum government contracts and intimidating farmers to sell agricultural land for their factories. One of the associations was with Lalit Modi, son of businessman K. K. Modi, who owned the Godfrey Philips tobacco company. Quite early on, even before he turned around cricket with the concept of Indian Premier League, Modi had set his eyes on entering into cricket administration. He tried to enter the Himachal Pradesh Cricket Association but had a fight with then chief minister and BJP veteran Prem Kumar Dhumal and was asked to leave. He then tried to enter the Rajasthan Cricket Association (RCA), which was under the control of the Rungta family. Author Alam Srinivas has explained the controversy around Modi and his proximity to Raje in his article 'Rise and fall: In Lalit Modi's never-ending brawls, some wins and many losses' for *Scroll.in*. 'Modi's fortunes changed in 2003, when Vasundhara Raje, a close friend of his wife and mother, became Rajasthan's chief minister. In August 2004, she promulgated the Rajasthan Sports (Registration, Recognition & Regulation of Associations) Ordinance. People familiar with the situation claim that one of its purposes was to eject the Rungtas from the RCA. One of its clauses stated that sport associations in the state had to be disbanded and registered afresh. Another stated that individual members would not be allowed to vote for posts in the associations. Another clause said that only office bearers of district-level sports associations and primary sports bodies could contest the elections. These clauses implied that the RCA's fifty-seven individual members, which included members of the Rungta family and their supporters, could not vote in the elections to its posts. Thus, the family, which had a majority, would not be able to influence future elections. The Rungtas challenged the Ordinance, but the Rajasthan High Court dismissed their petition in December 2004. The stage was set for Modi to become RCA's president in 2005. Modi claimed that he changed the fortunes of the association. He transformed the Sawai Mansingh Stadium, which became a regular venue for international matches. He turned the Rajasthan Cricket Association into a highly-profitable institution,' writes Srinivas.[3]

In *Outlook*'s October 2009 cover story, the senior journalist Smita Gupta writes that Modi ruled Rajasthan. 'He was able to do so because all powers during the BJP's five years of rule were apparently centralized in the chief minister's office—everything from transfers to change in land use to liquor licences and mining leases. Decisions on these issues had Modi's imprint. "It was a case of single window clearance," a fellow industrialist, cricket aficionado, and politician told *Outlook*. "Modi simply summoned civil servants with their files to his suite at the Rambagh Palace and told them what to do. And if anyone demurred, he'd simply say, "I'll have to talk to Vaasu (the name by which Vasundhara's close friends address her)....'" Modi was indeed a law unto himself. Like in the case of the Amer havelis. He is alleged to have manipulated government rules and pressured local officials to secure control of at least two of the havelis, with a view to renovating and converting these into a heritage resort,' writes Gupta.[4] The article recounts two public spats involving IAS officer Mahendra Surana and IPS officer R. P. Srivastava. '[Mahendra] Surana, who was secretary, employees' welfare, recalled that in 2007 he had accompanied friend Dr Hemendra Surana, a doctor in the army and a former Ranji player, to watch a match at SMS. Dr Surana had asked Modi for passes earlier but when his request was turned down, he procured them from minister Rajendra Singh Rathore. As the two waited to gain entry, Modi came in and saw the Suranas show their passes to the girl at the door. "He simply came up, asked the girl what was happening, grabbed our passes and tore them up." The reason for his anger: he thought Dr Surana was with the Rungta group (of Kishore Rungta, rival to Modi in the RCA). The Srivastava incident was similar.'[5]

The Congress started terming Modi as 'Super CM' and 'Shadow CM' and Gehlot called him an extra-constitutional authority. In the run-up to the 2008 assembly elections, Congress under Gehlot portrayed Raje as a maharani far removed from the grassroots, used to her palaces and wordly comforts, and entrusting her administration to rich businessmen. The serial blasts in Jaipur in May 2008 months before the assembly elections created an impression of deteriorating law and order in a peaceful state. The unassuming Gehlot, who was accessible to the electorate, became a natural choice for the people in 2008 and Raje was voted out.

WINNING BACK RAJASTHAN

Rajasthan has alternated power between the Congress and the BJP every five years for decades. It started with the Gehlot vs Shekhawat fight and later transformed into Gehlot vs Raje battle. The result is every chief minister spends largely the first one year in undoing what the predecessor has done and also instituting inquiries into corruption allegations of the previous regime. Once again in 2008, Gehlot followed the same pattern. He put Raje's signature big-ticket infrastructure projects— flyovers, shooting ranges, convention centres, rapid transport— on hold. He instituted the N. N. Mathur Commission in 2009 to investigate corruption charges to the tune of ₹20,000 crore during Raje's regime. The Rajasthan High Court held the three-member inquiry commission illegal in 2010. The order striking down the commission was upheld by the Supreme Court in 2011. By then Gehlot's term was riddled with increasing communal tensions within Rajasthan and saw the direct involvement of his ministers in mysterious disappearances and murders of women. Incidents of rape, murder, and molestation in police stations exhibited a state with poor law and order. Reforms in the power sector backfired and Gehlot's decision to increase power tariff ahead of elections became the proverbial last straw. Raje was voted back to power in 2013, winning 163 of the 200 seats. This was a historic mandate which not even Raje's mentor Shekhawat could boast of. The closest the Congress had come to this number was in 1998 when Gehlot led the party with a tally of 153 seats.

Raje had clearly left the ghosts of the first term behind. The second stint as the chief minister was marked by landmark decisions. She introduced key changes to laws to make Rajasthan an investment destination. She launched the shelved Bhamashah Yojana scheme and organized Resurgent Rajasthan, an investors' meet, in the state. Even when she was out of power, she had roped in technocrats to map the water grid of Rajasthan. Back in the saddle, Raje got water to the parched constituencies of

Churu and Nagaur. Raje has always been a hands-on boss with an eye for detail. Bureaucrats who served in the chief minister's office remember her spending hours finalizing the videos of 'Jaane Kya Dikh Jaaye' campaign of the Rajasthan tourism board, which marketed the state beyond its regal forts and palaces. Raje took inspiration from Tamil Nadu's Amma Canteens and introduced Annapura Rasoi Yojana, offering breakfast at ₹5 and lunch at ₹8 for the economically weaker sections. An officer, who did not wish to be identified, told this author how Raje even decided on the colour of the logo and the creatives for the scheme. She had a particular hue of red in mind and asked her officers to look for 'madder' for Annapurna logo. The officers suggested different shades of red for the new scheme and the chief minister went through several colour palettes before she settled on one, which remains the government's logo to date.

This is evident as she sits in her Lekha Vihar home in South Delhi. As she settles in her chair her eye catches a painting and she asks it to be straightened. Confused as the painting looks straight, the staff moves it slightly but Raje is not satisfied, 'A little to the left, a little more.' Finally, when the painting is straightened to her satisfaction she settles into the conversation. She is a big votary of women's empowerment. This is why barbs of 'No CM after 8 p.m.' by the Congress still rankle her. Raje, often described as high-handed, imperious, and autocratic by her own partymen, had come under attack from Congress MLA Raghu Sharma who, in 2009, had said that Raje had been known for being unavailable after 8 p.m.—a veiled reference to the whisky brand insinuating that the woman chief minister enjoys an evening drink while ignoring her administrative duties. 'Do you think anyone would have had the gall to say this for a man? Of course, women in politics have it very tough—political background or not. You have to be careful about how you conduct yourself,' says Raje.

Punctual to a fault, Raje is known to leave family members, officials, and politicians behind if they do not turn up on time. 'If she has to leave at 7 a.m., she will be there five minutes before time and leave exactly at 7 a.m.,' says an MLA who sheepishly admits he has been left behind. Deeply religious and a devotee of Lord Krishna, Raje is known to be an early riser who does not eat anything till she has prayed. An MLA, who has hosted Raje at his home during election tours, says, 'Vasundharaji has stayed at our place several times. Before her planned stay, two helpers would come and set up her room. No matter whatever you put in her room, her staff changes everything—even her doormat.' Her mandir is the first to be set up in the room.

Despite being an able administrator wielding a tight control over her bureaucracy, Raje found her government embroiled in two separate incidents of mob lynching of Muslim men in Alwar district by cow vigilantes. In April 2017, Pehlu Khan, a fifty-five-year-old dairy farmer who was returning from Jaipur to his village Nuh, was stopped and beaten to death by about 200 cow vigilantes who suspected him of buying cows for slaughter. Raje government's handling of the incident, her silence, and her home minister Gulab Chand Kataria's statement justifying the cow vigilantes' act triggered nationwide uproar. The following year, in July 2018, closer to the state assembly elections, another man, Akbar Khan (spelt as Rakbar in Aadhar card) was lynched in the Ramgarh area of Alwar district. This time, however, Raje had learnt her lesson and the government was quick in reacting to it by transferring officials, instituting inquiries, and arresting suspects. The damage, however, had been done.

Earlier on in her term Raje had once again been drawn into a controversy involving a visa for Lalit Modi, who had been banned for life from the Indian cricket board in 2013 and was wanted by investigative agencies. He had fled from India and taken refuge in UK. In 2015, *Times Now* news channel released a document, dating back to 2011, which was signed by Raje and endorsed Modi's application to stay on in UK to avoid arrest in India. The silence of Prime Minister Narendra Modi in this case added to Raje's woes and created an impression that she might be replaced. However, her clout within the organization and command over the state unit helped Raje survive the storm.

Rajasthan, however, stuck to its electoral pattern of voting out the incumbent government. The BJP lost to Gehlot's Congress but once again deprived him of a simple majority. Every time her party has lost the elections, Raje has always managed to retain her constituency. 'But 2018 saw a stalemate over the appointment of a new state BJP president. Incumbent Ashok Parnami's term had ended but no successor could be found even after meetings between Shah (Amit Shah) and Vasundhara…. As the deadlock continued, the services of the RSS supremo, Mohan Bhagwat, were reportedly sought. Vasundhara vetoed Arjun Meghwal and Gajendra Singh Shekhawat's nomination as state party chief but had to accept the appointment of Satish Poonia, who had a strong Sangh background and was her open critic. This was the first time since 2003, when she became chief minister for the first time, that someone with an RSS background had got prominence and an official post as the head of Rajasthan BJP.'[6]

Raje is holding onto her turf in Rajasthan. In the Modi–Shah BJP, Raje cannot be ignored. She was the first leader to hit the ground after the vicious second wave of Covid-19. In November 2021, she undertook a yatra touching six districts, visiting the families of BJP leaders who had lost their kin during the pandemic. She touched all major religious temples. Though she said it was a personal non-political yatra, it was seen as Raje setting the stage for the 2023 assembly elections. Her birthday celebrations on the banks of the Chambal River in Bundi in March 2022 became a show of strength of sorts. 'Raje's critics claim the large crowd at the venue, which caused traffic jams for several kilometres, had been drawn from all over the state. That, perhaps, is expected of any rally. What did not go unnoticed was the presence of the youth and the way Raje engaged them. There was the usual jostling to catch a glimpse of her. The political significance of the event was not to be missed. Of the BJP's seventy MLAs in the state, around forty-two, and ten of the twenty-five Lok Sabha MPs were in attendance. They had either entirely skipped the legislature meeting in Jaipur on 8 March or had left it midway to make it to Keshoraipatan on time.'[7] She remains a crowd puller. BJP is aware that an election in Rajasthan cannot be won without her support.

A voracious reader, Raje never comes out of Delhi's Khan Market bookstores in Delhi without carrying bags of books for herself and anyone around her who also shares her love of reading. Known to be an avid gardener, Raje tends to her plants and finds the greenery around her therapeutic. Her homes across cities are known for their manicured lawns, and chances are she has chosen the plants and their placement herself. She loves birds and is known to be worried about lone partridges and peacocks in her garden. If she sees a single bird, she is often heard wondering how lonely it might be.

SHEILA DIKSHIT

The Visionary Chief Minister

'**D**o you know these are fruit bats and they are really helpful in pollination?' she said pointing to the big pilkhan tree which was home to hundreds of fruit bats hanging upside down. Delhi Chief Minister Sheila Dikshit had been warned against taking up the 3 Motilal Nehru Marg bungalow in the heart of Lutyens' Delhi. Bats are a bad omen, her advisers had told her. After all, Dikshit was in the middle of her second term and no chief minister before her had completed a full term, in Delhi leave alone serve a second one. She needed to be careful, they warned her. 'But when I surveyed this house, I loved the space and the garden. I take a walk every day at 6 a.m.,' she told the author as she gave an exhaustive interview on her plans to turn around Delhi's transport system. I was a young reporter covering the Delhi government for the *Times of India* in 2006.

Seated in the garden, talking animatedly about turning around the debt-ridden Delhi Transport Corporation and making Delhi Metro the backbone of city's transport system, she smiled as a fruit bat swooshed above my head and startled me. 'They return home around dusk, you see,' she offered helpfully, adding, 'now I am thinking of opening a nature walk for children here.' When she first came to this house, she wasn't scared but curious. Instead of giving in to superstitions, she dialled the World Wildlife Fund and sought their help in identifying the species of bats. It turned out that this was a rare species of harmless fruit bats. In the coming months, Dikshit opened her home to schoolchildren and took them on nature walks to introduce them to the fruit bats.

This is how Dikshit was—decisive, experimental, not easily swayed by opinions or adversity, and a visionary. At the helm of the Delhi government for fifteen years (1998–2013), she turned India's national capital into a world-class city.

HOMING IN ON DELHI

In a way, Dikshit personified Delhi's cultural mix. She was born Sheila Kapoor in a Punjabi family in pre-partition Delhi in 1938. In her autobiography *Citizen Delhi: My Times, My Life*, Dikshit describes her carefree childhood which she spent cycling along the tree-lined avenues of Lutyens' Delhi, stuffing peanuts into bun-makhan to make her own version of peanut butter sandwiches. She and her two younger sisters, Pam and Rama, studied in one of Delhi's oldest schools—Convent of Jesus and Mary. After finishing school, Dikshit joined Miranda House, a prestigious girls' college under Delhi University. 'Our "gang" did everything together. We bunked class to go to the university coffee house where we would pool in our two annas and four annas for buns, coffee, lemonade, or ice cream soda.... We played ping-pong in college and watched cricket matches between arch-rivals, Hindu and St Stephen's, cheering the latter, for Miranda and Stephen's were most in tune with each other,'[1] she writes about her years in North Campus. It was while pursuing her master's that she met and fell in love with Vinod Dikshit, the son of freedom fighter and Congress veteran Uma Shankar Dikshit. The couple decided to get married after Vinod qualified for the Indian Administrative Service (IAS) in 1959. Like any inter-caste marriage in those days, hers also met with opposition from Vinod's parents. She describes in detail the opposition to her marriage. 'Dikshits, considered to be the highest of the high, orthodox Kanyakubj Brahmins from Unnao in Uttar Pradesh, were deeply rooted in a culture epitomized by the Hindi language. I, who was learning about such sociological categories for the first time, felt a twinge of alarm, but remained comforted by Vinod's unwavering support,'[2] she has said about reservations to their marriage. Finally, the couple tied the knot in 1962 with the blessings of both the families. They had son Sandeep in 1964 and daughter Latika in 1967. Dikshit spent these years as a bureaucrat's wife in Uttar Pradesh, watching politics from the ringside.

All this changed as her father-in-law Uma Shankar Dikshit or Dadda, as he was fondly called, got drawn into the battle between Prime Minister Indira Gandhi and the old guard or the Syndicate (as they were known) in 1969. President Zakir Hussain died in the middle of his term in May 1969. While the Syndicate supported N. Reddy for president, Indira Gandhi threw her weight behind Vice-president V. V. Giri. Uma Shankar Dikshit, who was a member of the Rajya Sabha and the Congress Working Committee, became the centre-point of the presidential campaign as Indira Gandhi asked him to rally support for Giri. This time is described by Sheila Dikshit in her autobiography as the beginning of her apprenticeship with Uma Shankar Dikshit. She started with managing Dadda's busy appointment diary and official telephone and ensuring tea for a stream of visitors—she gradually became the official hostess at dinners—giving her an opportunity to interact with a cross section of politicians and bureaucrats. On Indira Gandhi's insistence, she campaigned for the Congress in Rae Bareilly during the 1977 general elections.

Her real initiation in electoral politics came with a phone call from Rajiv Gandhi in November 1984 when he asked her to fight the Lok Sabha elections from Uttar Pradesh. Riding on a sympathy wave after the assassination of Indira Gandhi by her bodyguards, Dikshit won from Kannauj with a margin of 50,000 votes. In just over a year, Rajiv Gandhi inducted her as a minister of state for parliamentary affairs in 1986 and as a minister of state the prime minister's office in 1988. Dikshit, and not her husband Vinod, became the real political inheritor of Dadda. This is one of the few instances in Indian politics where the daughter-in-law and not the son inherited the political lineage. It could also have been what destiny chose for the Dikshit family as Vinod passed away after a heart attack in January 1987. He was forty-eight years old. A grief-stricken Dikshit immersed herself in family and work.

Dikshit lost her second parliamentary election from Kannauj in 1989 as the Congress was defeated following the Bofors scandal. Rajiv Gandhi's assassination in 1991 heralded years of turmoil and instability in the Congress. P. V. Narasimha Rao was sworn in as the prime minister of a minority government. Though he had a good relationship with Dadda, Dikshit was benched during his time as the prime minister. Sonia Gandhi refused to step into politics and take charge of the party, choosing to concentrate on her young children instead. But Dikshit always kept in touch with her during this time of grief, and they developed a rapport and trust. In 1992, Sonia appointed Dikshit as the secretary of the Indira Gandhi Memorial Trust, of which she was the chairperson and her trusted lieutenant Natwar Singh the vice-chairperson. India witnessed two years of political instability as successive coalition governments collapsed between 1996 and 1998. Finding their national leadership uninspiring and Sonia unwilling to step into politics, several Congress leaders resigned and floated smaller parties. Natwar Singh, Arjun Singh, M. L. Fotedar, and Dikshit broke away to form the All India Indira Congress (Tiwari).

Dikshit fought the 1996 parliamentary elections from Unnao in Uttar Pradesh on the new party's ticket and lost. This was a short-lived experiment as the breakaway faction came back into the Congress fold once Sonia took over the reins of the party in 1998.

What followed changed the political landscape of Delhi. Dikshit's son and former East Delhi member of parliament Sandeep Dikshit recounts, 'In 1997, various Delhi leaders— Dr A. K. Walia, Narendra Nath, Ram Babu Sharma called on her in our Nizamudddin East home. That was the time when Bhagatji (H. K. L. Bhagat) was a stalwart in Delhi. The sense amongst these leaders was that Bhagatiji's era is ending and the local leaders were looking for a worthy name to displace him. They thought of Amma as she was a known leader, close to Soniaji and a Brahmin, so they campaigned for her to contest from East Delhi parliamentary constituency saying that there is a big Brahmin vote bank.'[3] Dikshit did not make much of these visits as her politics had been in Uttar Pradesh. Then came a late night phone call. 'Amma had prepared to fight from Kannauj in 1998 parliamentary elections.... Closer to the date of filing nomination papers, quite late in the night around 10–10.30 p.m., the phone rang. I picked up and the person said, "Main George bol raha hoon. Sheilaji se baat karayein (George here. I want to speak to Sheilaji)."' Vincent George, Rajiv Gandhi's, and later Sonia's trusted private secretary, put her through to the party president who told Dikshit that she should fight from the East Delhi parliamentary constituency. Sandeep remembers that the decision did not take the Delhi leaders by surprise. 'All these Delhi leaders were prepared who would second her nomination— everything. Now, none of us knew East Delhi. When we went to file the nomination papers, we were looking for [the] SDM office. It was a huge constituency of about 25 lakh voters—usually the constituencies then were with 14–15 lakh voters. Amma lost by 44,000 votes to BJP's Lal Bihari Tiwari,' says Sandeep. It was during this election that Dikshit developed her local political contacts in Delhi.

Even though Dikshit lost the election, she successfully replaced the Congress strongman H. K. L. Bhagat, who was her senior cabinet minister in the parliamentary affairs ministry in Rajiv Gandhi's government. Ironically, Bhagat had been brought forward by Dadda against Chaudhary Brahm Prakash (the first chief minister of Delhi).

The highly-factionalized state Congress rallied behind her. Right before the Delhi assembly elections in November 1998, Dikshit was drafted in to head the state unit. This election is popularly termed as 'Pyaaz pe ladaa gaya chunaav (the election fought on onion prices)'. The price of essential commodities had increased over the months leading upto the polls. The humble onion touched ₹100 per kilogram. Dikshit, a seasoned politician, sensed the anger and was quick to make this the central issue, promising action on black marketers and hoarders if they voted the Congress to power. The incumbent BJP had changed two chief ministers—Sahib Singh Verma and Madan Lal Khurana—and brought in Sushma Swaraj just two months before the elections. In real terms, the pitch was ready for the Congress to bowl out the BJP.

'This was the first election when electronic voting machines (EVMs) were used,' remembers Sandeep. 'Amma's constituency, Gole Market, was one of the five constituencies where EVMs were used. So by 12.30–1 p.m. we knew Amma was winning but were glued to our televisions to see the rest of the state. By 5 p.m., Congress had won. Sajjan Kumar and Jagdish Tytler were the first ones to come late in the night and congratulate her,' he says, pointing to the fact that by then Dikshit had the support of all the different factions. 'It was later that Tripathi (Sheila Dikshit's aide for decades) took a phone call and declared loudly as he beamed, "Soniaji has declared Madam as chief minister." Just as this decision was declared, Sajjan Kumar walked in with a bouquet of flowers. So, somewhere everyone knew that Amma will lead the government and she had gained that acceptability,' says Sandeep.

SHAPING THE VISION

Dikshit inherited a Delhi which was struggling with basic civic problems—massive power cuts, a pilfered water supply system, an unreliable loss-ridden transport corporation, and air and water pollution. Politically, Delhi posed a tougher challenge. It is not a state but a union territory with its own legislature. As the chief minister, Dikshit did not have land matters or law and order under her control. While morally she could be held responsible for crime in the city, the Delhi Police was effectively under the union home ministry. All major legislative matters, including bills on taxation or transfer of bureaucrats needed the home ministry's approval. At the centre was the BJP-led National Democratic Alliance (NDA) government of Atal Bihari Vajpayee. In a way, she was the chief minister of the government of India's capital, but practically had no real power. 'Although people expected me to make their lives more secure, I had no control over Delhi Police, which reported to the union home ministry. Any desire to augment Delhi's water supply would necessitate turning to neighbouring states for help. Moreover, almost every file had to go to the lieutenant governor for approval. This cumbersome process of requiring so many levels of approval was unique to Delhi,' she says in her autobiography.[4]

Dikshit came up with an idea of participative governance—making people active participants in the development of their colonies and stakeholders in the development of the city. 'What we were thinking of was along the lines of a partnership—a two-way process—in which citizens would own programmes and acknowledge that they too were stakeholders in the development of their city.... My chief secretary, Mr Regunathan, and I detailed the idea. Ad-man Suhel Seth provided us with the name, Bhagidari, which means partnership in Hindi. Mr Regunathan located a consultancy, namely Accord, led by George Koreth and Kiron Wadhera, who went on to execute the scheme. Accord had the expertise of large group interactive processes.'[5] Bhagidari scheme was a direct citizen interface. It involved registering resident welfare associations (RWAs) and inviting them for interactions with the government officials to solve their every day problems related to electricity, water, sewage, and transport. In undermining this scheme, what Dikshit's adversaries did not realize was that the chief minister was directly reaching out to the people and lending them a sympathetic ear.

Former Delhi Chief Secretary Shailaja Chandra, whom Dikshit picked over six male batchmates in February 2002, remembers how sceptical she was about Bhagidari only to realize it was an exceptional policy. 'After taking over as chief secretary, when I called on lieutenant-governor Vijai Kapoor, he started our cold conversation by first pooh-poohing Mrs Dikshit's Bhagidari initiative. He called the programme "political rubbish" and I dutifully took notes. Within a week of my joining, the chief minister's office told me that the CM had desired I attend the next Bhagidari session on the coming Thursday. "What will I do there?" I thought to myself and remembered the L-G's dismissal of it. I went full of misgivings, wondering how I would keep such politically motivated programmes at arm's length,' says Chandra. Over the following three days, Chandra witnessed how office-bearers of the RWAs put down their grievances, interacted with government officials, and got acquainted with government processes. 'The telephone numbers of the key people, along with the location of the offices were shared. The RWAs were plied with tea, snacks, and lunch and made to feel important. By the time Saturday came, they had become good friends with the officials and were on card-exchanging terms. When Mrs Dikshit walked in she went up on stage, held hands with a few RWA representatives, and even danced to a catchy number. She personally handed them a potted plant as a giveaway gift.... It was a masterstroke to capture the imagination of the middle-class citizenry of Delhi despite having no control over some of the most important departments that affected their lives.'[6]

As Dikshit established a citizen interface, she realized that she needed to address the civic problems. This could be done only if Delhi was made financially secure. Dikshit appointed a committee of Ramesh Chandra, the principal secretary (finance), and Vivek Rae, secretary (planning and infrastructure development), to explore how to manage Delhi's finances. Ramesh Chandra says, 'After giving subsidies to Delhi Jal Board (DJB) and Delhi Vidyut Board (DVB), we hardly had any money left for developmental works. The subsidies were making Delhi bleed. No big bang work was possible. In our report, Vivek and I recommended to her to privatize DJB to reduce losses. While submitting the report I told her, "Ma'am kuch kariye. Losses bahut zyada hain. (Ma'am, do something. Losses are too much). Either you privatize DJB or you increase the tariff by 3–4 per cent every year." She told me, "Dekhiye Rameshji, paani ka bill main ek paise bhi nahin badhaaungi. Jis din main badhaaungi us din main haar jaungi. Meri party ke log hee mujhe hataa denge (Look Ramesh ji, I will not increase the water bill by a single paisa. The day I increase it, I will be defeated. My party people will remove me)." We realized that there were compulsions so we could not do anything.'

There was a growing realization within the government that if not DJB, power could be privatized in Delhi. It helped that officers at the helm in the Delhi administration were enthusiastic votaries of privatization. In 2001, Dikshit asked the Delhi Power Secretary Ashok Pradhan to explore if the DVB could be privatized. The first request for proposal got a good response from private distribution companies. But the companies started backing out gradually. 'On 1 January 2002, Mrs Dikshit called me and said she had decided to privatize power. She constituted a committee under my chairmanship with Jagdish Sagar and Rahul Khullar as members and the terms of reference were to privatize the DVB. Mrs Dikshit gave us time till June to privatize power,' says Ramesh Chandra.[7]

It wasn't a simple task. There were complex issues—the DVB employees' unions had fears about the private distribution companies not giving them their pensions or reducing the retirement age; entrusting distribution of the capital to one company could make it prone to blackmail; and dividing Delhi into different zones meant one or two zones could be loss-making ventures for the private company and the real estate assets of DVB. But above all was the timing of the move. It came when knives were out within the party against Dikshit. Earlier in April 2000, senior leaders like Jagdish Tytler, Deep Chand Bandhu, Ram Vir Singh Bidhuri, and a few newly-elected legislators claimed Dikshit was corrupt and incompetent and demanded her resignation. The party formed a coordination committee to iron out differences between the Delhi government and the state Congress unit. Though Sonia had conveyed that there won't be any change of leadership, Dikshit had to tread carefully. Ramesh Chandra says, 'Politically, Mrs Dikshit told us categorically that we had her full support. My request to her was to speak to her MLAs. At the same time, we requested her to get our proposal and all decisions on DVB privatization approved by the cabinet. With this, technically and legally on paper, the entire government became party to the decision,' says Ramesh Chandra.

Since private players were involved in the DVB privatization, Dikshit advised her officers to brief central ministers of the BJP government at the centre. 'The quality of political leadership was very important. We weren't the first ones to suggest DVB privatization. Before Mrs Dikshit, the political leadership did not have the courage and confidence to do it.... She told us that if you think correct, speak to Arun Shourieji (minister of disinvestment in Vajpayee's cabinet). Suresh Prabhu was the power minister in the first stage. Sagar and I met the secretary of disinvestment and Mr Shourie and we got full support. We had two–three meetings with Mr Shourie and he asked us to keep him in the loop. The privatization of power in Delhi is a perfect example that reflects what can be done through collaboration should not be done with confrontation,' says Ramesh Chandra.

On 1 July 2002, power distribution was privatized in Delhi. The initial months were chaotic. Dikshit kept a hawk's eye on the performance. Shailaja Chandra says, 'It was common for me to get a call from Mrs Dikshit as late as 10.30 or 11 p.m. "Shailajaji, I am returning from my sister's place in Noida after dinner. All streetlights are lit up in UP but as soon as I cross over to Delhi it is pitch dark. Not a single streetlight is working. Can you call a meeting of the power companies and tell them to get the lights working?" It was the cry of someone who wanted to see Delhi shining bright.' The power sector gradually settled down and now Delhi boasts of 24x7 power supply. But the biggest jolt for Dikshit came in 2004 when the Comptroller and Auditor General (CAG), in its report for 2002–2003, questioned the decision to choose SBI Caps as the consultant to map privatization and said that the state had suffered a loss of over ₹6,000 crore due to decisions made during the unbundling of the DVB.[8] Ramesh Chandra says the main controversy was over real estate owned by the DVB being given to power distribution companies for free. 'SBI Capital had recommended that you sell the business of power distribution in Delhi. The business means everything—transfer staff, real estate, and even sub-stations. Companies will bid and give a certain amount for taking over. Real estate was given away. It was a part of the business,' he explains. The committee members had met CAG before the privatization. 'It was Jagdish Sagar's idea. He pointed out that sooner or later CAG will look into it so it is better for us to brief him beforehand. After listening to us, CAG said this looks like a good model... so go ahead. It was part of his (CAG's) charter to find faults, if any. But at the end, nothing came out of it and no wrongdoing was proven,' says Ramesh Chandra.

> Even as Dikshit's officers were trying to privatize power distribution in Delhi, the Supreme Court was breathing fire over increasing air pollution in Delhi. Environmentalist M. C. Mehta had filed a public interest petition in the Supreme Court over pollution in Delhi. On 28 July 1998, the Supreme Court gave a detailed order on phasing out the entire diesel-driven city bus fleet and convert it to a single-fuel mode of Compressed Natural Gas or CNG by 31 March 2001. Delhi had to replace 200 diesel buses every month. Dikshit came to power four months later.

The task was not only administratively complicated but also politically daunting. Delhi needed access to CNG through long pipelines, the public transport had to be retrofitted, there were no safety or emission guidelines for CNG vehicles, manufacturers did not have the capacity to deliver buses, and the cost of conversion was prohibitively high. Initially, Dikshit thought that the courts would see the impossibility of the task at hand and extend the deadline to implement the order at its own pace. What her officers didn't expect was that the Supreme Court would take a grim view of the intent and doublespeak of the state government and private bus operators. Public transport came to a halt as the Supreme Court refused to extend the 31 March 2001 deadline and only one-fourth of the 12,000 city buses remained on road. Commuters were left stranded on bus stops and fought for space on over-crowded buses. Violence erupted in Delhi as irate passengers set buses on fire. 'Delhi Chief Minister Sheila Dikshit declared that her government was ready to "face punishment for contempt of court" but would not allow citizens to suffer.'[9]

Sindhushree Khullar, who took over as the transport commissioner and transport secretary in August 2001, remembers the chaos around the switchover. 'The Delhi government was reluctant to implement the Supreme Court order, with a stand-off being the preferred path.[10] The Supreme Court slapped a contempt of court order in April 2001. 'After the contempt of court order in April 2001, there appeared to be a change of course. There was a growing realization that confrontation with the apex court was not desirable and that the government could not continue to resist the switch to CNG. We crafted a doable timeline, giving every detail of the number and month-wise phasing out of diesel fleet and phase-in of CNG fleet. In this time, Ajay Maken took over as transport minister and we got the necessary backing for this plan. In December 2001, we filed an affidavit in the Supreme Court giving the plan, which was accepted by the court. It proved to be the turning point.' There were different expert opinions about the environmental benefits of CNG and powerful diesel lobbies were at work. 'Once we had committed to phasing out in the Supreme Court, the government started working earnestly towards the goal. The pressure from the diesel lobbies eased off considerably and the CNG lobbies began pulling their weight,' says Khullar.

Delhi was caught in a maze of administrative problems as it started implementing the CNG switch-over. 'Initially Delhi faced an acute problem of CNG supply. The CNG pipelines were very long and the availability of CNG for such a large fleet of buses and autos became an issue. Buses and autos would stand overnight at CNG filling stations. The queues became longer and public transport was hit, inconveniencing the people. These issues were smoothened out over time by coordinating with the Ministry of Petroleum and Natural Gas and Indraprastha Gas Limited,' says Khullar. By this time, the far-sighted politician in Dikshit had seen that there was no escaping the CNG order and she was on board. 'It was a tough and daunting task for Mrs Dikshit, but she rode the tiger,' says Khullar.

Dikshit introduced landmark initiatives in her first term. 'We approached Prime Minister Vajpayee to help rescue the Delhi Metro project from the comatose state into which it had fallen,' writes Dikshit.[11] Though the Delhi Metro was spearheaded by the union Union Urban Development Ministry (now renamed as the Housing and Urban Affairs Ministry), the Delhi government was a stakeholder and appointed E. Sreedharan as its managing director. 'Mrs Dikshit worked closely with "Team Metro" as she called them. I recall accompanying her into the labyrinths spreading under Chawri Bazaar as Mr Sreedharan took her down an unending staircase to show her the technology used to blast the tunnels and simultaneously erect the tunnel walls,' says Chandra. On 25 December 2002 the first stretch of 8.5 kilometres of the metro line from Shahdara to Tis Hazari opened. Curious Delhiites thronged the stations to take the first trip on the metro. People could believe that such a clean, fast, and

punctual facility could exist. Some people took away their first-
ride metro tokens with them and some other rowdy elements
tried to test the toughness of metro rail coaches' windows by
pounding on them with objects. 'There was bedlam. Mrs Dikshit
rang me and said I should immediately go on the train along
with Mr Sreedharan and find a way of cordoning off the public.
Her perception of the public mood was quicker than anyone
else's which was fortunate,' says Chandra.

There were many firsts to Dikshit's credit by the time she faced
the electorate again in November 2003. She implemented the unit
area method of paying property tax which categorized colonies
according to the civic amenities provided by the municipal
corporation, introduced Delhi's Right to Information Act before
the central government implemented it, addressed Delhi's water
woes by setting up the Sonia Vihar water treatment plant by
coordinating with the Uttar Pradesh Chief Minister Mayawati
for a plot of land in the neighbouring state, and built flyovers to
ease traffic. It was an easy victory for Dikshit as the electorate
rewarded her for the visible change they saw in governance and
the quality of life in Delhi. But what wasn't easy was staking
claim to the chief minister's post for a second time. Though the
Congress Party has always followed a policy of repeating chief
ministers who had led the party to victory a second time, Dikshit
had to wait for a good one week before being named the leader
of the legislature party. The announcement came only after Sonia
held a meeting with Dikshit and the Delhi state unit president,
Subhash Chopra—a known Dikshit baiter. But the dissidence
against Dikshit did not end here. Sandeep Dikshit's electoral
victory in the parliamentary elections of 2004 from the East
Delhi constituency further aggravated tensions between Sheila
Dikshit and the state Congress. There was a growing feeling in
a section of the state Congress that Dikshit was intentionally
keeping Subhash Chopra's loyalists out of the house committees
of the Delhi assembly and other plum posts. In April 2005, at an
outdoor meeting of the Delhi Pradesh Congress Committee, some
leaders and workers demanded the chief minister's resignation.

'I had never experienced anything like this onslaught. That the dissidents wanted to play it this way was their lookout; but to think that I would continue to sit through that one-sided meeting, grin and bear it, was a bit presumptuous,'[12] writes Dikshit about her famous walkout from this meeting. The proverbial last straw for Dikshit came when her bête noire, councillor, and state unit chief, Ram Babu Sharma, had her personal Nizamuddin East residence checked for building violations. 'One day I woke up knowing exactly what to do. I sent in my resignation to Mrs Sonia Gandhi...' writes Dikshit. The party high command moved with alacrity to defuse the crisis. Sonia's trusted political secretary Ahmed Patel visited Dikshit and pacified her by conveying that she had Sonia's support and that her resignation could not be accepted.[13]

STRENGTHENING REFORMS

In some ways, the second term was tougher for Dikshit. She was battling dissidence and her performance in office had raised the expectations of the people. Delhi was transforming at all levels. The chief minister wanted to provide an affordable, clean, and fast transport system to Delhi. The metro system was increasing its network, but Dikshit decided to explore the rapid bus transit system which involved segregating traffic into dedicated lanes with the bus lanes being next to the central median on the road. On 20 April 2008, a trial section of the first route, from Ambedkar Nagar to Moolchand Hospital in South Delhi opened up. 'In October, as work started on the rest of the route, the project was engulfed by a high decibel protest campaign. Car owners who realized that they were required to stick to lanes and go through longer pauses at traffic lights, as the system weighed in favour of buses, were most vocal,' writes Dikshit.[14]

Former transport department officials involved in the rollout, however, fault the hasty decisions that Dikshit made. The first pilot project was proposed from Moolchand to Jahangirpuri. Just a few kilometres from Moolchand was the then Delhi assembly speaker Chaudhary Prem Singh's constituency Ambedkar Nagar. Singh, a powerful Jat leader who held the Guinness world record for winning the most number of elections from the same constituency and political party, had seen the system at work in European countries. He wrote to Dikshit requesting that the first corridor be introduced from Ambedkar Nagar. After all, it was just a few kilometres down Moolchand, he had argued.

Dikshit got the new corridor examined—a 6 kilometre stretch from Moolchand to Ambedkar Nagar. This became the first stretch. Haroon Yusuf, the former transport minister in Dikshit's cabinet, says, 'Any system needs to settle down. There has to be behavioural change. Here we were trying to teach Delhi to drive in their lanes and giving dedicated space to buses for quicker movement. The main problem was that the editors of several newspapers and TV channels used to live in South Delhi—some in Sainik Farms. They took this route and witnessed first-hand the teething troubles. They never gave the system a chance, waging a war against it through their newspapers.'[15] It wasn't just the choice of the corridor that plagued the project. After travelling on the 6 kilometre stretch, the buses joined the same traffic chaos beyond Moolchand Hospital.

Furthermore, to Dikshit's surprise, Chaudhary Prem Singh wrote to the Delhi Lieutenant Governor Tejendra Khanna, blaming the project for traffic snarls and demanding it be scrapped. Yusuf remembers how Dikshit deputed him to persuade the speaker. Many say that Yusuf was armed with Singh's letters written to Dikshit demanding the route start from his constituency. Even as the chief minister could not persuade the speaker to not publicly criticize the project, she could not brush aside the public outcry. Sandeep says, 'After people started protesting against it, Pawan and I (Dikshit's political secretary Pawan Khera) took multiple journeys on the corridor—between 8.30 a.m. and 12 noon and 5–8 p.m. in the evening. Every time we took twenty-one to twenty-two minutes. This was the estimated time. We could not understand the criticism. But she decided to give in to people's demands and the project was never implemented beyond one corridor.' It was just seven months before the November election where she was eyeing a third term. 'She was instinctive about public perception. When she realized that the transport system had nobody's support, she asked me not to implement the remaining section of the pilot project,' says Yusuf. Right before the November 2008 elections, the people's chief minister announced her government may have to scrap the project. Delhi brought her back for yet another term. 'It did not harm us politically. Just for the record—Congress won all the seats along the corridor in the 2008 elections,' says Sandeep.

THE WEALTH TEST

Dikshit created history of sorts in 2008. She became the longest serving chief minister of Delhi after winning her third term. The electoral mandate came with a big responsibility—Delhi was going to host the Commonwealth Games, an international sporting event, in less than two years. The third term was the real test for the seasoned chief minister. Organizing the Commonwealth Games was a tough task for a chaotic city like Delhi which had multiple civic agencies and a complicated governance structure.

The bulk of responsibilities were with the centre and bodies like the Commonwealth Games Federation, Indian Olympic Association, and the Organizing Committee (OC). The Delhi government had a limited role in the upgradation of some stadia and in building a new sporting venue, the Thyagaraja Stadium. It had to complete flyovers, streetscaping, and upgrade streetlighting on the roads. By January 2009, the centre realized that about two-thirds of the projects were running behind schedule. Khullar, who took over as secretary in the union sports ministry in April 2009, says, 'The task in April 2009 was to somehow bring back on track projects which had been delayed since 2005 and just get the job done.' The deadline was 3 October 2010—the day of the opening ceremony.

Khullar describes how the Commonwealth Games were being managed by multiple agencies. 'Asian Games 1982 were coordinated by an organizing committee that was entirely from the government and headed by Rajiv Gandhi, with a close oversight by the prime minister's office. Commonwealth Games 2010 not only had an organizing committee that was outside the government's purview but also did not have the same buy-in at the highest levels of the central government. When Mrs Dikshit realized that things were not shaping up, she would often remark in our meetings, "I am responsible for Delhi. I am the face. We will look bad if the show is a flop." What should have been a commitment at the national level became limited to the Delhi government under Mrs Dikshit,' says Khullar. Dikshit also attributed the chaos to the lack of a clear chain of command, 'I had seen the work that had gone into the preparatons for the Asian Games of 1982, which triggered the first real transformation of Delhi. At that time, the PMO was clearly in charge.... This time it was different. There was no unified command overseeing the entire effort or even in the know of the larger picture and details at the same time.'[16]

The organizing committee was headed by Suresh Kalmadi from the Indian Olympic Association. The executive committee had the representation of several ministries, the Delhi government, sports federations, and the Commonwealth Games Federation. 'The OC was chaotic. It was unwieldy and unable to bring together the complicated decisions involving the conduct of the games and the readiness of venues. While Suresh Kalmadi seemed to wield a lot of clout both with the sports world and the political dispensation, he simply could not get things moving. He had an adversarial attitude towards government officials who did not take kindly to being given the short shrift despite the government providing financial and logistic support. By mid-2009, the sports minister M. S. Gill had prevailed upon the prime minister to appoint an experienced civil servant as CEO of the organizing committee. Jarnail Singh, a retired IAS officer who had worked in the PMO also, was brought in to bring a semblance of order into the functioning of the OC,' says Khullar. As agencies struggled to meet deadlines, monsoons hit Delhi. The capital received the highest recorded rainfall in thirty-two years in 2010, which further affected the pace of work. Dikshit started her night vigil. 'Weeks before completion...reaching the site at odd hours of the night, walking over slim planks of wood places as bridge between two sections, twenty-metres above ground, to check the status of work, became a regular after-dinner habit of mine,' writes Dikshit.[17]

The Delhi government under the chief minister was not responsible for many projects but as these remained incomplete, Dikshit took charge. 'When the Commonwealth Village remained incomplete, Mrs Dikshit started keeping a close watch and made several site visits. Even when the DDA and other central agencies were involved she would personally supervise the projects—asking officials what they needed. I have vivid memories of her in her elegant sari and sneakers, stubbornly sloshing through the wet mud and slush in the Games Village,' says Khullar.

This sense of ownership and responsibility is what set Dikshit apart. It did not go unnoticed. At the opening ceremony of the Commonwealth Games, every time an international dignitary made a speech and mentioned Dikshit's name, there would be loud cheers and claps from the crowds. What was embarrassing for the centre was the way Kalmadi was booed. Sandeep feels this is what did the three-time chief minister in. 'What I feel went against her was that people of Delhi recognized her hard work during the Commonwealth Games and celebrated her with gusto at the inaugural ceremony. The applause when her name was mentioned in speeches of leaders at Commonwealth Games opening ceremony was what made leaders insecure. I think even the PM felt insecure about this, especially his supporters and of course ably assisted by her detractors in Congress, like Ajay Maken, and even the then PCC President J. P. Aggarwal,' says Sandeep.

Within days of the successful completion of the 2010 Games,

Prime Minister Manmohan Singh appointed a committee under
V. K. Shunglu to investigate allegations of irregularities in the
Commonwealth Games organization. Yusuf says, 'She was only
defamed. She told the officers to make everything public. Even
if the Shunglu Committee hasn't asked for it, just put it up on
Delhi government's website. She gave a point-by-point rebuttal of
the report. But public got this impression that the administration
was corrupt.' Dikshit was emotionally hurt by the fact that her
own party's government instituted the inquiry. From the centre's
point of view, it had to be done as it couldn't gloss over the
allegations. Sandeep says, 'V. K. Shunglu's committee did not
send a draft to the Delhi government or give an opportunity to
the Delhi government to respond. This man and his team were
prejudiced from the very beginning and made some ridiculous
remarks in what was considered by all as a nonsensical report.'
Dikshit could foresee the attempt to find the fall guy. She asked
her officers to make all the documents public.

Just months later, an anti-corruption movement under the
leadership of the Gandhian Anna Hazare took shape. Social
rights activists Aruna Roy, Arvind Kejriwal, former cop Kiran
Bedi, and many others joined this movement. They demanded a
Jan Lokpal Bill to institute an independent body to investigate
corruption cases against bureaucrats and politicians within a
year. This caught the fancy of the people as it came at a time
when the Congress-led UPA government at the centre was under
the scanner for corruption in the 2G spectrum allocation, coal
block allocation, and an adverse CAG report on aviation. The
anti-corruption plank became formidable, and Kejriwal decided
to take the political plunge in Delhi. The AAP was formed in
November 2012. Right around this time, there were murmurs
within the Congress of Dikshit seeking a role at the centre. 'I
remember that after the Commonwealth Games, it was hinted
that she should move to the centre as a cabinet minister. If I
am not mistaken, this was conveyed by both the prime minister
and Congress president. She was quite happy with the promise
of a new assignment as she had had a fairly good run. She

was the longest serving chief minister of Delhi. But nothing was heard after that,' says Sandeep.

A month after the formation of the AAP, Delhi was jolted by the gangrape and brutalization of Jyoti Singh, a twenty-three-year-old physiotherapy student. The capital came on the streets. Protests and candlelight vigils were organized at Jantar Mantar and India Gate demanding justice for the young girl, who was christened 'Nirbhaya' (the fearless). As the young girl succumbed to the grave injuries inflicted by the six men, the anger boiled over. Dikshit could not dissociate herself from the deteriorating law and order situation in Delhi, a subject she did not have control over as it came under the purview of the Home Ministry, run by her own party's government. In her autobiography, Dikshit speaks about how she wanted to retire at this point because of her health. But had she resigned at that time, it would have seemed like she was admitting her fault. '...but I felt that such a move would be seen as running away from the battlefield. The centre had not wanted the blame to fall on it directly; and I, knowing well that our government would be blamed by the Opposition, decided to take it on the chin. Someone had to take the blame,' she writes.[18]

In the run-up to the 2013 assembly elections, Dikshit had lost touch with the people—what was considered her USP by many. Dikshit was known to sometimes take a morsel off the plate of journalists at a lunch or dinner while engaged in a conversation. That ease was gone. Her Bhagidari meetings had come down, and she had completely antagonized the state unit by refusing to accommodate partymen on the boards of corporations. At a time when Kejriwal was promising free electricity and water in Delhi, power and water meters were being changed in several colonies. J. P. Aggarwal, who took over as the Delhi state Congress president in 2007 and had massive differences with Dikshit, says, 'She was always very respectful towards me. But as professionals we had difference of opinion on one issue—I felt that since our party was in power, the partymen should be accommodated in different positions like boards or corporations. We never saw

eye to eye on this.' Dikshit's ministers, whom she had brought
forth, abandoned her side. 2013 was not a defeat. It was a rout.
Dikshit lost her New Delhi assembly constituency to Kejriwal
by 25,000 votes. Her party's tally plunged from 43 in 2008
to a mere 8 in 2013. Sandeep says Dikshit never regretted not
promising free electricity and water. 'The kind of environment
that was created was that your leaders are thieves. Towards the
end of campaigning in 2013, we had an inkling that we were
losing. But yes, Amma did not realize that free electricity and
water would get the kind of traction it did. She had no regrets
that she did not bite that free-electricity bait. Not even once did
she say that. She had always believed that "free" is instrumentally
a different path. She was very clear—we are social democrats,
we will price every service every commodity at a reasonable cost
but never free,' he says.

Many say Kejriwal was Dikshit's creation. It was supposedly
a master move to divide the Opposition votes. Kejriwal was
running his NGO Parivartan and working with slum dwellers
on ration cards—officials remember being asked to help him.
A senior official, who has retired now but did not wish to be
named, said, 'We used to get messages from the chief minister's
office asking us to give time to Arvind Kejriwal and hear the
points he was flagging about ration cards and public distribution
system. The chief minister felt that working with the non-profit
organizations always benefitted the government.' Yusuf, however,
denied Kejriwal was Dikshit's creation to divide the Opposition
votes. 'Not at all. The anti-corruption movement was a big bogey
created by the RSS, Baba Ramdev, and Kejriwal. It was a way to
discredit the Sheila Dikshit government,' he says. Even Sandeep
brushes aside these suggestions saying, 'She had nothing to do
with them. She could never understand the politics of Kejriwal
and Sisodia (present deputy chief minister). She was an old time
politician who enjoyed good relations with her opponents. Senior
BJP leader V. K. Malhotra had called her after the Shunglu
Committee report—even her opponents had the grace to call and
discuss. There was no vendetta. But these two fellows and their

lot, were leading a new culture in politics, of bad mouthing, of being liberal with lies and building a caucus with media and liberal activists.'

LIFE OUTSIDE DELHI

Dikshit's humiliating defeat did not deter the party from banking on her. In March 2014, months before the parliamentary elections, Dikshit was appointed the governor of Kerala. After the Congress-led UPA was trounced in the parliamentary elections, Dikshit resigned in August and returned to Delhi. As the Uttar Pradesh assembly elections approached in 2017, she was roped in to be the chief ministerial candidate. Though reluctant, she agreed. Sandeep says she would have never refused even if it meant putting the party above her health. 'In 2017, she wasn't excited about Uttar Pradesh elections. She had left UP politics long back and everything was in Delhi. She was seventy-nine and wasn't as active as she used to be. Then she was called and an entire machinery was set into motion. But we don't know what happened. The party started the campaign with so much excitement. Priyanka Gandhi was supposed to campaign with her. Then suddenly everybody lost interest. What was worse was that nobody told her anything. You know, it is like you declare a person captain of a team and then the captain later finds out that his team is not playing the match at all. Exactly this happened with her. I got the sense that the local UP leadership got insecure seeing the crowds at her public meetings. She did not like the way the party treated her,' he says.

This wasn't the last time that Dikshit bailed out her party. Once again in the 2019 Lok Sabha elections, Congress decided to field all party heavyweights and Dikshit contested from the North East Delhi constituency. 'She knew she would lose. It was a Modi wave. But she would have never said no,' says Sandeep. Within two months, Dikshit passed away at the age of eighty-one, working till the very last day. 'After she lost in the 2019 parliamentary elections, she started preparing for Delhi assembly elections. A day before her death, she was sitting in this home in this room and having a meeting with Ramakant Goswamiji, Mrs Kiran Walia, Mangat Ram Singhalji, and many others, and Jeetu (former councillor Jitender Kochar) discussing what the Congress should be doing till 9.30 p.m. She had a restless night. I had just come back from Bhopal and Maasi (Dikshit's sister Rama) told me the next day that Amma hadn't slept well and she had shortness of breath. We took her to the hospital around 10–10.30 a.m. By 1 p.m., she was gone. She passed away very peacefully, without suffering, working till the end,' remembers Sandeep adding, 'I feel she would have lived at least five years longer had she not got into the two elections.'

Dikshit has left an indelible mark on Delhi. From starting the practice of gifting plants to printing government diaries on recycled papers and even the kerbside tiles that the city uses, the green spaces, cultural festivals like Jahan-e-Khusrau, music in the park, a clean and spacious Delhi Secretariat, and kerosene-free Delhi are all her gifts to a city she grew up in and lovingly nurtured. Those who worked with her attribute her longevity in power to the way she handled opposition. 'She was not dictatorial,' says Yusuf. Officers remember how she efficiently handled tricky decisions which were opposed by her own ministers. She walked the political tightrope in 2004 when the Supreme Court ordered the shifting of the abattoir from old Delhi. The alternate site was found in Ghazipur—an area which bordered on the constituencies of two ministers (Arvinder Lovely and Dr A. K. Walia) and a vocal Congress legislator Naseeb Singh. During a cabinet meeting, Dr Walia protested against this as no MLA wanted an abattoir, even if it were a scientifically developed one, in his constituency. An officer present in the meeting remembers how, to everyone's surprise, Dikshit agreed with Dr Walia and sought an alternate site. When Dr Walia suggested it be shifted on the Ring Road near Salimgarh Fort area, Dikshit said, 'A Vishwa Shanti Stupa has already been planned there, how do we remove a monument for universal brotherhood with an abattoir?' As Dr Walia realized it would be a politically unpalatable decision to replace a green monument of peace with an abattoir, the matter was settled within one cabinet meeting.

Dikshit was a strong votary of women's empowerment. Her administration leaned towards women officers with over half the departments having women secretaries. Chandra, who remains the first and only woman chief secretary of Delhi to date, says, 'Unquestionably, Mrs Dikshit liked women and other things being equal, she tried to give visibility and greater responsibility to women officers. She had her own nicknames for some, but she used those names only in good humour. For example she referred to her woman environment secretary as Principal Jayaseelan (IAS Naini Jayaseelan) to her face because she was a no-nonsense civil servant, very vocal about the environment.'

Congress leaders involved in ticket distribution vividly remember Dikshit vociferously demanding more tickets for women candidates. In her autobiography Dikshit talks about how winnability is cited to deny tickets to women: '...that empathy for women has never found a corresponding echo in political parties when it comes to under-representation of women in Parliament. Whenever I raised the matter of having a larger number of women as election candidates, the discussions would invariably peter out. It was the same story in other parties as well. The "winnability" factor was always forwarded as being the sole reason why women's representation in Parliament was less than adequate.'[19]

With the passing of Dikshit, an era of political supremacy has ended for the Congress in Delhi. It has continued to cede ground to AAP in Delhi elections. From 8 seats in the 2013 elections, Congress does not have a single member in the legislative assembly in 2023. Suprisingly, there was no political inheritor of Dikshit's legacy—neither her son who had taken a political plunge nor any Congress leader.

MAYAWATI

The Dalit Icon

The intercom buzzed at around 11 p.m. The Uttar Pradesh Governor Moti Lal Vora had retired for the night. It had been an eventful summer day on 3 June 1995—he had sworn in Kumari Mayawati as the state's first Dalit chief minister. He was told she was at the Raj Bhawan to see him. Vora was surprised at this breach of protocol for chief ministers always sought time to meet the governors in advance. But then the events leading up to the change in regime had been nothing short of dramatic. Within two years of the Samajwadi Party (SP) and Bahujan Samaj Party (BSP) government led by Mulayam Singh Yadav, the BSP had pulled the plug and staked claim to form the government with the support of the BJP. On 2 June, a mob of irate SP MLAs had gone on a rampage in the state guesthouse in Lucknow where Mayawati was holding a meeting of BSP MLAs. Yadav wanted to split the BSP so that he could get the requisite numbers on his side. As Mayawati retired to her suites 1 and 2, the mob physically dragged the BSP MLAs out of the waiting hall and into cars to drive them to Yadav's home. Then they started pounding on the door of Mayawati's suite, hurling the choicest abuses and crudely detailing what would happen to the thirty-nine-year-old BSP leader once she is dragged out. It had taken several hours for District Magistrate Rajiv Kher and several police officers to push the mobsters out of the state guest house. After a lot of reassurance from Kher, Mayawati and a handful of MLAs locked inside the suite opened the doors. Vora had immediately provided a shaken Mayawati enhanced security. The next day, with her mentor Kanshi Ram and the BJP veteran Atal Bihari Vajpayee watching proudly, Mayawati had taken oath as the youngest and first Dalit chief minister of UP.

Now, just hours later she was at Vora's doorstep, unannounced. The Congress veteran, known for his astute political mind, came and greeted the new chief minister. She thanked him for the security provided at the time. A long-time confidante and former BSP Rajya Sabha MP Raashid Alvi says, 'Mayawatiji was so rattled by the incident that she told Voraji she did not feel safe and wanted to stay the night at the secure Raj Bhawan. Despite reassurances that she was the chief minister and no harm could come to her, she refused. The guest quarters of Raj Bhawan were opened up for the chief minister.'[1] The infamous state guest house incident went on to define Mayawati's politics and her four terms as the chief minister of India's most populous state, Uttar Pradesh.

STARTING AT THE BASE

Mayawati was born on 15 January 1956 in New Delhi. Her father Prabhu Das Dayal was a clerk in the posts and telegraph department and her mother Ramrati Devi was a housewife.

She and her eight siblings—two sisters and six brothers—were raised in Delhi in a slum cluster in Inderpuri. Her home was steeped in patriarchal biases very common in those times—her father had considered marrying a second time as her mother had three girls and could not give him a male heir—and in later years the family's meagre income was spent on educating Mayawati's brothers in private schools when she and her sisters went to the local government school to save money. Though Mayawati was raised in Delhi, her father hailed from Badalpur in the present-day Gautam Buddh Nagar district and her mother from Simrauli in the Hapur district of Uttar Pradesh. Trips to her grandparents' villages ensured that Mayawati was acutely aware of caste discrimination in India from a very young age. In her autobiography *Mere Sangharshmay Jeevan Evam Bahujan Movement ka Safarnama* (My Life of Struggle and the Path of the Bahujan Movement), published in 2006, she remembers how mohallas were divided on the basis of caste and when her parents would share that they lived in chamar mohalla (a Dalit sub-caste considered low in the Indian caste system), people travelling in buses would stop talking to them. From quite early on in her life, Mayawati was inspired by the work of Dalit icon and the architect of the Indian Constitution, Dr B.R. Ambedkar. Her family regularly attended functions on Ambedkar's birth anniversary and listened to speeches on his writings. While in school, she once asked her father if people would respect her if she fought social injustices like Dr Ambedkar did. Her father promptly told her about the importance of education and said that she needed to finish college and become an Indian Administrative Service (IAS) officer to earn the people's respect. Keen on embarking on this journey, Mayawati took exams for classes ninth, tenth, and eleventh together and jumped forward three years. She enrolled in a B.A. (Pass) course in Delhi University's Kalindi College. After graduation, she completed her B. Ed. course from a Ghaziabad college and started studying law at Delhi University's Faculty of Law. During this time, she began preparing for the UPSC exam while working as a teacher.

Mayawati belonged to the 1970s generation of educated young Dalit students who were well-read, politically aware, and had a sense of being wronged by the Congress, which was seen to be dominated by the so-called upper castes. These Dalit youths grew up bearing the consequences of a deeply-rooted caste system in a young nation which was desperately trying to fight social and economic iniquities. This generation saw Mahatma Gandhi's use of the word 'Harijan' (the children of God) for the lower castes in Indian society as an affront. In fact, Dalit scholars found Dr Ambedkar's constitutional term 'Scheduled Castes' more inclusive than Harijans. As a young student, Mayawati questioned the use of Harijan—if they were children of God, were the upper castes children of Satan? Several years later she would devote several pages in her autobiography to draw parallels with the word 'Devdasis' (God's slaves)—dancers who were supposedly kept in the temples to dance before the idols but were sexually exploited by Brahmin temple priests for years and often bore illegitimate children. The 1975 Emergency imposed by Prime Minister Indira Gandhi and faithfully executed by her brash son Sanjay proved to be the proverbial final straw for such young Dalits. The uprooting of slum clusters, which were largely inhabited by migrant labourers and socially and economically backward classes, in the name of beautification of Delhi during the Emergency years further aggravated the sense of being wronged. They found a vent in Jayaprakash Narayan's call for Total Revolution and later the Janata Party's attempt to offer a political alternative. In September 1977, a meeting was organized at the Constitution Club in the heart of New Delhi where Health Minister Raj Narain, who had famously won an electoral malpractice case against Indira Gandhi in 1975 leading to her disqualification and the Emergency, had been invited to speak. Mayawati was slated to speak after the senior leaders' speeches. Raj Narain extensively used the word 'Harijan' in his speech leading to murmurs in the packed hall. When Mayawati's turn to speak came, the twenty-one-year-old young girl ripped apart Raj Narain, questioning his audacity to use the word and hurt the feelings of Dalits. Mayawati had already earned the reputation of being a fiery speaker but this blistering attack on such a senior central minister in an open gathering sent ripples across political circles. A few days later, a man knocked on the door of her home in the middle of a cold winter night. The conversation that followed changed the course of Indian politics.

FINDING SAHEB

The man in his forties wearing a muffler around his neck saw Mayawati surrounded by books. He introduced himself as Kanshi Ram, a respected and well-known leader who was organizing the Dalit community—especially government servants—under the Backward and Minority Communities Employees Federation (BAMCEF). As her father wondered what Kanshi Ram could possibly want from his daughter, the Dalit leader asked Mayawati what she wanted to do after studying. She said she wanted to become an IAS officer and work for her community. At this, Kanshi Ram or Saheb, as he was known to all, is believed to have told her that he would make her such a big leader that several IAS officers would take orders from her. Mayawati was quite taken by this and was quick to forego of her dream of becoming an IAS officer. Mayawati's proximity to Kanshi Ram and her political work with the BAMCEF did not go down well with her father Prabhu Das who was disappointed to see his daughter give up on becoming an IAS officer. When the fights at home grew, Mayawati packed a small bag, carried savings from her teacher's salary, and left in a huff. She was forced to take refuge in the BAMCEF office as she had nowhere to go, and Kanshi Ram was travelling. Once back from his tour, Kanshi Ram told Mayawati to use his one-room tenement as her boarding place as he was mostly out of Delhi travelling. In the early 1980s, a single unmarried girl in her twenties, living in the house of a bachelor in his forties, did not go down well with society. Though Mayawati had brought along her younger brother Siddharth, she had already set tongues wagging.

Kanshi Ram and Mayawati shared a strong bond over their passion to fight for the rights of the Bahujan samaj and make them a political constituency. Gradually, Mayawati started wielding enough influence over Kanshi Ram for the other senior leaders to feel belittled and left out. Mayawati sometimes overturned Kanshi Ram's decisions, and he acquiesced. It further perpetuated the belief that it was more than a guru–shishya (mentor–disciple) relationship, as the two had publicly always maintained. There were claims by several BSP leaders, who had fallen out with Kanshi Ram over the years, of having seen framed photographs in Mayawati's bedroom of her lovingly feeding Saheb fruits. Some even claimed that the two had secretly married but never had the courage to accept it openly because of the age difference. But to confine a relationship that defined caste movements and politics in Uttar Pradesh in a narrow sexual sphere only furthers attempts to discredit Mayawati's achievements as a politician. The two were leaders with complementary qualities—he ran the organization like an army, borrowing heavily from his initial experience as a research assistant at the Pune-based Explosives Research and Development Laboratory and she was the public face with great oratorical ability. He was the Chanakya who believed in forging relationships, but she was the Ashoka being groomed for a greater role. He was calm and sociable, she was fiery and aggressive. After a stroke in 2003, Mayawati cut off almost everyone from Kanshi Ram's life. She cared for her mentor till his last breath. Her close aides say that she fed him and looked after him especially during his last days. 'She was like a mother tending to a sick child,' says a close aide.[2] Her bond with her mentor is evident in senior journalist Shekhar Gupta's May 2005 interview on NDTV. To a question on why she did not allow people and even Kanshi Ram's family to meet him, Mayawati says it was only on the doctor's advice. Further, on Gupta's request, she takes him to Kanshi Ram's room where she speaks to her mentor like a caregiver. She proudly declared, 'Saheb loves chole bhature and sweets but the doctor has said not to give him sweets'—Kanshi Ram passed away a year later in 2004. Till Kanshi Ram's stroke, Mayawati's rise within the party was looked at simplistically and unidimensionally as just the sexual interest of an older man in a much younger woman and not attributed to her calibre or political acumen.

Mayawati has always maintained that she never 'inherited' Saheb's legacy but worked hard for it. In interviews she has said that Saheb was her guru but neither he nor she inherited their politics—they worked together for it. Kanshi Ram had novel ways to involve Dalits in his outfits. He and his workers would fan out on bicycles in villages asking for donations. He felt that if a person gave him even a rupee, they felt he belonged to the outfit and had a stake in the political movement Kanshi Ram was bringing about. In 1980, the BAMCEF took the life story and teachings of Dr Ambedkar across several North Indian states under the banner 'Ambedkar on Wheels'. It made people aware of the injustices of the Indian caste system and how it should be fought. In 1981, he founded a social organization called DS-4 (Dalit Shoshit Samaj Sangharsh Samiti). It went with the catchy slogan, 'Thakur, Brahmin, Bania Chhod, Baaki Sab Hain DS4 (barring the upper castes of Thakur, Brahmin, Bania, the rest belong to DS4)'. Kanshi Ram believed that though Dalits and Other Backward Classes (OBCs) were numerically strong, parties dominated by the upper castes, like the Congress, did not give them a share in power despite relying on them as a vote bank. Not just Dalits, but OBCs and later Muslims were critical in Kanshi Ram's politics. The new outfit gave Dalits a sense of belonging. Slogans like 'Jiski jitni sankhya bhaari, uski utni bhagidari (roughly translated to the higher the population, the bigger should be share in power)' and 'Vote hamara, raj tumhara, nahin chalega, nahin chalega (Our Vote, your power. Won't work, won't work)' gave an electoral identity to the Dalits.

The DS4 participated in electoral politics for the first time in 1982, when forty-six independent candidates were fielded in the Haryana assembly elections and then in UP in 1983. Kanshi Ram organized a forty-day outreach across seven states through a cycle march of hundred community leaders the same year. The

DS4 gave way to the Bahujan Samaj Party (BSP) on 6 December 1984 and fought its first Lok Sabha election in the same year. Mayawati resigned from her post as a government school teacher and fought her first election from Kairana in Uttar Pradesh and Kanshi Ram from Janjgir Champa in Madhya Pradesh (now in Chhattisgarh). Mayawati came third, polling 44,445 votes. The next year, she entered a high-profile contest in Bijnor, which was fought between the Congress's Meira Kumar (daughter of Dalit icon Babu Jagjivan Ram) and Ram Vilas Paswan. Meira Kumar won and Mayawati stood third, polling 61,504 votes. This was an encouraging sign for the newly-formed political party as it showed that Dalits were shifting preferences to a little-known party over established players like the Congress. In May 1987, Mayawati fought the Haridwar by-election and polled 1,25,399 votes. The fine print of the results was even more interesting—she had relegated Paswan, another popular Dalit leader, to the third position and he had to forfeit his deposit. The mainstream media, however, did not notice this trend or probably chose to ignore it till the 1988 Allahabad by-election. Coming a year before the 1989 Lok Sabha elections and in the wake of the Bofors controversy, this election set the stage for V. P. Singh, who had openly taken on Prime Minister Rajiv Gandhi over corruption charges. The Congress had fielded Sunil Shastri and Kanshi Ram decided to enter the fray. Though the media attention was on V. P. Singh, two senior journalists, Vidya Subramaniam and Shekhar Gupta, have described Kanshi Ram's election campaign in detail. 'I had arrived in Allahabad to a mystifying blue welcome; the walls of the town were splattered with little blue elephants. Early next day, I saw a splash of blue again, and soon a cluster of cyclists, each carrying a blue flag came into view. I learnt later that they were volunteers of the BSP and were camping in Allahabad to campaign for Kanshi Ram, the BSP's founder and the third contestant in the by-election. The BSP was a tough party to cover but the experience overturned my world and exposed my scanty knowledge of harsh ground realities. The BSP abhorred the media and barred journalists from attending its rallies. At each rally venue I would be stopped by volunteers who'd accuse me of representing the manuwadi media,' writes Subramaniam.[3] Gupta recalls the innovative ways of money collection and the reasoning, 'For reporters like us, new to his method and energy, Kanshi Ram's campaign was a surprise, and by far the most vigorous of the three. His blue flag and elephant symbol dotted walls all over the constituency. The party's bicycle squads pedalled furiously and relentlessly through the countryside. His "begging" squads, carrying sealed collection boxes and banners proclaiming "The campaign to collect notes with votes" moved from one Dalit mohalla to another, collecting a little cash and plenty of loyalty. "The money collection is symbolic," said Kanshi Ram. "Once a poor sweeper pays me even two rupees he will have the self-respect to throw chappals at Congressmen who come to buy his vote."'[4]

The 1989 parliamentary election and the simultaneously-held Uttar Pradesh assembly elections were the first big test for the BSP. They won three Lok Sabha seats—Bijnor and Azamgarh in Uttar Pradesh and Phillaur in Punjab. Mayawati made her Lok Sabha debut, winning the Bijnor seat by polling 1,83,189 votes. In the UP assembly elections, BSP won 13 seats. Once again, the fine print of the election results was more interesting—the party had polled about 10 per cent of the votes in both parliamentary and assembly elections, which was higher than BJP's voteshare. With this began the BSP's struggle to come to power in Uttar Pradesh.

BY HOOK OR BY CROOK

In less than a decade of walking out of her Inderpuri home, Mayawati had entered the parliament of India. This was a new playground for the thirty-three-year-old first-time MP. 'With characteristic fortitude, she did not let the imposing facade of parliamentary democracy and its complicated rules intimidate her. For instance, she was fascinated by the practice—mostly adopted by Opposition MPs—where the lawmakers would rush to the well of the House when they were prevented by the Speaker from raising certain issues. Soon, Mayawati became an ardent exponent of this tactic and her first stint in Parliament is remembered for her noisy interventions.'[5] In some ways, she faced the same biases in the parliament that she was fighting outside in Uttar Pradesh. 'Her rough-and-ready ways in the House raised eyebrows and provoked criticism from traditionalists in Parliament who felt that she was a typical example of the deteriorating standards of parliamentary debate. Mayawati's oiled and plaited hair and casually dressed appearance reportedly affronted or amused other more 'sophisticated' women members of Parliament, most of whom came from royal houses and aristocratic families. They even complained she sweated too much and asked a senior MP to advise her to use a stronger perfume!'[6]

The 1990s were tumultuous years in national politics. The Janata Dal government, led by V. P. Singh, did not last long and Mayawati's parliamentary stint came to an end. Singh's decision to implement the Mandal Commission report to provide 27 per cent reservation to OBCs in government jobs and educational institutions triggered massive anti-reservation protests across India. In this new political landscape, the BSP found itself in a political wilderness. Around the same time, BJP President L. K. Advani initiated the Ram Janmabhoomi campaign and whipped up religious frenzy as he demanded the construction of a Ram Temple in place of the Babri Masjid in Ayodhya, Uttar Pradesh. Then right in the middle of the 1991 parliamentary elections came the biggest shock—Rajiv Gandhi was assassinated by LTTE suicide bombers at a rally in Sriperumbudur, Tamil Nadu. The Congress managed to come back to power at the centre on a sympathy vote. But the BJP rode to power in UP buoyed by its Kamandal politics—a term given to describe its largely upper-caste Hindu votebase as against the Mandal politics of V. P. Singh which wooed the OBCs. Kalyan Singh, a BJP OBC leader of the Lodh sub-caste, became the chief minister. On 6 December 1992, a mob of Hindu fundamentalists demolished the Babri Masjid violating the Supreme Court order. India was shocked and the BJP governments in several states started falling. Kalyan Singh resigned before he could be sacked. President's Rule was imposed in the state, necessitating a mid-term election in 1993. Mulayam Singh and Kanshi Ram struck a pre-poll alliance and decided that the SP will contest 256 seats and the BSP will contest 164. Together the alliance won 176 seats. The BJP still emerged as the single largest party and bagged 177 seats, but could not get support. This paved the way for Mulayam Singh to become the chief minister. Mayawati too won her first Rajya Sabha nomination in 1994 because of the increased numbers in the state assembly. Initially, the alliance worked fine with Mayawati shouldering the key responsibility of ironing out any differences between the two alliance partners without joining Mulayam's cabinet. However, the increasing number of atrocities against Dalits and the wily chief minister's bid to split the BSP and come to power on his own saw the BSP withdrawing support. Behind this was a backchannel deal with the BJP which was willing to accept a relative political greenhorn like Mayawati as the chief minister. Kanshi Ram was unwell and hospitalized at this time but coordinated the efforts from his hospital bed. On 1 June 1995, Mulayam Singh got word that Mayawati had met Governor Vora and withdrawn support. This led to the infamous guesthouse incident. Mayawati was sworn in as UP's first Dalit chief minister the next day. This was just one of the three times between 1995 and 2003 that the two ideologically opposed parties aligned to seize power in UP. The BSP grew at the expense of the BJP. In the Lok Sabha elections, the BJP's seat tally fell from 52 of 83 seats in 1996 to 10 of 80 seats in 2004.

The alliance lasted just four and a half months. Apart from the ideological differences, there were local factors that contributed to the parting of ways. BJP stalwart Kalyan Singh was always opposed to the alliance but gave in on the insistence of Atal Bihari Vajpayee and Murli Manohar Joshi. However, at the heart of the acrimony between the alliance partners was Mayawati's campaign to create a counter-culture to the Ayodhya Movement by giving Dalits a collective identity. She renamed public places after Dalit icons like Eklavya and Chhatrapati Shahuji Maharaj and organized programmes which ideologically irked her alliance partners. Mayawati introduced Periyar Mela to honour the memory of E. V. Ramaswamy Naicker or Periyar, who led the anti-Brahmin movement in Tamil Nadu and whose work *The The Ramayana: A True Reading* was considered blasphemous. The work, which was banned in Uttar Pradesh in 1969, challenged how Rama, Sita, and Ravana have been viewed in Ramayana with Rama being portrayed as weak and Ravana the true hero of the mythological epic. In her autobiography, Mayawati describes the step: 'Periyar Mela, Periyar ke naam ko Ram aur Sita ke "grih rajya" mein pratisthapit karne ka tatha Daliton ko ek jut va gatisheel karne ka prayas tha (Periyar Mela was an attempt to re-establish the name of Periyar in the home state of Ram and Sita and to unite Dalits and mobilize them).'[7] This rankled the BJP, which criticized its ally BSP in no uncertain terms.

The constant sniping and BJP's internal differences made the party withdraw support in October 1995. The 1996 assembly elections, which the BSP and Congress fought together, threw up a hung verdict and the BJP emerged as the single largest party. In February 1997, a wedding in Chennai became the meeting ground for L. K. Advani and Kanshi Ram, and the two parties came together once again and decided on a power-sharing agreement. This involved holding the chief minister's post for six months by rotation. Mayawati was sworn in on 20 March 1997, but once again the BSP withdrew support after six months. This time, the BJP was better prepared as Kalyan Singh had weaned away several MLAs from different political parties, including the BSP and Congress.

This phase was marked by political instability in UP and a mad scramble amongst political parties to somehow retain power with some permutation and combination. The BSP and BJP would come together a third time after the 2002 assembly elections but even this would not last long.

THE ADMINISTRATOR

In her first stint as chief minister, Mayawati, who had little administrative experience, depended on her bureaucrats to implement her agenda. She also used transfers as a threat to get officers in line. The chief minister's secretariat was run by a clutch of Scheduled Caste officers, led by the 1971 batch IAS officer P. L. Punia, who has since joined the Congress. Interestingly, Punia had served as the principal secretary to Mulayam Singh. Though Mayawati shunted out all officers who served Singh closely, Punia survived the regime change winning Mayawati's trust even before the power transfer.

Mayawati was a woman on a mission. She unveiled a slew of welfare schemes targeted towards the BSP's votebank of Dalits and Muslims. Dalit villages got dispensaries, schools, pucca houses, hand pumps, and metalled roads. If the upper-caste bias was visible in previous regimes, Mayawati turned the tables and made it evident in hers. So when she approved funds for resurfacing roads through Dalit villages, the same roads became unmetalled when they crossed through villages dominated by the upper castes. She resurrected the Ambedkar Village Scheme to channel funds in Dalit villages and bring overall development. Scholarships for meritorious Dalit and Muslim students and pensions for widows were also rolled out. Mayawati was nurturing her core constituency directly, but she soon acquired the image of a politician willing to bend the rules to pull favours for partymen and punish bureaucrats who came in the way. Anil Swarup, a retired 1981 batch IAS officer of the UP cadre who served in the chief minister's secretariat in her first stint, has written elaborately on her style of functioning in his book, the *Ethical Dilemmas of a Civil Servant*. 'On a particular issue regarding a favour to her party men, she sought my advice as I was readily available. I read the file that clearly outlined why such a favour could not be given. I concurred with the advice given by the departmental secretary as it would have been against the rules to provide the requested dispensation.

Once I explained to her the implications, she too concurred. I thought it was all over. But it wasn't. By the time I came out, another special secretary, a couple of years senior to me and considered to be close to the CM, had come over. I discussed the matter with him as well. He too seemed to agree with me. Meanwhile, I could hear Mayawati talking to someone on the phone (in those days we did not have mobile phones in India). And then she came out. She seems to have changed her mind on the issue that we had discussed a few moments ago. She had the file in her hand and asked the other officer to give his view. This officer was good at gauging what she wanted and advised accordingly. I was aghast, as what he was now suggesting was not only against the rules but totally contrary to my views that he had agreed to earlier. Mayawati looked at me with suspicion but was happy that her deal was done. The concerned secretary was asked to get the rules changed to "accommodate" the request. The rules were subsequently changed to ensure that no rule was violated and the favour was dispensed. Once the rules were changed, there was obviously no violation of rules in granting the dispensation...' writes Swarup.

Swarup, who had an impeccable reputation as an upright officer throughout his service, has also recounted how collectors carried briefcases for Mayawati—an indication that cash was collected and presented to the chief minister. 'I was on duty as day officer and as per the protocol, I reached the residence of Mayawati, the chief minister of Uttar Pradesh, early in the morning. I was informed that she was having breakfast, so I sat in the drawing-room waiting for her arrival. As I was waiting, in walked one of the collectors of a western district of UP. He had a briefcase in his hand. His gait as he entered was confident. However, the moment he saw me his gaze and his gait, both faltered. A sheepish look emerged on his face. I couldn't immediately fathom the reason for the abrupt change in his demeanour. Very surprisingly, he didn't even stop but simply walked past me straight into the room where the CM was having her breakfast. To be honest, having known the officer for the past few years, I had expected him to stop by and exchange a few pleasantries before proceeding. There wasn't much for me to do; so I sat in the room reading the newspaper. After a while, the officer came out but he didn't have the briefcase in his hand. I had no proof of what transpired inside but the absence of the briefcase made me suspicious. As I knew the officer personally, I confronted him and inquired about the briefcase he had brought with him, "It appears that you have left behind the briefcase by mistake." His response and demeanour gave it away. He nervously and haltingly responded, "No, no! It was for the chief...minister." "Briefcase for the chief minister? You got it all the way from the district?" I enquired. He smiled nervously but didn't respond verbally. I knew the answer. The briefcase obviously did not contain files. Files were not carried to the CM in briefcases. In any case, which file would a collector bring to the CM in a briefcase? The cat was out of the bag. I was livid. Here was a young collector demonstrating to a greenhorn chief minister that officers could deliver such "briefcases." I gave a piece of my mind to this young collector who was just a year junior to me. I told him bluntly, "You have demonstrated to the CM that she can expect such offerings from officers. What you have done is not merely wrong but a 'continuous wrong' as she would expect this from other officers as well." He heard me out and did not react at all. Thereafter he left. I was in a daze for a while. I did not have the mortification of serving in the secretariat of Mayawati when she became chief minister again. And during this period the horrid stories floating around of "briefcases" first turning into "suitcases" and then to "trunks" grew in intensity, manifold.'[8] In an interview, Swarup said, 'In my entire life I have never come across a more corrupt and petty person than her. A politician who only values money. Mayawati will go to any extent to amass wealth. I have been witness to so many instances when I saw how nazrana exchanged hands....'[9]

Mayawati's birthday celebrations that involved huge garlands of currency notes and elaborate tiered birthday cakes, videotapes released by political adversaries purportedly showing

her demanding money from MLAs from their funds, her bid to
immortalize Kanshi Ram and herself by spending public money
on their king-size statues in parks, uncorroborated anecdotes
of her treating businessmen brusquely after they did not turn
up with the promised amount of money, and the BSP allegedly
selling tickets for crores in every election gave the four-time chief
minister an image of being an unscrupulous politician presiding
over a corrupt administration. BSP leaders have blamed Kanshi
Ram and Mayawati's hostile relationship with the media for this
image. Close aides say Mayawati combs through all the Hindi
newspapers very carefully but feels that the manuwadi—a society
organized by the ethos of the Manusmriti—media is dominated
by so-called upper castes and is biased against Dalits. In an
interview to NDTV's Rahul Shrivastava in 2007, Mayawati spoke
about her morning routine and how she followed the newspapers
very carefully. Though she termed watching movies as a 'waste
of time', she said, 'I watch TV but I watch only news. I watch
which channel is showing what, which party is working behind
it.... I read the newspapers. I call for the papers as soon as I get
up and go through them carefully. I tell my staff also to monitor
the newspapers.'[10] Journalists who saw her successive terms as
chief ministers say that she interacted with the media through
her press conferences. Lucknow-based veteran journalist Brijesh
Shukla, who has followed Uttar Pradesh politics for decades,
says, 'Even during her press conferences she spoke from a written
paper and did not divert from the written text. She never fielded
any questions. If someone still asked, she would say, "Aap log
bhookhey honge, khana lag gaya hai, kha lein (You all must be
hungry, the food is laid out, go and eat)." She gave interviews
when she wanted to, which was usually around election time.
Five days before the slated day of the interview, the officials
would seek a list of question and prune it down.'

There have been several incidents which have only made
Mayawati more scornful of the media. Right after her first term
as the UP chief minister ended, *Dainik Jagran* carried an interview
with a former BSP leader in their 7 December 1995 edition

where it was insinuated that Mayawati had a twelve-year-old daughter out of wedlock. Mayawati was incensed and demanded an apology for the baseless news report. She had blamed the newspaper's editor Narendra Mohan Gupta of playing into the hands of the BJP, which later nominated him to the Rajya Sabha in November 1996. BSP activists attacked Jagran offices in UP, and 9,000 partymen were arrested. The paper later used the derogatory term 'chamarin' (a casteist slur for a woman belonging to the Chamar caste) for Mayawati in a headline in 2004. Mayawati again demanded an apology, and the paper printed it calling it a 'typographical error'.

Despite this impression, Mayawati did not lose sight of her electorate and is credited with planning the Delhi–Noida metro link, highway projects including the Yamuna Expressway, and the Buddha International Circuit which hosted the Formula One Indian Grand Prix. Moreover, in September 1995, the Vishwa Hindu Parishad (VHP), which had been agitating for removal of a mosque adjoining the Krishna temple in Mathura, decided to take over the site on Krishna Janmashtami. Pre-empting a communal clash, Mayawati forced the VHP to hold Janmashtami celebrations a few kilometres away from the mosque. Her handling of what could have been a second communally charged incident similar to the Ram Mandir–Babri Masjid incident remains a glowing example of her prowess as an able administrator willing to take hard decisions. With the help of Kanshi Ram she even won the support of BJP stalwarts such as Vajpayee.

BAHUJAN TO SARVJAN

In December 2001, Kanshi Ram passed on the baton to Mayawati at a massive rally in Lucknow's Laxman Mela Ground. He had been ailing, and Mayawati had already proved her credentials as a worthy political successor. Holding the reins, Mayawati led her party in the 2002 assembly elections. She unveiled a new experiment—so far Dalits formed her core voter base, but now she wanted to position the BSP as a sarvajan or universal party. She pored over the statistics of the past elections and studied demographics of each constituency. She finally gave tickets not only to Dalits and OBCs but also to the upper castes who held sway over their constituents. The BSP gave 38 tickets to Brahmin candidates, of whom 7 won and the party polled 4.7 per cent votes of 'sarvajans'.[11] This was a major shift for the BSP, which had cultivated Dalit pride and identity with the slogan 'Tilak, tarazu, aur talwar. Inko maaro jootey chaar (Thrash the Brahmins, Baniyas, and Kshatriyas with shoes).' This new social engineering helped her relegate the BJP to the third position in the assembly elections. But Mulayam's SP still emerged as the single largest party. Keen to keep Mulayam out, the BJP offered to support a Mayawati-led government. Despite the BSP's past dalliances with the BJP, the party had kept its secular credentials and the Muslim votebank intact. However, 2002 was different. The elections had followed the Godhra riots in Gujarat, which was led by a BJP government under Narendra Modi. At a time when the BJP's own allies deserted it, the BSP aligned with BJP, and Mayawati was sworn in as chief minister in May 2002.

It wasn't an easy alliance, and there were many pinpricks. Things came to a head after a newspaper reported in June 2003 that a corridor under construction on the Yamuna riverbed behind the Taj Mahal was flouting all environmental norms. Union Tourism and Culture Minister Jagmohan ordered to stop the works as the norms prohibited any construction close to a protected monument, and the corridor did not have the required environmental clearances. Initially, Mayawati made the right sounds. She held a press conference, dissociated herself from the project, and transferred officials in-charge under whose watch the corridor had been approved. But a Supreme Court order asking the CBI to institute an inquiry changed everything. Mayawati demanded Jagmohan's resignation, alleging that he was in the know of things and was involved in giving clearances to the controversial project. Raashid Alvi, then a BSP MP in the Lok Sabha, remembers getting a call from Mayawati. 'She told me that we should not allow the Lok Sabha to function. Enter the well, if need be, she told me and said we should demand Jagmohan's resignation. I reminded her that assembly elections were due in Delhi later in 2003 and he [Jagmohan] enjoyed a clean image. But she was firm,' says Alvi. The BSP MPs disrupted the proceedings, and there were repeated disruptions. 'During lunch, Sushmaji called me and said if you disrupt again and the House gets adjourned, we will withdraw support from the UP government. I conveyed this to Mayawatiji and she asked us to continue. I was told that the BJP is announcing the withdrawal of support. Once again, I conveyed this to Mayawatiji. She called prime minister (Vajpayee) and told him she was coming to Delhi. When she arrived, she put the entire onus on me saying that I acted unilaterally,' says Alvi. Later, Mayawati called a meeting of her party MPs and thanked everyone. 'She told us she will take revenge and not leave the BJP,' says Alvi. By August, the Supreme Court started monitoring the CBI probe. This irked Mayawati as she suspected a conspiracy. A former BSP leader, who has since joined the SP, says, 'Her natural instinct as a leader who has learnt her politics on the dusty roads of rural UP is "attack is the best defence." If you push Mayawati to a corner she always fights back like a wounded tigress. She suspected that the BJP wanted to corner her and go back on its promise of allowing her a full five-year term as CM.' She decided to pull the plug. At a cabinet meeting on 25 August 2003, Mayawati announced she was dissolving the assembly and recommending President's Rule. She was confident that if the state went to polls, she would come back with a clear majority. She had miscalculated. Mulayam came to power with the support of the BJP and belligerent BSP MLAs. Mayawati has always suspected a political conspiracy in the Taj corridor issue. 'The BJP got me implicated in this case in order to apply political pressure on me. In reality this project was not conceived by me. It was conceptualized by the BJP government when Rajnath Singh was the UP chief minister. The project was actually worth ₹175 crores but my government released only ₹17 crores. I had nothing to do with this project and I did not even approve it,' she told Gupta in May 2005.[12] Four years later, she explained her move to recommend President's Rule in an interview to NDTV's Rahul Shrivastava, 'BJP ke netaaon ne mujhe Dilli bulaakar yeh kahaa ki hum samay se pehle parliament ka chunaav karana chahtey hain. Hum aapko hamesha ke liye mukhyamantri banaake rakhenge aur koi shart nahin hai.... Aap centre mein hamesha banaake rakho hum UP mein aapko banaake rakhenge. Unhone kaha assi seat mein se saatth hamein de do aur 20 aap rakh lo. Maine kahaa aisa nahin hoga. Hum 50-50 ke liye toh maanne ke liye tayyar hain. Unhone kaha hum support withdraw kar lenge. Humne kahaa aap kya withdraw karte ho, maine phir 2003 mein apna isteefa de diya. Usee ke baad inhone Taj corridor ke maamle mein judiciary ka sahara lekar, CBI ka sahara lekar inhone mujhe galat tarah se fansaya. Lekin main jhuki nahin (BJP leaders called me to Delhi and told me that they wanted to advance parliament elections. They said that they would support me as chief minister of UP and I should support them at the Centre. They offered a seat sharing formula giving us 20 of 80 parliamentary seats. I refused. I told them we are ready for 50-50 seat sharing. They threatened to withdraw support. I told them what will you withdraw, I will resign and I resigned in 2003. Right after that they used the judiciary and the CBI to trap me).'[13]

By early 2005, Mayawati started giving shape to her sarvajan experiment. She cultivated a Brahmin leadership within the party by nominating Brahmin leaders to the Rajya Sabha. Central to this experiment was senior advocate S. C. Mishra, who over the years became her trusted lieutenant. Mayawati introduced Parshuram, the warrior saint who had vowed to kill all Kshatriyas to protect Brahmins, in the iconography. From the 'Jai Bhim' slogan, BSP moved to 'Jai Bhim, Jai Parshuram'. Multiple 'Brahmin Jodo Sammelan' were organized to involve Brahmins and upper castes with the BSP. These sammelans or membership drives culminated in a Brahmin maha rally in June 2005 in Lucknow. Describing the uniqueness of this rally and the tactical shift in Mayawati's politics, journalist Venkitesh Ramakrishnan writes, 'To start with, it was for the first time in the history of the state that a party professing essentially to champion the interests of "the oppressed Dalit community" organized a rally dedicated exclusively to the interests of the community at "the highest end" of the very caste system that the party used to term "oppressive". Second, and perhaps more interestingly, the response, in terms of numbers, from the Brahmin community to the call from the "Dalit party" was not insignificant. Third, the call and the response to it provoked discussions about the development of a new and powerful social combination, comprising Dalits, Brahmins and Muslims, capable of significantly impacting electoral equations in Uttar Pradesh.'[14] She changed the party's slogan from 'Jiski Jitni Sankhya Bhaari, Uski utni Bhagedaari (Representation of each caste according to its population)' to 'Jiski Jitni Taiyari, Uski Utni Bhagedaari (representation of each caste depending on their willingness to accept BSP ideology).' She constituted Bhaichara Badhaao committees (committees to improve brotherhood) in every assembly election.

The formula was put to test in 2007 when she gave tickets to eighty-six Brahmins in the assembly elections. Mayawati exacted her revenge from the BJP—a year after mentor Kanshi Ram's death. It was a historic victory when Mayawati won 206 of the 403 assembly constituencies and became the first leader to get a clear majority in the assembly elections since 1991. The biggest takeaway from the election was that the upper castes did not vote for the BJP and instead chose a Dalit party. Veteran journalist Brijesh Shukla says, 'Uttar Pradesh was largely a bipolar polity then—it was either Mulayam Singh Yadav or Mayawati. The upper castes looked at winnability and voted for Mayawati.'

She became the first chief minister of Uttar Pradesh to complete her full five-year tenure. But she could not win back the trust of the people as 2012 saw the SP return to power. The shrewd politician in Mayawati has always known to read which way the tide is turning. In the 2017 assembly elections, the BSP and SP were swept away in a saffron wave. The BJP won decisively, bagging 312 of 403 seats. In 2018, over two decades after the state guest house incident, Mayawati decided to bury the hatchet. She helped the SP in winning two by-elections in Phulpur and Gorakhpur. Mulayam's son Akhilesh thanked his 'buaji' (father's sister), and drove down to her home to congratulate her. In the 2019 parliamentary elections, the BSP, SP, and Rashtriya Lok Dal (RLD) formed a Mahagathbandhan to take on the might of the BJP but were decimated. Mayawati's BSP won 10 out of the 38 seats it contested. The SP's report card was worse as the party could win only five seats. Within a month, Mayawati had severed ties with Akhilesh. In a series of tweets on Twitter, Mayawati wrote, 'Everyone is aware that forgetting the differences in the past, as also the anti-BSP and anti-Dalit decisions like reservation in promotions and the law and order situaton during the SP rule in 2012–17, the BSP adhered to the 'gathbandhan dharma' with the SP in the interest of the country…. But the SP's behaviour after the Lok Sabha elections has forced the BSP to think whether it will be possible to defeat the BJP in the future. This is not possible. Therefore, in the interest of the party and the movement, the party will contest all small and big elections on its own strength.'

In June 2019, Mayawati shared her succession plan—she named her brother Anand Kumar as party's national vice-president and his son Akash as national coordinator. The biggest challenge for Akash is that BSP has been steadily declining. Its core votebank—the Dalits—have been successfully wooed by the BJP with its welfare schemes. The 2022 assembly elections, saw the BSP reduced to its worst tally of two seats. These polls were unique in that there was a committed votebank of the BJP which was later termed as 'labharthis' (or beneficiaries of government schemes).

Mayawati had built the party brick-by-brick with her mentor Kanshi Ram. Together they had pedalled through UP's villages taking the message of the Bahujan Samaj to the grassroots. She had inherited a cadre-based party with a robust organization and she had made it financially secure. Now her nephew Akash faces the test of resuscitating it.

III

The Lone Warriors

PRATIBHA PATIL

The Misjudged President

The Belgaum–Karwar border dispute between the Maharashtra and Karnataka has been an emotive issue since India started reorganizing states in 1953. At the time of Independence, the picturesque Belgaum, situated on Maharashtra's southern border with Karnataka, was a part of the Bombay State. But the 1956 State Reorganisation Act which divided states on the linguistic basis, included Belgaum and ten talukas (small administrative units) of Bombay State in the Mysore State (present-day Karnataka) contending that Kannada-speaking constituents far outnumbered the Marathi-speaking population in these areas. This paved the way for a long and bitterly fought Samyukta Maharashtra Movement from 1956 to 1960, which demanded a separate Marathi-speaking state. On 1 May 1960, Maharashtra was formed and held its first state assembly election in 1962. Belgaum, Karwar, Dharwad, and Bidar in northern Karnataka, remained as thorns in the flesh.

As the Maharashtra assembly held its first budget session in March 1962, the newly-elected members, a majority of whom had fought for a Marathi-speaking state, raised the inclusion of Belgaum. On 21 March, Chief Minister Yashwantrao Chavan faced angry members. 'It was a controversial issue and emotions were running high in the assembly,' remembers Madhukar Bhave, a senior Pune-based journalist who was covering the first assembly session for the *Maratha* newspaper. 'Mr Chavan tried to explain that negotiations were on. Vaata-ghaati, (discussions) he said, and tried to explain that the state government will raise it with the Centre. He repeated vaata-ghaati, as members shouted angrily,' says Bhave. Just then, a small voice from the last row of the hall said, 'Vaata konala milel, ghaati konala milel (Who will get a share, who will bear the loss)?' Bhave remembers how the smart wordplay brought smiles to the agitated members' faces. 'It was so relevant that everybody started smiling and tempers cooled down. The chief minister turned around to see who had said it,' says Bhave. It was a small-built, sari-clad, first-time member from northern Maharashtra's Jalgaon constituency—Pratibha Patil. The backbencher went on to serve as member of the Maharashtra assembly for five consecutive elections till 1985 and became India's first woman president in 2007.

Her first intervention earned the twenty-seven-year-old a meeting with the chief minister. He called her to his office after her remarks in the state assembly and enquired about her background. Young Pratibhatai (sister in Marathi), as she was fondly called by her constituents, had completed her master's in political science and economics and had enrolled herself in Government Law College, Bombay to better utilize her time during the long assembly sessions in Bombay. It was what her father had advised her. 'In the morning I would go to college and then attend Assembly. My father told me—don't just go to the assembly and occupy a seat, go contribute and make a difference. He advised me to go to the library, study on various topics, and prepare well for discussions. So in a way, even as an MLA I worked like a student,' remembers Patil, now eighty-seven years old and leading a quiet life in Pune.

THE POLITICAL CALL

Patil became a member of the legislative assembly at a time when politics was not a natural career choice for women, especially from middle-class families. Patil's father, Narayan Rao Patil, was a well-known advocate and social reformist. She had lost her mother when she was just nine years old. A promise to Patil's mother ensured that Narayan Rao provided the best education to his daughter. 'In those days girls did not get educated in our community. Before my mother died, she told my father that he should educate me—their only daughter. Growing up, though we always had our aunts taking care of us, my father paid a lot of attention to me, in fact more than he did to my five brothers,' says Patil. She was educated in her native town of Jalgaon. As she grew older, Patil wanted to become a doctor and enrol in a medical college for MBBS. 'My father was very conservative. He did not want me to travel outside Jalgaon so I did not pursue medicine,' says Patil. She was not allowed to travel alone outside Jalgaon, and a brother always accompanied her. During college, Patil was a table-tennis champion. She had to represent her college in inter-college competitions. 'One competition was in Nagar (a town in the Ahmednagar district of Maharashtra) and the other was in Nashik. When I told the principal that I wouldn't go as my father would not allow me to travel, he came home to seek permission. My father told him that he couldn't allow me to travel alone though there are other girls also travelling along. My two elder brothers took turns to accompany me to the competitions,' says Patil.

The conservative upbringing did not mean a lack of opportunities for the young educated girl. She remembers her first political speech even before she decided to join politics. 'In 1961, my father's friend and Rajya Sabha MP Sonu Singh Patil organized an all-India Rajput Conference in Chalisgaon (a town in Jalgaon district of Maharashtra). He wrote a letter to me and invited me to attend the conference and speak about the importance of educating girls, particularly from Rajput community. I read it and kept it aside thinking my father would not allow me to speak at such a conference. Next day, a news item about this conference appeared in the newspaper. My father started discussing with my brothers and suggested that they should go for the conference. I told him that I had been invited to attend. My father was surprised that I hadn't mentioned the letter to him. He encouraged me to go and give a good speech,' says Patil. But she had never spoken at such a large gathering. When she expressed apprehension, her father took it upon himself to prepare her. 'He was a very good orator during his college days. I went well prepared and that speech had quite an impact,' says Patil.

Many attribute the Chalisgaon speech for Patil joining politics. But she says it was really a call by Chief Minister Yashwantrao Chavan exhorting educated women to join the Congress Party in the early 1960s that inspired her. Sonu Singh Patil suggested Narayan Rao that with her educational qualifications Patil should seek a ticket from Jalgaon. Reading political books as part of curriculum was one thing but actual politics another— Patilremembers saying as she rejected their suggestion. 'My father tried to convince me. He said I was educated so I will get a job as a teacher or something similar but that won't be anything different. But if I were to join politics, he said, I will have a different career path and will be able to serve the people. He said I could show my merit and serve the country. This idea appealed to me and I agreed to contest the elections. Then the entire procedure followed—there were interviews with district Congress leaders and then the state Congress unit. Finally, I got a Congress ticket to contest from Jalgaon, which was a city and an urban constituency,' she says. She got elected as a member of the legislative assembly at the age of twenty-seven years.

As she stepped into politics, Pratibha Patil had no political grounding and had no godfathers. This meant she had to hit the ground running and learn the ropes on the job. 'It is how you imbibe the atmosphere and understand the sense around. You have to imbibe the spirit of a political environment. I had a very simple and straight approach—do things simply, work simply, study, prepare, and be honest. There are always groups in politics. When I entered politics, there weren't many women in politics. They did not expect me to belong to a particular group. Initially, nobody took me as a threat or a rival so I was allowed to do my work and what I was interested in. This changed as I got more experience and became a party senior. Then I started doing what was suitable to me,' she says. Even though she was an elected representative and twenty-seven years old, her father did not allow her to travel unaccompanied. In Bombay for the assembly sessions, Patil stayed at the government's MLA hostel but an aunt lived with her. One of her brothers always accompanied her to college. This did not deter Patil from visiting her constituency, planning for welfare projects, and forming a bond with the people. Clad in a traditional sari, with a pallu firmly in place over her head, Patil endeared herself to the women voters. 'People used to love and respect me like a sister. They never thought that she is a woman and what would she do for the constituency. In fact, they would welcome me, especially women in the constituency. I got a better response from my rural constituency. I always had my head covered with my pallu (sari edge). This endeared me to the people who always thought I was one of them,' she says remembering fondly her time as a first-time MLA. Her trademark style of full-sleeve blouses worn with elegant silk saris with embroidered borders came later when she moved to Delhi as a member of the parliament.

In the very first year of her term, the Indo-China War of 1962 overtook Indian politics. Patil, a committed political worker, felt restless sitting in Jalgaon. A suggestion from her friend's husband, who was a commander in the district Home Guards, saw the young MLA raising an all-women's Home Guard unit in her district. 'We went to the state Home Guards commandant and as a special case he allowed women to raise a unit and train as home guards. They gave us training and thereafter a camp of ten days was held at Goregaon on firefighting, parade, and how to fire a rifle. We used 303 rifles and I stood second in rifle shooting,' she says, beaming about her achievement.

In the middle of her first term, Patil's father discussed marriage with Patil. 'I had told my father that I will marry whoever you choose for me. But I put two conditions—first, he will not give any dowry and second, I will continue my political career. My father sent a proposal to my husband's family in Amravati conveying my conditions. They took a lot of time to say yes,' she says remembering the apprehensions of her husband Devisingh Shekhawat's family. Patil and Shekhawat tied the knot in a traditional ceremony in 1965. Once married, Shekhawat, an educationist and a politician, stood beside her as a supportive husband, shouldering responsibility of their children and never envying her years in the limelight. Bhave, who has observed the family closely while covering the proceedings of the Maharashtra assembly as a journalist, says, 'Traditionally, in politics we see a woman supporting her husband's career. But in this case, Mr Shekhawat has been an understanding husband. After taking oath as the president of India, Pratibhatai had to travel alone in her car as the supreme commander of armed forces and taking the salute. Mr Shekhawat, as the first gentleman, travelled in a car behind her official car. This was acceptable to him.'

FINDING HER FOOTING IN POLITICS

She had her son Rajendra in 1966 while she was an MLA. Within a year she started preparing for the assembly elections in 1967. This time, Patil sought a ticket from a rural constituency. After winning her second term, she was appointed as the deputy minister of public health, prohibition, tourism, housing, and parliamentary affairs. Her reponsbilities grew as she handled her ministerial work, constituency, and home. 'I was an MLA when I had my son and a deputy minister when I had my daughter Jyoti. I remember an earthquake of high intensity had hit Koyna Dam (Koynanagar earthquake in 1967). I was the health minister and was seven months pregnant with my daughter. I was asked to oversee medical facilities for survivors. The health secretary and I took a special plane from Bombay, came to Koyna Dam, and took a round to ensure all healthcare facilities were in place and then went back the same day,' she says.

Patil vividly remembers juggling multiple responsibilities, working till the end of both pregnancies, calling office files home to get back to work within three days of delivering her daughter, leaving her young children in the care of an aunt to attend political meetings, and still carrying the working mother's guilt. Yet she remained undefeated, winning successive terms in the assembly between 1962 and 1985 and serving as a cabinet minister in the Congress Party's governments in Maharashtra till 1985. In 1980, Maharashtra missed a chance of getting its first woman chief minister in Pratibha Patil. She was so close to the finish line that Shekhawat brought their two young children Rajendra and Jyoti in an unreserved train compartment, seating them on a newspaper spread on the floor to Bombay in time for the swearing-in ceremony. But that was a swearing-in that never happened. The 1980 assembly elections in Maharashtra had followed the January parliamentary polls which saw Indira Gandhi's Congress (I) faction sweeping to power. A few months later, Maharashtra mimicked the political trend voting Congress (I) in the 288-member legislative assembly. Prime Minister Indira Gandhi's son Sanjay Gandhi, who had a stranglehold on the party, was in favour of making a Muslim leader the state's chief minister. A. R. Antulay was his favoured candidate. Following party procedures, senior Congressman Sitaram Kesri was deputed as an observer to Bombay to get the views of the elected members.

Vasantrao Naik, who had served as the chief minister from 1963–75, did not want to cede space and called Pratibha Patil, advising her to stake claim as she was the leader of the Opposition in the previous assembly. 'Vasant Dada called me and said that Antulay will be made the chief minister but we don't support him. I was the leader of the Opposition at that time and Dada indicated that he would support me as the chief minister and asked me to inform Indiraji about it. I told Dada it would be better if he were to go and convey this to Indiraji. He agreed to come with me. We went to Indiraji and he told her that MLAs did not want Antulay and instead she should consider him (Vasant Dada) for the CM. But Indiraji expressed apprehension over Vasant Dada's name. So he suggested my name. She agreed. She called Mr R. K. Dhawan and asked him to send a union minister as an observer. Sitaram Kesri was already in Maharashtra as an observer and was conducting the exercise of seeking MLAs' opinion. Somehow this news was leaked that another observer was flying on a special plane to Maharashtra. The plane was deliberately delayed. It was sent back midway, and by that time Kesri had completed his exercise. He declared that there was consensus on Antulay's name. Once the name was declared, Congress could not have gone back and declared a new name.'

Many thought that Patil's political career would never recover from this shock. But Antulay's term ended abruptly when he was convicted by the Bombay High Court in 1982 of extorting money from builders for receiving more cement than the quota set by the state government. He was succeeded briefly by Babasaheb Bhosale. A year later, Vasantrao Naik was back in the chief minister's seat in 1983 and entrusted Pratibha Patil with civil supplies and social welfare portfolios. This was a time when Maharashtra was rocked by agitation against the Mandal Commission Report. The commission had been established in 1979 by the Janata Party government under Prime Minister Morarji Desai to identify socially and economically backward classes. (It was accepted only in 1990 when India introduced 27 per cent reservation for OBCs in government jobs and educational institutions.)

The Opposition demanded the commission report be tabled and discussed in the assembly. Naik was firm and refused to give in to a discussion. The Opposition parties created a furore in the assembly and the house did not function for a week. Unlike present-day parliamentary proceedings which are not allowed to run for weeks, those days were different. The deadlock had to be broken. There was a business advisory committee meeting at the end of the week to discuss the assembly's agenda for the following week. Patil says she was present at the meeting when the Opposition again demanded a discussion on the report. She suggested to Naik that a discussion be offered with a reply from her and not the chief minister to break the deadlock. 'I had read the report for two days and gone into every minute detail so I knew I would be able to handle the Opposition. Vasant Dada was surprised and asked if I was sure. Seeing my confidence, Dada offered the Opposition a discussion but clarified that the minister (Pratibha Patil) and not chief minister will reply,' she says. With her fine oratory skills and well-argued points she satisfied the Opposition in her ninety-minute speech and normal proceedings started.

IN THE NATIONAL ARENA

After an uninterrupted stint in state politics, Patil was sent to Delhi. She became a member of the Rajya Sabha, the upper house of the parliament, between 1986 and 1990. During these years, she also presided over the house's proceedings as the deputy chairman of the Rajya Sabha from 1986 to 1988. Patil agrees that there is a bias against women parliamentarians as they are not taken seriously when they speak on subjects like finance. 'But then you have to break the glass ceiling. You have to show that you can speak on serious subjects like finance. They may think that women cannot handle serious portfolios, but then you have to show them your ability and interest. You need to carve out a space for yourself by showing your interest to the party when they decide on speakers on a specific issue. When you are given an opportunity you cannot just bank on oratory skills, you need to give a very serious speech after preparation.

I used to work very hard on my speeches,' she remembers about her years in the parliament.

Despite her Delhi assignment, she remained rooted in state politics. She headed the Maharashtra state unit of the Congress from 1988 to 1990. A former member of legislative council (MLC), Ulhas Pawar, who has worked closely with Patil since the beginning of her career, describes her as a leader who worked at the grassroots to build the party organization. The following year she got a Congress ticket to contest her first Lok Sabha election from Amravati, her husband's native town.

The tumultuous phase of coalition politics, unstable governments at the centre, and the lack of leadership in the Congress during the mid-1990s saw a hiatus in Patil's political career. But the Gandhi family loyalist was appointed as the Rajasthan governor in 2004 as soon as the Congress-led United Progressive Alliance (UPA) coalition government came to power. Congress's rainbow alliance faced a major challenge in 2007— they had to choose an able successor to Dr A. P. J. Abdul Kalam. The Congress had proposed names of party veterans Dr Karan Singh and Shivraj Patil. In fact, political circles were abuzz with rumours that Shivraj Patil, known for his sarotorial indulgence, had even got a special achkan (traditional high-necked long coat) stitched for his swearing-in ceremony. However, the Left Front, comprising of the Communist Party of India (Marxist), Communist Party of India, All India Forward Bloc, and the Revolutionary Socialist Party, vetoed the two names and proposed Pranab Mukherjee's name. Congress President Sonia Gandhi and Prime Minister Manmohan Singh could not spare their chief troubleshooter Mukherjee. The Left Front again asked the Congress leadership to consider party treasurer Motilal Vora or veteran Arjun Singh. Both were ruled out by their party due to ill-health. It was then that CPI leader D. Raja suggested in a meeting of the UPA that if the alliance partners could not agree on a man's name they should consider a woman.[1] The suggestion found instant support.

In June 2007, the Congress leaders drew up a list of women

candidates, including Mohsina Kidwai and Pratibha Patil. As Prime Minister Singh read out Patil's name, CPI General Secretary A. B. Bardhan recalled her instantly. 'I had worked closely with Bardhanji in the Maharashtra assembly and later in many other initiatives,' says Patil. Bardhan's endorsement was adequate for CPI(M)'s Prakash Karat. What really clinched it for Patil was not just her gender but her husband's caste. The Opposition had decided to field the senior Bharatiya Janata Party (BJP) leader and India's Vice-president Bhairon Singh Shekhawat as their presidential nominee. NCP chief and Maratha strongman Sharad Pawar, whose party was a part of UPA government, felt that Pratibha Patil, who was married to a Shekhawat, would pose a formidable challenge to the BJP leader. Pratibha Patil was announced as the ruling coalition's presidential nominee on 14 June 2007. With this began a month-long campaign to elect the twelfth president of India, which is, by far, the most bitterly-fought and acrimonious presidential election in India.

THE FIRST CITIZEN

The president of India is elected by the members of an electoral college, comprising elected members of both houses of the parliament and legislative assemblies of states and union territories. Though the Congress-led UPA government had the required numbers, it did not want to leave anything to chance. Following set precedents, Pratibha Patil was required to visit each state and request the MLAs for their votes. It was a whirlwind campaign which required covering two to three states every day. Patil was clearly not prepared for what followed.

The BJP launched a website called 'Know Pratibha Patil'. The online onslaught sought to inform the common people, who vote indirectly through their elected representatives, about Patil's background. With photographs of Sonia Gandhi and Patil on the landing page, the BJP raised the question, 'Does this lady, hand-picked by Sonia Gandhi, deserve to become the president of India?' It posed the question on the basis of media reports that dug out waivers of the Pratibha Mahila Sahakari Bank to Pratibha Patil's relatives[2] and her remarks on purdah being introduced in India to protect women from Mughal invaders.[3] The vicious campaign created a divide within the BJP. While the BJP chief, Rajnath Singh General Secretary expressed reluctance over such a personal attack, party Arun Jaitley personally launched the website at the home of veteran M. Venkaiah Naidu.[4]

Looking back at the campaign, Patil says she had not imagined how murky it would be. 'I was shocked with the kind of campaign that was run against me in 2007. It was a nightmare for me. It felt that the level was that of a sarpanch election. Baseless allegations were levelled against me,' she says adding that there came a point when she thought of withdrawing from the presidential race. 'Yes I did consider withdrawing. I thought it was disgusting and would wonder why at all was I fighting the election and putting myself in such disrepute. I don't even like to remember those days now,' she says. The personal attacks were shocking for the septuagenarian, who had never witnessed anything so malicious even during the no-confidence motion debates in the Maharashtra state assembly. What rankled the family more was that the Congress did not reply to any of the allegations. 'We would collect proof, frame a reply from our side, and give it to party leaders who were helping in the campaign. They would collect the papers and that's all. There would be nothing from our side in the newspapers or anywhere. The party felt that my mother's work would speak for itself and the controversies would die down,' says daughter Jyoti.

The Opposition's nominee Shekhawat gave a call for a conscience vote. Despite the campaign against her, Pratibha Patil won the presidential elections with a margin of 3,06,810 votes. Though the electoral college was tipped heavily in favour of the Congress-led UPA, there was cross-voting with the BJP ally Shiv Sena unwilling to vote against a woman presidential nominee from Maharashtra. Pratibha Patil took oath as the first woman president of India on 25 July 2007.

Rashtrapati Bhavan started preparing for its first woman

occupant. Squadron Leader Ankur Naik, who served as the Aide-de-Camp (ADC) to Dr Kalam and later to Patil, reminisces, 'President Pratibha Patil was the first lady president who came with a male spouse. So far, the President House had never seen a male spouse. So we were at sea as to how to handle the changed scenario. Usually, the system was in place to help the head of the state and a spouse who would appear in ceremonial capacity but was otherwise happy to be left on her own. Here, the spouse was a professor, former mayor, and an active politician. Since we did not know how to handle this, we spoke to the family on their requirements.'

Shekhawat conveyed his requirement of a functional office since he had been in public life and people wanted to meet him. 'He said he wouldn't want to disturb the president so we needed to set up a separate office. This also meant very busy years ahead for Rashtrapati Bhavan staff. Here, for the first time, the Rashtrapati Bhavan had two very active individuals,' says Naik.

As Rashtrapati Bhavan made arrangements, the next question was how to address a lady president. While the ADCs did not face any problem since they were using a gender-neutral term 'President', other staff took time in finding the right term to address her. Patil remembers the issue with much amusement, 'They used to call me H. E. (Her Excellency). Sometimes when the staff would interact with me, they would brief me and refer to me as "Sahab" in a generic manner. They used to call him (husband Devisingh Shekhawat) "Bade Sahab". When we used to have our meals, he would take the place of the host and I would be at the head of the table. Once he said jokingly, "Oh you are H. E." I said, 'I am sahab, but you are badey sahib."'

Patil took over as the president when farmers' suicides in Maharashtra's Vidarbha region were at an all-time high. 'When farmers started committing suicides due to debt, I was disturbed. I got representations from people in Maharashtra. They invited me to come to Maharashtra and I agreed. They organized a meeting near Nagpur, and farmers from all across Vidarbha came and I listened to their problems. I came back to New Delhi and spoke to Prime Minister Manmohan Singh and told him that farmers' suicide is a blemish on our country and something needed to be done. Different options were discussed and one of them was a farm loan waiver,' she says. Later, in 2012, Patil once again discussed with Prime Minister Manmohan Singh the possibility of holding a conference in the Rashtrapati Bhavan on rainfed or dryland farming and invited him to address it. A one-day conference was called in the Rashtrapati Bhavan in February 2012, where Patil invited chief ministers, governors, representatives of the farming community, agricultural universities, the Reserve Bank of India, State Bank of India, National Bank for Agricultural and Rural Development Fund (NABARD), and union ministries. Union ministers, including then Agriculture Minister Sharad Pawar, attended the conference. 'I appointed a committee of all governors (in November 2011) to examine how to make rainfed farming sustainable. A report was drafted and submitted to the government which asked Planning Commission to study it,' she says.

Within seven months of taking over as the president of India, Patil took up the cause of women's empowerment—an issue, she says, is the closest to her heart. As early as February 2008 she decided to have detailed discussions on different schemes for gender equality. The discussions led to the formation of a committee of secretaries for the coordination of government schemes. Later that year she formed a committee of governors to study and recommend strategies for speedy socio-economic development and empowerment of women. 'In 2009, I called a meeting of governors in Rashtrapati Bhavan on the empowerment of women. The committee of governors gave a report suggesting formation of a national mission for empowerment of women. The prime minister accepted the suggestion and the National Mission for Empowerment of Women was launched in 2010. Similar commissions were launched in some other states as well,' she says. Patil feels that women's empowerment comes from education and financial independence and that the government should increase the involvement of self-help groups and non-governmental organizations (NGOs) in governance. 'This gives women an opportunity to become financially independent. As a state minister I took the lead in setting up all the women's banks in Maharashtra and they are still working so well. We set up Mahila Aarthik Vikas Mandal to help women trying to set up small entrepreneurial ventures. With financial independence comes awareness and confidence. This is when women can truly become people's representatives.' As all women leaders, Patil supported the Women's Reservation Bill. 'Whenever Women's Reservation Bill is introduced, it elicits a very strong response from the male MPs. It is a very human response. Nobody wants to forego their share in education, employment, or political representation for anybody else. Had reservation for Scheduled Castes and Scheduled Tribes not been prescribed in the Constitution, nobody would have given up their share. I think it will help if Women's Reservation Bill is passed,' she says.

Pratibha Patil tried to set an example for other women to emulate. She became the first woman head of state to fly in a warplane in 2009 when she took off in a frontline Sukhoi-30 MKI fighter jet from the air force base in Pune. Squadron Leader Ankur Naik recalls how the decision brought into focus the question of allowing women in armed forces. 'When we were in the aircraft to fly to the base, she asked me, "You are from the Indian Air Force, what do you feel about having a lady in the cockpit flying a fighter jet?" I answered, "Ma'am if operationally and physically the person sitting next to me in my aircraft is competent and has gone through the training required to fly the aircraft, it does not matter whether it is a man or a woman. The machine doesn't differentiate between a man or woman, your adversary doesn't know whether a man or woman is flying the plane. As long as the standards or training are not lowered for anyone, it does not matter who is with me in the cockpit or alongside me in the war." She was very satisfied and said, "Nobody has echoed these sentiments to me." She completed her flight and said the same when she interacted with the media, "Involving women in any service should not be for showcasing purposes only and that she had no doubt about the capability of women but the technical requirements and qualifications had to be considered by experts."'

As Patil neared the end of her term, she was once again mired in controversies. The political rumour mills had it that Patil may be given a second term. Daggers were out, some say, within the Congress. But it was really the social rights activists, who actively used the Right to Information (RTI) Act to seek details from Patil's secretariat, that did her in. It started early in 2012 with six months for Patil's term to end. Subhash Agrawal, a well-known Delhi-based RTI activist, filed an application in the president's secretariat to get the number of mercy petitions pending before Patil and how many death penalties were commuted after her intervention. Article 72 of Indian Constitution gives the president of India power to grant pardons, to suspend, remit, or commute sentences after a person has been convicted of a crime. In February 2012, Patil was termed as the most 'merciful President' having commuted death sentences of twenty-three petitioners and criticized for being 'merciful' towards even those who had been convicted of heinous crimes against children.[5] But Patil has no regrets. She says she did not want to be called a 'Butcher President'. 'When I took over as President, there were twenty-three mercy petitions pending and nine more came to me. So I had thirty-two mercy petitions pending before me. Out of these thirty-two, I disposed of twenty-two petitions commuting nineteen and rejecting three. My disposal rate was 200 per cent. I don't want to name any presidents before me but my predecessor (Dr A. P. J. Abdul Kalam) disposed of two and the president before my predecessor disposed of one. Their backlog came to me.'

Though there is no time limit under Article 72 of the Constitution in which a president must decide on the mercy petitions, Patil remembers how a question was raised in the parliament on mercy petition pendency. 'This was the time when Supreme Court had made observations in several cases that mercy petitions for prisoners on death rows should be addressed to spare them any mental agony. When the question was raised in parliament, then Home Minister P. Chidambaram came to meet me asking for these to be expedited. I told him that I did not want to be called a "Butcher President" and I would like the home ministry to review all of them. I sent all mercy petitions to the government for their comments. I granted commutations going completely by the advice of the government of the day. I did not commute death sentence of terrorists. But when I saw young people or those who had committed a crime in a fit of anger, I commuted their sentences on the recommendation of the government.'

Within a month, the RTI activist had released another set of statistics that brought focus on Patil's foreign trips. An application filed under the Right to Information Act revealed Patil undertook twelve foreign trips across twenty-two countries and her foreign visits cost the exchequer ₹205 crores.[6] Since her family members, her son, daughter and sometimes grandchildren, accompanied Patil on these foreign trips, questions were raised on her integrity. Patil, who has never spoken about these controversies, says she went by the rulebook. 'Carrying your spouse or a family member on an official trip has always been the practice and I followed it. Sometimes I took my spouse and sometimes my children. I don't know why it was criticized. This was at the end of my term and I felt it was politically motivated. There were rumours that I might be given a second term as president and some people wanted to criticize everything I did,' Patil told this author in an extensive interview.

She links her foreign trips with the improvement of business relations with other countries. 'It was I who started the practice of taking a business delegation for improving our business and commerce relations with other countries. Therefore, I asked FICCI, CII, and ASSOCHAM [all commerce consortiums led by industrialists] to send their delegations to whichever state or country I was visiting. They would send their delegations at their own cost to that country and not in my plane. They would meet their counterparts and work out the difficulties they and their counterparts in other countries were facing in terms of government policy. When I visited these countries we would call a common meeting of our business delegation and their counterparts and work out issues. Some MoUs were signed before us. After we returned, we sent notes to central ministries apprising them of our progress and suggesting policy interventions. My first foreign trip, which included a business delegation, was to Latin America. I visited Brazil, Chile, and Mexico. There were about seventeen to eighteen delegates in the business delegation. By the last visit of my tenure—which was to South Africa— the number of delegates had increased to sixty. They saw the advantage of being a part of these delegations and took interest,' she says showing a booklet, *Pratibha Devisingh Patil: Engaging the World*, taken out by the three chambers of commerce. In the booklet, Chandrajt Banerjee, director general of the CII, called the decision to take a business delegation, 'A landmark step, which has strengthened the bilateral trade and economic cooperation between India and that country.' This, however has not addressed the impression that Patil travelled extensively at the expense of the exchequer.

Around the same time, the government started the search for a retirement home for Patil. Like her predecessors, she was given a choice to live in New Delhi or her home town. Patil chose Pune. Due to security concerns, the government chose a defence plot in Khadki, the cantonment area. An RTI activist and army veteran, Colonel (Retired) Suresh Patil, filed an RTI application to find out the president's entitlement if the residence has to be taken on lease. The president's secretariat replied to Colonel Patil's application saying 'where suitable government residence is not available for allotment to a retired president, the size of the residence to be taken on lease to be provided to a retired president shall have a living area not exceeding 2,000 sq ft.'[7] The government planned to demolish two bungalows on two adjacent plots of land and amalgamate the plots. When the wall between the plots was razed, newspapers carried photographs and RTI activists felt the area was more than the president's entitlement. Patil, who has never spoken on any of the controversies, says,

'Somebody pointed out that president's retirement home will deprive war widows of their housing project. At that time I decided to refuse it. I had worked so extensively for war widows during my tenure as Rajasthan governor. It is surprising that the moment I refused, the demand for a war widows project vanished suddenly. If there was really such a project they should have pushed it on the plot and completed it. But that did not happen.' Patil declared she did not want the bungalow on the plot in April 2012. The plot now houses the Rajendra Sinhji Army Mess and Institution, which was inaugurated in 2017.[8] Once Patil refused, the government found a new plot near the CID Office in Pune on Pashan Road.

Patil never got a second term in the Rashtrapati Bhavan. She was succeeded by the Congress veteran and chief troubleshooter Pranab Mukherjee. But Patil seemed to be controversy's favourite child. Even after demitting office, controversies did not stop. In August 2012, she was accused of shifting out gifts received by her as a president to a museum in Amravati, which was run by a family-owned trust.[9] Patil returned all the gifts as media questioned the need for a museum and such gifts to be showcased. She, however, cites precedents of Rajendra Prasad and her predecessor Kalam. 'When Rajendra Babu (first president of India Rajendra Prasad) demited office his gifts were taken for a museum. Dr A. P. J. Abdul Kalam had an exhibition centre which was set up at Brahmos Centre in Delhi Cantonment. Several items of Rashtrapati Bhavan were taken and displayed there. The gift items given to Amravati museum were on a temporary basis. An agreement was signed on a stamp paper listing out how long the gift items will be there. In case of Rajendra Babu and A. P. J. Kalam, no such agreements were signed. Amravati museum wasn't a private museum but it was planned by the government and the district collector headed the committee. Our educational organization was supposed to only maintain the museum. All the items were returned to Rashtrapati Bhavan as per agreement. The controversy was a deliberate attempt to malign me,' she defends.

As she leads a quiet retired life, keeping her social and political engagements to a bare minimum in pandemic times, Patil sometimes feels a twinge of sadness recalling her stint as president. 'I feel very bad about my stint as president. I had such a fulfilling political career and then my years in Rajasthan as a governor. But in Rashtrapati Bhavan there were too many controversies,' she recalls. As she thinks, her daughter Jyoti adds helpfully about her people outreach. 'Yes, thankfully I got immense support from the people. I got close to 1.5 lakh visitors in Rashtrapsti Bhavan. My secretariat used to tell me that never had they seen such a stream of people wishing to see the president,' she adds with a smile. back back

SUSHMA SWARAJ

The People's Minister

'What is your opinion about the strained relations between India and Pakistan?' the immigration officer asked peace activist Aliya Harir at the Attari checkpoint on the India–Pakistan border. Harir had never been asked this question on her previous visits to India. But back then the atmosphere was never this tense. Just days before, on 18 September, militants had entered an army base camp at Uri and killed nineteen soldiers. India blamed Pakistan for allowing militant groups to operate in its territory. Harir steered clear of any controversial statement and said, 'Conflict should not affect the common people like us. What do you think?' The officer smiled and said, 'India and Pakistan are like paen-pra (sister and brother).' He stamped on the visa, and Harir entered India on 27 September 2016.

She was leading a delegation of nineteen young women from the different provinces of Pakistan to participate in the Global Youth Peace Festival, an annual festival organized by the Chandigarh-based NGO Yuvsatta. It was a five-day trip. Aliya remembers there were threatening remarks against them on social media. 'Though the organizers were very careful and we had tight security, there were several comments like, "Inhone hamaare unnees ko maara hai toh hum inke unnees ko maarenge (Pakistan has killed our nineteen soldiers in Uri so we will now kill their nineteen)" directed towards us. Though it was my fifth trip to India and third to attend this annual festival, it was the first for the rest of the young women in the delegation. In fact, the families of these women were very worried when we were coming here. Some had dropped out before the trip. Mothers of girls part of the delegation had called me asking, "Kaun India jaata hai aise mahaul mein? (Who goes to India in such a vitiated atmosphere)" and "I hope you all return safely."' [1]

A day after the delegation arrived for the festival, India had carried out surgical strikes across the Line of Control (LoC). 'We were watching news and had WiFi in the hotel we were staying in. We were worried and many girls thought a war had broken out and we would not be able to return. We called our families. But the news on this side of the border was very different from what we heard from our families and they told us they had not heard anything about a war. But we were very worried,' says Harir.

Harir's delegation reached the conference venue. In the middle of a session, organizer Pramod Sharma passed on the phone to Harir, 'Our external affairs minister Sushma Swarajji is on the line. She wants to speak to you.' Harir was stumped. What would she want to say to Harir? 'I was so surprised. I got flustered initially that what would I speak to her about? Also, she was considered a tough minister in Pakistan, giving hard political statements. She asked me, "Aliya, kaisi ho? Kaisa lag raha hai

Hindustan (How are you, Aliya? How are you liking India)?" I remember replying, "Bahut achcha lag raha hai. Lekin jo tension hai woh political lag rahi hai, logon ke beech mein kuch nahin hai (I am really liking it here. The tension between the two countries looks political and not between the common people)." She acknowledged this and said, "Beta, main samajhti hoon ki logon ke beech kuch nahin hai (Yes there is nothing between the people)." She was so kind and there was a soft maternal side to her queries about our well-being. I was reminded of her visit to Pakistan the previous year and how she had met then Prime Minister Nawaz Sharif's mother. She assured me that we will cross the border safely.' For Harir, it was overwhelming to have received a call from a senior minister of the Indian government. 'It showed the level of concern. I could not imagine any minister, leave alone such a senior minister, calling a lay person like me to assure me.' The security of her delegation was increased. The conference concluded peacefully without any untoward incident.

Harir took to social networking site Twitter to thank the minister, 'Extremely overwhelmed. Spoke to @SushmaSwarajji who assured that Pakistani delegation of #GYPF2016 will reach Pakistan back safe.' She was pleasantly surprised when Swaraj wrote back, 'Aliya—I was concerned about your well being kyonki betiyan to sabki sanjhi hoti hain (because daughters belong to all).' Harir's delegation was escorted safely to the border, and they returned home carrying fond memories of their visit to India. Swaraj, the firebrand leader, had won hearts in Pakistan. She had a direct connect with people in distress, struggling with bureaucratese at passport offices or desperate to be rescued from a foreign land. As she once wrote on Twitter, 'Even if you are stuck on the Mars, Indian Embassy there will help you.' Swaraj brought the so-far unapproachable external affairs minister's office close to the people during her stint in the first Modi government from 2014–19.

THE ORATOR

Swaraj was born on 14 February 1952 in Ambala, Haryana. Not many know that she was adopted within the family by Hardev Sharma and his wife Laxmi Devi. Her biological mother had been raised by her own maternal uncle and aunt. When she got married she promised her first born to Hardev Sharma and Laxmi Devi as they did not have children of their own. Swaraj's brother was born first and was adopted by Hardev Sharma. Later, Swaraj was born and happily included in the Sharma family. When Swaraj's biological mother passed away, her other two siblings too found a home in the growing household. Sharma was an RSS leader, and Swaraj's upbringing was steeped in Sangh values. In a way, Swaraj inherited her political beliefs. Her parents, especially her father, recognized very early on that she had the gift of the gab. Swaraj's daughter Bansuri, a Supreme Court advocate, says, 'My grandfather used to say, "Meri beti vakeel banegi kyunki Saraswati ka vaas hai iske kanthh mein (My daughter will become a lawyer because she has Goddess Saraswati's blessings)."' She majored in political science and Sanskrit at the Sanatan Dharma College in Ambala Cantonment. She joined the BJP's student wing Akhil Bharatiya Vidyarthi Parishad (ABVP) in her undergraduate years. 'She used to tell me these interesting tales about how she used to be the only girl who would go to protests and dharnas by ABVP in Ambala. In fact, she came from Ambala to campaign for Arun Jaitleyji in Delhi,' says Bansuri. After her graduation, she pursued law at Panjab University, Chandigarh.

At university, the young girl from Ambala met Swaraj Kaushal. They were on the debating team together. While she debated in Hindi, Kaushal was the English speaker. Congress leader Pawan Bansal, who studied with Swaraj and Kaushal and engaged with her later as UPA-II's parliamentary affairs minister when she was the leader of Opposition in the Lok Sabha, remembers what a fiery speaker Swaraj was and how nervous her opponents used to be pitted against her.[2] Love blossomed while working closely on debates. Those were the heady days of Jayaprakash Narayan's Sampoorna Kranti and students from across India were joining in. Bansuri describes her mother as a child of the revolution. Swaraj and Kaushal joined the JP Movement. 'They wanted to participate in anti-Emergency protests in New Delhi. But my Naani (maternal grandmother) put her foot down saying that she would not allow them to step outside together without getting married. It was a sweet and simple wedding in Ambala which my father describes as, "Saat logon ki baraat gayi thi, aath log waapis aa gaye (A wedding procession of seven people went and eight came back)."' The young lawyers got married and started practising in Chandigarh and then moved to New Delhi to practice in the Supreme Court. Even while practising as lawyers they remained an integral part of the anti-Emergency front in their own way. They fought the Baroda Dynamite case for George Fernandes, who was arrested in June 1976 for a conspiracy to procure dynamite sticks to blow up bridges and vital rail and road infrastructure, and the case was handed over to the CBI. When Indira Gandhi lifted the Emergency and called for elections in 1977, Swaraj and Fernandes's mother campaigned together for the jailed leader. Swaraj gave slogans like 'Jail ka taala tootega, George hamara chhootega (The jail lock would be broken and our George will be released).' She mesmerized the crowds with her oratory prowess. There is an oft-repeated tale of how she kept the crowds in Muzaffarpur seated throughout the night, taking the dais six times when the speaker was ten hours late.[3] The popular slogan became, 'George ki jannani zindabad, George ki bhagini zindabad (Long live George's mother, Long Live George's sister-in-law).' Many attributed Fernandes's victory from behind the bars to Swaraj's tireless campaigning.

Later that year, Swaraj fought the Haryana assembly elections on a Janata Party ticket and won from Ambala Cantonment. Bansuri says, 'It was JP who requested for a ticket for her in the Janata Party.' At twenty-five, Swaraj was the youngest cabinet minister handling labour and employment. Within three years of formation of a government at the centre and in states, the

Janata Party started disintegrating. The original members of the
Bharatiya Jana Sangh formed the Bharatiya Janata Party in 1980,
and Swaraj joined in 1984.

BJP veteran L. K. Advani had recognized the bright spark
in Swaraj very early on in his first term as the BJP president
from 1986–90. In 1987, Swaraj contested the Haryana assembly
elections from her Ambala Cantonment seat again, but this time
on a BJP ticket. She was included in the cabinet in the coalition
government and got education and food and civil supplies
portfolios. The 1984 elections after Indira Gandhi's assassination,
termed by the BJP veteran L. K. Advani as 'Shok Sabha and not
Lok Sabha elections'[4], had seen the BJP's tally fall to a mere
two. The saffron party improved manifold, rising to eighty-five in
the 1989 parliamentary elections. Later in June 1989, the BJP's
national executive at Palampur, Himachal Pradesh, adopted a
resolution where the party openly decided to support the Ram
Temple at Ayodhya, 'The Bharatiya Janata Party calls upon
the Rajiv government to adopt the same positive approach in
respect of Ayodhya that the Nehru government did with regard
to Somnath. The sentiments of the people must be respected,
and Ram Janmasthan handed over to the Hindus—if possible,
through a negotiated settlement or else, by legislation. Litigation
certainly is no answer.'[5] When Advani constituted his team he
promoted youngsters including Swaraj, Pramod Mahajan, M.
Venkaiah Naidu, Ananth Kumar, and Arun Jaitley. Swaraj was
initiated into an organizational role as a secretary but quickly
moved to being a general secretary.

TAKING CENTRESTAGE

Swaraj entered the arena of national politics in 1990 when
she was elected to the Rajya Sabha from her home state of
Haryana. Swaraj's interventions and initiatives as a first-term
member of the parliament reveal her interest in administration,
far-sightedness in identifying administrative issues that could
crop up, and awareness towards constitutional processes. Her

private members' resolutions give a peek into her interest areas as a parliamentarian. On 7 September 1990, she introduced a resolution which demanded a time limit for the grant of presidential assents to bills Though it was withdrawn, it generated a lot of discussion in the Rajya Sabha. On 8 May 1992, Swaraj moved another resolution on the creation of two separate states of Uttaranchal and Vananchal to ensure the balanced development of Uttar Pradesh and Bihar. Though the resolution lapsed, the two states of Uttarakhand and Jharkhand were carved out eight years later in 2000 when the BJP-led NDA government came to power at the centre.

Arvind Bharadwaj, a resident of Green Park, remembers how he got a call from the then South Delhi BJP President Radhey Shyam Sharma in 1996 asking him for the basement of his home. Swaraj had just been declared the party's candidate from the South Delhi parliamentary constituency. 'Radhey Shyamji said "Behenji aa rahey hain. Basement de do apna office ke liye. Hawan bhi karenge (Sushmaji is coming today. Give us the basement for the election office. We will also do a hawan today)." She came and we had a hawan at 5 p.m. My wife Neelima was not there. After the hawan, Sushmaji asked, "Yeh jagah kiski hai (Who does this place belong to)?" I came forward and replied, "Bhagwan Krishna ki (It belongs to Lord Krishna)."' A Krishna bhakt herself, Swaraj was quite taken by this reply and thus began a life-long association. Bharadwaj's basement became Swaraj's election office, and she went on to win her first Lok Sabha election from South Delhi. 'It has been my experience that nobody turns around and visits anyone after victory,' says Bharadwaj. But Swaraj was known to treasure and nurture relationships. She paid a visit. 'One evening she came visiting. She met my wife and told her she had come only to meet her as she wasn't there on the day of the hawan,' says Bharadwaj.

As Swaraj took charge of the Information and Broadcasting Ministry in what was to be the thirteen-day Vajpayee government, she asked Bharadwaj to help her with constituency work. 'My work was to scan the newspapers and invites for her and make a list of all funerals, mundans, weddings—all occasions especially in her South Delhi constituency. She would go to as many as she could and the rest were assigned to me. I used to joke that my formal designation is "personal assistant (chautha) (the fourth day of mourning)."' Swaraj's gifts at a wedding were thoughtful—an ornate silver box with sindoor in it for the bride and 'Compliments from Sushma Swaraj' written on it. She used to think about small things. 'She would say the bride would keep it with her and every day she dresses up she would remember me and the husband's family would know that there is somebody behind her,' remembers Bharadwaj. Swaraj won two consecutive Lok Sabha elections from the South Delhi parliamentary constituency in 1996 and later in March 1998.

Swaraj was an established MP when, in October 1998, the party called her to take over as the Delhi chief minister—elections were just two months away and it was near impossible to swing it for BJP. 'A meeting was called by Vajpayeeji and Advaniji with all senior BJP leaders from Delhi—Sahib Singh Verma, Madan Lal Khurana, and Sushmaji. She openly said she didn't want to be chief minister "Yeh log mera saath nahin denge (These people will not support me),"' says Bharadwaj. As the two leaders vouched support for Swaraj, she was sworn in as Delhi's first woman chief minister. This was the election fought in the wake of spiralling onion prices and deteriorating law and order situation. 'When she became the chief minister, law and order was a big issue in Delhi. She decided that all ministers, including herself, would patrol the streets of Delhi at night. She declared, "Jab tak Dilli surakshit nahin hogi main nahin soungi (I will not sleep till Delhi is safe)." It was a part of her campaign,' says Bansuri. Though she fought an aggressive campaign against Sheila Dikshit in the election, her differences were only ideological. 'She and Sheila Dikshit were very good friends. They used to call each other sakhi (friend). They used to bump into each other at some Diwali mela and shop for diyas together. Sheilaji even called me to wish me luck before my class tenth board exams,' recalls Bansuri. Swaraj fought her election from the Hauz Khas assembly constituency and defeated Kiran Walia by 2,615 votes. Though Swaraj won her seat, the BJP was trounced by the Congress. In a few months, Bharadwaj got a call from Swaraj asking him to give her resignation from the Delhi assembly to the speaker.

In less than a year, the party called its loyal foot soldier again. In August 1999, she got a call from M. Venkaiah Naidu telling her that the party wanted her to fight against the Congress President Sonia Gandhi. This was Gandhi's maiden election and she was expected to fight from a Congress bastion. The toss-up was between Cuddapah in Andhra Pradesh and Bellary in neighbouring Karnataka. 'We were told to reach Bangalore and a chopper would be kept ready for her. She was told to fly wherever Sonia Gandhi filed her nomination from. There was a lot of suspense. At the last moment Sonia Gandhi decided on Bellary and Sushmaji went and filed her nomination from there,' says Bharadwaj. She checked into a hotel. During the night she felt unwell as the hotel food had not agreed with her. Renowned physician Dr B. K. Sreenivasa Murthy was consulted and she felt better. In the morning she asked Dr Murthy if she could come and stay at his house as she did not want to live in the hotel. She celebrated the traditional Varmahalakshmi vrata pooja at Dr Murthy's home—a tradition she continued till her death in 2019. Dr Murthy's family still refers to a room where Swaraj had stayed in their home as 'Sushmaji's room'.

Swaraj knew the BJP had lost every parliamentary election from Bellary by two to three lakh votes so she had to work hard. Just like Gandhi, she was an outsider to the constituency. Dressing in her best kanjeevarams was not going to work. She had to connect with the people in their language. She was determined to make it a 'Bharatiya Beti versus Videshi Bahu' election. She asked Dr Murthy to teach her Kannada. Swaraj was fluent in Sanskrit and that helped her. 'She learnt the language in four days. She learnt enough to hold a conversation,' remembers Bharadwaj. When Vajpayee came to campaign for her in Bellary, Swaraj gave an entire speech in Kannada. She had an eighteen-day whirlwind campaign in Bellary. But she lost by 54,000 votes to Gandhi.

She returned to Delhi dejected, as per her aides. A year later, she was informed that the party had decided to nominate her to the Rajya Sabha from Uttar Pradesh. She was nominated in September 2000 and was inducted into the cabinet as the information and broadcasting minister. Swaraj and her husband Kaushal were members of the Rajya Sabha together—one of the rare occasions in parliament when a couple was together in the same house.[6]

In her two stints as the information and broadcasting minister, Swaraj is credited with giving an industry status to Bollywood and attempting to release it from the clutches of underworld. She also hosted glitzy Bollywood nights at the Cannes Festival and improved India's presence at the international festival. In the last year of the Vajpayee-led NDA's term, Swaraj was given the ministries of health and family welfare and parliamentary affairs. She got six new AIIMS hospitals cleared as the health minister.

THE POLITICS OF OPPOSITION

Buoyed by opinion polls and electoral victories in assembly polls, Vajpayee decided to advance the parliamentary polls due in November 2004 to May. It turned out that Vajpayee and his team had misread the people's mood. There was a clear disconnect with the electorate and the BJP's India Shining campaign fell flat—the Congress-led UPA emerged as a clear winner and formed the government at the centre in 2004. The hardliner in Swaraj came to the fore to protest against Gandhi becoming the prime minister. Swaraj said she would shave her head, live like a sanyasin, and eat only dry gram if an Italian took over as India's prime minister. Her tresses remained intact as Manmohan Singh became the unlikely prime minister.

The BJP emerged as an effective Opposition with its leaders like Murli Manohar Joshi, Advani, and Swaraj tackling the government by raising issues of price rise, unemployment, and internal security threat inside parliament. Though marred by controversies like cash-for-votes scandal, the Congress-led UPA got a second term at the centre in May 2009. BJP had asked all its senior leaders to fight the Lok Sabha elections. Swaraj fought from Vidisha and won. During his term as leader of opposition in Lok Sabha from 2004–2009, Advani had perpetuated the belief that the leader of opposition is the party's prime ministerial candidate. Since Advani was the NDA's prime ministerial candidate, voices of dissent against his leadership could be heard within the party. The BJP brought an amendment to the party constitution creating a post for Advani as chairman of the BJP's parliamentary wing. He stepped down as the party president and gave way to the younger guard he had nurtured over the years, nominating his trusted lieutenants Swaraj and Jaitley as leaders of the Opposition in the Lok Sabha and Rajya Sabha respectively.

The rivalry between Swaraj and Jaitley was well-known but this nomination, which was seen as Advani giving his place to Swaraj, further deepened the mistrust between the two. Many within the party compare it with sibling rivalry with both children fighting for the affection of a parent who clearly prefers one over the other. Much to Jaitley's frustration, Advani's soft corner for Swaraj was evident to everyone and became more pronounced as Jaitley switched loyalties to then Gujarat Chief Minister Narendra Modi as the BJP's prime ministerial candidate in the 2014 parliamentary elections. Deepak Chopra, Advani's close aide since 1989, says, 'Advaniji loves his daughter Pratibha. I think the attachment with Sushmaji was a manifestation of that natural attachment to a daughter. He used to be so proud when she would give a speech in parliament—his eyes would well up and he would get emotional.' Later as external affairs minister when Swaraj got embroiled in a controversy for giving Lalit Modi a visa, she would blame Jaitley for leaking information to the media and waging a proxy war to malign her.

As the leader of the Opposition in the Lok Sabha, Swaraj spearheaded protests on the 2G spectrum and coal block allocation, stalling the parliament for numerous sittings, and demanding the government give a statement. This, however, never vitiated her relationships with the leaders of political parties. 'In the midst of a parliament logjam over 2G scam, one day while Swaraj was interacting with MPs in the Central Hall, Sonia Gandhi entered unnoticed from the other side and embraced the leader of opposition leading the charge against the Manmohan Singh government.'[7] The reason was her wit and warmth. Even when she criticized, it remained factual and sometimes poetic. Her exchanges with then Prime Minister Manmohan Singh remain the most memorable.

In March 2011, the parliament was rocked by protests by the BJP after allegations by Wikileaks revealed that the Congress was purchasing MPs to win the confidence vote in 2008. Swaraj tore into the government and ended her speech with a scathing attack on the prime minister. She quoted Shahb Jafri's famous Urdu couplet, 'Tu idhar udhar ki na baat kar, yeh bataa ki karwaan kyun luta. Mujhe rehjano se gila nahin, teri rehbari ka savaal hai (Do not subterfuge, tell us why the caravan was looted. We have no complaint with the passersby, it is a question of your leadership).' The next day, Manmohan Singh took on the challenge and quoted an Urdu couplet by Allama Iqbal, 'Maana ki teri deed ke kabil nahin hoon main. Tu mera shauk toh dekh intezaar toh dekh (I agree I am not worthy of a glance from you. But you see my passion and see my perseverance).'

Soon these became the most awaited exchanges in the Lok Sabha with even the treasury benches refusing to interrupt Swaraj's couplets. In March 2013, the prime minister took on Swaraj and the BJP in his speech during the motion of thanks to the president's address in parliament. In his forty-minute reply, Dr Singh said his government's performance was better than the NDA's and the BJP had made unwarranted attacks on his government. He used a couplet by Mirza Ghalib to poke Swaraj, 'Humko hai unse wafa ki umeed, jo nahi jaante wafa kya hai (We hope for loyalty from those who do not know the meaning of the word).' Not one to take it lying down, Swaraj used a verse from Bashir Badr, 'Kuch to majbooriyaan rahi hongi yun koi bewafa nahi hota (There must have been some compulsions, one is not disloyal for no reason at all).' She then broke into a second verse, 'Tumhe wafaa yaad nahin, humein jafaa yaad nahin, zindagi or maut ke toh do hee taraane hain, ek tumhein yaad nahin, ek humein yaad nahin (You don't remember loyalty, we don't remember disloyalty, life and death have two rhythms, you don't remember one, we don't remember the other).'

No one, not even her husband Kaushal, was spared on the floor of the house. On 22 August 2003, Swaraj was bidding farewell to retiring members of the Rajya Sabha, including the noted actor Shabana Azmi. While heaping praises on Azmi, Swaraj said, 'I had never imagined that I would get a chance to work with her as a member of parliament, friend, and colleague but when I got that chance, the introduction was turned into friendship and friendship into intimacy very soon.... Today she is leaving this house and I will feel her absence but this absence will be more intensely felt by my husband because she was one of the few lady colleagues who used to sit with him in the Central Hall.' At this Swaraj Kaushal interrupted to say, 'Sir, this is not the forum for making complaints. This topic has been discussed extensively at home.' Then Rajya Sabha Chairman Bhairon Singh Shekhawat said, 'It can be termed as a complaint only if she is jealous of her meeting with you.' Swaraj, however, quipped, 'This is not a complaint, Mr Chairman. It is a feeling of greater responsibility because the little time she used to share with him will now have to be shared by me.'[8]

THE METICULOUS LEADER

Swaraj was an epitome of Indianness. There wasn't a teej when a flower-laden swing did not adorn her garden. There wasn't a Karva Chauth that she did not dress up in her finery—bangles, bright and ornate sari, her trademark big bindi, and ample sindoor in the middle parting of her hair, pulled back in a neat bun. 'That was her mantra—nothing in excess. Ek hee zindagi hai ruj ke jiyo (You have one life, live to the fullest),' says Bansuri.

A working mother all her life, Swaraj was a hands-on parent. 'Every report card, every recital, every cultural programme—

she was always there to cheer me on,' says Bansuri, Swaraj's only child. Bansuri attributes this facet of Swaraj to her time management. 'She never allowed decision fatigue to kick in. Everything was sorted—we had a fixed menu at home. Monday will be choley kulche, Tuesday rajma chawal, Wednesday dal palak, Thursday will be kadhi, Friday arhar dal. Sunday was always a South Indian food day. Nobody would ask, "*Aaj kya banega khane mein* (What will be cooked today)?" Everybody knew what will be cooked because it was a fixed menu,' says Bansuri who has still not changed the way the household runs. Behind her trademark style of a sari and a sleeveless matching jacket of the same colour was a wardrobe meticulously arranged according to the days of the week. It wasn't astrological considerations but really which God is worshipped on that day of the week according to Hindu belief system. For instance, Monday is considered day of the moon so she preferred white or cream colour, Lord Hanuman is worshipped on Tuesdays so she wore any shade of orange or red, Wednesday would be green, Thursday yellow, Friday grey or mauve and Saturday blue or black. As a busy minister she had to travel frequently or sometimes suddenly. Bansuri remembers her mother calling home and specifying what days of the week she had to travel. 'The wardrobe was organized in such a manner that the person packing for her just needed to pick it up from her almirah and just put it in. This is how structured and organized she was,' says Bansuri.

There was always an emphasis on studies at home, says Bansuri. But she has fond memories of going for campaigning with her mother. 'The most vivid memory is of going to Karnal with my mother as a toddler. Advaniji was on the stage and I threw a tantrum that I wanted to sit with her on the stage. One of the karyakarta's wife was handling me and she said, 'Oopar stage pe baithna hai toh kuch karna padega (You have to do something if you want to sit on the stage).' There was a massive poster of Krishna as Saarthi (charioteer) of Arjuna and at that time B R Chopra's *Mahabharata* serial was a rage.

So I decided to sing the title song of Mahabharata. I ended it with a long poo sound to imitate the shankhnaad. Of course, everybody had a hearty laugh. Kudos to Advaniji who told my mother "Sushma, ab isko neeche mat bhejo (Sushma, now don't send her off the stage)." I happily sat on the stage with her throughout the meeting,' remembers Bansuri. Campaign trails were an introduction to Indian culture. Bansuri remembers sitting in the middle of a field near a tubewell and having senghdana poli in Shirur, Maharashtra, and visiting a weavers colony in Mysore. 'She ensured I wasn't a generation that grew up only on western culture. She wanted me to see the rich culture and diversity of India as she believed that the language and food changes every 1.5 kilometres in India. She wanted me to know the difference between aloo chokha and jeera aloo,' she says.

It isn't a surprise that Swaraj has left behind a notebook for Bansuri titled *Parampara* (tradition). 'She has handwritten how to celebrate every festival. But at the same time it is not a dictat. I am allowed to change it. For example, during Covid it wasn't safe to give cooked food to the children on kanjak (a pooja done on the eighth day of the Hindu observance of Navratras) so I gave away packed boxes of biscuits,' says Bansuri.

Deepak Chopra remembers the little gestures that endeared Swaraj to people. 'She used to call me chhotte praaji (younger brother). I remember Advaniji and Sushmaji were going in a private plane. She used to always carry home-cooked food. She offered it to everyone and insisted on us trying a mango pickle. I loved it. I told her this pickle has made everything taste nice. From that time till her death in 2019 I used to get one big jar of aam ka achaar every year. When she became the external affairs minister she would come on the line and tell me "aapka aam ka achaar taiyyar hai, chhotte praaji' (your mango pickle is ready),"' says Chopra.

On 8 November, Advani's birthday, Swaraj would take a chocolate cake to wish him and have breakfast at his home. Bansuri has continued this tradition after Swaraj's death. She says, 'The first year right after Ma's death, I reached after court in the evening and not in the morning. It was an emotional moment for all of us. They said, "Hamein lagaa is baar cake nahin aayega (We thought the cake won't come this time)." I said, "Yeh meethi reet kabhi nahin tootegi (This sweet tradition will never break)." I saw it was difficult for Dada (Advani). But now I have made it a point to visit him before the day starts.'

Every Friday evening was date night with her daughter. 'In her calendar it was marked as "EG" and struck out. It stood for "Exclusive with Gudda" (Bansuri's nickname). If she couldn't do a Friday, it would be compensated with time on a Saturday or Sunday. My Dad was not allowed. Either we would stay in or go out or watch a movie. This was all throughout school,' says Bansuri. There was never any working mother's guilt. This was probably because Swaraj had the unwavering support of her husband throughout the career. Theirs was a partnership based on love and mutual trust. Every evening after dinner, Swaraj would be clearing files or reading something and Kaushal would play her favourite Kishore Kumar songs or other old Hindi music on YouTube or just recite Urdu couplets.

THE ACCESSIBLE MINISTER

The anti-incumbency against the Congress-led UPA government was evident by 2013. The BJP had sniffed an opportunity, so far elusive for a decade now. But the run-up to the 2014 parliamentary elections saw an unprecedented churning within the BJP. The party was divided into camps—the Modi camp and Advani camp. The octogenarian clearly could not match up to Modi's popularity. Swaraj firmly remained behind her mentor Advani—an act that was read as defiance by Modi and remained a thorn-in-the flesh even when he inducted her in his cabinet. India gave an unprecedented mandate to the BJP in 2014—the first time that the saffron party did not really need its regional allies to assume power at the centre. This also meant that the prime minister had enough leeway to choose his own team. Swaraj did not expect to be entrusted with a substantial portfolio. Chopra says Swaraj visited Advani at his residence after victory in 2019 and discussed her position in the party in detail. 'She told him that she did not expect any major portfolio in the cabinet. Advaniji told her that she is efficient and capable and she would be entrusted with a major responsibility in the cabinet,' says Chopra.

All party seniors found a place in Modi's first cabinet and Swaraj was assigned the external affairs ministry. The governance under Modi was highly centralized with most decisions being driven by the prime minister and his team of hand-picked officers at the Prime Minister's Office (PMO). Despite finding a place at the high table, Swaraj had minimal role in policy, which was largely the preserve of Modi and the National Security Adviser Ajit Doval. However, she tried to carve a niche for herself in governance and a new aggressive BJP under Modi and Amit Shah. She went from being one of the top contenders in the prime ministerial race to a minister struggling to remain relevant with her octogenarian mentor sidelined from the party he had created. It was difficult for Modi to trust Swaraj initially as she had been reluctant in accepting him as the prime ministerial candidate in 2013. In this, her rival Jaitley had stolen a march over her. He had been quick in foreseeing the turn in the tide and was the first to throw his weight behind Modi. Swaraj kept a low profile, starting with what she was best at—engaging with the common people. She focused on resolving passport and visa problems of the people and ensuring help to those in trouble abroad. All one had to do was to tweet the problem on Twitter and tag the ministry of external affairs and Swaraj.

In fact, her most famous rescue of Geeta, a deaf and mute girl, was initiated on Twitter. Geeta had accidentally strayed into Pakistan about twenty years ago and was found on the Lahore railway station. She was handed over to the Edhi Foundation. Pakistani activist Ansar Burney tweeted on 2 August 2015 saying '@SushmaSwaraj in search of a family of a missing girl.' Swaraj immediately responded and asked then Indian High Commissioner to Pakistan Dr T. C. A. Raghavan to visit Karachi and meet Geeta. After Raghavan confirmed that the girl was Indian, Swaraj made efforts to bring her back and reunite with her family. Geeta was brought back to India three months later in October and was given the name 'Daughter of India' by Swaraj. Today, she lives in an institution in Indore as repeated attempts to find her family have failed.

The most notable rescue, which required diplomatic initiative, came within a month of Swaraj taking over as the external affairs minister. About forty-six Indian nurses had been held hostage by the Islamic State of Iraq and the Levant (ISIS) in Iraq's Tikrit, Saddam Hussein's hometown. The ISIS militants had launched an offensive in the region on 9 June 2014. Even as India started diplomatic efforts to rescue the nurses, ISIS moved them to the ISIS-controlled city of Mosul, 250 kilometres from Tikrit. Swaraj opened backchannel talks with the ISIS and all major Gulf countries to bring the nurses back. After intense efforts by Swaraj and her ministry officials, the nurses were evacuated in buses to Erbil International airport, 70 kilometres from Mosul. They landed in Mumbai and were then taken to Kochi in a special flight. Bansuri remembers how her mother waited by the phone through the night for news on the nurses. 'She slept only when her officers called and told her the nurses had landed safely. She loved the assignment as foreign minister as she liked helping people. It gave her a sense of purpose,' says Bansuri.

Equally dramatic was how the Mumbai techie Hamid Ansari was brought back to India. Ansari was arrested in Pakistan in 2012 for entering the country illegally from Afghanistan. While he maintained that he had come to meet a girl he had befriended online and who was being forcibly married off, the Pakistani agencies suspected him of being an Indian intelligence agent. In 2015, he was sentenced to three years in jail. When his prison term ended in December 2018, he was unable to return to India as he did not have the proper travel documents. Swaraj's ministry stepped in and India issued ninety-six notes verbales to Pakistan for consular access to Ansari. With Swaraj's involvement and diplomatic pressure, Ansari was back to India in a matter of days. After he returned, his mother Fauzia said: 'Mera Bharat mahaan, meri madam mahaan, sab madam ne hi kiya hai (My India is great, my madam is great. Madam did everything).'[9]

Even as she kept her head down and worked diligently to straighten the passport system, Swaraj and her family got embroiled in a controversy over helping the scam-tainted former Indian Premier League (IPL) Chief Lalit Modi obtain British travel documents when he was being investigated for financial impropriety by income tax authorities. 'According to a report in a UK English daily, Labour MP Keith Vaz used Swaraj's name to put pressure on a top immigration official to grant British travel documents to Lalit Modi. Citing a leaked correspondence, the report in the daily revealed how Vaz cited Swaraj's name in an effort to expedite the case of Lalit. Vaz had earlier allegedly offered to help Swaraj's nephew to apply for a British law degree course, it claimed. According to the British daily report, Vaz personally wrote to Sarah Rapson, the director-general of UK Visas and Immigration, in an effort to expedite the case of Lalit Modi, former commissioner of the IPL cricket tournament. The report also claimed that Lalit got his travel papers after Vaz invoked Swaraj's name and that of Sir James Bevan, the British High Commissioner to India.'[10] There were allegations that Bansuri represented Modi in Delhi High Court between April 2012 and August 2014 while the legal row over Modi's travel documents was on.[11] Swaraj took to Twitter to clarify that she had done nothing wrong and had taken the decision on humanitarian grounds. The Opposition was quick to seek Swaraj's resignation but the party rallied behind her. Then BJP president Amit Shah said, 'There were no moral grounds involved.... The help was based on humanitarian grounds.' The Rashtriya Swayamsevak Sangh, also rushed to her aid, stating that the minister was clearly guided by her 'humane nature and nationalistic spirit'.[12] Even though she had the support of the party, Swaraj insisted on putting her side of the story on record—she insisted on giving a statement in parliament. Bansuri explains the decision, 'She never believed in running away from anything. She believed in the Sanskrit phrase—Na Dainyam Na Palayanam (Never be helpless and never run away). There was nothing to hide.... Her entire political record was blemish free. Parliament was her space so she wanted to put her side of the story. This way her version would be on record till eternity.' On 3 August 2015, Swaraj gave a statement in the parliament, 'I did not request the British government for any travel documents for Lalit Modi. The allegations levelled against me are baseless.' The scrutiny on the family was intense. In September, Bansuri had a brain stroke and was admitted to AIIMS, New Delhi. 'As far as my involvement is concerned, I happened to be a junior lawyer on that case (Lalit Modi's defence team).... She was the victim of the controversy, we (Kaushal and Bansuri) were just collateral damage,' says Bansuri.

On 25 December 2015, the prime minister stunned the world as he made a brief stopover in Islamabad and gave a warm hug to his Pakistani counterpart Nawaz Sharif. It wasn't just the audacity of the move by a head of the state that made the world sit up but also the fact that Modi was the first prime minister in almost twelve years to have visited Pakistan. But what many thought was an impromptu stopover after a brief meeting at a climate summit in Paris came after a backchannel outreach by Swaraj. Journalist Archis Mohan deconstructs the groundwork done by Swaraj, which paved the way for the warm hug shared by Modi and Sharif his article in *Business Standard*. 'Swaraj has worked assiduously to build good relations with Sharif and his family. In November-end, Swaraj was in Valletta, capital of the Mediterranean island-nation of Malta that hosted the Commonwealth Heads of Government Meeting, or CHOGM. There, as a South Block source recounted, the dignitaries were made to sit in the order that they receive the first rays of the rising sun.'[13]

It meant the Bangladesh foreign minister, Abul Hassan Mahmood, sat on the right of Swaraj and the Pakistan prime minister on her left. Sharif and Swaraj chatted endlessly, the source said. By the second day, the seating arrangement was somewhat changed. The Bangladeshi minister now sat at some distance from Swaraj and Sharif because of a gap in the circular table. This helped Swaraj and Sharif to talk with more ease. Swaraj's proficiency in Urdu and Punjabi helped the conversation build up. Sharif had travelled to Valletta with his mother Shamim Akhtar, wife Kalsoom, and daughter Maryam. Swaraj was invited to meet them. It helped that no journalists and camera crews from India or Pakistan were present when Swaraj broke the ice with the Sharif family. Swaraj returned home from Malta, Kalsoom and others left for London to be present for the law exam results of Maryam's daughter Mehr-un-Nisa and Sharif headed for Paris to attend the climate change talks. A day later, Sharif had an unscheduled but animated discussion with Modi for two minutes in Paris. The two national security advisors met in Bangkok on 6 December, and Swaraj was in Islamabad to attend a conference on Afghanistan on 8 and 9 December. Apart from her meetings with Sharif and her Pakistani counterpart Sartaj Aziz, she again spent over four hours with Sharif's family in Islamabad. Aziz even complemented Swaraj for her command over Urdu, confessing that in his case, his Punjabi at times interfered with his Urdu pronunciation. 'Yes, subah (morning) becomes suvere-suvere (Punjabi),' Swaraj joked.

She again called on Sharif's mother. 'Tu mere watan se aayi hai, vaada kar rishte theek karke jayegi (You have come from my homeland, promise me you will try improve relations),' she told Swaraj, and spoke with nostalgia about her birthplace, Bheem ki Katra, in Amritsar. She said neither had she visited Amritsar after the Partition nor met any from her watan before Swaraj. The two spoke at length about Amritsar, a city Swaraj would visit often when growing up in her Ambala hometown and later during her political career. Akhtar also recalled Modi and told Swaraj that the Indian prime minister had sent her a shawl and asked about her well-being whenever speaking to her son. Swaraj also met Sharif's wife, daughter, and granddaughters. Swaraj's meeting with Aziz led to the decision to resume comprehensive bilateral dialogue. Before returning, Swaraj met Sharif's daughter,

Maryam. 'Tell your grandmother that I have kept my promise (on improving relations),' she told her.[14] Not once did Swaraj take the credit for this. She merely tweeted about Modi's statesmanship, 'That's like a statesman. Padosi se aise hi rishte hone chahiyen (That's the kind of warm relations neighbours should have).'

A year later, Swaraj offered her resignation to Modi. She needed a kidney transplant and was not keeping well. Bansuri says, 'When she was unwell, she offered her resignation to the prime minister. He refused and said you get your operation done and come back after full recovery.' Swaraj broke another taboo— unlike politicians who keep their health problems especially surgeries a closely guarded secret, Swaraj declared on Twitter that she was undergoing a surgery.

HANGING HER BOOTS

She was campaigning for the Madhya Pradesh assembly elections in November 2018 when she shocked everyone—the firebrand leader decided to hang her boots. At a press conference in Indore on 20 November 2018, Swaraj said, 'It is the party which decides, but I have made up my mind not to contest the next (Lok Sabha) elections.' She said her health was fine but she had been advised to stay away from dust since her kidney transplant in 2016. Bansuri says even she was not aware of her mother's decision till it was announced. Her closest aides were shocked. She was not even sixty-seven. Her husband supported her decision, comparing her to Indian track and field sprinter Milkha Singh, who was nicknamed the 'Flying Sikh'. In a series of tweets, Kaushal said, 'Madam—thank you very much for your decision not to contest any more elections. I remember there came a time when even Milkha Singh stopped running.' He followed it up with tweets on her political journey. 'You have been four terms in Lok Sabha, three terms in Rajya Sabha, and thrice elected to state assembly. You are contesting elections since you were twenty-five and fighting elections for forty-one years is quite a marathon,' he said adding, 'Madam—I am running behind you for the last forty-six years. I am no longer a nineteen-year-old. Please, I am also running out of breath. Thank you.'

Many party veterans did not fight the 2019 parliamentary elections. But Modi won a never-before mandate with the BJP winning 303 seats and once again emerging capable of forming the government on its own without the support of its NDA allies. As Modi and Shah got down to the complicated exercise of balancing the caste math and regional representation in the council of ministers, Swaraj waited for a call offering her a cabinet berth. But the call never came. Despite not contesting the parliamentary elections, Swaraj did not expect to be left out and the secretary reporting to her in external affairs—S. Jaishankar—became the external affairs minister. Jaitley found a place in the cabinet. Bharadwaj says, 'She was expecting a call when the cabinet names were being finalized. In fact, she checked if a call had come on the landline in case the mobile network was not working. She went to the Rashtrapati Bhavan swearing-in ceremony of the council of ministers half expecting that there had been some slip up in calling her.' It may have been this heartbreak that made her vacate the official residence within a fortnight of the government formation. 'The official residence was packed up in a hurry even when she could have easily retained it as a former minister. We got her personal flat vacated and she moved,' said Bharadwaj.

Within three months of the 2019 general elections, on 6 August, she took ill and was rushed to AIIMS, Delhi. She had a cardiac arrest and passed away. 'It was all so sudden,' says Bharadwaj. 'The driver had been sent away at the regular time around 8–8.30 p.m. She started feeling uneasy. A neighbour's car and driver had to be borrowed to take her. I reached the hospital but by then she had passed away.' Swaraj was a leader whose illustrious career path had paled the boundaries of gender and regions and inspired many to keep fighting for the ideas and ideology they believed in.

MAMATA BANERJEE

The Streetfighter

Place: New Delhi
Time: November 1984

On 31 October, India was mourning the assassination of its first and only woman prime minister, Indira Gandhi. Her son Rajiv, whom Indira had initiated into politics three years ago in 1981, had taken his oath as the new prime minister. The parliamentary elections were due in January 1985. The Congress was planning to advance the parliamentary elections to December 1984. In a room in the heart of Lutyens' Delhi, Rajiv and senior Congress leaders were discussing statewise candidates. Rajiv's trusted advisor, popularly known as his computer boy, Arun Nehru was preparing the list. Suddenly, there was a commotion outside the room, the doors opened and a young woman barged inside raising slogans. The security personnel quickly came in and removed her. Two leaders walked outside to pacify her. A shocked Rajiv asked in disbelief, 'Yeh kaun hain (Who is this)?' Nehru said, 'Woh sab theek hai. Himmat dekho. (All that aside, look at her courage). If she could barge into this office, yeh ladki aafat kar degi (this girl can spell trouble).' It so turned out that her name had been recommended by the West Bengal state unit president, Subrata Mukherjee, for the parliamentary election. 'I feel we should field her against Somnath Chatterjee. She won't win but she will give a good fight,' a former Congressman and friend of Rajiv's recalls Nehru as saying.[1] The short, petite, cotton sari-clad young lady was fielded by the Congress from the Jadavpur parliamentary constituency against CPI(M) stalwart Somnath Chatterjee. Riding on a sympathy wave after Indira Gandhi's death, Congress won an unprecedented mandate, sweeping 404 of 514 seats. Mamata Banerjee, the young lady who had barged in, emerged as a giant slayer defeating Chatterjee. This was just the beginning of a tumultuous but illustrious career for the young woman who had the conviction to leave a national political party to float her own outfit and the courage to face violence on the streets of Bengal to emerge as a people's leader.

HUMBLE BEGINNINGS

The unusual life story of Mamata Banerjee cannot start the usual way of when she was born. Like her life, even this is an interesting tale. Mamata was not born in a hospital. Like several children in the young India of the fifties, she was born at home in rural Bengal. She was very small when she was brought to Calcutta by her parents Promileswar Banerjee and Gayetri Banerjee. Like most mothers, Gayetri Devi went by the tithi (Indian date) on which Mamata was born and celebrated her daughter's birthday on ashtami (the eighth day of the auspicious navratras). Mamata was homeschooled till class three with a private tutor coming home to give lessons. Then her elder brother and she were enrolled in adjacent schools. At the time of enrolment her birth date was given as 5 January—it had no real reason. Mamata's horoscope declares her birthday as 5 October. Mamata had written her class twelfth exam when she was not even fifteen years and could have been disqualified for being underage. Her father got around that problem by giving her a date of birth and year—5 January 1955—which added five years to her age. Till date, she reluctantly accepts birthday wishes on 5 January.

Mamata was brought by her parents to 30B Harish Chatterjee Street in southern Kolkata—a lower-middle-class locality parallel to the 15-kilometre-long Tolly's nullah. Her father was a government contractor in the construction business. She and her six siblings had a modest but comfortable upbringing. The single storey family home has witnessed Mamata's childhood, heady days of students politics, her first election, the establishment of the Trinamool Congress, and when she ended the Left hegemony in Bengal to become the chief minister. It has been her official residence even as the West Bengal chief minister where, until recently, she lived with her mother, brothers, sisters-in-law, and their children. She lives alone here after the death of her mother. Mamata remembers a happy childhood, but all this changed when her father died after being operated for a gastric ulcer. Her father was a big influence on her and she wanted to emulate his altruistic ways. Mamata, fondly called Monababa by her father, was shattered by his death. Mamata believes in divinity and supernatural beings, and one gets the first glimpse into this side of her at the time of her father's death in her autobiography. 'Often you come across experiences for which there is no logical explanation. Some people believe in the supernatural, some do not. For those who believe, no proof is needed, for those who do not, no proof is enough. As for me, I believe because I have faced enough situations in my life to convince me that some things cannot be explained by science or logic,' she writes in *My Unforgettable Memories*.[2]

Though Mamata's family faced tough times after her father's death, the children continued their education. Mamata's eldest brother took over the family business after selling ancestral land in the village. Mamata enrolled in Calcutta University for her undergraduate studies and it was here she was introduced to student politics. Bengal had a Congress government between 1972 and 1977. Mamata's father was a Congress worker, so for her joining the party was a natural choice. Mamata worked very hard to establish the Congress' students wing, Chhatra Parishad, in several colleges to take on the All-India Democratic Students' Organization (DSO), the students' arm of the Socialist Unity Centre of India. Trinamool Congress veteran and Lok Sabha MP Saugata Roy, who has seen Mamata from her college days, says, 'After her father's death, she supported the family by taking private tuitions. I was teaching in the day section of the college when Mamata was a college student. I was associated with Congress at that time. I remember she fought very hard to establish Chhatra Parishad when DSO ruled the campuses. She was a student leader and then a trade unionist.' The university campuses across India saw a rise in student activism as Prime Minister Indira Gandhi imposed the Emergency in 1975 and Jayaprakash Narayan gave his call of total revolution. Mamata, who because of her Congress leanings was at the other side of these political agitations, shot into prominence when she climbed atop Narayan's car to protest against his visit to Calcutta University. In the 1977 elections, the Congress was routed and the Left came to power in Bengal. Interestingly, she never stopped her studies. She completed her master's and then B.Ed. and got a law degree from Calcutta University. Even as she actively participated in political protests she would carry her books with her, get arrested, and prepare for examinations in the lock up. Roy says Mamata was known to go out at night to put up posters against the Left Front government and in support of Indira Gandhi which would be torn the next morning by the CPI(M) party workers.

'But she would doggedly go back to putting them on the walls the following night,' he says. Seeing her zeal for street politics, Subrata Mukherjee inducted her in the Indian National Trade Union Congress (INTUC).

Mamata caught the eye of party seniors during the All India Congress Committee (AICC) session in Kolkata in 1983. As one of the volunteers she was deputed to take care of party seniors. This story, once again, gives an intriguing insight into Mamata's character. She was told by Subrata Mukherjee that the Congress veteran Kamlapati Tripathi's meals would need to be cooked by a Brahmin. She passed on the instructions to her colleague Anima Chatterjee. When Anima said she would need two helpers, Mamata came up with a novel idea—two non-Brahmin volunteers could cook and Anima could serve the meal. 'Everything went according to plan. Perhaps what we had done was wrong! Tripathiji is no more. If he was alive he would have fired me.'[3] But a young and brash activist could be least bothered then.

The next year, the parliamentary elections following Indira's assassination saw Mamata being fielded against the Left veteran Somnath Chatterjee in Jadavpur, a communist citadel. On 29 December 1984, Mamata managed the unthinkable—the twenty-nine-year-old feisty political activist had taken on the organized and well-oiled CPI(M) election machinery and defeated the unassailable Chatterjee in her maiden election. The 1984 elections had seen the electoral debut of many political fledglings including Sheila Dikshit, who went on to become Delhi's three-term chief minister. But Mamata's case was different—she had no political background or a mentor and had worked her way up from student politics. In Prime Minister Rajiv Gandhi she found a benefactor who recognized her talent and gave her opportunities. Rajiv personally assigned her the responsibility of the general secretary of the Indian Youth Congress (IYC) in 1985. Senior Congress leader and former union minister Anand Sharma, who was the Indian Youth Congress president then, remembers, 'She was always a very brave and gutsy woman. I distinctly remember an incident when she and another IYC office bearer, who was in-charge of Punjab, barged into my room visibly agitated. Mamata had wanted to go to Punjab, which the Punjab in-charge did not approve of as terrorism was at its peak. I met them both separately. She was undeterred. Finally, I persuaded him to let Mamata go. We gave her a jeep and she finalized a tour programme. She went there for two weeks and the tour was a great success.'[4]

Mamata lost her Jadavpur parliamentary constituency in the 1989 parliamentary elections fought in the aftermath of Bofors gun controversy. However, this did not deter her from protesting against the CPI(M) government in Bengal. On 16 August 1990, Mamata and her party colleagues gave a bandh call to protest against the deaths of Congress workers Raghunandan Tiwari, Manash Banerjee, and Bimala. Mamata and other protesters wound their way through the city and reached Hazra. Suddenly, Mamata saw a few people carrying iron rods and firearms approaching them. She recognized one of them as Lalu Alam, a CPI(M) worker. Eye witnesses later recalled that four to five taxis with armed men had landed at the Hazra crossing and taken over the area. Mamata has described this attack in detail. 'I was expecting this so I calmly waited for them. The first thing that Lalu Alam did was to hit me on the head with the iron rod. I was drenched in my own blood but somehow I did not feel the pain.... Before I knew what was happening, there was a second blow on my head. I did not lose my cool even then although the second hit came pretty close to my brain. When I saw them bring down the rods for the third time, I covered my head with my arms, and blacked out.'[5] Mamata was confined to a hospital bed for a month. Later, she appeared in public with her head bandaged for quite some time. Mamata has attributed her insomnia in later years to the head injury sustained in the attack. She recuperated gradually. During this phase, Rajiv was concerned about her well-being and even offered to send her to the US for treatment and bear the expense personally. He appointed her the West Bengal Youth Congress president after the deadly attack.

Mamata has described Rajiv as 'a proverbial banyan tree over our heads' as he intervened to address factionalism and sometimes ease her way into the Bengal state Congress. This bond with the Nehru–Gandhi family continued even after Mamata walked out of the Congress.

DISILLUSIONMENT WITH THE CONGRESS

At a certain level, Mamata's disillusionment with the Congress began in the early 1980s. After the Left Front's stranglehold on Bengal seemed evident, she felt that the Congress's pushback was half-hearted as senior leaders were busy striking backchannel deals with Left leaders to survive in their constituencies. 'But after 1983, suddenly the movement started to fizzle out. I do not know why Congress initiatives in Bengal simply lost steam. The culture in the party is that when any regional faction gets too active it is immediately censored by the top leadership.... The party's top leadership expected us to be quiet and calm, give the occasional speeches, write the occasional report, make some money, and share some of it with the party—this was the party's idea of political activism. This was the reality within the party super structure.'[6]

Within a year of the attack on her, Mamata had started wielding power in the affairs of the state Congress. However, she could never be a part of any clique. She was her own coterie. In 1991, when West Bengal went in for both parliamentary and assembly elections, she once again insinuated that the Congress had a tacit understanding with the Left and was intentionally fielding weak candidates in some constituencies. 'I finally woke up with a jolt one day when I went to meet a well-known leader at a premium hotel where he used to stay. He had called me and another respected leader for some special discussions to his room.... In the room, I, as flanked by these two senior leaders.... One of them said, "Listen, CPM's Shymol Chakravorty has sent us a proposal. If you accept it, they will not 'disturb' south Calcutta (Mamata's constituency)." The deal? In Shymol's constituency

Manicktolla, we will not choose your candidate. If we do, then they will not let you win from south Calcutta.'[7] Mamata was incensed with this offer and turned it down. In the middle of the elections, Rajiv Gandhi was assassinated. Congress came back to power and formed the government under P. V. Narasimha Rao. Mamata returned to the parliament in this election, winning from the South Kolkata seat. She got a pleasant surprise when she was inducted as a junior minister incharge of youth and sports affairs in Rao's council of ministers.

In private conversations with this author, her party colleagues, some of whom left the Congress with her to form the Trinamool Congress, say Mamata was always focused on one thing—overthrowing the Left government in Bengal. She may have experimented with alliances with the BJP and Congress at the centre but every decision she took and every word she uttered as a central minister was measured on how it affected her politics in Bengal and brought her closer to her ultimate goal. Her assignment at the centre did not gel with her goal—in fact, in a way it took her away from state politics. In 1992, the West Bengal state Congress witnessed one of the most bitterly-fought elections for the post of state president and Mamata decided to contest. This story has been told by the two main protagonists—Mamata and the former President of India Pranab Mukherjee—in two different ways. It brings to the fore the factionalism in the state Congress and Mamata's ambition. In his book *The Coalition Years: 1996-2012*, Mukherjee writes, 'In 1991, I was the deputy chairman of the Planning Commission and was not taking much interest in the day-to-day politics of the WBPCC. But before the organizational election, there was an interesting development. There were some media reports that important Congress leaders of West Bengal, including P. R. Dasmunsi, Ajit Panja, Somen Mitra, Subrata Mukherjee, Mamata Banerjee, and Atish Sinha (then leader of the Congress Legislative Party) had approached Prime Minister and Congress president P. V. Narasimha Rao with a written request to persuade me to work out an alternative to avoid an open contest at various levels of the state Congress organization. Open contest, they reportedly said, only resulted in ugly factionalism, and sometimes also violence, thus bringing disrepute to the party. They further stated that the signatories represented all major factions of the WBPCC and also those of four frontal organizations, namely Mahila Congress, Yuva Congress, Chhatra Parishad, and Bengal Provincial National Trade Union Congress. They insisted that since I did not belong to any faction or group, I would inspire confidence in the minds of ordinary Congressmen and any compromise formula put forward by me would be accepted by all.... P. V. called me and told me to work out a mechanism in consultation with the leaders. Initially Mamata Banerjee did not have any objection, in fact, she had signed the proposal. Siddhartha Shankar Ray, who was then president of WBPCC, also told me personally that Mamata Banerjee would support me wholeheartedly.... One day during the winter of that year, I requested Mamata Banerjee for a meeting to discuss some of the observations she had made about the process. G. K. Moopanar and K. T. Ramachandran were also to be part of the meeting. During the discussion, Mamata suddenly flared up and accused me along with other leaders of a conspiracy against her. She now demanded organizational election, and said she had always stood for elections so that grassroots level workers could have their say in organizational matters. She went on to accuse me and others of distributing organizational positions amongst ourselves, thereby thwarting the electoral process. I was flabbergasted by her reaction and wild allegations. She, however, said that she was totally opposed to my approach and wanted open elections. Having said that, she left the meeting in a huff. I was stunned, and felt humiliated and insulted.'

Mamata, however, has a different take. She said she and many others were supporting Pranab Mukherjee as the state Congress chief and had no inkling that the candidate was Somen Mitra. 'As I was depending on Pranabda blindly, I was both distressed and offended with him rather than anyone else. That is when the mistrust crept in. I started wondering whether Pranabda wanted someone else as Pradesh Congress chief instead of himself,' she has written in her autobiography. She decided to contest the election against Somen Mitra but lost. It was a humiliating defeat. But the indefatigable street fighter was back within months. She organized a rally in Kolkata's iconic Brigade Parade Ground later the same year. She had no support from the central party leadership and the rally was her own show. And what a success it was. From here, Mamata announced her resignation as union minister. She wanted to work for Bengal, she said. These years as an Opposition leader in the Left-ruled Bengal were chequered with street fights, dharnas, and physical assaults. In 1993, the Indian Youth Congress, under Mamata organized marches demanding voter identity cards as the only identification to vote in the elections. When the IYC activists tried to gherao the Writer's Building, the seat of power of the Bengal government, they were fired at and fourteen people were killed. Mamata and several Trinamool Congress activists was arrested. Her party remembers the fourteen party workers every 21 July, which is observed as Martyrs Day in Bengal.

Four years after the firing incident, this Martyrs Day rally at Esplanade in 1997 became the venue of Mamata's open defiance against the Congress. Just as the Congress was gearing up to hold the AICC's 80th Plenary Session at Netaji Indoor stadium, the high-profile meeting where Rajiv's widow Sonia was formally joining the party, Mamata declared that she would hold a parallel session at Brigade Parade Ground. She had already started calling her supporters 'Trinamool Congress' or the Grassroot Congress. Somen Mitra and Bengal Congress leaders went to Delhi to meet Sitaram Kesri, then Congress president. But by then Mamata was defiant and was gaining mass popularity. A senior leader who was in Mamata's core team, told this author, 'About two days before the session many senior Congress leaders including Jitendra Prasada, Ahmed Patel, Ambika Soni, and Aslam Khan came to my place for dinner. I wanted them to ensure Mamata didn't leave the Congress. I requested them to ask her what she wanted. I took them to her Kalighat residence at midnight. But I think there was a realization among the senior leaders that no matter what the Congress would give her, she would still leave the party. She had tasted blood. The attacks on her had made her stronger in the state and very popular. It was a perception that Sonia Gandhi had a soft corner for her and that is why the senior leaders had come to pacify Mamata. But the party leaders knew that even if she would have been made the state Congress chief she would leave the party. Her ambition was not to become the chief of West Bengal Congress but to become chief minister of Bengal.' Persuasion didn't work. The leader says Kesri offered Mamata an olive branch—hold the rally under the Youth Congress banner. But Mamata refused. Her pitch was leaders will meet 'inside' Netaji indoor stadium and the workers will meet 'outside'. With this she clearly positioned herself separate from the classes, the bhadralok of Bengal who had supported the Left Front. She epitomized the masses, the grassroots—the Trinamool. Her call to the people elicited an enormous response and lakhs turned up at the venue to hear her speak. She became Didi to the young and old. What endeared the mercurial street fighter to the masses was her austere and almost-ascetic lifestyle. She was always clad in her crumpled white cotton sari with a thin border and rubber slippers and was single. Her histrionics, lampooned by the Left bhadralok, made the common man from rural Bengal feel she was fighting for him and was being unfairly dismissed as cacophonic. She had travelled extensively through Bengal. Another former Trinamool Congress leader, who has now joined the BJP, told this author, 'She was connected to the people. She did it through her simple ways. She has a photographic memory. She remembers every person's name. She will start addressing a public meeting and she will say, "Aye Poltu, Dada kothaye. Ja deke aano (Poltu, where is your elder brother? Go call him)." Now tell me if a political leader remembers your name, will you ever forget it? She did that in villages. This was in contrast with the Left leaders who remained far removed from their constituents.'

Certain that the Congress will not give her a substantial organizational role, Mamata was determined to float her own political party. Sonia stepped in to intervene and broker peace. The deadline for submitting papers for a new political party before the 1998 parliamentary elections was 17 December 1997. Mamata drafted her application, and leaders close to her drafted the party constitution. She was summoned to Delhi and along with Ajit Panja and Sudip Bandyopadhyay met Sonia at her 10 Janpath residence on 12 December. Sonia assigned Oscar Fernandes to find a solution. Fernandes had two meetings with Mamata and her supporters on 13 and 14 December. However, Mamata did not hear anything from the party leadership, making her suspect that the Congress was trying to ensure she missed the 17 December deadline for submitting her papers. Mamata got time with the Election Commission for 17 December. Just a day before, Sonia's office sought out Panja and asked him to carry a message to Mamata and ask her not to keep her appointment with the Election Commission. Though she was in a dilemma, Mamata agreed. She, however, quietly sent Mukul Roy and another confidant to the Election Commission to file the papers before deadline. The Congress hammered out a solution and Mamata returned to Kolkata. However, Mamata said that Congress went back on its promise. 'Instead on 21 December, the Congress president (Sitaram Kesri) went to Hyderabad and said the exact opposite.... Sometime later I heard they were readying the papers to expel me from the party and would announce it at 4 p.m. When I heard this, I first checked the veracity of this information and decided to call a press conference on 22 December. We announced that we would contest the election as Trinamool Congress candidates, no matter what.'[8] While she was addressing the press conference, she got news about her expulsion from the party. Mamata has written in her autobiography that till this day her mother did not support her decision to quit the Congress. 'When I met her, my mother hugged me and burst into uncontrollable tears, I was crying too. The party that I had worked for so many years kept us hanging for days and then finally expelled me. My mother was hurt, she said, "I will never ask you to work for the Congress again...go ahead and work for

Trinamool and my blessings will always be with you."' Leaders close to Mamata say that though at a certain level Mamata was hopeful of a solution in the Congress, a big part of her had made peace with breaking off all ties and branching out on her own.

'The idea of the party was crystal clear in Mamata's head. The objective was to defeat the CPI(M). When we left the Congress, we sat down and we asked her what do you want to name it and what should the symbol be? Inspite of coming from a humble background her aesthetics were very refined. She took a paper and drew the symbol of two flowers growing out of the grassroots. She said 'Trinamool'—meaning the grassroots in Bangla. This was our symbol and how everyone around her ensured she got that,' said the leader. On 1 January 1998, holding aloft the symbol made from paper cutouts by Panja, a visibly elated Mamata emerged out of the Election Commission office to announce the formation of her own party, the West Bengal Trinamool Congress.

OVERTHROWING THE LEFT

The next month in February 1998, the Trinamool Congress fought its first parliamentary election and won seven seats. Trying to find a foothold for her fledgling outfit, Mamata began experimenting with election alliances. In 1999, the Trinamool Congress improved the tally and won eight seats. It supported the BJP-led NDA government under Atal Bihari Vajpayee and Mamata was assigned the plum railways portfolio. The feisty Opposition leader, who had infamously flung her black shawl at Ram Vilas Paswan when he was presenting his railway budget in 1997 as he had not kept Bengal in mind, now had the opportunity to keep her promises to her state. She presented her first budget in 2000, rolling out a number of new trains and increasing the frequency of certain trains to Bengal. But in September 2000, she and Panja resigned from the cabinet in protest against the petroleum price hike. They were back within a week without any justification. Mamata was a whimsical ally.

Before this, she had suspended support to Vajpayee during the previous regime in May 1998 after panchayat poll violence in Bengal. She had also threatened to walk out of the NDA after the Christian missionary Graham Staines was murdered in January 1999 by right-wing groups. In 2001, a sting operation called the Operation West End caught the BJP National President Bangaru Laxman taking bribes on camera from journalists posing as arms dealers. Defence Minister George Fernandes, the NDA convenor and Vajpayee's trusted lieutenant, was forced to resign in March 2001. Mamata made Operation West End a major issue and resigned and walked out of the NDA. Mamata's resignation was a well thought out strategy—she had decided to forge an alliance with the Congress for the upcoming West Bengal assembly elections in May 2001. Mamata looked at an alliance with the BJP as a liability—a factor that could come in the way of wooing her dedicated Muslim electorate. However, the poll math did not work out and Mamata's Trinamool Congress could not pose a formidable challenge to the Left Front. She was back in the NDA fold in August 2001. She remained the voice of the Opposition within the government— she expressed her reservations on the Prevention of Terrorism Ordinance (POTO) when she said that allies were not consulted and later, in July 2002, agitated on new railway zones triggering a Bihar–Bengal fight. She was inducted in the cabinet in September 2003 but remained without portfolio till she accepted coal in January 2004. Internally, the Trinamool Congress had its fair share of rebellions with several leaders, including Founding Chairman Pankaj Banerjee, Panja, and Sudip Bandyopadhyay, branching out on their own by returning to the Congress or floating their own party or bargaining for a cabinet berth at the centre. These rebellions were also quelled and saw a majority of leaders returning to the party fold over the years. Mamata is known to forgive if an old ally returns and admits his mistake but she never forgets. Aides say Mamata has an elephantine memory.

The road to oust the entrenched Left Front was paved with

cobblestones of protracted people's movements. It saw Mamata graduate from a shrieky Opposite leader to a mature politician fighting alongside the people, lending her support to the cause of people's homes, livelihood, and land. Her struggle from 2004 till 2011 is summed up in the slogan 'Ma, Mati, Manush (Mother, Motherland, and People)' that she coined in 2009. As the former Trinamool Congress leader, who has joined the BJP, says, 'The turning point of Mamata's political career was Nandigram and clinching point was Singur.' On 18 May 2006, the day CPI(M)'s Buddhadeb Bhattacharya took oath as the West Bengal chief minister for another term, then Tata group chairman Ratan Tata announced his Nano car project at Singur. Within days, farmers started protesting against the forcible the acquisition by the government. Sensing the anger on ground, Mamata sowed paddy near the Tata factory site in Singur in July 2006. The government was in no mood to relent. Farmers started organizing themselves in groups to protest against acquisition. Rights activists like Medha Patkar also threw their weight behind the farmers. Mamata started an indefinite hunger strike on 3 December 2006. At the same time, about 150 kilometres away, the government announced its plan to develop a chemical hub in a special economic zone in Nandigram, in East Midnapore district, close to Haldia. It was supposed to play host to one of the state's most prestigious special economic zones (SEZ) of the Indonesian real-estate giant Salim Group. In all, over 14,500 acres of land was required for the proposed zone, out of which 10,000 acre had to be given to the Salim Group and another 4,500 acre to the Ruia Group for a shipping project, among others. The farmers, largely from the Muslim community, felt cheated as they found the compensation meagre and felt the Left Front had given up its ideology by supporting the capitalists against them. The farmers started forming small groups such as the Krishijami Raksha Committee and the Bhoomi Uchhed Pratirodh Committee with the help of the Trinamool Congress to protest the acquisition of farmland for the SEZ. Much to the alarm of the state government, Mamata's indefinite fast continued.

In Delhi, the Trinamool Congress raised the issue of forcible land acquisition in the parliament. Prime Minister Manmohan Singh and President A. P. J. Abdul Kalam expressed worry over Mamata's health and appealed to her to call off the fast. Finally, on 29 December, Mamata ended her fast and was rushed to the hospital. She stayed there till 3 January 2007.

In Nandigram, the farmers started blocking access to their villages. 'It wasn't until 2 January, however, that protests turned violent with police opening fifteen rounds of fire and one of their jeeps being burnt in the process. The locals then barricaded the entrance to some of the villages where land had to be acquired. In the meantime, around 250 Left cadres set up camps in village Tekhali, opposite Sonachura, where the farmers' protests were mainly taking place with the Trinamool's backing. They gathered arms and men to attack Sonachura. Around 3.30 a.m. on 6 January, bombs started being hurled on Sonachura from Tekhali. The cadres even started firing on the villagers. There were direct clashes, which claimed six lives. Though the CPI(M) claims that the killed were their cadres, locals say the dead were actually farmers who were fighting the CPI(M). The next day, on the morning of the bandh, there was more firing, but no one was killed this time. The police, till 8 January, had not been able to enter the villages.'[9] Even as the protests in the two areas continued, the West Bengal government signed the Singur land lease with the Tata Group on 9 March 2007. Several kilometres away, Nandigram was simmering. A former Trinamool Congress MP told this author, 'We had an uncanny feeling that something would happen as the administration wanted to open the roads captured by the villagers. The police action was very unfortunate. Those who were fired at were mostly Muslims and they instantly changed their allegiance from CPI(M) to Mamata Banerjee.' On 14 March 2007, fourteen people died in police firing and subsequent violence. What began as an agitation over rumours of land acquisition for a proposed chemical hub turned into a bloody turf war between the CPI(M) and the Trinamool Congress-led Bhumi Uchhed Pratirodh Committee—a grouping of Maoists, Trinamool supporters, the Socialist Unity Centre of India (SUCI), and others. Though the official figure is fourteen, many went missing and villagers alleged that women were raped and molested by the CPI(M) cadres. Seeing the backlash, the SEZ was shelved. There was a fresh round of violence as displaced villagers started returning after eight months in November 2007. In Singur the protests intensified as the government dug in its heels and in February 2008, the Tatas announced that the first car will roll out of Singur factory in October 2008. The talks between the state government and Mamata failed and in September 2008, the Tatas suspended work on Singur site. Seeing the face-off, Governor Gopalkrishna Gandhi intervened and the government announced enhanced compensation for farmers. But the solution didn't dissuade the Tatas from moving the factory in October 2008 to Gujarat. Mamata emerged victorious out of her second struggle in two years.

On 2 November 2008, there was a failed assassination attempt on Chief Minister Buddhadeb Bhattacharya at Kalaichand in West Medinipur near the forested Lalgarh area. A number of local tribals were arrested by the police in Lalgarh. In protest, the tribals began a violent agitation with the support of Maoists and refused to allow the police or government administration officials to enter the area. It was a clear sign that the Maoists were attempting to establish a Muktanchal (liberated zone) as they had successfully done for nearly a year in Nandigram in the neighbouring East Medinipur district. With no police presence, the Maoist-backed People's Committee Against Police Atrocities (PCPA) started killing CPI(M) cadres and targeting police stations to declare the Lalgarh region free and establish their own administration. In February 2009, Mamata visited the area to express her party's solidarity with the tribal movement in the area and shared dais with PCPA leader Chhatradhar Mahato, who was a former Trinamool Congress member.[10] It was an eight-month long reign of terror in 2009. Finally, the union government deputed the Central Reserve Police Force (CRPF) and the Combat Battalion for Resolute Action (COBRA) and started flushing out Maoists.

The violence had compelled thousands of villagers in and around the area to leave their homes and live in relief camps. Maoist leader Koteshwar Rao, popularly known as Kishenji, put Mamata in an uncomfortable position when he asked her to clarify her stance on the centre sending security forces to Lalgarh. Mamata took a nuanced stand. In June 2009, she charged the CPI(M) government with using central forces to recapture lost political ground in the state. Banerjee also questioned the motive behind the police action in Lalgarh. She claimed this was a game plan of the CPI(M)-led Left government, and the central forces were playing into their hands. 'The CPI(M)'s plan is to use Central forces to recapture lost ground in the region. This was planned before the CM left for Delhi three days ago,' said Banerjee.[11] The Trinamool chief said: 'The chief minister knows he will get money in the pretext of resisting Maoist activities. The most unfortunate part is the sufferings of villagers. On one side you have Maoists, on the other the paramilitary forces. Villagers have become hostages.' Alleging that the CPI(M) was committing atrocities across the state, she asked why nothing was being done to check the state-sponsored terror. 'Is only Lalgarh the issue? The same condition is in Garbeta and Keshpur. The centre should declare the region as a disturbed area. More arms will be recovered from houses of CPI(M) cadres in the coming days,' she said.[12] An MP remembers the violence on ground, 'Mamata bore the brunt of CPI(M)'s goons. She had the courage to fight against them. I still remember how once our car was stopped in Keshpur and the goons spat on Mamata's face. She was rattled but she refused to go back and continued her journey. This is what she is made of.'

The struggles for land drew in the intelligentsia or the bhadralok of Bengal. Theatre groups and intellectuals openly supported Mamata. In a way, Mamata had breached the Left citadel even before the 2011 assembly elections. This time, she aligned with the Congress and SUCI to fight the elections against CPI(M) and secured 227 seats with her party cornering 184. The 34-year-old Left rule had ended in Bengal.

INSIDE WRITER'S BUILDING

Once in the seat of power, Mamata started working on her reforms agenda. Her focus was social welfare, power sector reforms, transport, and livelihood. She introduced a slew of schemes to keep girl students in schools and ensure they completed their studies. She also provided financial support to elderly women and people belonging to the minority community. During the years of struggle against the Left, Mamata was seen as an ally of the Maoists. However, she did an about turn in 2011 after taking over as the chief minister and refused to bow down to the Maoists' demand to withdraw security forces from Jangalmahal. In her biography of Mamata, author Monobina Gupta speaks about the chief minister's handling of Maoists after assuming power. 'During the tribal upsurge in Lalgarh, the CPI(M) had launched an acidic campaign, accusing Mamata of aiding and abetting Maoist violence in Jangalmahal. Undoubtedly, her political rhetoric at that time was ambivalent. She did indeed play down the issue in the interest of her ultimate goal of defeating the Left Front government. But to describe Mamata as being hand-in-glove with the insurrectionists would be a gross exaggeration. Her polemical claims aimed at the CPI(M)—that there were no Maoists in Bengal—on the eve of assembly elections should not be taken at face value. It was part of the rhetoric of political performance at the time. Let's not forget that Mamata—despite her recent alliances with Left-leaning intellectuals, artistes, and activists—has always been essentially a political centrist at heart. The recent escalation in tension between her and the Maoists needs to be grounded in a context where after assuming power Mamata had given them enough leeway to abandon arms and come to the negotiating table for talks. She had kept the central and state joint security forces operation in abeyance, which was one of her key manifesto commitments. But the negotiations did not work. Even as the chief minister announced a slew of development packages for Jangalmahal, the Maoists stepped up their offensive. With

Mamata sanctioning resumption of security operations against
the Maoists, the bonds between her and a sizeable section of
Left-leaning intellectuals and human rights activists seem to be
on the verge of snapping. The growing distance was manifest
when the government-appointed interlocutors, mandated
to negotiate with the Maoists, quit following the killing of
prominent Maoist leader Koteshwar Rao, popularly known as
Kishenji.'[13]

Mamata is a stubborn street fighter. Once she sets her
mind to something she achieves it. In her sixties, Mamata as
the chief minister had been leading a stressful lifestyle and was
advised to include daily brisk walks. Even if she has to travel,
Mamata never misses her morning routine of walks. In the run-
up to the 2019 parliamentary elections, this author met her
at the Vishakhapatnam airport after her rally with the TDP
Chief N. Chandrababu Naidu and Delhi Chief Minister Arvind
Kejriwal. With her chief secretary and three senior officials
briefing her about administrative issues, Mamata was walking
briskly, following a 200 metre stretch at the terminal. Balancing
files, officers were finding it tough to keep pace with her. When
asked why the airport, she said, 'I am travelling so much, where
else will I complete my steps?' Banerjee is a nervous flier. An aide
said, 'Even if there is a little turbulence in the flight, she thinks it
is really a conspiracy to kill her. As late as 2016, when she was
the chief minister, she was flying from Patna to Kolkata and her
flight was circling over the airport due to congestion. The party
demanded an inquiry as it thought there was a conspiracy in an
aircraft running low on fuel. She has always felt insecure while
flying. There have been times when I had landed in Kolkata at
9–10 a.m. and have had to fly to Delhi with her at 11.30 a.m.
just to reassure her.'

After remaining in power for a decade, Mamata faced her
toughest challenge in the 2021 assembly elections from the BJP,
which won 18 out of 42 parliamentary seats in Bengal in the
2019 elections (a marked improvement from its 2014 tally of
two seats). The BJP's election micromanagement was on full

display with Prime Minister Narendra Modi and union Home Minister Amit Shah fully involved in the state.

On the advice of her nephew Abhishek Banerjee, Mamata decided to rope in election strategist Prashant Kishor's I-PAC for the assembly elections in the state in 2021. Like every election, Mamata earmarked over 40 per cent of the seats for women candidates. It was one of the most bitterly-fought elections in Bengal. The BJP weaned away at least fifteen disgruntled Trinamool Congress MLAs. Modi was the star campaigner trying to rile Mamata with his sarcastic calls of 'Didi O Didi'. Mamata's masterstroke was her wheelchair. At a public meeting in Nandigram, Mamata hurt her leg and was admitted in the hospital. With her leg in plaster, she led her rallies from a wheelchair, gaining the sympathy of the electorate. Many suspected that the injury had healed and Mamata wore the plaster a little too long, but these suggestions didn't matter to the people. Trinamool's war cry of 'Khela hobey (Game on)' saw Mamata winning a decisive 213 of the 290 seats contested, leaving the BJP at 77 seats.

THE SUCCESSION PLAN

Mamata's nephew Abhishek, the thirty-four-year-old member of parliament from Diamond Harbour, is seen as her heir-apparent. Abhishek joined the Trinamool Congress in 2011, the year Mamata became the chief minister of West Bengal. He was made the president of the youth wing of the party. He climbed the organizational hierarchy quickly and has emerged as a power centre. The bhaipo (nephew) has been responsible for several desertions from the party, including that of Mukul Roy and Suvendu Adhikari, people who had been with Mamata from the time she formed the party. Several have been persuaded to return, but Abhishek's influence on party workings is evident. The fact that Mamata ceded decision-making ground and allowed inputs from I-PAC in deciding candidates reflected Abhishek's rising stature within the party. The old-timers, however, have been uncomfortable with the meddlesome and often brash ways of Abhishek. His involvement in the party has exposed the Trinamool Congress and Mamata to attacks from the BJP over corruption. It is alleged that his businesses have illegally benefitted because of his links to Mamata and he is often referred by the BJP as 'tolabaaz bhaipo (extortionist nephew)'. Abhishek and his supporters have actively worked towards edging out the old guard in the Trinamool Congress by insisting on one-man-one-post principle (which means one person could either be a part of the state government or hold a party post) and a maximum age for holding party posts. Mamata has been quick in gauging the rumblings of dissent within her party—the mark of a grassroots leader with an ear to the ground. In 2022, she clipped Abhishek's wings in an organizational exercise of rejigging the National Working Committee. She struck a fine balance between accommodating the old guard and younger leaders but deputed three national vice-presidents, limiting Abhishek's influence as the national general secretary of the Trinamool Congress.

Mamata thinks of herself as a pilgrim in her political journey. But this pilgrim has had the courage to follow her convictions and chart her own course without any sage.

BRINDA KARAT

The Comrade

A religious procession of about 500 people and 40–50 two-wheelers was making its way through Jahangirpuri in northwest Delhi. The devotees, some of them armed, were taking out a planned yatra on the occasion of Hanuman Jayanti on 16 April 2022. The policemen were tense. Jahangirpuri has a sizeable population of Bengali-speaking Muslims who have been here for fifty years. The yatra came just six days after incidents of communal clashes during Ram Navami in the states of Gujarat, Madhya Pradesh, Jharkhand, and West Bengal. As the procession made its way in front of a mosque around 6 p.m., an argument broke out between two groups. Before the policemen could realize, stones were being pelted on both sides. A wireless message was relayed to the police control room flagging a law and order situation. Rioters torched vehicles on the road. The heavily outnumbered policemen were caught in stone pelting from both sides. As reinforcements came, forty to fifty teargas shells were fired and gradually the crowds dissipated. The injured, including policemen, were taken to the hospital.

Four days later, nine bulldozers rolled into Jahangirpuri at 9 a.m. with fourteen civic teams. About 1,500 police officers, most in riot gear, surrounded the area. A day earlier, then Delhi BJP President Adesh Gupta had shot off a letter to the North Delhi Municipal Corporation Mayor Raja Iqbal Singh demanding identification and demolition of 'illegal encroachment' and construction by those arrested in the Jahangirpuri violence. The corporation had sought police personnel to conduct the drive the same day. The requisite police force could not be provided in Jahangirpuri so the action was planned for 16 and 17 April. It was curious that the civic body had taken note of encroachments only in this decrepit colony in a city which has for decades turned a blind eye towards the posh and illegal Sainik Farms. It was reminiscent of the 'bulldozer justice' meted out by the BJP's Uttar Pradesh Chief Minister Yogi Adityanath against suspected riot-accused. The model was implemented by another BJP Chief Minister Shivraj Chouhan in Madhya Pradesh's riot-hit Khargone where fifty homes of allegedly riot-accused men were demolished in the same week.

On 16 April at 9.30 a.m., former Rajya Sabha MP and the Communist Party of India (Marxist) leader Brinda Karat was sitting in her second floor office at A. K. Gopalan Bhawan near Gole Market in Central Delhi. She had come to know about the demolition a night before and had called the senior advocate and All India Lawyers Union General Secretary P. V. Surendranath. Both had decided to take the matter to the Delhi High Court and the Supreme Court of India. While Surendranath was in the Supreme Court, Karat's lawyer Tara Narula went to the Delhi High Court. Then Chief Justice of India N. V. Ramana was due to hear a plea filed by the Jamiat Ulama-i-Hind against the demolition in Khargone. Senior advocates Dushyant Dave, Kapil Sibal, P. V. Surendranath, and Prashant Bhushan mentioned the Jahangirpuri drive and said no demolition notices had been given to residents. 'Maintain status quo and let the matter be heard tomorrow,' said Justice Ramana. Surendranath called Karat and conveyed the order around 10.50 a.m. She rushed to Jahangirpuri. The demolition drive, which was earlier planned for 2 p.m., had already started. Bulldozers were destroying shops owned by Muslims—their only source of income. It took Karat over an hour from Central Delhi to reach Jahangirpuri, which is towards the other end of northwest Delhi. Bulldozers were still rolling despite the Supreme Court order. Dushyant Dave informed the Chief Justice that the demolition drive had not stopped. Justice Ramana asked the Supreme Court registry to communicate the stay order to the commissioner of the Delhi Police North Delhi municipal commissioner, and mayor.

As Karat reached Jahangirpuri, crowds had swelled up. At 11.45 a.m., jostling for space with people and armed policemen, Karat stood in front of the bulldozer—'Roko, Supreme Court ka order hai (Stop, it is the Supreme Court's order).' Within half an hour, the Special Commissioner of Police (law and order) Dependra Pathak reached the spot and Karat briefed him. Finally, the drive stopped. Clad in an off-white sari, a photo of the seventy-four-year-old Karat standing in front of the bulldozer with her arms raised is one of the lasting images of the Jahangirpuri demolitions. While the rest of the Opposition was on Twitter berating the government for 'bulldozer justice', Karat was doing what she has known best—fighting on the streets for the rights of the poorest of the poor.

Not many know that the bylanes of Jahangirpuri are not new to Karat. She has worked extensively with worker unions during the Emergency years and has seen them being uprooted in the name of beautification of Delhi and moved to the resettlement colonies of Jahangirpuri, Mangolpuri, Nand Nagri, and Dakshinpuri. Karat and other women leaders fought for functional schools, toilets for women, and hygienic living conditions in these colonies in the 1970s. She terms her years as a trade unionist from 1975 to 1985 as the best learning years of her life which laid the foundation for all her party work. But it all started with a mini rebellion over skirts in London of the 1970s.

LAYING THE FOUNDATION

Karat remembers a carefree childhood in Calcutta—being raised by her father and aunts, closely supervised but without any strict code of parental dos and don'ts. Her mother died when Karat was five years old, but her influence lived on in the household. Her father Suraj Lall Dass, originally from Lahore, had come to Calcutta looking for a job. Karat's home was always filled with people, his friends, relatives, Punjabis and Bengalis, her elder brother, elder sister, and a younger sister. 'So there was no dominant culture but a kind of mix. As far as political influences are concerned, one of my father's friends was standing for elections and although I can't recall which party he was representing, I have a distinct memory of my younger sister and I marching around the house, shouting "Vote for Uncle Dan". That was the extent of politics in my childhood,' she says.

Karat studied in Loreto House, Calcutta, till she was twelve and then joined the Welham Girls School in Dehradun. She did her college from Delhi University's Miranda House in between 1963 and 1966. Her first introduction to gender issues was during her years in college. 'When I was in college the issue of woman as property and the aggression when a girl says no came home to me in a very stark and tragic way. I had a group of close friends in the college hostel where we stayed. One of them was in a relationship with someone in the army. He was much older than her. She decided that she wanted to break it off with him. There was an exchange of letters. The man was insistent that they should meet and then take the decision. We were all against it and she too was hesitant,' remembers Karat. 'On the morning of the day she was to meet him we had a discussion and suggested that one of us should go along with her, but she felt she should deal with it herself. She went to the university cafe to meet him and he shot her dead. Then he shot himself.... It was such a brutal introduction into a world in which you suddenly realize that there are issues about being a woman, there is a price to pay when you take your own decisions, when you refuse to be subordinate, when you say no. It affected all of us deeply,' Karat told the author. Those times were different, Karat says there were cases of sexual harassment but there were not many movements at that time.

Since her main interest was theatre in college, she wanted to train at the London Academy of Music and Dramatic Arts (LAMDA) to become an actor. 'But my father believed that his daughters should first be economically independent and since there were no scholarships available, he promised as a consolation to help me get a job in London which would pay for my evening classes,' says Karat. She got a job in Air India in London. She stayed as a paying guest with a relative who had other Indian girls staying with her. 'My first posting was at Heathrow Airport, not the London head office in the city. I was disappointed because I had to work different shifts which meant that I could not join evening classes,' she says. At nineteen, Karat's first protest was a personal one. 'When I reported for duty I was told that I had to wear a skirt which was the rule for Air India ground staff at the airport. I had nothing against wearing a skirt as such, but I asked my manager, a really kind man called Alan, "When I am working with the national airline of India, why can't I wear a sari?" He said it was the rule, and he couldn't do anything about it. I felt it was wrong and an illogical rule and I refused to obey it. I was lucky he didn't sack me on the spot! I guess he felt I had a point, so he wrote to the legendary Bobby Kooka, the commercial director of Air India at the Bombay head office. There was quite a furore. The other girls didn't really support me, most of them were British and thought it was a non-issue. Finally, after six weeks, there was a letter from Bobby Kooka saying "Not only this girl can wear a sari at the airport, but any girl posted at the airport can wear one." I got such beautiful saris as uniform from Air India and then one after another, the British girls signed up for wearing saris too,' says Karat, who soon had a queue of girls waiting for her in the rest room, wanting to be taught how to wear a sari. Within a few months, Karat got transferred to the city office and thought she could finally start theatre classes. But instead, she got introduced to Marxism.

'My very close friend from Welham, Mala Sen (author of the biography of *Phoolan Devi: Bandit Queen*), lived just down the road from me. She and her brilliant husband Farrukh Dhondy had a wide circle of friends, many of them students. Their small home was always full of young people engaged in political discussions about organizing and mobilizing,' says Karat about her first introduction to Marxism. This was the London of the late sixties and there was an outrage against the Vietnam War. Karat started reading Marxist literature and began to understand the division of classes and became aware of 'my own elitist background and the privileges I had taken for granted.' Most of the students Karat met in London were scornful of the organized Left in general and were more attracted to the Naxal Movement. Though she could not connect with pro-Communist Party sympathizers in London, she knew CPI(M) was the party for her. 'I was inspired by Jyoti Basu and his role in the late sixties in leading the huge class struggles that were shaking Bengal and also representing that struggle in parliamentary politics. There was a huge attack on the CPI(M). But the courage of the people holding the red flag inspired me. I wanted to go back to Bengal, my birthplace, and join the movement. I decided to give up my job and come back to India and join the party,' says Karat. Despite stiff opposition from her father, Karat quit her job at twenty-three and came back to India to join CPI(M). She lived with her elder sister as her father did not speak to her for six months. But gradually everyone in the family came around.

JOINING THE PARTY

So how does a twenty-three-year-old young woman with no political background join a party? In the Bengal of the 1970s, where the CPI(M) was under severe attack, it was difficult to walk into a party office and express one's willingness to do political work. 'Becoming a member of a party like the CPI(M) is not a "missed call membership". One has to work hard for it. In the CPI(M) party membership is earned through one's work in the area in which one lives, or in the institution one is in, like a student or teacher in college would join the party through their political work in the mass organizations,' says Karat. After a misadventure, which involved meeting a 'sham person' who was more interested in meeting in cafes than taking her to the party office, Karat's friend Subhashini Ali (now the All India Democratic Women's Association president) gave her the contact of a party member in Calcutta. The party leadership suggested she join the university and work among students. Karat enrolled in the MA history department as what was called then a 'casual student'. 'It was a dangerous time when the CPI(M) cadre were under attack both by the police under the Siddharth Ray-led Congress government and also by the Naxalites who considered us their main enemy. Literally when we left home in the morning, we were never sure whether we would return. It was trial by fire, and it was a great training for me. It was through the recommendation of the comrades I worked with, that I was given party membership within a year,' says Karat.

After working for two years in the university, Karat worked as an editor on the party's English weekly and did area-based work, including in the Calcutta Port area where Hindi-speaking workers lived. She expressed her keenness to work with trade unions. 'The then CPI(M) General Secretary P. Sundarayya was sympathetic to my request, but he felt it would be better if I shifted to Delhi. That discussion was on when in June 1975, the Emergency was declared. All our leaders went underground. I was sent a message to go to Delhi and given the name of a comrade at whose place I could stay. The room where I was staying in Calcutta—I had shifted out of my sister's home some years earlier—was used as a meeting place for our underground leaders. The police broke into the place some weeks later. I was already in Delhi by then. Comrade Surjeet, who was semi-underground in Delhi, asked me to meet him at a pre-destined place and told me that I was to work in the Textile Workers Union (Lal Jhanda Kapda Workers Union),' says Karat. She had been assigned her dream job.

LEARNING AT THE GRASSROOTS

These years were challenging—the political leadership was either in jail or had gone underground or like Karat, they were working discreetly under assumed names. 'I was advised to adopt another name as a precautionary measure after the police broke into my room in Kolkata. I was at a party branch meeting with textile workers when the decision to change my name was taken. I suggested I be called Sheila. The workers looked uncomfortable with this suggestion, and then one of them said that this would cause confusion, since the name of the wife of the union president was also Sheila and workers may think I was his wife! Another senior worker, Chandrabhan said, please give her a name we can easily pronounce, the best name for her would be Rita. And so for three years I was known as Comrade Rita,' says Karat. Even today the old associates from union days call her Rita.

During the Emergency, workers colonies near textile mills and industrial areas were demolished and the workers moved to resettlement colonies on the outskirts of Delhi. The workers lived in squalor and abject poverty in these colonies with no proper sewage system, blocked drains, lack of toilets, and no schools. With a ban on trade union activity during the Emergency, mill owners pushed greater productivity norms on workers without increasing their wages. There were widespread retrenchments and women workers bore the brunt. By the time Karat joined, a majority of the handloom and textile mill workers were men. Karat and other comrades would visit workers' homes and interact with women, forming lifelong bonds. The homes became secret meetings places. 'I often stayed in workers' homes. At night we would go out with stencils and a box of black paint and a brush and would stencil slogans on the mill walls on our demands. We used to hold branch meetings late into the night in the different areas where workers lived,' says Karat.

As she interacted with women in those families, Karat understood the necessity of organizing women. The small green shoots of the women's movement were only becoming visible on the national platform. The Committee on the Status of Women in India, led by the iconic Dr Vina Mazumdar and Dr Lotika Sarkar, had just submitted its 'Towards Equality' report. These years saw feminist women's groups fighting against domestic violence, pushing for an anti-dowry legislation, equal wages, better working conditions, and driving campaigns against female foeticide. From being a movement driven by the educated upper-middle-class women, it soon became a movement powered by working-class women. These movements were spearheaded by fiery women leaders who were members of CPI(M). The party's state units conveyed the need for a national women's organization. The CPI(M) founded a dedicated women's organization, the All India Democratic Women's Association (AIDWA), in 1981. Karat says, 'It was an organically felt need of women working at the ground level in many states. The CPI(M) only facilitated this process since many of the women concerned were important leaders of the party. I became the founding secretary of the Delhi Committee. Our membership was drawn from the working class bastis (settlements) where we had worked.'

During this time, Karat met her future husband Prakash, who was deputed to work with the Delhi party state centre since the secretary had been arrested. 'Our wedding was held at the home of the mother of one of our comrades, who generously and also fearlessly offered her home as the venue. There were twenty guests and those who presided over this "party wedding" were comrades Surjeet, A. K. Gopalan, and Suseela Gopalan. A "party wedding" means that we read out self-written vows and exchange garlands and those presiding made speeches,' says Karat.

SHAPING THE WOMEN'S MOVEMENT

Karat emerged as a fiery activist championing the cause of women in the 1980s and 1990s. In the late 1970s and early 1980s, Dahej Virodhi Chetna Manch was formed by a diverse group of women's organizations to spread awareness against the dowry system and demand an anti-dowry legislation. Dr Indu Agnihotri, a fellow women's rights activist and former director of the Centre for Women's Development Studies, says, 'We used to start at 8–8.30 a.m. on tempos, holding nukkad sabhas and nataks to spread awareness amongst women. We would return home late at 9 p.m. Gradually, we saw a change when women in bastis started stopping families from mistreating their daughter-in-laws. I remember how once in a resettlement colony women took a tape recorder and recorded a mother-in-law beating up her daughter-in-law and then they told her firmly to stop or she would be reported to the police. It was so heartening to see women standing up for themselves.'

The developments in the mid-1980s brought several women-related issues to the fore and women's organizations founded forums to push for changes in legislations. One of the most prominent mass campaigns for women's rights focused on Muslim women after the famous Shah Bano case verdict. Shah Bano, a Muslim lady, had taken her husband Mohammad Ahmad Khan, a prominent Indore lawyer, to court in 1978 demanding maintenance for herself and her five children. The lawyer husband had married a second time and lived with both wives for several years before divorcing Shah Bano. After his divorce, he paid Shah Bano ₹200 per month but in 1978 stopped all payment necessitating the then sixty-two-year-old Shah Bano to approach the local court demanding a monthly maintenance of ₹500. Khan said before the court that he had paid Shah Bano what was prescribed under the Islamic law. The local court directed Khan to pay ₹25 per month. Shah Bano filed a review petition before the Madhya Pradesh High Court which granted an enhanced maintenance. Khan, however, appealed against the high court order and filed a petition in the Supreme Court. He argued that Muslim Personal Law in India required the husband to pay maintenance for the iddat period after divorce. Iddat is roughly a ninety-day period for which a woman has to wait after divorce or the death of her husband to remarry. The appeal before the Supreme Court also saw the All India Muslim Personal Law Board and Jamiat Ulema-e-Hind intervening in the matter. On 23 April 1985, a five judge bench dismissed the appeal while taking a grim view of the All India Muslim Personal Law Board's submission that it was irrelevant to inquire as to how a Muslim divorcee should maintain herself. The Supreme Court asked Khan to bear the cost of the appeal of ₹10,000 and upheld the maintenance awarded by Madhya Pradesh High Court.

The judgment, especially the observations of the Supreme Court bench on the need for a uniform civil code, triggered widespread protests by Muslim bodies who saw this as an infringement of the community's right to have their personal laws. The Congress government under Rajiv Gandhi, which had won a landslide victory, winning 404 of 514 seats in the 1984 parliamentary elections, feared a backlash from the Muslim community, a dedicated party votebank. The government passed the Muslim Women (Protection of Rights on Divorce) Act, 1986,[1] which turned the clock back on the Supreme Court judgment and allowed maintenance only for the iddat period of ninety days as prescribed in the Muslim personal laws. AIDWA organized protests across the country. 'We formed the Muslim Women's Rights Forum to spread awareness and launch nationwide protests against this regressive move,' says Karat. Similar protests were organized when the eighteen-year-old girl Roop Kanwar was burnt alive on the funeral pyre of her deceased husband in Deorala village in Sikar district of Rajasthan. She was hailed by villagers as 'sati'—an orthodox practice in pre-Independence

India when the woman sat on the funeral pyre with her husband and was burnt alive. Though there were conflicting versions of the events around Roop Kanwar's death, it shook the conscience of the nation as people realized that such heinous practices still existed in India. 'These years were marked by various protests and mass movements for women's rights. Various organizations got together to run these campaigns. Our interventions were taken on board and brought about several changes in law,' remembers Karat. She was the general secretary of the AIDWA from 1993–2004 and later the vice-president.

THE PARLIAMENTARIAN

Karat's life has always been at the grassroots' level and she never gravitated towards electoral politics. Bengal has been the centre of Left politics, but Karat's politics has always centred around Delhi. In August 2005, she was elected to the Rajya Sabha as a member from Bengal. 'The pattern of my work and responsibility in the party has been in class and mass organizations and in responsible roles in party committees. This has kept me in Delhi and also functioning from the party centre. In 2005, for one term I was elected to the Rajya Sabha as a member from Bengal. Being a member in the parliament or the state assembly certainly provides an important platform to fight for policy changes to empower women. But in my experience, it is the women's movements and united efforts which really push the agenda of women's equality forward,' she says. The year 2005 was significant as Karat broke the proverbial glass ceiling within the party—she became the first woman to be elected to CPI(M) politbureau, the highest decision-making body of the Left party. 'The decision to elect a woman in the politbureau is a product of the times, not a personal achievement. It just means that socially and in a broader sense women's assertions through struggle challenged exisiting norms. There were great women communist leaders who did not get this opportunity. Our path was made easier by communist women before us. They were path breaking women. It was unfortunate that it took the party so many years till 2004 to realize that women should be a part of the highest decision-making body,' she says. At present, the seventeen-member politbureau has two women members—Karat and Subhashini Ali.

Karat's Rajya Sabha term saw a significant development. In March 2010, the house passed the Women's Reservation Bill. Cutting across party lines, women MPs Sushma Swaraj and Najma Heptullah and Karat holding their hands up to mark the victory has become an iconic photograph capturing the joy of women MPs as they moved an inch closer to reservation in the parliament and in legislative assemblies. 'The Bill is critical to push forward the longstanding demand against male privilege and overwhelming domination in decision making bodies, including the parliament and state assemblies. It is a shame that we are celebrating seventy-five years of Independence but women still are just 12 per cent in the parliament and in many state assemblies less than even 10 per cent. The change that is required can only come through a law and constitutional amendment since no party will willingly change an MP from a sitting seat unless it is reserved for a woman,' she says. The women's movement post-independence has gradually changed its stance on reservation. The women leaders of the 1940s, who were progressive and educated women largely affiliated to Left-leaning organizations, felt that reservation goes against the concept of equality. Over successive elections, the women leaders realized that political parties were not keen on giving tickets to women candidates and very few were getting elected to the parliament and legislative assemblies. 'After Emergency and the awareness generated in the fight for restoration of democracy, the issue of political participation of women to strengthen democracy was foregrounded. Since Independence the experience was the denial of tickets to women in the arena of parliamentary politics. We realized that women were mobilizers and participants in the democratic process but never part of decision-making. The experience of women's reservations in the panchayats was very positive. It was a logical step to demand reservations in parliament and in state assemblies,' says Karat.

Giving more tickets does not guarantee increased representation, she feels. 'It is no point having political parties reserve seats in their lists in the present system. Unless there is a proportional representation system, party lists with women do not guarantee an increase in women's numbers in the parliament, because there is no guarantee that the woman in the party list will be given a winning seat. This can only be achieved if seats are reserved. The bill was passed in the Rajya Sabha in March 2010. Since then it is in cold storage. The conclusion is clear: there is neither the political will nor the intention to increase women's representation to at least one third in elected bodies at the state and national level,' says Karat. The Left leader acknowledges the inherent bias against women in politics. 'It is true that women have to work much harder to get heard whether in an elected body or outside and are often not even considered eligible to speak on a so-called serious matter or shoulder a responsibility. This is reflective of the inherent bias that women face in politics. We have seen how women's opinions are often treated with a dismissive or patronizing attitude. This happens in parliament as well as within the party. The general attitude makes it difficult for women in politics,' she says.

Karat, however, feels that women in Left politics have an advantage over women in other political formations because ideologically Left parties have a strong commitment to gender equality. 'This is not to say that patriarchal influences and behaviour are absent. But it is considered a collective responsibility of all party members both men and women to root out what is considered an alien trend in a Communist party. The most empowering aspect of being in the party is the comradeship that develops, based on common goals. Participation in struggles, sometimes risking one's life, developing powerful relationships driven by shared principles and ideals,' says Karat adding, 'This experience is quite different from women in bourgeois parties who must rely on family connections or other factors and when all politics is geared towards individual goals women do feel disadvantaged. Sexism is also rampant at different levels in many of these parties making it difficult for women.'

Karat and her husband Prakash have been considered the power couple of CPI(M). Being married to a comrade in the same party has left Karat open to comments sometimes conveying that she has risen through the ranks because of her husband, who held the top post of the CPI(M) general secretary from 2005 to 2015. Karat feels that women have to work harder than men in every field. 'There will always be a section of opinion which would diminish your work by saying that you achieved it because of your spouse. This does not ever happen to men. Women, in any field, have to work harder than men and it is no different in politics. You have to be true to yourself and develop a thick skin when such comments are made, otherwise it would be difficult to work. In a society where patriarchal notions remain dominant, it is essential for women to fight it in every sphere, at every level. There is often a default attitude of men in positions of power being dismissive of a woman or her work or patronizing about it. Yes, I have faced it in my own political journey, but predominantly from those outside such as the anti-communist sections of the media, than within my own party,' says Karat adding she can't imagine being married to someone not in the party. 'When one's whole life is dedicated and practically 24x7 hours and days in party work, I can't see how one could live with a partner who was outside this world. As far as the actual spheres of responsibility are concerned, Prakash's work has been on a different trajectory. He has been at the party centre and all the responsibilities of central work for decades whereas I have been more involved in mass work such as in trade unions, then the women's organization, and now am working with the Adivasi platform,' says Karat.

There is more to be achieved within the party. 'We have more women now in the Central Committee. But we are barely 20 per cent as far as party membership is concerned. We are trying to push a sensitive approach to enable a bigger recruitment of women. This mandatory inclusion of more women in committees will be reflected in the party constitution too,' says Karat.

AMBIKA SONI

The Loyalist

A Sikh should be the chief minister of Punjab—this was the argument Ambika Soni gave to Sonia Gandhi as she declined to take over the reins of the government in the northwestern border state. It was September 2021 and the assembly elections were just five months away in Punjab, one of the six states the politically marginalized national party was in power in. The Grand Old Party was battling a crisis—its reliable Chief Minister Captain Amarinder Singh had clearly lost popularity with the electorate and partymen; it was trying to balance the political ambitions of the rebelling cricketer-turned-politician Navjot Singh Sidhu who had the support of a majority of the Congress's members of Legislative Assembly (MLAs); and the restless party workers who were exploring an opportunity in a resurgent rival, the Aam Aadmi Party (AAP).

Captain Amarinder Singh dramatically resigned as Punjab chief minister on 18 September and Gandhi turned to her trusted lieutenant—the five-term Rajya Sabha member Ambika Soni. Born in Lahore, in undivided Punjab, Soni hailed from a Punjabi–Sikh family, had a bond with Hoshiarpur, contested and lost the 2014 parliamentary elections from Punjab's Anandpur Sahib constituency and had donated ten acres of land in her husband's Bajwara village in Hoshiarpur for an armed forces training institute in 2019. Above all, she was acceptable to most MLAs and a belligerent Sidhu. 'If you do not make a Sikh chief minister in Punjab, which state will you make one in? It was an attempt to maintain the cultural identity of the state,' Soni explains her decision. Punjab has had only three non-Sikh chief ministers in Gopi Chand Bhargava, Bhim Sen Sachar, and Ram Kishan. Following the reorganization of states on a linguistic basis in 1967, Punjab has never had a non-Sikh chief minister. 'Mrs Gandhi called me to say that she was convinced I should take charge. I explained that it is only now that the Congress has become acceptable to the Sikh community. After the 1984 riots, Congress has formed the government twice in Punjab. The community would have felt wronged if a Sikh had not been made the chief minister,' she says. After explaining to her party president, Soni emerged out of her Lodhi Estate residence to tell the waiting media that only a Sikh would be the chief minister of Punjab. Many within the Congress likened it to Sonia Gandhi's sacrifice in 2004 when she declined to become the prime minister after the Congress-led UPA's victory in the parliamentary elections.

Soni did not become the king but the kingmaker in Punjab. She recommended the name of Charanjit Singh Channi, and Punjab got its first chief minister from the socially and economically backward Ramdasia Sikh community. She feels had she accepted the chief ministerial assignment, the next five months would have been spent warding off attacks from the Opposition parties on how a non-Sikh had been sent from Delhi to the state. 'Shiromani Akali Dal's candidate was a Sikh—Sukhbir Singh Badal. Though AAP had not declared its candidate till then but everyone knew the party would back Bhagwant Mann, who is a Sikh. The BJP came in the reckoning only when it aligned with Sikh leaders like Captain Amarinder Singh and S. S. Dhindsa. Congress just could not take the risk,' she says. Over the months, Channi's unassuming ways as a chief minister put the Congress back in the game for February 2022 elections. The party, however, was routed when the fledgling AAP got a landslide mandate. 'For me it was enough that the party had thought I was suitable to be the chief minister. I have only wanted a place for myself in the Congress and I have got it—not through sycophancy but by hard work, honesty, and sacrifice,' says Soni. It was a masterstroke. The seventy-nine-year-old Congresswoman had shown why she has survived so long in politics. After decades of serving the Gandhi family so loyally, she had gently but firmly declined to play into their hands and lead the party to an impending defeat.

A NEW WORLD

Soni is one of the few politicians who has worked closely with every member of the powerful Gandhi family. But growing up, joining politics was not even a remote possibility for Soni. 'I had a very protected and sheltered upbringing. Politics was not a consideration for me,' she says. Soni's father Nakul Sen Wadhwa was an Indian Civil Services officer. At the time of Partition, he was posted as the Amritsar collector and worked assiduously for the rehabilitation of refugees pouring in from across the border. Over the years, Wadhwa endeared himself to Jawaharlal Nehru, India's first prime minister. Soni considers her progressive father a very big influence in her life. Ambo, as he called her, studied in Welham Girls School in Dehradun. She later did her college from Delhi University's Indraprastha College.

Young Ambika Sen (as she was known then) met Uday Soni, an Indian Foreign Service officer, and love blossomed over some couplets of Urdu. Though she confesses that with her English boarding school education she was not familiar with the Urdu poetry of Ghalib and Iqbal, she was quite taken by her persistent suitor. Equally keen to impress him, she persuaded her cousin to teach her some lines of romantic Urdu poetry. She memorized them without understanding the meaning and then recited before Uday. But the poetry had just the opposite effect. The mischievous cousin had taught her a couplet which spoke about parting ways. Soni quickly cleared the air when Uday explained the meaning, and all was well between the lovestruck couple. The courtship was just three months long and the two got married. Soni was nineteen and happily took to the life of a diplomat's wife. She travelled the world with him, picking up languages and pursuing academic courses. When Uday was posted in Cuba, Soni did her master's in Spanish art and literature.

In 1968, Uday returned to India and Soni joined the reservation section of Air France. This was a time when Prime Minister Indira Gandhi had initiated massive reforms like the nationalization of banks. 'We were the generation which was in awe of Indiraji. Her economic programme, especially bank nationalization and abolition of privy purses had inspired an entire generation. She was such a charismatic mass leader that many of us joined politics to volunteer for the Congress,' says Soni. Shankar Dayal Sharma was the party president. Soni's first job was to cut newspaper clippings and flag important news items for the party. This was also the time when women did not join politics. The reaction from her relatives was that of shock. 'They thought I had gone mad. But my parents, especially my father, were very supportive. He gave me the best advice—join politics if you can make a difference and be different, don't join if you will be like the rest of them,' she says. Soni describes her husband's views as progressive. 'Neither was permission sought nor expected to be sought. He (Uday Soni) was too progressive to think that I would be the coy wife following him around the world. Follow him around I did for quite a few years. But when this opportunity came, he did not stop me,' she says. He had, in fact, surprised her with his views quite early on in marriage. 'As soon as we got married he spoke about freedom and charting out one's own course to develop one's full potential. I was so shocked. I thought he was having an affair and wanted me out of the way. I asked him why was he saying all this?' she says laughing heartily at her nineteen-year-old young self.

What helped her was the watchful eye of Gandhi. 'I knew nothing about politics and could not boast of a political legacy. It was a tough world for women. But I had the reassurance that Indiraji was watching over me. There is an instance I remember when some of us volunteers were receiving a dignitary at the airport. Everyone carried a rose to give but I was a novice and I did not carry anything. Indiraji noticed my discomfort and instead gave me the bouquet which she had been given. These little gestures really gave me confidence,' says Soni. Soon after she joined the Congress, Uday was summoned and objections were raised by his seniors over Soni working with a political party. He was given different reasons including it being a violation of service rules and how he would not go too far as this may be considered a subversive service. The young couple sat down with the service rules but could not find anything that forbade Soni from working for a political party. 'There was a session of the All India Congress Committee (AICC) in Patna and all the volunteers were sitting on the ground waiting for the leaders. Indiraji entered and stood on the dais looking out for someone. Then she gestured in our direction asking someone to come and see her. We were all confused till a Seva Dal volunteer asked me to come and see her. All eyes were on me. She asked, "I believe you have a problem." I don't know how she got to know about this incident. Then she asked me to go meet Nandini Satpathy,' says Soni, who met Satpathy. After this, Soni never faced a problem.

Soon she realized that she enjoyed her political work more than her day-time job and quit Air France. Soni worked as joint convenor of the party's foreign affairs department with Mukul Banerjee as convenor. As the Congress readied to face the 1971 parliamentary elections, Soni wrote a letter to Gandhi making a case for Banerjee, a woman candidate from the New Delhi parliamentary constituency. Gandhi asked her principal secretary, P. N. Haksar, to look into Soni's recommendation. 'I told her how we should fight New Delhi parliamentary constituency and she told P. N. Haksar (principal secretary to Indira Gandhi) to look into it. This is how Indiraji was, a true leader,' says Soni who remembers seeing the letter decades later. 'Recently Jairam (former union minister Jairam Ramesh) showed me the same letter. He had found it in the archives while researching for his book on P. N. Haksar,' (*Intertwined Lives: P N Haksar and Indira Gandhi*) she says. Mukul Banerjee got a ticket from the New Delhi parliamentary seat in the 1971 elections and Soni campaigned energetically for her. Following Banerjee's victory, Soni was asked to fight the Delhi Metropolitan Council election in 1972 (Delhi did not have a legislative assembly then). 'I did not know anything about elections and I did not want to fight one. So I went back and joined my husband on his posting abroad. There were no cell phones those days so nobody could really contact you immediately,' she remembers with amusement. But she was back soon.

THE FIERY RETURN

It was a chance meeting with Prime Minister Indira Gandhi in Rome that brought her back into politics. 'Indiraji was travelling to Europe. There was a problem with the plane and her stopover in Rome was longer than expected. She spotted me when the embassy officials were being introduced and asked "What are you doing here?" And I told her that my husband was posted in Rome. During that brief halt I was asked to escort her to a few places. I remember she asked me again "What are you doing here?" When I repeated my answer, she said, "I know what he is doing here but what are you doing?" She asked me to go along with her and work for Congress,' says Soni remembering distinctly how her explanation of having a three-year-old son and husband was brushed aside. 'I went home and packed my bags and got onto the prime minister's plane with my son. We flew to Hungary,' she says. The prime minister's delegation was staying at the ambassador's home. Soni remembers wondering what was expected of her on the trip. 'I just went into my room with my son. Indiraji knocked on the door and like all curious three-year-olds my son rushed and answered the door. She told him, "Leave your mother here and come with me." She just took him around. This is how she was,' says Soni. She came to New Delhi and started living with her parents, who took care of her young son while she manoeuvred the world of politics.

Soni joined the Indian Youth Congress, which was considered Gandhi's younger son Sanjay's brigade. A fast learner, fluent in several languages, and articulate, the fiery attractive woman became a part of Sanjay's coterie. While others were scared of Sanjay, Soni matched steps with him delivering on every task assigned to her. It was a comfortable relationship which was construed in the political circles as having romantic undertones. 'There was no such thing,' Soni says attributing the comfortable relationship to her habit of speaking her mind. 'He was a colleague and we worked together on Indiraji's vision and the Youth Congress five-point programme.[1] I used to speak my mind in front of him and often stood up to him. He respected that.' She does not make much of the rumour mills. 'The easiest way to bring a woman down is not to run faster than her but to assassinate her character. A woman will never stoop down to that level because she always has a family to look after and answer to,' she says.

Those were the heady days of aggressive youth politics. But fear wasn't something Soni felt. 'I remember there was a Youth Congress convention in New Delhi in 1976 and I got a call in the middle of the night saying youth delegates from one state were clashing with another state's delegates. My father had given me an old Matador to drive. I just took that in the dead of the night, picked up the person who had called me and we drove to the venue. Bottles were being smashed. I just shouted "Haan kya ho raha hai (Yes, what is happening here)?" A woman's booming voice in the middle of the night shocked everyone. This had the effect I wanted and then I told everyone to just calm down. Then other leaders came in and took charge. No, I never felt fear then,' she says. Facing an angry crowd was a part of life as an Indian Youth Congress volunteer. 'We were once asked to go to Uttar Pradesh to campaign in an election. When we reached the ground, there were tall sturdy men standing with latths (big sticks) and they asked us to return. Women cannot campaign, they said. That was because in those days women did not. But we did,' she says.

Soni became the first woman president of the Indian Youth Congress in 1975—the year Prime Minister Indira Gandhi declared a state of Emergency. On 12 June 1975, the Allahabad High Court delivered a shocking verdict in the State of Uttar Pradesh vs Raj Narain case—it found Gandhi guilty of electoral malpractices. Sanjay's coterie rallied behind Gandhi and advised her not to resign. A massive rally was organized the next day in New Delhi, diverting all public transport to ferry people from neighbouring states as a show of support. On the day, a group of socialist youth were marching towards Gandhi's 1 Safdarjung Road residence raising slogans of, 'Indira Gandhi murdabad. Indira Gandhi isteefa do (Down with Indira Gandhi. Resign Indira Gandhi).' Soni was standing across the road with Youth Congress activists. She crossed the road with fellow partymen and a scuffle followed. A black and white photograph of a young Soni raising her hand to hit a youth is one of the lasting images of the Emergency, which was to be imposed in less than two weeks. Decades later Soni accepts there was a scuffle, 'We were young. The youth were raising slogans against our leader, our prime minister. We couldn't have looked the other way. I remember crossing the road with the other activists, catching hold of one of them and raising my hand. Had I been a Youth Congress man would anyone have thought twice about this street scuffle? No.'

During this time from June 1975 till March 1977, most of Gandhi's political opponents were imprisoned and the press muzzled. Sanjay implemented several programmes including mass sterilization camps, which many accused of being involuntary, through his coterie. Soni being the Youth Congress president was at the forefront of putting into effect Sanjay's vision. In her book *The Emergency: A Personal History*, Coomi Kapoor has written how Soni had acquired a reputation of being 'free with her hands'.

Soni's power during the years has been elaborately described by Kapoor through an incident with her husband Virendra at a function in Red Fort, Delhi. 'On that evening at the Red Fort function, Soni and a couple of her Youth Congress activists got hold of a boy who was barely out of his teens. She ordered the others present, including the police, to thrash the boy. Virendra being Virendra felt it necessary to intervene and chide Soni: "Why are you beating this boy? What has he done? If he has broken any law, the police will look after it. You are not the police." Soni stopped for a second, assuming he was a plain-clothes policeman. But when she saw him walking away from the scene, she was taken aback by his effrontery and asked who he was. He nonchalantly replied, "I am an ordinary citizen like you." "But don't you think that instead of helping me arrest these boys, you were preventing me from getting hold of them?" she shot back. Bajwa came running up to her and the two went into a huddle. Within a split second Bajwa ordered the police to arrest Virendra as well.'[2] Soni, however, denies wielding such power. 'This didn't happen. I have sat with Virendra later to discuss this. What authority will a Youth Congress activist have to direct the police?' she says.

The Emergency years saw Soni's real rise to power. The firebrand leader organized several rallies to show public support for Gandhi's decision to impose the Emergency. 'It was Sanjay's coterie that went into overdrive to protect his mother's position. Between 12 and 24 June, daily pro-Indira Gandhi demonstrations, rallies, and public meetings were held, the usual rent-a-crowd shows organized by Congressmen... writes Kapoor describing the role of the Indian Youth Congress and Sanjay's aides during the

Emergency.[3] With Gandhi's benevolent gaze and Sanjay's firm backing, Soni became a force to reckon with. In 1976, thirty-four-year-old Soni was elected to the Rajya Sabha. In November 1976, the AICC session at Gauhati (present day Guwahati in Assam) established Soni as a power centre. The most significant event was the emergence of the Youth Congress as a force. Officially, it was accorded a status and granted a blessing. In the prime minister's words, the Youth Congress 'had stolen the thunder out of us'. 'The fire of the youth has been lit,' said Youth Congress president Ambika Soni in a stirring address.[4] Both Sanjay Gandhi and she were accorded a welcome as big as the prime minister and Congress president D. K. Barooah. The roads were lined with banners and Sanjay and Ambika both appeared on luridly coloured calendars, doing the rows of deities and film stars,' Sunil Sethi wrote in his report on the session.[5] Soni's elevation had left several die-hard Congressmen bitter. One of them was Priya Ranjan Dasmunsi, whom Soni had replaced as the Youth Congress president. Dasmunsi and Kerala Congress President A. K. Antony were the only leaders to criticize the aggressive ways of the Youth Congress under Soni and the stranglehold of Sanjay Gandhi during the Emergency at the Gauhati session.[6] The criticism, however, did little in dampening the spirits of an aggressive Youth Congress. Within two months of the Gauhati session, Prime Minister Indira Gandhi called for the parliamentary elections.

The March 1977 parliamentary elections, which was fought by the Janata Party on the Emergency plank, saw the Congress routed and Gandhi defeated from her seat in Rae Bareilly, Uttar Pradesh.

THE FALLING OUT

The Janata Party government instituted a commission of inquiry under the former Chief Justice of India J. C. Shah to inquire into the infringement of civil liberties and excesses committed during the twenty-one-month-long Emergency. The knives were out

against Sanjay's brigade within the Congress. Soni, with her easy
access to Gandhi and Sanjay and her stupendous rise within the
Congress, had earned herself vicious enemies. Soni remembers
those months of hectic meetings within the party and at homes
of several leaders and says, 'I used to send Youth Congress
leaders to different meetings to ensure our side was also put
forward. I don't think this was taken too kindly by leaders.
There were people around Indiraji who were instigating her
constantly.' Soni says Gandhi used to come out of her residential
quarters and walk through a corridor to a room full of leaders
and meet them. 'She used to instantly greet me and take me
aside to talk. I remember one day she came out and just walked
past me. I was shocked. I kept standing there waiting. She took
a round and when she was returning, she turned and remarked,
"You must be very busy. I heard you have been meeting a lot of
people." I was so hurt. I just stood there. She was the one who
brought me into politics and sustained me. I drew my strength
from her,' remembers Soni. She saw herself gradually edged out
of the inner circle and very quickly in political wilderness.

Congress saw bitter in-fighting, open blame games, and palace
intrigues in the months after electoral defeat. 'Admitting her
cynicism about national politics, Mrs Soni said that she had not
met Mrs Gandhi and Sanjay since April. But she was determined
to make the best of her two years in parliament. "I feel liberated
as a member of the Opposition in some ways," she said. "One
can say things which one could not as a member of the ruling
party for fear of embarrassing your colleagues." The year had not
been too promising for her. Her husband, Uday Soni, now India's
Ambassador to Morocco, has left to take up his post. Mrs Soni
thinks that she "can hardly represent the people flying between
Morocco and New Delhi". "It's a big conflict in my life. I have
to be with him in Morocco although being an ambassador's
wife is really no more than being a glorified housekeeper. And
I want to stay on in Parliament here as well. After my term,
maybe I'll decide to quit politics, or perhaps I'll give up my seat
earlier. I think we politicians have spoilt the game for ourselves.

I've seen a lot in the last two years. I'm not sure I want to stay in the game,"' an *India Today* cover story from January 1978 issue quotes her as saying.[7]

As Gandhi walked out of the Congress with loyalists to form her own party, Soni stayed behind in the faction which came to be known as the Indian National Congress (Socialist) or Congress (S). Sharad Pawar, A. K. Antony, Priya Ranjan Dasmunsi, and Chandrajit Yadav were a part of this faction. Soni found a mentor in Pawar and later in Chandrajit Yadav. The fallout with Gandhi was final. Soni appeared before the Shah Commission to clear her name. 'Law had to take its course. Had I not appeared before the commission of inquiry it would have seemed that I had something to hide. I did not,' she says. Soni maintains that she was not aware of forced sterilizations, a programme she was associated with. 'It was a lesson we learnt the hard way. When political representatives are not involved in any programme run by an overzealous administration which does not fear the wrath of people, excesses can happen. I learnt of these much later,' she says.

India's experiment with the Janata Party government was short-lived. Early elections were called in January 1980 and Gandhi, Sanjay, and his loyalists swept back to power. Within six months, Sanjay died in a tragic air crash. Gandhi initiated son Rajiv into politics. Many former Congressmen returned to the party fold. But not Soni. 'I couldn't have gone crawling back just because I couldn't stay out of a party in power. I had taken a decision and I stuck to it,' she says on why she never returned to the Congress till Gandhi was alive. 'There was mutual respect,' she says recalling how she had written to Gandhi to complain about a bunch of Youth Congress activists heckling her on Rajpath. 'I was driving from parliament in my car and four to five young men started following my car. I stopped at the traffic signal on Rajpath and they came beside me, opened the car door and started raising slogans against me. I answered back and got into my car and drove away with the door open. I was incensed and wrote to Indiraji complaining about the incident and how it was unacceptable. She wrote back to me saying if what I was saying was true, it was unfortunate and she had no political differences with me,' remembers Soni of her political mentor.

The Congress (S) and Gandhi's Congress (I) even wrangled over plots of land for the party office. The Congress's headquarters at Jawahar Bhawan were planned on two plots of land—1 and 3 Raisina Road (opposite Shastri Bhawan near Parliament House in the heart of Delhi). However, Congress (S) did not part with 3 Raisina Road. In 1986, a charming Rajiv Gandhi persuaded Pawar to merge Congress (S) with the parent party and return of the plot was spelt out in the terms of merger. After eight years, Soni returned to her parent party to work with yet another generation of the Gandhi family.

A COMEBACK

Soni made a political comeback of sorts when Rajiv formed a panel under V. N. Gadgil to explore the possibility of lowering India's voting age from twenty-one. Vishvjit Singh, Pawan Bansal, Jayanthi Natarajan, and Soni were members. Incidentally, Bansal, Natarajan, and Soni went on to become ministers when the Congress-led United Progressive Alliance (UPA) came to power in 2004.

Soni has remained an astute Gandhi family loyalist over the years. If Gandhi initiated her into politics, Sanjay propelled her into prominence, Rajiv fell back upon her and later his wife Sonia Gandhi depended on her for tough assignments. 'I strongly feel that the people who support the Congress recognize the Congress led by the Gandhi family. That is why all those who broke away at different times to form Congress parties of their own had to come back and rejoin the mainstream Congress. I do feel that the leadership of the Gandhis is iconic,' she explains. It is this unquestioned loyalty and impeccable organizational skills that saw her being entrusted with major responsibilities after Sonia staged a coup of sorts and took over as Congress president in March 1998. Soni became the president of the All India Mahila Congress, the women's wing of the party, in 1998. She took on the role of Sonia's political secretary—a powerful post which she held for one and a half years when she gave way to Ahmed Patel.

What entrenched her in Sonia's inner circle was her vociferous support during a May 1999 Congress Working Committee (CWC) meeting, where the Congress president's foreign origin was discussed in detail. This meeting had paved the way for the ouster of Pawar, P. A. Sangma, and Tariq Anwar from the Congress. 'On 15 May 1999, the Congress President called a meeting of the CWC. For no apparent reason, she suddenly pulled out a sheet of paper and read out aloud: "I was born outside India. If this becomes an issue in the campaign, how would it impact our party's performance in the election?" She requested CWC members to voice their opinion candidly,' Pawar has written in his book *On My Terms: From the Grassroot to the Corridors of Power.*[8] 'Arjun Singh was first to speak. "You may be foreigner by birth but you became a domicile of this country after marriage. You did not leave the country even after your husband and mother-in-law were assassinated. Just as you embraced this country, the people of India also have accepted you as one of them. For them, you are the Rashtra maata (the mother of the nation). You alone deserve to lead the nation and the party." Arjun Singh more or less set the tone of the speeches that followed. A. K. Antony, Ghulam Nabi Azad, and Ambika Soni were all one to express their loyalty,' says Pawar in the book.[9]

Soni climbed up the organizational ladder quickly under Sonia and was one of the eight general secretaries who are given charge of states in the Congress. Within a year, she was back in the Rajya Sabha in January 2000—after a twenty-four-year hiatus. This time, the political pitch was very different—the Congress was in the Opposition and the BJP-led National Democratic Alliance (NDA) under Atal Bihari Vajpayee had formed a stable non-Congress government at the centre. Soni had also graduated from her aggressive street politics to tactfully tackling the government inside the parliament. From saffronization of education under the BJP to electricity reforms, Soni raked up several issues in the Rajya Sabha to corner the NDA government.

Riding high on his development agenda, Vajpayee decided to advance the parliamentary elections of 2004 by six months. A well-crafted election strategy saw the Congress-led UPA come to power for the next decade. Internally, the victory led to a clamour for Sonia to take over as the prime minister. However, she chose to be the power behind the throne. Prime Minister Manmohan Singh constituted his council of ministers and Soni got a letter. She went to Sonia Gandhi's 10 Janpath Road residence and declined the offer. 'I was always an organizational person. Party work excited me. So I requested Sonia ji to allow me to work as a general secretary,' she says. Sonia agreed. But it wasn't for long that Soni could stay out of government. She joined as the tourism and culture minister in Singh's first major cabinet reshuffle in January 2006.

THE GOVERNANCE EXPERIENCE

Soni's stint in the government began when the Congress-led UPA alliance, the first alliance the party formed with outside support of the Left Front, was fairly comfortable at the centre. She came with a brief—to improve hotel infrastructure and make India an attractive tourist destination ahead of the Commonwealth Games which New Delhi was slated to host four years later in 2010. This was no mean task. Incredible India, the government's international campaign to attract foreign tourists since 2002, had failed to become a brand. India had a shortage of 100,000 rooms to cater to foreign and domestic tourists. On top of this, bomb blasts and the law and order in states had made several countries issue travel advisories against going to India. The World Trade and Travel Council had declared India as one of the fastest-growing sector economies. Soni knew the potential and challenges of her first assignment in the government. 'This was an assignment very close to my heart and it was the most satisfying amongst all my portfolios,' says Soni.

Known to be a demanding but reasonable boss, Soni worked closely with her officers to deliver on the targets. She took the first step by engaging with the major players of the tourism industry. The inputs were specific—India needed to increase hotel rooms available, work on its image to attract foreign tourists, address law and order, and introduce new concepts to tap different tourist segments. Armed with these inputs, Soni rebranded Incredible India with attractive media campaigns. Medical tourism, rural tourism, and wellness tourism—three new concepts were introduced by Soni to market India as a safe and cheap destination.

She persuaded states with high tourist inflow to set up a separate tourist police force. 'The idea was to ensure that the tourists had a place—a specific police station or tourist police officers—who could address their complaints,' she says. An IAS officer, closely involved with Soni throughout her term as tourism minister, spoke extensively about the turnaround. 'We began with rebranding Incredible India with a powerful media campaign. The emphasis was on impressive visuals like a tiger in Ranthambore or beautiful images of the Taj Mahal. Then we used the theme 'Atithi Devo Bhava (Guest is God)' to give a glimpse of Indian hospitality and warmth to international and national tourists,' says the officer, who spoke on condition of anonymity. India shone on the international stage with these campaigns. 'Incredible India was taken to the world and it went viral. We developed new tourism circuits and destinations,' says Soni. With her team of hard working officers, Soni managed to get the UNESCO World Heritage Site status for the Red Fort in 2007 and for the Kalka–Shimla railway line in 2008. Soni considers getting elected as chairman of the executive council of General Assembly of United Nations World Tourism Organisation (UNWTO) in 2007 as a big achievement. 'What more could one ask for? It was recognition of our efforts,' she says. During her stint, India saw a 12 to 14 per cent increase in foreign tourist arrivals.

However, the first-time minister could not address the problem of infrastructure shortage. Her 'bed and breakfast' scheme, which allowed Delhi's homeowners to get a star rating from the tourism ministry to give out their rooms on rent to tourists failed.

While tourism brought her recognition, Soni courted her first controversy as the minister of culture in 2007. At the heart of the political storm was the Ram Setu or Adam's bridge, a mythological site that is supposed to have been built in the treta yuga by an army of monkeys for Lord Rama to reach Lanka and rescue Sita from the clutches of the demon king Ravana. It is a 30 kilometre stretch comprising of limestone shoals from the Rameswaram Island in Tamil Nadu to Mannar Island in Sri Lanka. On the insistence of its crucial southern alliance partner Dravida Munnetra Kazhagam (DMK), the Congress-led UPA launched the Sethusamudram Shipping Canal Project, which proposed a 167-kilometre-long shipping canal across the Gulf of Mannar, Palk Bay, and the Palk Strait linking the Arabian Sea to the Bay of Bengal, thereby opening the shallow Sethusamudram Sea for large ships to ease trade with Sri Lanka. Large ships from the west have to go around Sri Lanka to reach India's eastern coast now and the project proposed a shorter sea route saving the circumnavigation of about 400 kilometres. The alignment of Sethusamudram shipping canal, as proposed in 2005 by the UPA, would have meant dredging and the removal of limestone shoals. The project was challenged in the Supreme Court in 2005 on environmental and religious grounds. Petitioners argued that the government had not considered any of the other six alternate routes and the alignment under consideration could cause environmental damage.

The more politically potent challenge came from Dr Subramanian Swamy, then Janata Party president who later joined BJP in 2013. Dr Swamy filed a public interest litigation (PIL) arguing that any dredging of Ram Setu would hurt the sentiments of Hindus and the Setu should be declared a national monument. The Supreme Court sought the culture ministry's view on this. On 12 September 2007, the Archaeological Survey

of India (ASI), which comes under the culture ministry, filed
an affidavit which questioned the existence of Lord Rama and
termed Ram Setu as a natural formation of limestone shoals.
ASI Director (Monuments) C. Dorjee stated, 'The petitioners
while seeking relief have primarily relied upon the contents of
the Valimiki Ramayana, the Ram Charit Manas by Tulsidas and
mythological texts, which formed an important part of ancient
Indian literature, but which cannot be said to be historical records
to incontrovertibly prove the existence of the characters or the
occurrence of the event, depicted therein. Whereas it is submitted
that the ASI is aware of and duly respects the deep religious
import bestowed upon these texts by the Hindu community across
the globe, it is also submitted that the study of human history,
which is the primary object of the ASI, like other sciences and
fields of study, must be carried out in a scientific manner using
available technological aids, and its findings must be based on
tangible material evidence.'[10]

The Opposition BJP was quick to jump on this affidavit. It
was a gaffe which almost cost Soni her ministry. She says it was
her habit of reading every file before signing it or sending it for
cabinet approval that saved her. 'I emerged unscathed because
of my remarks that I had pencilled in the margin. After reading
the affidavit I had written carefully asking officers to check the
claims. I had reviewed the affidavit and suggested three deletions.
While two were carried out, one wasn't,' she remembers about
the controversy. Soni was in Japan when the affidavit was filed.
She got a call from Prime Minister Manmohan Singh on how
such an affidavit had been filed. 'After I returned from Japan,
I went back to the ministry and sought the original file. It was
kept safely. I saw my remarks were in the column and the
suggested changes had not been made. I sought time from the
prime minister and went with the original file and showed him
the file notings. I was prepared to resign. After all, the affidavit
had been filed by my ministry. But resignation was never asked
for,' she says. The government withdrew the affidavit. It was
a different matter that the Sethusamudram project was first

proposed during the British Raj in 1860 and then launched much later by the BJP-led NDA government under Atal Bihari Vajpayee in 1998. The UPA's attempt to challenge Lord Rama gave the BJP enough ammunition to push the ruling government into a corner and form a committee to look into the realignment of the Sethusamudram shipping canal. Fifteen years on, the project remains stalled.

Despite such political controversies, the Congress-led UPA government won a second term in May 2009. With this victory, Soni got what she terms as her most challenging assignment. She was handpicked by Gandhi to take charge as the information and broadcasting (I&B) minister. It may not be what is considered the 'big five portfolios', but internally for every government I&B is a sensitive assignment as it deals with the government's public image. 'It is not an easy ministry. There are many pressures. Government advertisements are a revenue source for several newspapers. Around this time, there was a sudden increase in the number of television channels, especially regional channels. It made my job tougher,' says Soni. As I&B minister, Soni remembers how a serving minister once asked her to cancel the licence of a channel. 'When I asked him why. He said that they were running false propaganda against him trying to extort money. But when I asked him to file a complaint and take it up formally, there was no action from his side. It revealed the other side of media and politics to me,' she says. Soni completed the complicated task of digitalization of cable television.

Challenging as the I&B may have been, Soni did not get the tougher job of government's image management in the last mile when the UPA was bogged down by numerous corruption scandals and a belligerent BJP. In a major cabinet reshuffle in October 2012, the Congress veterans including Mukul Wasnik and Soni were asked to make way for fresh faces. Soni went back to the organization in 2013 as the general secretary in-charge of states, a charge she held till 2020.

THE CHANGING POLITICS

The political landscape of India changed completely in 2014. Congress went for parliamentary elections bearing on its back the burden of scams, anti-incumbency of a ten-year reign, and tainted alliance partners. Rahul Gandhi's 'Idea of India' was pitted against the majoritarian brand of politics being promised by a resurgent BJP under then Gujarat Chief Minister Narendra Modi. Congress pressed its heavyweights into service and Soni was asked to contest a Lok Sabha election from Anandpur Sahib constituency in Punjab. Soni remembers how Sonia had asked her to rope her family in for the campaign. 'What family, ma'am? I had asked her. In all my years in the Congress and later in government, I had taken pains to keep my family out of the world of politics. My son did not ever step into my office in Shastri Bhawan when I was a minister,' she says. The strategy fell apart under the mammoth Modi wave India witnessed and Soni, like many others in the Congress, was defeated. She, however, remained in the Rajya Sabha.

In all her years in politics, Soni has always rallied for women's political empowerment. 'Women's empowerment is not possible till they are politically empowered. This is why there is an urgent need for the parliament to pass the Women's Reservation Bill. We have seen how reservation in panchayats and local bodies have brought forth women leaders,' she says. Soni had once 'gifted' the demand for 33 per cent reservation for women in legislatures and the parliament to Sonia. After taking over as the president of All India Mahila Congress in 1998, Soni came up with the idea of collecting signatures of women across India demanding reservation and gift them to Sonia on her birthday. The women's wing collected 33 lakh signatures and gifted the document to Sonia on 9 December 1998. It took Sonia a decade before she could finally rally enough support within her party and the Congress government to introduce the Bill in 2008. Soni is still waiting for it to be passed by the parliament.

IV

The Future Leaders

SMRITI Z. IRANI

The Giant Slayer

'I can't find my bicycle,' the eleven-year-old girl was exasperated. The realization that it could have been stolen from outside her home broke her heart. She went to her grandfather, 'Dadu, I think it has been stolen.' The indulgent Navy veteran tried to pacify the child, 'Who do you think stole it?' She insisted a neighbour's son had. But Dadu wanted to divert his favourite granddaughter's attention and told her about the mechanisms put in place to report a crime. You have to go to a police station and file a complaint, he told her thinking he would distract the child. Little did he know that the eleven-year-old would walk to the R. K. Puram Sector 8 police station and demand her complaint be filed. But then she was the same girl who walked two kilometres daily from the Malai Mandir to the Little Flower School in R. K. Puram. When Dadu told her that they had money only for the movie tickets and not for the ride home, she happily walked the five kilometres from home to the Chanakya Cinema Hall. After all, it was a treat for a perpetually cash-strapped family. It is hardly suprising then that the girl who went to Mumbai to run a courier logistics company went on to become a Miss India finalist, Indian television's favourite bahu, the youngest minister in Prime Minister Narendra Modi's first cabinet, and the woman who dealt a body blow to the Nehru–Gandhi family by wresting their borough Amethi from the dynast, Rahul Gandhi, in the 2019 parliamentary elections.

You can love the approachable minister or hate the articulate you-can't-fault-my-beliefs power woman, but you can never ignore Smriti Zubin Irani. Known to have ruffled enough feathers within the Bharatiya Janata Party (BJP) and made many a stalwarts insecure with her proximity to the top leaders of the saffron party, Smriti's story has all the masala of a never-ending serial from the stables of Ekta Kapoor, her telly mentor and a close friend.

FINDING HER PLACE

She was born Smriti Malhotra to a Punjabi-Maharashtrian father and a Bengali mother. The oldest of three daughters, Smriti was close to her Dadu, who was a swayam sewak of the RSS. Her initial years were spent in Little Flower School that her grandfather had helped in establishing. Growing up, there were financial constraints as her father did not have a stable income and her mother worked multiple jobs, including as a housekeeper in Taj Mahal Hotel on Mansingh Road. She remembers eyeing the big school across the road from Little Flower and wondering what it would take for her to go there. 'A lot of money,' her mother had told her. She finally cornered a kind nun at the Holy Child Auxilium School and enquired the details. She was told she had to clear an exam to get admission in class sixth. 'Will you put me in if I clear the exam?' she remembers asking her mother. 'But it is expensive,' her mother repeated. Smriti sat for the exam and cleared it. Her mother found a scholarship meant for the children of Tata employees and Smriti studied at the premier school. She was the quintessential Delhi girl who tried her hand at everything. Her first job was selling cosmetics for Naturence outside a shop on Janpath. She remembers how a lady, after buying the cosmetics, came back to her and said she spoke very well. Her father owned a courier company, and Smriti told him she wanted to help. She started from the bottom, picking up what is known in logistics as 'load' from Mahipalpur and the Old Delhi railway station at odd hours. Ask her if as an eighteen-year-old school girl she felt insecure or awkward or had an untoward incident. 'No. None. Nobody messed with me,' she shoots back.

After getting a hang of how things worked in logistics, she came to Mumbai to run a courier agency in Parle. 'Those were the days when no courier reached Thane in less than two days. I first charted all the trains from Parle. Then I realized that the workers were not coming on time. If they came on time and caught the train, a courier could be delivered in less than two days,' she says. So she threatened pay cuts, attracted the wrath of the workers union, but in the end, cut the delivery time to Thane to one-and-a-half days. She returned to Delhi and responded to a newspaper advertisement for Miss India. 'I hadn't even worn heels till then leave alone knowing the walk. I lived in my T-shirt and jeans,' she laughs. Her father deputed his office assistant to chaperone Smriti to the contest. 'After every round she and I thought it was over and I would be walking out to the gate till I was called back,' she says remembering how she surprised everyone, including her own family, by ending up in the top twenty. Then began the struggle of finding her true calling. For a good eighteen months she did the rounds of production houses auditioning for roles, took up small jobs hosting events, and mopped and cleaned at McDonald's. Smriti is not one to hide her humble beginnings. In fact, she talks about it proudly.

'I openly say that I have worked my way up from the trenches. Why not? What's the shame in it?' she asks.

She had borrowed a lakh from her father to make it on her own and the money was depleting soon. Come back and get married, she was told on the phone. The day she agreed, she was offered the role of Tulsi Virani, the priest's sanskari daughter who glued Indians to their television sets like probably only B. R. Chopra's Ramayana and Mahabharata serials had in the 1980s. 'I had gone to Balaji Productions to sign a contract to play some side character in *Ghar Ek Mandir*, which had actors Ram Kapoor and Gautami. They were going to pay me ₹1,500 per day. I remember the day well as it was 23 March, my birthday. A face reader was sitting with Ekta Kapoor in her office—it is all glass and she can look outside. The face reader asked her—"Who is that girl who is standing there, catch her, she will be big,"' she recalls. Ekta Kapoor walked out and asked what she was signing and asked the office to prepare a new contract. 'She asked me how much will I charge? I was quickly doing the math and I couldn't think of a number and just rattled off—₹2,000 per day. She said "done" and before I could realize I was the leading lady in *Kyunki Saas Bhi Kabhi Bahu Thi*. But Ekta paid ₹1,800 no matter the ₹2,000 I asked for,' says Smriti. In her twenties, Smriti did not mind playing a much older character of the ideal *bahu* with sindoor, mangalsutra, and seedha pallu sari. The following years were spent shooting for Ekta Kapoor's Balaji Productions. She met and married Parsi businessman Zubin Irani in 2001. This was Irani's second marriage and he already had a daughter Shanelle from his previous marriage. Smriti remembers how she was shooting even on the day of the wedding. 'I was very clear—there are loans to be paid and I had to work. Ours was a marriage of equals. We split even the cost of the marriage reception. I told him at the outset that I owed my father money and would not be able to contribute to household expenses initially. Not that Zubin ever thought I needed to,' she laughs. The couple had their son Zohr in 2001 and daughter Zoish in 2003. Smriti remembers balancing home, children, and her shoots.

'I also did Vishwa Hindu Parishad (VHP) work on water and women's health in these years,' she says.

Smriti was expecting her daughter Zoish and wanted to complete shooting for as many episodes of *Kyunki* before she took some time off. She invited her cast and crew to her husband's farmhouse in Dahanu outside Mumbai so she could wrap up her schedule. 'Word travelled fast across Dahanu, and soon, excited residents gathered to watch the shoot. Among those who dropped by at the mansion was Manisha Chaudhari, a member of the BJP's Maharashtra wing and currently the MLA from Dahisar.... Recounting the 2003 shoot in Dahanu, Chaudhari said, 'I decided I will go invite her into the BJP,' Chaudhari said. She gathered a group of women, and went to the Irani house. 'I just introduced myself and told her about our party. Smriti said she liked the work of Atalji.' Ashish Shelar, currently the president of the BJP's Mumbai unit, confirmed that Manisha was the one who first introduced Smriti to the BJP. Smriti herself has admitted this in her speeches.[1] But what pushed her to join BJP formally was a statement by the party's Maharashtra veteran Gopinath Munde. 'He said, "Kitni bhi koshish kar lo agar policy nahin badlegi toh kuch nahin badlega aur aap sirf saalon tak sewa hee karoge (No matter how much you try, if the policy does not change, nothing will change and you will keep serving the people for years)." I decided to join the BJP,' says Smriti. She joined the BJP in 2003 in the presence of Pramod Mahajan, Munde, and Mukhtar Abbas Naqvi. Almost two decades later, Smriti would replace Naqvi as minority affairs minister in Modi's second cabinet in 2022.

THE VOICE ON THE STREETS

When Smriti joined the BJP, the party was in power at the Centre and was eyeing to wrest power from the Congress in several states. Her first big assignment was the Rajasthan assembly elections. In the run-up to the 2003 assembly elections, the BJP had decided to bring Vasundhara Raje into state politics and make her the state unit chief. Mahajan had foreseen a rebellion within the state unit and flew down about hundred young BJP activists from his home state Maharastra to micromanage Raje's campaign and election. Smriti was one of these activists. Mahajan was hesitant in drafting in Smriti as her daughter Zoish was just two months old. But an eager Smriti decided to work for the party. She was still an actor and actively shooting for her serials. 'I would shoot through the night. Come home in the early hours of morning, feed my baby, align everything at home and be at the airport by 8.30 a.m. to take the plane assigned by the party and then campaign the whole day. I would return at 6–6.30 p.m., bathe and feed my little one, and go back to my shoots,' she says remembering how she got into the habit of catching up on her sleep on flights—something she still does. Did she ever feel stressed? Smriti says, 'Life does not give everyone opportunities. It was giving me opportunities. How could I have refused or complained?' This balancing act caught the eye of the BJP seniors. Within a year she was made vice-president of the BJP's Maharashtra youth wing. 'I felt that when people said "youth wing", somehow only a male activist came to mind. I told Mundeji that we should involve more women in the youth wing. He assigned me the job of finding Yuvati Pramukhs in each district. We started with Vidarbha and within six months, every district of Maharashtra had a Yuvati Pramukh in place,' says Smriti.

In the national arena, the BJP was on a high. It had won elections in Rajasthan, Madhya Pradesh, and Chhattisgarh in 2003 and Mahajan advised Prime Minister Atal Bihari Vajpayee to advance the parliamentary polls by six months to April–May 2004. Smriti was given a ticket from the Chandni Chowk parliamentary constituency against the Congress veteran and lawyer Kapil Sibal. The BJP was routed and the Congress-led UPA came to power at the centre. Smriti lost her first election to Sibal. In December 2004, Smriti took a political misstep. In Surat to inaugurate a jewellery store, she linked the party's defeat to the 2002 Gujarat riots and said, 'If Narendra Bhai gives up the post of the chief minister of Gujarat, it would prove that the BJP is a party with a difference.' She went on to announce a fast unto death on Vajpayee's birthday if Modi did not step down. It sent shock waves in the party—a political greenhorn had taken on Modi in his home turf of Gujarat. Smriti had clearly tried to choose sides, in this case Vajpayee's camp. However, by later that evening Smriti had to retract her statement. Two months later, L. K. Advani hosted a screening of a documentary at his home and Smriti bent down to touch Modi's feet, who accepted the gesture and blessed her by calling her 'Gujarat ki beti'. Many felt that this would end Irani's career, some said that she was made to give that statement, others said she clearly tried to choose a camp. In a 2016 interview with the well-known television journalist Barkha Dutt, Smriti cleared the air, 'At that time, I was just a young kid,' she said, while Mr Modi was 'a star of the BJP'. He could very well have told the organization that this upstart of a girl has said something, kindly have her sacked, or kindly put her in a place from where she never politically rises,' she said. Instead, Irani recalled, 'He sat down with me, he said, "Tell me how you reached this conclusion." When she replied that she had been influenced by what was reported in the media, she says Mr Modi replied, "Don't judge me by editorials" and then advised her, "You ensure you see me by the programs that I roll out, see me by the effectiveness, or if there is a gap, tell me what the gap in that program is, help me work so that I can deliver on the promise of development."' Irani said that the PM advised her, 'I am not looking for apologies, explanations. If you can apply yourself to any one program and help me make it a success, that is something you should do for the party.'[2] She was appointed the national secretary and later the head of the BJP's Mahila Morcha in 2010. Within eight years of joining the party, she was nominated to the Rajya Sabha from Gujarat in 2011. The nomination had Modi's blessings—he was present when Smriti filed her nomination papers. A little-known fact is that Smriti began her close association with Gujarat with this nomination and as an MP nurtured and closely monitored tribal-dominated areas such as Kevadia, where the world's tallest monument, the Statue of Unity was planned and constructed.

Her spectacular rise through the echelons of the saffron party, which is perceived as patriarchal, started rumours objectifying Smriti as yet another actor charming her way into power. She had attracted the ire of the entrenched old guard. There were ludicrous claims of a tunnel running between Smriti's and a senior leader's home in New Delhi. But Smriti is never known to have bothered. 'The problem is that when a woman gets attacked, she gets attacked for her character but never for her policymaking. Have you ever seen any criticism of a woman in politics about her policies?' she asks. Putting in eighteen-hour days, balancing politics and home as a hands-on parent, reading voraciously about different issues, managing her party's ideological stand, and her fluency in multiple languages saw Smriti emerge as an indefatigable, fiery, and dependable leader of the BJP.

THE GLASS CLIFF

There is a well-known concept of a glass cliff in the corporate world. In this phenomenon, companies prefer women over men in leadership roles when the chances of failure are exceptionally high. Informally, in board rooms it is known as the 'Think crisis, Think women' phenomenon. In the 2014 parliamentary elections, Smriti was brought in to scale this glass cliff. In a high-profile electoral contest, she was pitted against Rahul Gandhi in Amethi. With barely twenty days to plan her entire campaign, Smriti managed to narrow Rahul's victory margin and polled over 3 lakh votes—the highest a BJP candidate had ever got in Amethi. Smriti vividly remembers how she was told that she could be shot during the campaign. 'I never conveyed it to the party but Zubin knew,' she says. Zubin charted out an elaborate plan in consultation with doctors at Gurugram's Medanta hospital on how to get Smriti to a hospital in case she was shot at. It involved finding the shortest route from Amethi to Lucknow airport and then flying out to Gurugram. Smriti says she was shocked when she saw the state of the parliamentary constituency of the Gandhis. 'There is a halo around the family which is absolutely unnecessary. I was shocked to see how the family has not worked for the constituency they represent,' she says. In Smriti people found an approachable leader who was willing to get her hands dirty in bringing solutions to the constituency's chronic problems of transport, irrigation, flood, drinking water, and the lack of employment opportunities. Though she lost, Smriti did not give up on Amethi. 'I had promised the people of Amethi that I will return and work for their constituency no matter I win or lose. They told me to my face that nobody returns after losing an election. I did not know whether the party would field me in 2019 but I had given my word and my word should mean something,' says Smriti. From Smritiji she gradually became Amethi's didi. She started building her team and then bringing small projects to Amethi and finally scaling up. It helped her when the BJP seized Uttar Pradesh in 2017 and formed a government under Adityanath.

Even though she lost Amethi in 2014, Smriti was given the portfolio of education in Modi's first cabinet. Smriti, who in her 2014 election affidavit had declared her educational qualifications as 'Bachelor of Commerce, Part-1, School of Open Learning (Correspondence), University of Delhi, 1994', came under attack for not being qualified enough to head education ministry (then the human resource development ministry). Congress leader Ajay Maken took to Twitter to say, 'HRD minister Smriti Irani is not even a graduate! Look at her affidavit at the ECI site – page 11.' Indian academician Madhu Kishwar was the first to point out the discrepancy in Smriti's different affidavits—2004 affidavit had declared her 'BA 1996 Delhi University (School of Correspondence)'. Congress was quick to point out that misrepresentation of facts on an election affidavit was a criminal offence and Smriti was liable for disqualification. This spawned applications under the Right to Information (RTI) Act to access her educational records in Delhi University. Though there is no minimum qualification for a member of parliament in India, the controversy took different turns over the years as the matter reached the Central Information Commission and even the Delhi High Court. Smriti had famously declared that people were free to even scrutinize her nursery records.

Smriti was unlike any other education minister before her—she read cabinet notes, pored through files, sat with her bureaucrats to draft and redraft affidavits to be filed in court, followed an open-door policy with her bureaucrats, casually dropping in on the junior staff to chat and comment on the saris worn and food carried in tiffins. But all this changed very quickly. A journalist covering education in a leading national daily in New Delhi told this author, 'From Day 1 Smriti was on the defensive because of the controversy on her educational qualifications. Her way of dealing with officers and academicians was coloured by that. Smriti was in a hurry. She opened several fronts and wanted to change too many things at once. Education as a sector does not do well with sudden and numerous disruptions. Eminent academicians started objecting not only to her bid to change policies but also the way she was speaking to them.' Smriti tried to turn the clock back on several decisions taken by her predecessors, including scrapping of the four-year undergraduate programme, replacing German with Sanskrit as third language in the Kendriya Vidyalayas in the middle of the academic year (a decision which was challenged in court and allowed only from the following academic session), and initiating a move to scrap the no-detention policy. She questioned spending the Indian taxpayer's money to fund an off-shore IIT Delhi campus in Mauritius.

Suddenly, there were requests of transfers by bureaucrats working under her and a spate of resignations from the heads of institutions, including the IIT Delhi Director R. K. Shevgaonkar and IIT Bombay Chairman Anil Kakodkar. Aides and consultants, who worked closely with Smriti in the education ministry, however, have a different take. 'As soon as she was challenged on her educational qualifications, academicians felt that they could challenge the minister's decisions. In one of the meetings, a senior academician told her "You can lean on me, I can guide you." It gave the impression that she was not only academically bereft but also a dainty little lady in need of academic rescue. The minister was shocked. She made her displeasure known. There was another instance when she questioned why there was no woman in the IIT Council as she entered a meeting. When the director said there was no woman qualified, she got on the phone immediately and found a woman scientist,' said a consultant, involved closely with Smriti during her education ministry stint. Smriti says she was very clear that she had to clean up policy. 'I was not there to win a popularity contest. My brief was to clear up policy and make it more transparent,' says Smriti indicating that her boss was on her side.

This was evident as an embattled Smriti tried to defuse the tension after Rohith Vemula's death. In August 2015, the BJP's student wing Akhil Bharatiya Vidyarthi Parishad (ABVP) activists protested against the screening of a documentary *Muzaffarnagar Abhi Baaki Hai* (a documentary on 2013 Muzaffarnagar riots) by the Ambedkar Students Association (ASA) in Hyderabad Central University. It led to a clash where students were injured. A proctorial board inquiry cleared the ASA students of charges. However, the BJP MP and union minister Bandaru Dattatreya wrote a letter to Smriti saying that the university had become a den of anti-national politics. Uncharacteristically, the ministry swung into action and ordered a fresh inquiry under newly-appointed Vice-chancellor Appa Rao Podile. Five Dalit students, including Vemula, were suspended and barred from the hostel and mess premises and restricted from contesting student elections. Mostly first-generation scholars, the suspended students were asked to vacate hostel rooms. In January 2016, Rohith died by suicide, leaving behind a pained note which read, 'The value of a man was reduced to his immediate identity and nearest possibility. To a vote. To a number. To a thing. Never was a man treated as a mind.' This triggered widespread protests in university campuses across India. The Opposition accused the government of unnecessarily meddling in the affairs of educational institutions and targeting the socially and economically backward communities. Smriti defended her actions in a fifty-minute speech in the Lok Sabha, which saw her angry, on the verge of tears ,and beating her chest to show how she had been wrongfully accused of targeting a Dalit student. 'My name is Smriti Irani. I challenge you to tell me what my caste is. You won't be able to tell. I am angry today because when you accuse a mother of murder she will break from inside,' she said in the Lok Sabha on 24 February 2016. It was evident that she had the backing of Modi as the prime minister tweeted the link to her speech. Around the same time, another controversy broke out in Left-leaning Jawaharlal Nehru University in New Delhi. A group of students, including the students' union president Kanhaiya Kumar, were caught on video, which has since been proven to have been doctored before being telecast on TV news channels, during an on-campus protest against the hanging of Afzal Guru for his role in the parliament attack. The students were booked for sedition and arrested. When Smriti rejected the Opposition's demand to reconsider the punishment meted out to students across universities, it cemented her image of an obdurate minister unwilling to engage.

Though Smriti was toeing the party's ideological line, the numerous controversies did not augur well for her. The last straw was the ministry's skirmishes with the PMO. The Indian Institute of Management Bill and the Institutes of Eminence were on the anvil. In case of Institutes of Eminence, Smriti wanted the letter of intent issued to an institute to be non-transferable. However, the PMO had their inputs in this case. Similarly, the PMO had sent specific inputs on the IIM Bill which would have put in place a company-like structure in IIMs and given them sweeping autonomy. Smriti felt that the government needed to have some control over the workings of the IIMs. 'The PMO had recommended more than five changes to the draft law—which aims to empower the premier B-schools to award degrees instead of diplomas—to dilute the scope of government control over the institutes. But the HRD Ministry under Irani's leadership had not accepted all the suggested changes. While it agreed to increase the number of alumni and female members on the board of governors of every IIM from three to five and from one to three, respectively, the ministry had retained the provision which makes the HRD minister the head of the IIM Coordinating Forum. The PMO was not in favour of this.[3] Smriti, who had turned around her relationship with the officials heading the higher education department of her ministry, went by her officials' advise. More than her political bosses, many say, she had rubbed PMO bureaucrats the wrong way by insisting on retaining certain clauses despite inputs. In July 2016, Smriti was eased out of education ministry and given textiles. The journalist, quoted earlier, told this author, 'I think the party just got tired of the controversies because some were created when there was no need at all. For the first three months after she was eased out, Prakash Javadekar (the amiable minister who took over from Smriti) kept saying, "Koi controversy nahin chahiye (I don't want any controversy)" or sometimes asking us what we were writing as he did not want any more controversies. It was an indication of the fact that somewhere the party wanted somebody to just toe the line unquestioningly.'

Once again, people had written her off. Within a year, she was given the politically crucial information and broadcasting portfolio in July 2017. But her stint was dotted with controversies. She initiated an overhaul of the Press Information Bureau, the government's arm handling press publicity. She started interviewing Indian Information Service officers attached to ministries asking them whether they had ever been posted in other cities. Her common refrain was—why should plum Delhi postings be the preserve of a few? She shook things up by transferring people out of Delhi and irking the bureaucracy. But she understood the importance of media coverage. Smaller autonomous organizations under ministries which never had information officers suddenly got officers to handle media and publicity. Smriti used her film industry relationships and organized one of the most successful

International Film Festival of India (IFFI) in 2017. This was the only time that superstars like Amitabh Bachchan and Shah Rukh Khan were all present at IFFI, an annual festival. Even in the information and broadcasting ministry, Smriti opened too many fronts. She had frequent run-ins with public broadcaster Prasar Bharati. But what proved to be her undoing was her bid to curb fake news in April 2018. Though on the face of it the move still seems like something that needs to be addressed, her ministry proposed harsh measures like the immediate suspension of accreditation while charges of fake news were being investigated and the loss of accreditation in case of three fake news instances. The circular on fake news came just a year before the 2019 parliamentary elections and was seen as an age-old tactic by a government to muzzle the press. Smriti had to withdraw the circular after the prime minister stepped in to put a lid on the controversy. Her aides blamed Jaitley, who had held the portfolio from November 2014 to July 2016 when M. Venkaiah Naidu took over. Within a month of the fake news circular, Smriti found herself drawn in another controversy with over fifty recipients of the National Film Awards skipping the ceremony. The recipients were unhappy when they found out that President Ram Nath Kovind would present awards to only a select few winners and not follow the set procedure till then. The Rashtrapati Bhavan had complained to PMO that it was unnecessarily drawn into a controversy due to mismanagement by the I&B ministry. Within days, Smriti was relieved of I&B and her junior minister Rajyavardhan Rathore took charge. She held the textiles portfolio for the remaining term. A BJP leader, who did not wish to be identified, told the author, 'Arun Jaitley's shadow loomed large on I&B ministry especially because he had good relations with senior journalists. Smriti was never comfortable in this ministry and was always fighting one crisis or the other. But it is unfair to blame every crisis on Jaitley—a lot was Smriti's own doing.' But once again her critics made the same mistake of writing her off. You can pull her down but you can never write off Smriti. In a year's time in 2019 she was back in the fighting arena, battle ready as ever. After all, her party had entrusted her with Amethi.

THE FINAL FRONTIER

Smriti took on Nehru-Gandhi family scion Rahul in Amethi in the 2019 parliamentary elections. But this time, it was different. Smriti had become didi in Amethi and the people had seen what change could mean. In a way, the Congress expected to be embarassed in Amethi—Rahul decided to contest from a second seat of Wayanad, considered a safe constituency for the Congress in Kerala. Author Anant Vijay has detailed out the strategy in Amethi in his book *Dynasty to Democracy: The Untold Story of Smriti Irani's Triumph* and how the BJP planned the entire campaign meticulously with the involvement of the RSS grassroot workers. 'When Irani was declared the BJP candidate from Amethi again for the 2019 Lok Sabha elections, the RSS gave the responsibility of managing the election to Parmeshwarji, who used to be a zila pracharak in Amethi. The RSS workers had become active long before the 2019 elections. The RSS had started to work in Amethi from November 2018. The entire constituency was divided into 116 nyay panchayats, and more than half of them were assigned to a full-timer (poornakalik) and mandal karyawahs of the Sangh. Immediately after the dates were announced for the 2019 Lok Sabha elections, sixteen blocks of the Amethi constituency were placed under full-time pracharaks of the Sangh,' Vijay writes.

Smriti camped in the constituency throughout the campaign, keeping a gruelling schedule, sometimes addressing twenty to twenty-five public meetings in a day. She would get up at 7 a.m., do her puja, and get ready to start her meetings at 8 a.m. According to her party colleague Pragya Tripathi, 'Didi took care of everybody herself during the entire campaign. The election was happening in the summer, and she would prepare Rasna herself and serve it to the team members. After conferencing with the party workers in the morning, she would get into the

car at half past ten. She would eat breakfast in the car itself.
But she used to be mindful of whether those travelling with her
had eaten or not.'[4] Her team members in Amethi have many
vignettes to share about the hectic campaign. The favourite one,
which endeared her to many, is about how she returned in the
middle of the night after a hectic day of campaigning and didn't
think twice before squatting in the kitchen to make pooris for
the party workers when she saw others working in the kitchen.
'She remembers our names, sometimes the names of our children
and which class they study in. You tell didi about one incident
in your life, and she will recall it when you meet her next. She
has a photographic memory and a genuine concern about you,'
a member says.

'After meetings and interactions throughout the day, she
would return to her Gauriganj home by nine in the night and
after half an hour, leave to meet prominent residents of the area.
These were people who could influence voters. These meetings
could go on until midnight and sometimes longer. From midnight
to the wee hours, she would prepare materials for the media
and respond to the messages of journalists. After taking care of
media work, she would retire around half past two or three in
the night.'[5] She would be back to business at 7 a.m. Ask her
how she kept such a gruelling routine, Smriti says she does not
need much sleep. 'Two hours is fine,' she says.

RSS pracharaks fanned out in the constituency and went
booth-wise, trying to make it an election fought on nationalism
and not on caste, which is intrinsic to all elections in UP.
'Voting in Amethi was scheduled on 6 May 2019. Booth-level
preparations were done. The election-day challenge that was
set for the swayamsevaks and BJP workers was to reach out to
voters in every polling booth and tell them that they should vote
keeping in mind the national interests. A district-level official
of the Sangh, Satyendraji tells me, "People from all castes and
communities were brought together and encouraged to vote as
Indians. Based on the election list, responsibilites were assigned
to conduct 100 per cent polling. The RSS representatives used to

speak about the upliftment of the Hindu society. They did not take the name of any political party. Neither were sides taken nor was any party denigrated. National interest was stressed upon and the people were told that voting was their right. In the Dalit neighbourhoods too, the Sangh representatives used to talk about the nation and society.'"[6]

'In the Lok Sabha elections, before 2019, Congress candidates used to visit Amethi for seven to ten days during which some outreach time was kept aside. Then they would go back to the special rooms arranged for them in the guesthouse, meet a few selected people and leave. After the Congress candidates filed their nominations and were back, the real game would begin. A week before voting, envelope politics would start at the block level. The BJP or any other prominent opposition party never took the Amethi Lok Sabha elections seriously, and this allowed for Congress walkovers. The media across the country tended to portray Amethi as the Gandhi family bastion. The RSS had readied its workers to counter this strategy of the Congress during the 2019 elections. Whenever the RSS workers came to know that a Congress car was on its way to dole out money, they would follow with cameras.'[7]

On 23 May 2019, the fortress was breached. Smriti defeated Rahul Gandhi by over 55,000 votes. But Smriti did not declare victory till the wee hours of 24 May. As the votes were being counted in booths, she sat inside her room listening to music. 'I told my party workers—it is your election, you go to the booth. I was very tired. I sat listening to music,' she recalls. Rahul conceded defeat at 5.30 p.m. and congratulated Smriti. There was a knock on the door. Pragya, Smriti's aide, said there should be a statement from Smriti. 'Wait, let the Election Commission declare the victory,' Smriti said. Pragya insisted. In half an hour, Smriti took to Twitter and borrowed a line from the poet Dushyant Singh's inspirational poem, 'Kaun kehta hai aasman mein surakh ho nahin sakta (Who says you can't make a hole in the sky).' As her team insisted, she went to the counting centre but the votes were still being counted. Her victory came 2.30 a.m. on

24 May. Why didn't she celebrate till then even when Rahul had conceded defeat? 'The Opposition accuses the BJP of subverting democracy and democratic institutions. Votes were being counted and counted again. How could I have been presumptuous and declared victory before the authority—Election Commission— had declared it?' she explains.

Smriti had emerged as the giant slayer of the election. Seeing the enormity of the victory it was expected that Smriti would be given a big-ticket portfolio. She was given the women and child development and textiles portfolios—considered lightweight portfolios. But then again, every time you dismiss Smriti at your own peril. The second stint at the centre saw her in a new avatar—that of a tight-lipped controversy-free minister. Smriti has streamlined the information flow in both her ministries and it is amply clear to officials that they are not supposed to speak to the media. She comes well prepared for her press briefings, takes pains to answer all the media queries, and even arranges the information sought for. But reporters looking for controversial statements or a misstep by the minister have been disappointed. Smriti's biggest moment in this stint came during Covid-19 outbreak in 2020. Suddenly, India was short of personal protective equipment (PPE) and masks required by healthcare professionals. Textiles ministry stepped in and personally called manufacturers from across the sector, many of whom did not have any prior experience in manufacturing PPEs. The textiles ministry handheld knitwear and home textile manufacturers to manufacture PPE kits. In three months, from being an importer of PPE kits, India had become the second largest producer of PPE suits in the world. Later, in the middle of 2022 she was also entrusted with the minority affairs ministry.

SETTING AN EXAMPLE

With no family background in politics, Smriti found her way about by herself. Very early on in her career, she had been invited for tea by the BJP veteran Jaswant Singh and given some friendly advice—cultivate a few journalists around you. She says she has chosen to ignore this advice. In fact, she has fiercely guarded her privacy and kept the media at bay. She is one of the rare ministers who does not have hangers-on. There is no clutter around her—of people or of things. 'I cannot mollycoddle people. I am a straight talker. Ask anyone in Amethi also—if I can get something done I say it clearly and I never give false hopes,' she says matter-of-factly.

Irani feels that women politicians have it easier in political parties like the BJP than parties like the Congress. 'If you work hard, nobody can ignore you. Right now, the need for us is to not bring forth women for the sake of increasing women representation. The need is to bring women who are representative of not just women but of men, who know their politics, who have a vision,' she says.

SUPRIYA SULE

The Influencer

On 13 May 2022, then Maharashtra Health Minister Rajesh Tope announced a landmark step—gender affirming or sex reassignment surgeries would be carried out free for members of the transgender community in the state. Speaking at a conference organized by the public health department and the Yashwantrao Chavan Centre, Tope said, 'I would like to tell you on this occasion that we will carry out surgeries for transgenders 100 per cent free.' With this Maharashtra became one of the few states after Tamil Nadu and Kerala to offer this facility to transgender people.

Behind the announcement was a slip passed by the transgender rights activist Priya Patil to Supriya Sule, the

Nationalist Congress Party (NCP) MP from Baramati, at the conference briefly mentioning point-wise health challenges faced by the transgender community. Patil, who was Mumbai's first transgender candidate in the 2017 Brihanmumbai Municipal Corporation elections, says, 'Within five minutes Supriyaji had passed on the message to the health minister who discussed that there could be a provision under Mahatma Jyotirao Phule Jan Arogya Yojana (the state government's health scheme).' Tope announced the move. 'This is what Supriyaji is all about—she does not take up causes to show off. She genuinely feels for these causes,' says Patil. It is this confidence in Sule that made Patil walk into the MP's office in 2020 to propose a separate wing for transgender people in the party. 'The pandemic had hit transgender people hard. Apart from social discrimination our community has been facing, the lockdown exposed the community to financial and mental hardships. I thought when the party has cells for women, youth, minorities, and all sections, why not for transgender people. This way our community can hope to get better political representation,' says Patil. She put up the proposal before Sule and by the time Patil finished, the MP was on the phone with the NCP Maharashtra State President Jayant Patil. Within two months the idea became a reality and NCP became the first political party in India to have a separate cell for lesbian, gay, bisexual, transgender, queer, intersex, and allies (LGBTQIA+).

Of course, when you are the Maratha strongman and NCP President Sharad Pawar's only child it helps to get the wheels of the party and governance churning. But it would be unfair to attribute Sule's passion for social service and achievements as a people's representative to only her political inheritance.

THE LINEAGE

Sule is proud of this political inheritance and wears it on her sleeve. During a debate in the Lok Sabha on 9 February 2022, she took on the BJP MP Tejasvi Surya who had said that before

Prime Minister Narendra Modi the country was under the control of dynasts. 'Jyotiraditya Scindia, who is also a minister, Piyush Goyal, Dharmendra Pradhan—all my very good friends. I am very proud of them. The one thing I have in common with them—we were all born in political families. And I am not ashamed of being born in a political family,' Sule cheekily said, pointing out all the dynastic BJP parliamentarians.

Over the years, Sule has worked diligently to use this lineage to nurture the family's constituency and bring about policy changes. Sule, the parliamentarian, has ground to dust the entire debate on nepotism. Track her record in her first term in the Rajya Sabha and successive three terms in the Lok Sabha and you realize that the parliament is her playground. She is like an excited child going to school after summer vacations—first in and last out. She has the immense capacity to tirelessly sit through long-winding debates and participate with pertinent interventions. Ask the research team behind her and they tell you how she puts in long hours poring over detailed briefs prepared on government bills and subjects coming up for discussion in the house. She says it helps her understand people and problems from across India. 'It is like any other job, any other profession—you need to work hard and do a lot of homework. I have an entire team working to do research and do the groundwork before any debate. An MP has to read a lot to make a meaningful intervention in any discussion,' says Sule. Her private members' bills give a peek into what Sule stands for. She has introduced the Right to Disconnect Bill in Lok Sabha twice—once in 2014 and then in 2022. The bill seeks to respect the personal space of the employees by giving them the right not to respond to their employer's calls and emails during out-of-work hours. She also introduced an amendment to the Special Marriage Act to legalize same sex marriages and provide legal recognition to LGBTQIA+ couples.

Like her father, who is considered a man of all seasons, Sule has friends across the political spectrum. She has an understated style of functioning. Hers is not the politics of confrontation but of compassion and taking everyone along. The differences are only ideological. So she may blow apart the BJP MP Nishikant Dubey's argument inside the Lok Sabha but a few hours later she may hitch a ride with him back to her 6 Janpath Road residence in New Delhi discussing nuances of a policy. 'We all have our ideologies but that doesn't mean that I can't be friendly towards a person. I have friends across political parties—we sit together, share our food, and some friendly banter. We are professionals working together. I learn something new about an ideology from each one of them. That is the beauty of a democracy. For us to call it a vibrant democracy, you should be friendlier across party lines and ideologies. I don't find it difficult to get along with people,' she says.

Sule was born in Pune in the powerful Pawar family of Baramati on 30 June 1969. Pawar had famously declared that he would undergo a vasectomy. At the time, there was a nationwide campaign on family planning and emphasis on a two-child policy. Pawar tried to send two signals way ahead of the times—it was alright to have only a girl child and contraception need not always be a woman's responsibility. When people asked him who would conduct his last rites as he did not have a son, he announced that his daughter would light the funeral pyre. To understand his views one needs to go back a generation to Pawar's mother Sharadabai Govindrao Pawar, who was a member of the Pune Local Board in pre-independent India. In his autobiography, Pawar has described his mother as feisty, dynamic, and a left-leaning social and political activist. He recounts his mother's political involvement and dedication with an anecdote. 'I had my first brush with administration when I was barely three days old, cradled in the arms of my mother. Sharadabai Govindrao Pawar had a meeting to attend at the Pune Local Board, of which she was a member, on 15 December 1940. Although she had delivered a baby boy just three days earlier, she was not one to miss her call of duty. Neither the hard winter nor the four-hour-long arduous journey, in a crowded bus, from the tehsil town of Baramati to the district headquarters in Pune could deter her from attending the crucial meet.'[1] Owing to his mother's progressive outlook, Pawar grew up in a household where his sisters were encouraged to finish graduation so that they could become financially independent. 'Looking back, I realize how all this has imperceptibly guided me through life,' he says.[2]

Sule studied microbiology in Mumbai's Jai Hindi college. At the age of twenty-two, right out of college, she married Sadanand, son of the former Mahindra and Mahindra managing director Bhalchandra R. Sule. Sadanand was a US-based IT consultant. The newly-married couple moved to California. Sule studied at the University of California, Berkeley and did research on water pollution. Work took them to Singapore and Indonesia before they returned in 2001 to Mumbai with their daughter Revati. Their son Vijay was born a year later. Sule says the thought of joining politics at this time had never crossed her mind. She began working at the grassroots with women self-help groups (SHGs) and for tribal children. Within five years, Sule had fast tracked the common political trajectory of fighting municipal and state assembly elections and straightaway got a nomination to the Rajya Sabha in 2006. She created a stir when she filed her affidavit for the Rajya Sabha elections declaring assets worth ₹41.52 crore. This made her one of the richest politicians in India with two homes on the premium and elite Peddar Road in Mumbai. In trademark Pawar style, Sule was elected unopposed to the Rajya Sabha. So far, Pawar's firebrand nephew Ajit, his elder brother Anantrao's son, had been looked at as his political successor. With Pawar's only child making a foray in politics, the equations were certainly going to change.

THE GRASSROOT CONNECT

During Sule's first term as a Rajya Sabha MP, her party was a part of the Congress-led United Progressive Alliance, which was in power at the centre. This did not deter Sule from posing tough questions on her areas of interest such as education, the mid day meal scheme, the problem of deafness among children, the power crisis in Maharashtra, and increasing fratricide cases among armed forces personnel. In a way, Sule had a sheltered political debut—something like a soft launch. But within three years, Sule was ready for the real rough and tumble of politics. Her father vacated his family pocketborough of Baramati Lok Sabha constituency for Sule and she contested her first Lok Sabha election in May 2009. She polled over 66 per cent of the votes, even more than her father's previous election from the constituency in 2004. It was a clear testimony of how the family has invested for decades in Baramati. 'After my election to the Lok Sabha, his advice to me was: "As you walk up the steps of Parliament, remember the people of Baramati who have voted you as their representative. As an MP, work with a sense of commitment and gratitude to those who have elected you. Bond with people. Work to better their lives,"' writes Sule.[3]

Baramati is largely a rural parliamentary constituency. It comprises of six assembly segments—Baramati, Indapur, Daund, Khadakwasala, Bhor, and Purandar. About 120 kilometres from Pune, Baramati town has been developed by the Pawar family as an education and employment hub. The family speaks through its various institutions. The towering presence of Pawar is evident in Baramati. There is a two-floor curated museum housing gifts received by Pawar from famous personalities—an entire section is devoted to the numerous expensive pens Pawar has received as gifts, including one from the well-known singer Lata Mangeshkar.

The Sharad Pawar-run Vidya Pratishthan Trust has opened a medical college, school of architecture, engineering college, girls and boys hostels, school of biotechnology, and a law college in Baramati. Spread over 120 acres, the sylvan campus is impressive. It boasts of a nakshtra udyan—planetarium—and a herbal garden, which emanates smells of medicinal plants early in the morning. Uday Vinayak Thombare, Vidya Pratishthan's hostel coordinator, says, 'Many students come here and meditate. It has a therapeutic effect.' Till a few years back, students had to travel to Pune or Mumbai to pursue higher education but the educational institutions set up by the Pawar family have changed it all. 'Now Baramati has become self-sufficient with state-of-the-art facilities,' says Thombare. There is an emphasis on greenery and cleanliness with not even a speck of plastic strewn anywhere on the campus. The entire town of Baramati bears a similar look with tree-lined roads and bougainvillea shrubs on the central verge.

It is evident that the Pawar family has invested in employment generation in Baramati. In 2005, the centre launched the Scheme for Integrated Textile Parks (SITP) to provide the industry good infrastructure to set up textile units in a dedicated area. Pawar's intervention ensured that Baramati was included in the first phase under SITP. M. B. Sankeshwarkar, CEO of the Baramati Hi-Tech Textile Park (BHTPL), says the first factory to begin production in the initial phase was in Baramati even though the town's textile park was included in the scheme eighteen months later than all other planned parks in India. Ajit Pawar's wife Sunetra is the chairperson of BHTPL which is spread over sixty acres of land and has sixty plots. About 75 per cent of the workers are semi-literate women. 'The average woman worker earns about ₹30,000 per month and she is earning more than her husband,' says Sankeshwarkar, who has been involved with the BHTPL since 2007. Now, Sankeshwarkar and his team are trying to restart units which were shut down during the Covid-19 pandemic. Another major initiative in Baramati is the Schreiber Dynamix Dairy, India's largest milk production and milk products complex which buys about 500,000 litres of milk daily from a dairy cooperative, the Baramati Doodh Utpadak Sangh.

Quite early on, the Pawar family realized the challenges of the agriculture-dependent region. Pawar's elder brother Dinkarrao Pawar had instituted the Agriculture Development Trust to understand the problems faced by farmers and introduce new technologies for improving agricultural production and help in irrigation. Decades later, Baramati is now known for its drip irrigation system and a variety of produce including seedless grapes. As this author travelled to Baramati in mid-February 2022, it was hosting Krushik, an annual farmers fair exhibiting new technologies for the farming community and innovations to help them improve yield. It was a crowded fair with farmers and representatives of non-profit organizations coming from far off parts of Maharashtra to look at the options available under organic farming and natural farming. While larger than normal sized vegetables exhibits drew farmers, the biggest attraction was drone farming, which showed how drones could be used to sprinkle fertilizers and pesticides uniformly across fields. The government's top cabinet ministers and the Pawar family were all present at different times of the day, some even seeking views of women on problems they faced.

Like her father, Sule is a hands-on MP. Pawar famously travelled to fifty-four villages of his Baramati constituency to invite people to Sule's wedding. Over a lakh constituents came and five tonnes of pedas (Indian sweetmeat) were distributed.[4] Sule works through a well-oiled machinery, personally spending about ten to twelve days a month in the constituency. Every Monday, she sits in her office in Pune from 10 a.m. to 5 p.m. listening to grievances and demands ranging from road widening to additional stops at a railway station and training programmes for employment generation. 'I love the people contact. It is essential for an MP to go to the constituency and have direct contact with people. It helps in understanding how government schemes function and if something more can be done to get funds to the constituency. If you take Jal Shakti Mission—it is a great scheme which promises an investment of ₹3 lakh crore. But now I am getting feedback from the ground that there is no clause for operation and maintenance of the network you create. It is based on this that we are raising the issue. You realize all these finer details only when you interact with your constituents, your zila parishad CEO, anganwadi workers. This is why this direct contact with people in the constituency is very important,' says Sule.

Baramati is the epicentre of the Pawar family's politics. Rashmi Kamtekar, Sule's personal assistant in Pune since the MP's debut in Lok Sabha in 2009, says it is Sule's push and constant follow-ups with central agencies that have ensured the electrification of railway sections and widening of highways. With a number of historical and religious places dotting the Baramati parliamentary constituency, Sule has realized that tourism could be an employment generator but developing certain places as tourist spots requires better infrastructure. Sule is actively working for facilities like a better railway station for the temple town of Jejuri which has Khandoba temple, a ropeway project, conservation of forests inside the Maratha king Shivaji's first fort at Sinhagad, the development of the Ujani Dam backwaters at Indapur as a tourist spot for birders to watch flamingos and bar headed geese from Mongolia, and the restoration of several ancient temples in the constituency.

Sule brings a sensitivity to project planning and problem solving. Taking forward her father's motto of women's empowerment through financial independence, Sule has conceived projects like Gaurang and Tai's Kitchen. Gaurang is a food festival which showcases the region's cuisine in Pune. Women from across the region travel to Pune city for a three-day festival where they offer local and regional delicacies like crab, fish, varieties of rice, and chilapi fish from Indapur. Kamtekar says that in three days women report a profit of ₹70,000 to ₹80,000. Women entrepreneurs trying to start out on their own are also provided small tempos at three fixed spots in Pune to offer home-cooked meals at ₹20 to 40. 'This took a hit during Covid-19 but it has started out again gradually,' says Kamtekar. During the Covid-19 lockdowns, Sule started receiving complaints of domestic violence in her largely-rural constituency. She spoke to the local body representatives and formed the Mahila Suraksha Samitis (women protection cells) in villages. About 9,000 cases of domestic violence were reported in these samitis and with the intervention of village elders and counselling, the issue of domestic violence was addressed.

Ask Sule what she feels most strongly about and pat comes the reply—malnutrition. 'I want my constituency to be the best in all social sector schemes. More specifically, zero malnutrition—

that will be a great gamechanger. The moment you have zero malnutrition, you check a lot of boxes in terms of several social indicators,' says Sule. During her first term as the Rajya Sabha MP in 2007, Sule came together with Jay Panda (then an MP from BJD), the BJP's Shahnawaz Hussain, and Congress's Sachin Pilot to form the Citizens' Alliance to Fight Against Hunger. About 20–25 MPs joined under this umbrella and even asked actor Aamir Khan to endorse this cause. The MPs toured several states to check the extent of malnutrition. Sule has been involved with this cause since then. Kamtekar says that through the government's Child Health Tracking System, 3 lakh children have been screened in the parliamentary constituency and 404 were found malnourished. 'We have been stressing on counselling of mothers and proper follow-ups if a child is found malnourished,' says Kamtekar.

Sule easily shifts between slick Mumbai and her Baramati constituency. Clad in a neatly pinned sari, exhibiting her elegant taste for Indian weaves, she is often seen having a meal or partying with her friends, the industrialist Anil Ambani and his wife Tina, Rima Jain, and her husband Manoj Jain. She is, however, equally at ease 250 kilometres away in Jejuri town enjoying mutton at former corporator Mehboob Pansare's home.

THE GENDER QUESTION

Sule has grown up in a family where gender has never been an issue for her. She brushes aside any suggestions of facing discrimination on the basis of gender inside or outside home. 'See, I am a Mumbai girl. Maharashtrian society is a gender equal society. In public space my gender does not define me. I don't get trapped in a gender specific role—I don't allow myself to enter that zone. I am not an abla naari (helpless woman),' she says. Though many women leaders complain of sexism and even discrimination in elected bodies, Sule says she has never felt it. 'My philosophy has always been to treat people the way you would like them to treat you,' she says adding that since

Maharashtra has seen a lot of strong women in all walks of life, she hasn't faced discrimination on the basis of gender.

But Sule has been a champion of increasing women's representation in elected bodies. In her first term as a Lok Sabha MP, she started the Nationalist Yuvati Congress in 2012. 'I realized that while there is place and platform for young women, there was no such place for girls. In fact, families still have a problem in allowing their daughters to participate in politics. We are talking about women reservation in legislatures and parliament. Where will these future leaders come from?' says Sule. The Nationalist Yuvati Congress is a specific forum for women in the eighteen to thirty-five age group.

Aditi Nalawade, who heads the Mumbai wing of the Nationalist Yuvati Congress, remembers the unusual launch of the wing in Mumbai. 'NCP gave the platform to young girls to express their grievances and what they thought was missing from public discourse. It was a ten-day programme and young girls gave speeches on several issues including the lack of sports infrastructure and educational facilities and health issues. But the common thread in all these speeches was that there are not enough clean and hygienic public toilets for women. On the spot, deputy chief minister Ajit Pawarji announced that all NCP MLAs and corporators will identify spaces for public toilets for women and earmark funds to build them at the earliest,' says Nalawade. For a fledgling organization it was quite encouraging to see its voice being heard. Sule travelled across Maharashtra from 11 June to 27 October, holding fifty public meetings exhorting young women to join the new wing. Sule elicited a good response with her meetings attracting huge crowds.

Nalawade, who has majored in business psychology, says that a majority of the young women who have joined the Yuvati Congress are professionals who want to be involved in policy making and politics. 'I studied business psychology abroad. After I returned to India I knew I wanted to get into politics but there was no forum for young women like me. The youth wings of most political parties have about twenty to twenty-five girls to a hundred boys. So when it comes to expressing their problems or taking up women-related issues, young women do not find these youth wings a credible or sympathetic platform. At the same time, women wings of most parties predominantly raise issues relating to older women. Yuvati wing provided me the perfect forum to talk about issues pertaining to young professionals,' says Nalawade. Yuvati Congress has targeted programmes to train young girls in public speaking and how to influence policy making. Nalawade says Yuvati Congress is a self-sufficient political venture. 'We don't outsource anything. If there is an event and we want to put together promotional material or compose a song, we will use a copywriter or an artist among ourselves to do this. It helps all of us to grow,' she says. Unlike other political wings, Yuvati Congress has got political opportunities with its members getting tickets to fight corporation and assembly elections.

Sule feels that passing the Women's Reservation Bill is the only way to increase women's representation in legislatures and the parliament. 'Women need a foot in the door. Unless we reserve constituencies for women, political parties will not give tickets. Another form could be to make it mandatory on political parties, through a change in our laws, to reserve a certain percentage of tickets in every election for women,' she says. Terming this as a 'big social change', the four-term MP says it could mean that initially women from political families would come forward. 'We need to increase the representation of women. If we need to do this, we need to begin somewhere. It is not just a change in political representation. It is a big social change. It will take time. Initially political parties may field women from political families citing winnability but gradually it will bring forth women leaders in public spaces,' says Sule.

Being in public life comes with its share of controversies. Sule has also courted a few—some by association with the Pawar family. In 2010, when financial irregularities in the functioning of cricket's Indian Premier League (IPL) surfaced, there were allegations that her husband owned a 10 per cent share in a firm that had exclusive broadcasting rights for IPL matches. 'In 2010, a deal between WSG and Multi Screen Media (formally known as Sony Entertainment) came under the tax authorities' scanner. The global broadcast rights for the IPL were originally bought in 2008 by WSG for ten years for more than 900 million dollars. The TV rights for India were then allotted by WSG to MSM. However, in 2009, the IPL cancelled the MSM contract, citing, among other reasons, poor-quality broadcasts. MSM went to court, but after a tough legal battle, decided on an out-of-court settlement. The new deal saw MSM paying more than a billion dollars to hold onto the TV rights for the remaining nine years. MSM also gave WSG an 80 million dollar (₹425 crore) facilitation fee as part of its agreement. The smallest of the chinks being probed in this deal is that WSG should pay 40 crores in tax for the facilitation fee it benefitted from.'[5] Sule's father-in-law was a part of a consortium called Atlas Equifin, which owns a third of MSM. B. R. Sule, as part of Atlas Equifin, invested in MSM. However, after he fell sick, he assigned signing rights to Sadanand. Sule had defended her husband saying, 'My husband's only role is that he is a cricket fan. He has no other role...please read my lips.'[6]

Her father's dream project of Lavasa Hill City has also seen Sule and Sadanand being dragged in another controversy. 'As the story goes, while being flown from Mumbai to Pune in a helicopter, Pawar spotted a large tract of vacant land in the Mulshi valley area of the Sahyadri mountain range in Maharashtra. Thinking of it as an ideal spot to plant a new, model city (as conceived by his friend, Aniruddha Deshpande), Pawar took the proposal to realty baron Ajit Gulabchand and his company, HCC. Gulabchand is an old friend of Pawar's, and Lavasa City Corporation (LCC), the firm responsible for the city's construction, is part of HCC's real estate wing. In 2001, the Maharashtra government sanctioned 10,000 acres of land for the construction of this modern city, which would be spread over twenty villages and hamlets. The first phase of construction, Dasve, on 1,700 acres, began in 2005 and has been completed. Work on the second phase, Mugaon, is stalled because of regulatory issues.'[7] Over the years, the project was mired in several environmental and regulatory issues and became a bargaining chip of sorts between the NCP and the Congress at the centre and the NCP and the BJP–Shiv Sena government in Maharashtra. Sadanand owned a 12.7 per cent stake in the project until 2007. 'For her part, Supriya Sule, Sharad Pawar's daughter, has washed her hands of the project, saying that her husband Sadanand had "very very nominal" shares in Lavasa which he sold ages ago. 'I don't have a view on the Lavasa development,' she says. 'We sold [our] shares ages ago, before the project became large. We personally have zero financial association with it.'[8]

A spate of public interest litigations (PILs) saw activists dragging the Pawar family—Pawar, Ajit, and Sule—to court for allegedly using their influence to push the project through. On 26 February 2022, the Bombay High Court refused to pass any order in the PIL seeking to declare as 'illegal, arbitrary' the special permission granted in 2002 to the corporation for purchasing lands for developing the hill city. But at the same time the court observed both father and daughter exerted influence in the project. 'It cannot be said that exertion of influence and clout by Sharad Pawar and Supriya Sule is an unreasonable inference that cannot be drawn from the facts.... Sharad Pawar and Supriya Sule being personally interested in the project, it is proved by preponderance of probability that the allegations are true,' the bench noted.[9]

THE CROWN

It is believed in political circles that it is Pawar's dream to see his daughter as the first woman chief minister of Maharashtra. Since her political debut in 2006, the turfs were clearly divided between Sule and her cousin Ajit—she was the party's face in New Delhi and Ajit the regional satrap. But with Pawar's political influence in the national capital significantly diminished during the Modi years, he is involving Sule more in Maharashtra's regional politics. She was by his side throughout the 2019 parliamentary election—a change that many in Maharashtra thought showed her growing influence in state politics.

The cracks began to show in the closely knit Pawar family after the October 2019 Maharashtra assembly elections, which threw up a fractured mandate. The BJP had emerged as the single largest party with 105 seats in the 288-member assembly. The Shiv Sena won 56 seats, the NCP 54, and the Congress 44 seats. The BJP could not stake claim to form the government because of differences over rotational chief ministership and equal sharing of cabinet berths with its long-time ally Shiv Sena. On 11 November, the alliance broke and Governor Bhagat Singh Koshyari invited the NCP to form a government. When the NCP could not cobble up the numbers, Koshyari recommended imposition of President's Rule in the state. Pawar started backroom talks to get the Congress and the Shiv Sena to the table to form the government. Just when it seemed that the unlikely alliance could be stitched up, Ajit rebelled with his loyalists and decided to support the BJP. In the early hours of 23 November, Devendra Fadnavis was sworn in for his second term and Ajit took over as deputy chief minister. The governor gave the BJP and the breakaway faction of the NCP time till November 30 to prove their majority. The Pawar family was shocked. Whatever had been the differences, they had never come out in the open. A heartbroken Sule's WhatsApp status read 'Party and family split'.

Over the next two days, Pawar sent at least five emissaries to persuade Ajit. But nothing worked. On 26 November, Ajit left his home in the early hours presumably to attend a government function to pay homage to martyrs of the deadly 26/11 Mumbai terrorist attacks. In his book *36 Days: A Political Chronicle of Ambition, Deception, Trust and Betrayal*, journalist Kamlesh Sutar reveals how Pawar brought back his nephew. 'After leaving his house, Ajit started towards Nariman Point. The media cameras followed him, expecting him to head towards the

26/11 memorial. But his car, rather than taking a right towards Girgaum Chowpatty, took a left turn towards the end of Nariman Point. He straightaway headed into the hotel, where someone was waiting for him. The moment Ajit saw the person, he bent forward and touched the person's feet. There had never been such an awkward moment between him and his Kaki in the past. There was a long silence as Pratibha Pawar, Sharad Pawar's wife, saw Ajit for the first time since the coup. Pratibha Pawar had seen how the events had distressed her daughter. She was now sitting with the man at the centre of the coup—the nephew who she has always treated like her son. Caught in the silence was Supriya Sule's husband, Sadanand, who also shared an excellent bond with Ajit. Pratibha Pawar wasn't the first person from the Pawar family to speak to Ajit. Several other family members had approached him with a single line message: family first, politics later! ...No doubt that Ajit's rebellion had not only hit the party hard, but it had hurt the family immensely. The meeting between Ajit Pawar and his aunt wasn't a very long one. Very few words were spoken, but a long message was conveyed. No politics was discussed between Ajit and his Kaki; there were no requests or deals. It was just an uncomfortable hush that communicated a thousand words. While leaving, there was a positive smile on Ajit Pawar's face. He left with a renewed poise....' A meeting followed at the NCP leader Praful Patel's home just as the Supreme Court was hearing the appeal demanding a floor test. By afternoon, Ajit had decided to return to the NCP and conveyed this to Fadnavis. He resigned as the deputy chief minister and Fadnavis faced the embarrassment of heading the most short-lived government in Maharashtra.

Sule dismisses the rebellion by Ajit as an issue which was sorted out. 'It didn't need much persuasion. It was decided after a healthy discussion within the family. It wasn't insecurity but a decision my brother took. He felt differently about an issue but then he saw what the family felt and it all worked out,' she says adding, 'there is no mistrust. We were and still remain a close knit family. Life has a lot of surprises. Every family goes through issues and so did ours. The only difference is that ours come out in the newspapers and others' do not.' But is she the true inheritor of her father's political legacy or that mantle will be donned by Ajit? 'This is public life and it cannot be so shallow. You have to earn the trust of the people you represent. Y. B. Chavan's legacy was inherited by my father Sharad Pawar even when there was no blood relation. So people and time decide who inherits what. People of Maharashtra will decide what role I play,' says Sule.

KAVITHA KALVAKUNTLA

The Cultural Ambassador

For Ravi a job in Saudi Arabia was his ticket out of Chepur village in the Armoor mandal. His family had always struggled with basic necessities such as educating their children and making a decent living in a remote village of Nizamabad district in northern Telangana. A placement agency, one of the innumerable that dot the Nizamabad landscape, got Ravi a job to tend to the camels of a rich sheikh in Saudi Arabia. He got a two-year employment visa and left. He was quick in sending money back home. As years passed, Ravi did not get his visa renewed and overstayed for about six years. He wanted to return, but the employer refused to allow him to go. When Ravi insisted, he was beaten up. He called home weeping and wondered if he would ever be able to return. The family desperately reached out to community leaders who, in turn, approached Kavitha Kalvakuntla, Nizamabad's former member of parliament. Kalvakuntla moved swiftly, calling India's ambassador to Saudi Arabia. The local police intervened and Ravi was rescued. His employer volunteered to get his papers corrected at his own expense and paid for Ravi's medical treatment. Ravi says he owes his life to Kalvakuntla. 'I don't know if any leader is so involved in a common man's life,' he says.

From the ill-treatment by employers in Gulf countries to sudden deaths during the Covid-19 lockdown and confinement in prison for flouting visa conditions—there are several stories like Ravi's in Nizamabad district. After all, the district has roughly two lakh families who have sent at least one member to the Gulf countries for work. Over the years, Kalvakuntla has helped many in need through her non-governmental organization Telangana Jagruthi. 'We have clear instructions from Kavithaji that every person in distress needs to be helped,' says Shaik Ahmed Shahdullah, UAE Jagruthi Charity coordinator. 'Over the years the systems have been put in place. There are so many workers from Nizamabad who pass away in hospitals in Gulf countries. It is not only expensive to bring back their dead bodies but the paperwork can be overwhelming for the families. When a family approaches us with a problem like someone with a false case, visa overstay issue, or a death in a prison or hospital, we do the paperwork till the person is on the flight home,' he says. The expenses can go upto 9,000 dirhams (roughly about ₹1.50 lakh). 'Kavithaji bears the expense in every genuine case where a person is in distress,' says Ahmed. 'Our Jagruthi volunteers are now so involved that Indian consulate officials and local police know them well and realize that we want to help people reach home,' he says.

Starting Telangana Jagruthi in 2005 was Kalvakuntla's idea to involve more women in the Telangana Movement. Till then, she was a non-resident Indian (NRI) who had taken the impromptu decision to return to Hyderabad with her family on her son's first birthday celebrations. She had no intention of joining politics despite the fact that her father, K. Chandrasekhar Rao, was leading a movement to carve a separate state of Telangana from Andhra Pradesh.

THE CULTURAL CONNECT

Kalvakuntla grew up in a political family. K. Chandrasekhar Rao or KCR, as he is fondly called, was a member of legislative assembly (MLA) in a united Andhra Pradesh. He had started as a Youth Congress leader and later joined N. T. Rama Rao's Telugu Desam Party (TDP) only to quit it to form his own regional party, the Telangana Rashtra Samithi (TRS), to fight for a separate Telangana state. Despite growing up mostly in the MLA quarters in the state capital of Hyderabad, Kalvakuntla says she was never politically inclined. 'I did my schooling from Stanley Girls School in Hyderabad. My generation was the dollar dreams generation. It was a simple formula—take MCP (Maths, Chemistry, Physics) in class eleventh, pursue engineering, take GRE and TOEFL, and go to America. So I followed this formula to the dot. I went to US for my masters. Unfortunately, in the final year just before my dissertation, I met with an accident. I had to come back to India and I couldn't complete my masters,' she says. Kalvakuntla got married and returned to the US. 'My son was born in September 2003. We came to India to celebrate his first birthday in September 2004. When we looked at everybody we realized what we had been missing. So we decided to move back. I never went back to even pack up. My husband packed up everything and quit his job. It was an impulsive decision but it was the best decision. What used to irritate me the most was the people could never get my name right—Kaveeta, they would call me. You always feel alien in that country,' says Kalvakuntla.

2004, the year Kalvakuntla returned to India, was a crucial one in the fight for a separate Telangana state. The Congress-led

UPA had deprived the Atal Bihari Vajpayee-led NDA of a second term at the centre. The UPA's National Common Minimum Programme, which outlined the objectives of the coalition government, acknowledged the demand for a separate state of Telangana. 'The UPA government will consider the demand for the formation of a Telangana state at an appropriate time after due consultations and consensus,' the document laid down. This brought hope to KCR who wanted to take the statehood demand to the national level. 'It was the highest point anyone could take it to the national level. Indira Gandhi had earlier crushed it mercilessly,' says Kalvakuntla. Though most partymen thought she had returned to help her father, Kalvakuntla had no such plans. 'In 2004, joining politics wasn't even an option before me. I always wanted to be an entrepreneur. I brought the Lakme salon franchise to Hyderabad,' she says. But gradually she got drawn into the Telangana Movement. The first year after her return was spent travelling through Andhra Pradesh to understand the problems faced by the people. 'During this time I met many women who said to me that all they needed was ₹1,000 per month to lead a decent life. I thought what is ₹1,000 for me? It is a dinner with my family. I knew I had to do something for these women and I started my own non-governmental organization—the Telangana Jagruthi,' she says.

Her travels revealed a surprising ground reality for Kalvakuntla—women were not closely involved in the Telangana Movement. They did not feel connected to the cause of a separate state. While reading a book on the Indian freedom struggle, Kalvakuntla chanced upon Bal Gangadhar Tilak's idea of celebrating Ganesh Chaturthi. Tilak, who is popularly known as the father of Indian unrest, had successfully made Ganesh Chaturthi a community festival and a forum to talk about nationalism to fight against the British. 'I realized that I needed to take an indigenous festival and ensure women identified with it and participated in it. I found Bathukamma,' she says. Bathukamma is a nine-day festival of flowers which is celebrated during the auspicious time of Navratras in end-September or

October. It is a festival to thank Goddess Parvati for nature's bounty and to seek her blessings for the next year. Traditionally, the men of the household bring home seasonal flowers and the women make Bathukamma, which is a beautiful arrangement of flowers in seven concentric layers in the shape of a temple's gopuram (the entrance tower in South Indian architecture).

Kalvakuntla distinctly remembers celebrating the festival till she was in third standard when her family moved from the village to Hyderabad. 'Even after we moved to Hyderabad, we used to go back to the village to celebrate Bathukamma till my grandmother was alive. But then after her death we almost stopped celebrating. Nobody celebrated it in Hyderabad. We were in MLA quarters and there were representatives from Rayalaseema and other parts of Andhra Pradesh where Bathukamma is not celebrated. I realized that I had a big challenge before me. I had to remind my mother's generation about this festival, inform my generation, and inspire the future generation to celebrate it,' she says. Kalvakuntla gave women a cause to identify with. 'We need to market properly any cause or a plank you want to take to the people,' she says. This was the turning point for Kalvakuntla. She carefully planned a media strategy. 'I realized that our festivals were not being covered by mainstream media, which gave enough space to Andhra festivals like Sakranti. In 2007, I decided to spend money on buying slots on television. I bought half an hour slot from 8–8.30 p.m. for the nine days of Bathukamma festival during Navratras. I had only one chance—I knew if one TV channel showed us, the next year many channels would be open to the idea. I also roped in a newspaper. I travelled to nine of the ten districts of Telangana region and every day we used to send photographs of the festival being celebrated for publishing in the newspaper.'

Celebrating it in the first year was not an easy task. Kalvakuntla says she did not get permission to hold massive celebrations at Tank Bund (a landmark in Hyderabad) despite there being a Bathukamma ghat. Undeterred, she went to the High Court to get permission and was allowed to hold the celebrations. 'This is how oppressive regimes put down people—they first ensure that people forget their language and culture,' she says. It took just one year for the mainstream media to sit up and take notice. 'Next year, TV channels and newspapers approached us for buying space. We have come a long way—now celebrating Bathukamma is a fashion statement,' she says. The festival brought women on the streets through a traditional route. Once they met and bonded, identifying with a demand for Telangana was easy. It earned Kalvakuntla the nickname 'Bathukamma Kavithamma'.

THE YEARS OF STRUGGLE

As Kalvakuntla worked diligently at the grassroots, giving the people of Telangana region a social and cultural platform, her father fought politically for statehood. Between 2004 and 2009, KCR collected letters of support from thirty-two political parties to push for the division of Andhra Pradesh. 'My father had always told me that we will take our voice to the people through the political medium. If political medium does not give what you want, then you take to the roads and follow the agitation route. He says he visited (Bahujan Samaj Party supremo) Mayawatiji nineteen times to convince her to give a letter of support and the nineteenth time she gave the letter,' says Kalvakuntla. Though the Congress was in power at the centre and in Andhra Pradesh, it could not build a consensus on dividing the state. Its powerful Chief Minister Y. S. Rajasekhara Reddy did not support the move and gave feedback to the centre that bifurcation would mean the return of naxalism to the state. Seeing the Congress's reluctance to address the thorny issue, KCR walked out of UPA in 2006. In September 2009, the powerful YSR died in a helicopter crash. As the Congress struggled to keep its house in order after losing a grassroots leader, KCR declared a fast unto death on 29 November to force the UPA's hand. 'It was a very difficult time for the family. He is a frugal eater anyways. He fasted for eleven days and survived only because of his will power,' she says. Looking at KCR's health, the UPA decided to accede to the demand. On 9 December, then Home Minister P. Chidambaram issued a midnight statement giving an impression that Telangana would be created. KCR ended his hunger strike. However, within days on 23 December, Chidambaram clarified his 9 December statement and bought more time for any final call on bifurcation. Widespread protests and resignations from both camps of MLAs followed in the state. KCR called for the formation of a Joint Action Committee (JAC) on Telangana. He asked all political parties to join it to push for statehood. In February 2010, the centre formed the Srikrishna Committee to examine bifurcation of Andhra Pradesh.

Kalvakuntla's Telangana Jagruthi worked extensively to spread awareness about the movement. It brought out books on the history of the movement. 'We actively participated in interventions like forming a human chain from Adilabad (a district near Maharashtra border) to Mehboobnagar (the district on Karnataka border). We involved women by giving a call to make one crore Bathukammas on the eighteen days of the festival (originally Bathukamma was celebrated for eighteen days) and put tags of "Jai Telangana" on each Bathukamma. When the Srikrishna Committee was formed and started hearing all stakeholders, Jagruthi was one of the major organizations which represented how even in school syllabus they do not talk about Telangana culture,' Kalvakuntla recalls the years of struggle.

Over the years, the Congress lost significant ground in Andhra Pradesh. The ruling party did not want to give in to YSR's son, Y S Jaganmohan Reddy, who was pressuring the Congress leadership to make him the state's chief minister. The Congress's K. Rosaiah, who took over after YSR's death, was replaced by N. Kiran Kumar Reddy in a year's time. This paved the way for Jagan floating his own party, the YSR Congress Party (YSRCP), in March 2011. At the same time, KCR's TRS was fast gaining popularity with its demand for bifurcation. The Congress realized it would need to divide the state if it wanted to remain politically relevant. In July 2013, the Congress Working Committee (CWC) passed a resolution calling for the creation of Telangana. It clearly showed the intention of the ruling party. On 3 October 2013, the union cabinet approved the bifurcation of Andhra Pradesh and constituted a Group of Ministers (GoM) to hold consultations and finalize a Reorganisation Bill. The parliament passed the Andhra Pradesh Reorganisation Bill in February 2014, months before the Lok Sabha elections. It was notified in the gazette on 1 March 2014. This was a major victory for KCR's TRS.

STEPPING INTO POLITICS

Since KCR had formed his party to give voice to regional aspirations, there was a big question before him—should the party fight the first elections independently or merge with the Congress. 'The opinion across the state was that regional aspirations can be represented and protected better by a regional party like TRS. People felt that if we merged with Congress the decisions will all be centralized,' says Kalvakuntla about her father's decision to fight the new state's assembly and parliamentary elections. KCR turned to his children, son K T Rama Rao and Kalvakuntla. 'Until Telangana formation, I didn't think I would step into politics. I was just running my organization very actively. The party needed known faces to fight elections. My father asked me to contest from Nizamabad and I accepted the task,' she says.

The first elections were a cakewalk for the TRS, which won 11 out of the 17 Lok Sabha seats and 63 of the 119 assembly constituencies in the newly-formed state. Kalvakuntla beat her closest rival, the Congress's Madhu Yaskhi Goud, bagging 42.49 per cent of the votes. The political scenario for the TRS MPs entering the parliament was very interesting. The results were declared in May, but the state came into existence on 2 June 2014. This was a curious case of representing a state in the parliament without the state formally coming into existence. Kalvakuntla remembers the paradoxical situation the TRS MPs found themselves in. 'When we entered parliament, we were told that even after the formation of the state we will still be called the Andhra Pradesh MPs. We were crestfallen. We didn't want to be called Andhra Pradesh MPs—that was our entire battle. But they told us that division was a long drawn and complicated process and for a month we will be called Andhra Pradesh MPs,' she says.

The bifurcation of Andhra Pradesh had been high on drama, street protests, and violence. The division of assets was difficult. But the TRS was not pulling punches now. 'The first one year we wanted to ensure that the terms on which the state was divided should be fulfilled. Formation of a high court was a big issue for us. I remember standing in parliament for twenty days holding a placard "We want our high court". The central government was not fulfilling that promise. Till date there are unfulfilled promises like industrial incentives, a steel factory in Khammam, a railway coach factory, and a tribal university,' she says.

But parliamentary procedures were new for Kalvakuntla, who had only been introduced to street and agitation politics. If experienced Lok Sabha MPs like N. K. Premachandran guided her on rules and procedures, there were senior university professors who helped her in grasping the nuances of public policy, finance, and international affairs. 'I deliberately chose subjects like finance and international policy to speak in parliament. I took proper lessons when I came to Delhi. I had a brilliant people connect but then I did not know about policy making,' she says. The maiden speech of an MP is always special. It is like a film star's debut. First-time MPs put in several days of work—coordinating closely with their research team and perfecting on speech delivery. If you are from a political family, the maiden speech provides an opportunity to political leaders across party lines for a direct comparison with the entrenched parent or sibling. Kalvakuntla, however, was thrown into the deep end by her father who sprung a surprise by suddenly telling her to speak in the parliament. 'The first time I spoke in parliament was on a motion of thanks to the President's address. This was the time when they had taken nine mandals from Telangana and given away to Andhra Pradesh through an Ordinance as Chandrababu Naidu's TDP (who had come to power in Andhra Pradesh after 2014 elections) was in alliance with BJP. My father called me in the morning and told me to give a speech. I remember I had only half an hour to prepare and reach the House in time. Through Jagruthi I had filed several petitions against Polavaram Dam pointing out that building it would deprive Telangana of its water share. My father said you have worked extensively on this and these mandals are being taken away to build Polavaram,' she remembers. After the call from her father, the young MP went to the parliament library to sit peacefully and write down the speech. 'There wasn't much scope for research but we had struggled for the state so much that every issue is etched in our minds. Luckily, the speech was received very well. At least forty to fifty MPs sent me a congratulatory note saying I had spoken well. Many senior MPs verbally congratulated. The maiden speech is considered special but I didn't know all that. I learnt on the job,' she says. Gradually, Kalvakuntla started grasping parliamentary procedures and decorum.

Kalvakuntla made quite an impression with the choice of subjects she spoke on. In the second session of the new Lok Sabha in August 2014, Kalvakuntla raised the issue of the rehabilitation of Kashmiri Pandits. While the BJP government at the centre maintained that rehabilitation of Kashmiri Pandits was a continuous process, the Telangana MP's speech centred around how Kashmiri Pandits died of sunstroke, snake bites, and out of depression in makeshift tents created for their rehabilitation. She demanded a retrial in the case of Farooq Ahmed Dar (alias Bitta Karate), who was accused of killing over twenty people, including many Kashmiri Pandits. The BJP patriarch L. K. Advani was so impressed by the speech that he stood in the Lok Sabha to support the young MP and said, 'I feel that everything that Kavithaji has said today carries a lot of weight.'

Despite being the Telangana chief minister's daughter, Kalvakuntla never had the privilege of being introduced to any political leader by her father. 'My father never introduced me to anybody. When you belong to a political family, there is a huge burden on you. There will be an obvious comparison between you and your parent. I carried the burden of performing in my very first speech in parliament. It is compared to their (parent's) forty–fifty years in public life. I am not cribbing about it. There are obvious privileges of being born in a political family. I must have picked up some things naturally while growing up in a house with him (KCR) around,' she says.

NURTURING NIZAMABAD

With the electoral victory came big responsibilities. Being KCR's daughter meant a general expectation that the Nizamabad constituency will get drinking water, better educational and healthcare institutions, and infrastructure projects. Kalvakuntla gave her own manifesto in the run-up to the 2014 elections. 'The biggest promise I made was piped water supply and drinking water to every household. I did not want women to carry water because it is a lot of productive hours wasted. Our state government took this up and we have delivered. In my district, agricultural land was about four lakh acres. I had promised that I will double this to 8 lakh acres because we wanted more surface water to flow into our fields. But thanks to our irrigation projects, it has trebled to 12 lakh acres. The third was getting turmeric board as there are more than 60,000 turmeric farmers,' she recalls.[1]

Even before she had won the election, she had scored a victory with the women. During her travels through the state, Kalvakuntla had noticed that a number of women work in the fields and factories the entire day and when they return home they start rolling bidis. 'Rolling bidis is like a second income for these women. They get a paltry ₹500–600 per month. They don't give this extra income to their husbands but use it to put their children into English medium schools,' she says. KCR was coming to campaign for Kalvakuntla in Nizamabad in 2014.

Sitting with her father in the helicopter Kalvakuntla pitched the idea of a state pension for these women. She requested he announce it in Nizamabad. 'When the chopper was just landing, he calculated that there were 4 lakh women bidi workers in the state and giving them ₹1,000 will mean a burden of ₹450 crore. He agreed as we landed and he announced the pension.'

The newly-formed state saw a spate of welfare schemes being rolled out between 2014 and 2019. The government provided 6 kilograms of rice per family member at ₹1, introduced Kalyana Lakshmi or Shaadi Mubarak scheme to give financial assistance of ₹1 lakh to get girls from poor families married, Rythu Bandhu scheme to support farmers investment for two crop cycles, free electricity for agriculture sector, and free housing for homeless poor. The TRS state government invested heavily in irrigation projects, piped water supply, roads and building district administration infrastructure. The development initiatives helped Kalvakuntla in her constituency. Shweta, a bidi worker in Borgaon village in Nizamabad, sums up the impact of KCR's governance model. 'Every household has at least two beneficiaries of KCR's schemes. My husband works in the Gulf and I have two college going children. I get good quality of rice every month, bidi worker pension and the government dispensary and hospital is very well-equipped. My neighbours have benefitted from Kalyana Lakshmi scheme,' she says as she rolls bidis and places them meticulously in a basket. This, however, did not stop Shweta and several like her in Nizamabad from voting against the TRS and Kalvakuntla in the 2019 parliamentary elections. One of the few in her village who can converse in Hindi, Shweta translates for her fellow bidi workers, 'We were told that the bidi pension will stop if we did not vote for the BJP. We believed them.'

THE SHOCKING MANDATE

It was a shock defeat for Kalvakuntla in the 2019 parliamentary elections. Telangana had given a second term to the TRS and her father just four months earlier in December 2018. The

TRS lost on only two seats in the parliamentary elections—one was Kalvakuntla's Nizamabad. The BJP's Dharmapuri Arvind defeated Kalvakuntla by 70,000 votes.

Behind the loss was a farmer's demand—the establishment of a turmeric board. A prominent farmer leader from Nizamabad Narasimha Naidu explains, 'Nizamabad farmers grow commercial crops like turmeric and red jowar. But they do not get remunerative price for their crop. There is a long-pending demand to have a separate turmeric board. Though there is a Spice Board, a turmeric board will get better funding and price for these farmers.' During her term as an MP, Kalvakuntla was aware of the sensitivity of this demand. She approached chief ministers of other states including Tamil Nadu and Maharashtra and rallied support for a separate turmeric board. She had also moved a private member's bill—the Turmeric Board Bill 2017—in the Lok Sabha in March 2017 trying to show her intention in pushing the move. In 2019, the BJP candidate Arvind caught the attention of the farmers as he signed on a stamp paper and promised a Turmeric Board if he is elected. It became an election issue. Farmers were miffed. About 200 farmers decided to file their nomination papers from Nizamabad and challenge the chief minister's daughter. After the scrutiny of nominations, 179 farmers remained in fray, apart from seven other candidates representing political parties. There were 186 candidates, including Kalvakuntla, fighting in the Nizamabad parliamentary constituency. Naveed Iqbal, a two-term former corporator in Nizamabad district and a prominent minorities leader, says, 'The polling centres were changing very often in Nizamabad because a rescheduling exercise of housing colonies had taken place. We had flagged this to the party.' He says the party workers had taken it for granted that Kalvakuntla will win. 'Madam ko jeetna hee hai (Madam has to win)—this was the general feeling. So many committed voters did not turn up,' he says. When the names of 186 candidates were arranged, multiple electronic voting machines (EVMs) had to be arranged sequentially. 'On the ground this became a practical election management problem. Since there were so many nominations, there were twenty-four electronic voting machines (EVMs) which were kept in an L-shaped formation in the room for the voter. My name was first on the list. The practical problem that arose was that in some places the L-shaped formation was inverted and many voters just pressed the first button they saw. The votes were scattered. My estimate is that we lost about 1 lakh votes because of this. The most interesting aspect was that my voteshare increased by 30,000 votes in 2019 over my 2014 election,' says Kalvakuntla. The party had clearly underestimated the groundswell over farmers issue. The 179 farmers cornered 96,000 votes. 'Whatever it was I could not see. So I take full responsibility for the loss. It has taught a great lesson to me for life. I can confidently say that I will never lose an election if I fight one,' she says.

After her defeat in the elections, Kalvakuntla has drastically reduced her visits to Nizamabad. She has continued her work through an efficient team. She spearheads campaigns emphasizing the need for institutional deliveries, wearing helmets while driving, and works closely to improve healthcare facilities in the government hospital. The step closest to her heart is providing free food to attendants of patients coming for treatment. There is a mechanized kitchen which prepares food to serve to the family members of patients. Ask her why she has not been visiting the constituency or pushing her own schemes and she says she wants to give space to the people and the new MP. 'The new representative should be given time and space to perform. It is democracy and one should respect the choice of the people and not start criticizing the very next day. Now I will start visiting the people.... I think a child's biggest fear is of disappointing one's parents.... When I lost the election in 2019 this was the first thought in my head. My father has never lost an election. The only election he lost was his first one when he was fresh out of student politics. But after that he has never lost an election. He was not disappointed. It was a technical loss not an ethical loss for me.'

She feels that a weak heart can never survive in politics.

'You have to love your job,' she says. A big votary for increasing representation for women in legislature and parliament, Kalvakuntla feels it needs to be a bottoms-up approach. 'Having women in parliament is important but having women in panchayats is necessary. Initially, probably twice, somebody's mother, sister, and daughter will be elected but the next time it will be a woman leader who deserves to be there. Another important step is the formation of women self-help groups which help in the financial empowerment of women. Telangana has introduced 50 per cent reservation for women in agricultural marketing committees,' she says. But rather than a fixed set of constituencies being reserved for women cyclically, as is proposed in the Women's Reservation Bill pending in parliament, Kalvakuntla feels the political parties should be given the freedom to choose the seat and the percentage to be allocated. 'This is not my party's opinion but my own—political parties should be given freedom to select whatever percentage 33 per cent or 50 per cent, which can be agreed upon by parties, to field women candidates. If you reserve a seat, two or three women fight against each other and only one emerges victorious. If the scene is reversed and political parties are given the freedom then they look for winnable women candidates,' she explains.

Kalvakuntla got elected as a member of the legislative council from the Nizamabad Local Authorities constituency in a by-election in October 2020. The next year in December, she was elected unopposed. She has identified education and employment generation as two key areas for her to work on.

KANIMOZHI KARUNANIDHI

The Poet Politician

A group of transgender rights activists were waiting at Namakkal Kavingnar Maligai, which houses the secretariat of the Tamil Nadu government in the historic Fort St George complex in Chennai. The Dravida Munnetra Kazhagam (DMK) had formed the government a fifth time under M. Karunanidhi in 2006. His youngest daughter Kanimozhi had brought this delegation to meet the education minister K. Ponmudi. Thirty-nine-year-old Kanimozhi wanted Ponmudi to solve a problem—the transgender people did not have access to admission in colleges as they had to declare their gender and the form specified only two options—male or female. As Ponmudi was in a meeting with the chief minister, the delegation waited patiently in the common waiting area. As the meeting finished, Karunanidhi and Ponmudi emerged together from the room and the chief minister spotted his daughter. 'What are you doing here? Have you come to see me?' he asked. Kanimozhi said, 'No I have brought these people to meet the minister and make a representation.' Karunanidhi left the secretariat and the delegation met the education minister to explain their struggle to get college admissions. Hours later when Kanimozhi returned home, she found her father waiting. Curious about the issue, he asked her and Kanimozhi explained how transgender people were forced to drop out of school, how many become beggars and prostitutes and did not have any identification.

Kanimozhi remembers how her father constituted a committee and Tamil Nadu became the first state to establish the Transgender Persons Welfare Board in 2008, introduce the third gender option in college admission forms, and issue Aravani (transgender) cards which became the gateway for getting voter IDs, family cards, and passports. These documents helped transgender people to tap into the government's welfare schemes. It wasn't just documentation but the respect that Karunanidhi gave. He called transgender people 'Thirunangai'—'Thiru' is used to show respect to someone and 'nangai' means woman.[1] The understated Kanimozhi, a two-term Rajya Sabha MP and Lok Sabha MP from the Thoothukudi constituency, is known as a champion of social issues and is a vocal campaigner of the rights for the differently-abled and the lesbian, gay, bisexual, and transgender (LGBT) community. This could easily be an attribute of her upbringing.

THE SWEET ONE

The name Kanimozhi literally means 'sweet or honeyed language' in Tamil. Karunanidhi had married Dayalu Ammal[2] after the death of his first wife Padmavathi Ammal but fell in love with Rajathi Ammal during an election campaign in the 1960s. In January 1968, Rajathi Ammal gave birth to Kanimozhi and when the hospital asked for the father's name she gave the name 'M. Karunanidhi'. Fresh out of a humiliating defeat in the 1967 assembly elections, the Congress was looking to embarrass the DMK, which had formed the government in Tamil Nadu under C. N. Annadurai. A Congress MLA tried to confront Karunanidhi during an assembly session and asked, 'Who is Rajathi?' The legendary response from the quick-witted Karunanidhi was, 'En magal Kanimozhiyin thaayaar (She is the mother of my daughter Kanimozhi).' He had silenced his critics. Karunanidhi had married Rajathi Ammal as per a tradition started by the DMK known as Swayam Maryada Kalyamam (roughly translated to marriage of self-respect). It did not require the presence of priests and only the blessings of party elders. By law, these marriages are not legal if the spouse is alive. This did not mean growing up was easy for Kanimozhi. 'Yes, it was not easy. A lot of people use it to hurt you. But one thing it has taught me is to never stand in judgement of anybody. And I am very grateful to both my parents for that,' says Kanimozhi.[3] She did her schooling from Chennai's Church Park Presentation Convent.

The youngest child in the family, Kanimozhi was considered Karunanidhi's literary heir and his favourite. He was very open about the living arrangement with his two wives. Even as chief minister, he spent his evenings at Rajathi Ammal and Kanimozhi's home at CIT colony and mornings at his Gopalapuram home where Dayalu Ammal lived. DMK leaders say he referred to Dayalu Ammal as 'Manaivi' (wife) and Rajathi Ammal as 'Thunaivi' (companion), giving equal importance and respect to both. Kanimozhi remembers growing up in an open house surrounded by politics. 'Growing up I was surrounded by politics. It was an open house to political leaders and party cadres who would keep coming throughout the day to meet my father,' Kanimozhi told this author. 'These leaders were your family and your family friends and relatives. I got an opportunity to see different people from various parts of the country. It was a learning experience about life itself—what politics can really do, how an election victory earns you a lot of new friends and once you lose an election how people abandon you. It teaches you how short lived power is. It can be real and unreal at the same time,' she says.

Though Kanimozhi doesn't think she had a sheltered life, Karunanidhi was fiercely protective of his daughter, especially her privacy. 'It wasn't a protected upbringing. But I did not go out to my friends' homes so freely—like walk out and go to somebody's house. One thing I could not tolerate was having security personnel around me. As I started growing up, my parents would ask me to take some security along, but I somehow never liked that. In fact, in college I would hail an auto and go to a friend's place or to attend classes. There were cars but sometimes it used to happen that I didn't want to wait for the car to come back after dropping my father or my mother somewhere,' she says. Like all young adults, Kanimozhi says even she did not see her parent's point of view. 'Finally my father came down to a point when he said exasperatedly, "If you really want to travel alone, take a bus and but don't take an auto." He felt it was safer for me to travel in a bus with more number of people around,' laughs Kanimozhi remembering the college days.

Sandhya Ravishankar has described Kanimozhi has 'an awkward child in the Karunanidhi family' in her book *Karunanidhi: A Life in Politics*. She does not share a close bond with her stepbrothers and stepsister. 'He (Karunanidhi) has never made me feel alienated,' says Kanimozhi. 'He has never made me feel anything that way. He has never given me any reason for him to explain anything. He has never let my mother down either. There are many politicians who make mistakes or do things. And they try to hide it under the carpet or they even hurt the person. Their children are neglected. I know children who do not have the courage to say who the father is because they may not live for another day if they did. So, if you look at all of that, my father was a very, very good man that way. I am not justifying it or saying that what he did was right or wrong. But I am grateful for what I learnt from it—never to judge.'[4]

She has inherited her love for the written word from her father. Kanimozhi says he introduced her to Periyar's thought and his writings. She started composing poetry from a very young age, expressing pain and feelings beyond her years. Naturally inclined towards the written word, it wasn't a surprise that she did not venture into politics. She did her master's in economics from Ethiraj College for Women at the Madras University. When she was barely twenty-one years, she got married to Athiban Bose in 1989. The marriage, however, did not last long and ended in divorce. In 1992, Kanimozhi started working as sub-editor with south India's leading national daily *The Hindu*. 'Growing up, I was very clear that I did not want to get into politics. I was always into art and poetry and was fascinated by the way films and theatre could influence people. DMK also has a culture for using art forms and films to talk about social issues,' says Kanimozhi. She found love again in G. Aravindan and tied the knot in 1997. 'Our love for art, music, and the written word is what brought us together,' says Kanimozhi. As Aravindan was settled in Singapore, Kanimozhi moved there with him. She was gone for about two years but was called back by her family as she needed to take care of her mother. 'My husband started dividing his time between Singapore and India. My son Aditya was born and I never returned to Singapore,' she says.

Over the years, Kanimozhi evolved as the party's cultural ambassador. Karunanidhi's political arrest in 2001 by the AIADMK government saw the daughter squatting alongwith her father in front of Chennai Central Prison. The photograph became a lasting image of Tamil Nadu's vendetta politics between the AIADMK and DMK. About a decade later, Kanimozhi would remember the episode on Twitter, posting the same image of her young self next to her father saying, 'The lesson I learnt from the rebel (Karunanidhi) was that prison and throne are the same for people who defy fear. Though I was sitting alone with him, thousands of udanpirapus (party workers) were facing a lathicharge for him.'[5] She was always a sensitive and expressive poet, but she evolved into a rights activist during these years.

In 2005, she launched a website on free speech, *Karuthu*, with then union minister P. Chidambaram's son Karti. Though she remained apolitical and removed from politics, she became a focal point of several social causes. In 2006, disability rights activists and people with disabilities held a huge meeting in Cuddalore. After this meeting, they took their representation to Kanimozhi, who took the demands to Karunanidhi and the chief minister who constituted a separate board. She thought of providing employment opportunities and organized the Kalaignar 85 job fairs in small towns. In September 2006, Kanimozhi thought of showcasing Tamil Nadu's culture, cuisine, martial arts, street plays, drama, and performing arts, and in early 2007, launched the biggest cultural initiative in Tamil Nadu—the Chennai Sangamam, a week-long cultural extravaganza marking Pongal celebrations in the state. She brought artistes from across the state to showcase their art forms in an open festival organized at various places in Chennai, including beaches, parks, colleges, and shopping malls.

Even as she worked quietly, largely as an influencer nudging the government towards people-friendly policies, Karunanidhi thought of pushing her towards politics. 'My father wanted me to get into direct politics and come to Delhi. I was very hesitant. I feel that involvement in electoral politics comes with a lot of compromises and sacrifices. As a writer, you are an individual answerable only to yourself. Participating in politics comes with its responsibilities. I had seen my father's involvement. His entire day belonged to the people and he had to steal moments from his day for himself. I did not want to be under the microscope. My son was young. I wasn't sure if I would be able to devote time to active politics,' says Kanimozhi. 'Since I was involved in a number of social campaigns, I had realized over the years that when you are a part of a political system, it is easier to influence government decisions. I had seen it when we used to take up issues like bus passes or hurdle-free environment for differently-abled people. During this time all this was also playing in my mind. A few party seniors also spoke to me expressing their keenness for me to become a part of the party structure. There was a seat coming up in Rajya Sabha and on my father's insistence I stepped into politics.'

TRIAL BY FIRE

Kanimozhi entered the Rajya Sabha in 2007 when the DMK was an alliance partner in the ruling UPA government. As soon as Kanimozhi stepped into active public life, she was drawn into the 2G spectrum allocation scandal. To understand Kanimozhi's initial years, it is essential to know the basics of what is often termed as India's biggest political corruption scam. At the centre of this corruption scandal was the DMK MP and Telecom Minister Andimuthu Raja, considered close to Kanimozhi. Raja took over as the telecom minister in May 2007 and initiated the process of allotment of 2G Spectrum for telecom along with Universal Access Service (UAS) Licences in September 2007. His ministry fixed the deadline as 1 October 2007 for application. The department of telecommunciations decided to issue licenses on a first-come first-serve basis and advanced the application deadline from 1 October to 25 September. The entire process came under a cloud when the department posted a notice on its website on the same day that any company applying for a licence between 3.30 p.m. and 4.30 p.m. will be given a licence on a first-come first-serves basis. In November 2007, Prime Minister Manmohan Singh and the finance ministry pointed out problem areas, but Raja rejected the suggestions. In May 2009, the scam hit headlines when the Central Vigilance Commission (CVC) acted on complaints from an NGO named Telecom Watchdog and an activist alleging that the spectrum had been allocated at throwaway prices to Swan Telecom and Loop Telecom and asked the Central Bureau of Investigation (CBI) to investigate any irregularities. The CBI registered an FIR against unnamed officials of the department. In 2010, the Comptroller and Auditor General of India (CAG) presented its report questioning the first-come first-serve policy and pegging the loss to the exchequer at ₹1.76 lakh crore. The CBI chargesheeted Raja and others in April 2011 and the CBI calculated the 2G spectrum allocation loss at ₹30,984 crore.[6] While the CBI was investigating the spectrum allocation, the Enforcement Directorate started a money laundering investigation and alleged that ₹214 crore was paid as bribe by Swan Telecom promoters which was routed through Karunanidhi family-owned Kalaignar TV. Kanimozhi and Kalaignar TV MD Sharath Kumar held 20 per cent stake each in Kalaignar TV, while Karunanidhi's wife and Kanimozhi's stepmother Dayalu Ammal held 60 per cent share. Kanimozhi was denied bail and arrested on 21 May 2011. She spent 193 days in jail and was released on bail in November 2011. On 21 December 2017, all accused, including Kanimozhi were acquitted by a special court.[7]

Speaking about the allegations, Kanimozhi says, 'The takeaway from that episode for me was that women are dispensable. When I stepped into politics I was not sure whether I wanted to continue in politics after one term or whether I wanted to go back to writing or work in art. This episode made me decide. I realized if it is happening to me it may be happening to so many women. I wanted to be there if in any way I could help the cause of other women. Somehow it gives you the resolve and makes you a very strong person. I felt if I can go through this I can go through anything.' Kanimozhi remembers how the scandal had hurt her father. 'I did not want to be a part of Kalaignar TV at all. So I was resisting it initially. My father felt it is not right that I am not in the venture. He thought it is a family venture so I should be a part of it. He talked me into it. Later when this happened he felt bad that because of his insistence I got into Kalaignar TV and then had to go through a long-drawn case because of it,' she remembers. Kanimozhi honestly admits being disturbed by the scandal. 'It does hurt a lot when you come to know what happened around you. I won't say that there were not days that I was disturbed but then I did not want to let it bring me down. I was very clear about that. It took ten years for the case to end. As the trial goes on, it is so long drawn.

It is taxing in many ways. There is so much of uncertainty around you. It is not easy. Till the verdict comes you are not sure. Especially in political cases it is not just the law which is at work. You can never be sure. It is very difficult for people around you. You feel so guilty for making people who love you go through it,' she says. Kanimozhi drew her strength from her husband. 'He was there with me all throughout. It gives you so much strength that there is somebody who understands you and you can share what you are going through. It makes a lot of difference. He was my connect to the entire world,' she says. At this time, her closest friends held onto her. 'You still realize that when the world has turned against you, there are still some friends left who will be with you,' she says.

After two successive terms as a Rajya Sabha MP, Kanimozhi finally decided to get into electoral politics and fight her first Lok Sabha election from the Thoothukudi parliamentary constituency in 2019.

THE DEBUT

Thoothukudi parliamentary constituency comprises six assembly segments—Thoothukudi, Tiruchendur, Vilathikulam, Kovilpatti, Ottapidaram, and Srivaikuntam. The choice of the constituency was curious as it wasn't a party stronghold as such. The DMK had won the seat in 2009 but had been upstaged by the AIADMK in subsequent elections. In the 2014 parliamentary polls, the AIADMK had won the seat and later in the 2016 assembly elections the AIADMK had won 4 out of 6 segments. 'I discussed with my brother (M K Stalin). He advised me to take this one,' she explains the choice. Kanimozhi had not been paratrooped into an uncharted territory. She was in-charge of southern districts of Tamil Nadu, including Thoothukudi, in the 2016 assembly elections. A well-known environment crusader, Kanimozhi had been raising the issue of mercury contamination in Kodaikanal with the union ministry of environment, forest, and climate change since 2016. So when police opened fire killing fourteen persons protesting against the expansion of a copper smelter plant run by the Sterlite Corporation in Thoothukudi in May 2018, Kanimozhi stood with the bereaved families. An aide, who handles her constituency work, says: 'She is a very soft and dignified person. She feels for people in grief and quietly works behind the scenes to help them.' Kanimozhi remained in touch with the families and once the DMK came to power in Tamil Nadu in 2021, she ensured a government job for the next of kin of all victims. Kanimozhi was pitted against the BJP's state unit president Thamizhisai Soundarajan in the 2019 parliamentary elections. Though Soundarajan put up a fight, she was no match in a state which refused to mirror the national Modi wave in the 2014 and 2019 parliamentary elections.

Kanimozhi has been nurturing the constituency with major impact projects. Since she feels strongly about climate change, Kanimozhi has planned projects like the rejuvenation of water bodies being fed from Thamirabarani River to improve their retaining capacity and removing weeds from lakes by tapping funds under corporate social responsibility (CSR). She has also set up mega water tanks for deficient areas of her constituency and created employment opportunities by training women in making handicrafts from water hyacinth and palm tree climbers. 'We have a lot of educated young people in the constituency as southern Tamil Nadu is known for good education institutions. My constituency is largely rural—agrarian in some parts and some dry land. This is why employment generation is a top of agenda for me,' says Kanimozhi. The enthusiastic MP spends a lot of time in the constituency every week. 'According to my party seniors I spend too much time. I go there every week except when parliament is in session,' she says. Projects on the expansion of roads and the Thoothukudi airport, allowing night landing at the airport, new bridges, and schools are on the anvil.

Her involvement in the constituency is evident on the ground. During the Covid-19 lockdown in June 2020, custodial deaths of a father and son in Sathankulam town near Thoothukudi had triggered protests and anger across the state. The two victims—

father Jeyaraj and son Fenix—used to run a mobile repair shop and had been taken into custody for flouting lockdown rules and keeping the shop running beyond hours. They died in police custody allegedly after torture. The AIADMK government was in power in the state. Kanimozhi reached the home of the victims in her constituency and helped them with the paperwork. Over the following days she donned masks with 'Justice for Jeyaraj and Fenix' and demanded that the FIR mentions the names of the police officers. Her masks triggered a hashtag demanding justice for the family on social media. She wrote to the National Human Rights Commission (NHRC) highlighting the police atrocity and pushing for a probe. The pandemic curbs did not deter Kanimozhi from working in her constituency. When flight operations were suspended, she would travel the 600 kilometres from Chennai to Thoothukudi by road to ensure relief measures were in place in her constituency. She opened a kitchen in her constituency to provide freshly-prepared meals free of cost to the economically weaker sections. During the second wave, when the shortage of oxygen hit Indian hospitals, the centre started exploring the option of reopening shut plants like Sterlite's Thoothukudi copper smelter plant for oxygen production. Kanimozhi had the unenviable task of convincing her constituents that the plant would only reopen for oxygen production. Since it was a highly emotive issue, Kanimozhi travelled to her constituency and met workers and the bereaved families, assuring them that the plant will only reopen for oxygen production and nothing else.

THE DIE-HARD FEMINIST

The soft-spoken, always smiling Kanimozhi has emerged as the DMK's face in Delhi. Unlike Tamil politicians, she is easily accessible to the media. But don't let that affable demeanour fool you. Kanimozhi is known to fight any sexist remark tooth and nail. She is never seen losing her cool inside the parliament but has always made her point emphatically. Senior Janata Dal (United) leader Sharad Yadav, who is known to have made demeaning remarks about women inside the parliament, has also been at the receiving end. On 12 March 2015, during a debate on the government's Insurance Bill in the Rajya Sabha, Yadav said, 'The women of the south are dark but they are as beautiful as their bodies.... We don't see it here. They know dance.... Your god is dark like Ravi Shankar Prasad (present in the house), but your matrmonial ads insist on white-skinned brides,' he said.[8] Kanimozhi immediately got up and objected even as the male MPs began laughing at Yadav's comments. She demanded the remarks be expunged and the MP apologize. Kanimozhi remembers the episode even now and how fellow MPs were trying to pacify her rather than correct Yadav. Ask her if she has ever felt any gender bias inside the parliament and she stuns with her reply, 'Every day.' Despite her family background—her father a five-term chief minister and her stepbrother a serving chief minister—Kanimozhi feels the gender bias is ingrained in people inside and outside the parliament. 'I am a proud feminist. But this doesn't mean that I can't raise other issues. It seems that we are there in parliament and legislatures to raise only women's issues. Yes, we will raise women's issues because they must be raised like many other issues in this country. But why am I getting slotted? Which man gets slotted? Be it parliament or legislative bodies or standing committee meetings, unless the person chairing the meeting is conscious that women should not be denied an opportunity to speak or they should be listened to, nobody takes women politicians seriously. A political party or a house would much rather allow a junior male colleague to speak than a senior woman politician,' says Kanimozhi adding, 'You will be surprised that my political background does not make a difference. Despite my political family background, if I have to go through this then imagine those women who have no such backing.'

Kanimozhi says political parties look towards women MPs when they have to raise gender issues. 'There are so many times we women MPs get up and point out inappropriate or sexist remarks. When a woman MP is speaking, they sometimes say

"This is not the way a woman should be behaving." It is not the parliament alone, it is everywhere. What I wear, what I speak, how I speak, how I sit, how I cry, how I smile, how I relate to my colleagues. Everything has been charted out for women. We have frames for everything,' she says. 'I see it even outside parliament when you work with others within the party or with other political parties. The point I may have made is repeated by a male colleague but in a meeting he is the one who will be heard and acknowledged. Some of our party seniors cannot hear a woman's voice unless it is high and shrill.'

Kanimozhi distinctly remembers the animosity when the Women's Reservation Bill was passed in the Rajya Sabha. 'It was unbelievable. I have never seen such strong emotions and opposition for any other bill,' she says. Since then, the MP has asked the question four times about the status of the bill in the parliament. She gets a standard response each time. 'The government didn't think farm laws needed wider consultations. It didn't think labour code laws needed wider consultations. When it comes to Women's Reservation Bill, a legislation that all political parties say they support, only that needs wider consultations! This is one bill that can be passed with 95 per cent of votes but then why aren't you bringing it even in the list of business. This is a way of men saying that they do not want to share the space where we make laws of the country,' says Kanimozhi. Like most women in politics, Kanimozhi feels reservation is essential for women to get a foot in the door. Increasing the number of tickets given to women can be just a stop gap measure. 'I think it would be better if we reserved seats for women. Every political party has seats which are hopeless and not winnable. The parties will be inclined to field women from there. Then they don't reach the decision-making bodies of legislatures and the parliament.' Kanimozhi brushes aside suggestions that men in the family of elected women representatives wield power by proxy. She takes the example of 33 per cent reservation for women in local bodies. 'The first batch of women representatives who came were not interested in politics. But gradually successive elections have brought forth women leaders at the grassroots. This churning will take place even in legislatures and parliament once the process begins.'

What sets Kanimozhi apart is her zeal for understanding future issues. In December 2021, she initiated a discussion on climate change and its repercussions. She terms it as a climate emergency. 'We do not realize that the time to address climate change is now. It is climate emergency right now,' she says passionately. 'Our oceans are heating up, rains are acidic, forests are burning, sea level is rising, and people are displaced, that is the truth.'

AMPAREEN LYNGDOH

The Torchbearer

When a baby is born in Meghalaya, the neighbours wait eagerly—is it a boy or a girl? As the family announces the birth of a baby girl, there are celebrations all around and a beaming mother rests happy that the family name will now be carried forward. Surprising as it may sound in a largely patriarchal country, the picturesque hill state of Meghalaya in the Northeast India is a matrilineal society. A woman, not her husband, is the head of the household. A man marries a woman and moves into her home and the children carry the name of their mother. The youngest daughter, or khatduh, is the anchor of the family—she inherits the property and shoulders the responsibility of looking after elderly parents and grandparents. Meghalaya reflects a trend rarely witnessed in India—women pray for daughters. The National Family Health Survey 5, 2019–21, data shows that amongst all states Meghalaya has the highest percentage of women (21.2 per cent) who want more daughters than sons. The national average is 3.4 per cent. For a society which cherishes women, one expects to see at least half of the elected members in the state assembly to be women. There are only three women in the sixty-member Meghalaya assembly—that is just 8 per cent of the total elected legislators. The highest number ever elected to the state assembly is four in 2013. 'We are called a matrilineal society but if there is a son he will always be preferred over a daughter,' says Mazel Ampareen Lyngdoh, a National People's Party MLA and minister in several Meghalaya governments.

The fifty-seven-year-old short-haired and fairly-outspoken MLA of the East Shillong assembly constituency personifies the contradictions in Meghalaya's society. At forty-three, Lyngdoh had a late initiation into politics in 2008 when she fought and won the first election. She was the only woman in the assembly from 2008 to 2013.

THE YOUNG MANAGER

Lyngdoh was born into politics. Her father, Peter G. Marbaniang, was an academician, legislator, and a parliamentarian during the 1970s and 1980s. A respected Congress politician, he had represented the Shillong parliamentary constituency in the Lok Sabha from 1989 to 1996. Marbaniang was a progressive and inspiring leader. Patricia Mukhim, a veteran editor of the *Shillong Times* and the journalist who challenged India's controversial sedition law in the Supreme Court in 2021, remembers, 'I was associated with the Congress from 1978 to 1994. I was a school teacher and involved in politics. I would come back from school and just have a cup of tea and during the campaign just rush to take part in election rallies. This is how inspiring Ampareen's father Peter G. Marbaniang was. He was a person of integrity and a born leader.' Marbaniang was a great supporter of women's empowerment. 'He believed that nobody can win elections in Meghalaya without the support of women—women drive and support all campaigns and unlike men do not succumb to bribery.' Lyngdoh's initiation started under him at a very young age. 'I was always surrounded by political activity because of my father. In fact, I was the person who helped him in his constituency work. From the time I was fourteen years, my father would take me everywhere. If somebody died and he was expected to visit and pay condolences or somebody was getting married, I would brief my father on the details and often attend these representing him. My father and I had a close relationship. I was an extension of his mind,' says Lyngdoh.

In Meghalaya, people's representatives start the day very early. Mukhim says that as government infrastructure remains poor the constituents look towards their representatives in the assembly and parliament for help, particularly financial help for buying uniforms, paying college tuition fee, and medical bills. Attached to her father as his young assistant, Lyngdoh would have an early start to the day. 'Every day in the morning my father would start meeting people from his constituency at 7.30 a.m. My father would make me meet them first and understand their problems. I would brief him and then he would spend some time with them,' she says. Quite early on, she started firefighting for him. 'My father had a very short temper so he would often snap at people. I would then go to the families and by noon of the same day I would make amends and say "Don't mind my father. You know he means well." I would patch up many of his messes. I was very connected to his politics,' says Lyngdoh. By the time she was eighteen, she had started giving inputs for his speeches.

Lyngdoh completed her schooling in Shillong and then shifted to New Delhi to enrol in college. She graduated from Jesus and Mary College and then went on to do her postgraduation in mass communication from Jamia Millia Islamia. On her father's insistence she became a member of the Congress-affiliated student's party, the Nationalist Students Union of India (NSUI) and later the Indian Youth Congress (IYC). However, she wasn't politically active during her years in New Delhi. After finishing her postgraduation, she worked with the television channel NDTV and later assisted filmmaker Mike Pandey with his documentaries in New Delhi. She returned to Shillong and started working with Doordarshan Kendra. Lyngdoh got married to one of one of her father's political aides and had two children. Though this seemed like a fairly-settled life, Lyngdoh says she was not enjoying work. 'It was very bureaucratic. We were allowed to do just certain type of programmes. My children were very young then and I remember I had to trek through a forest to get to the Kendra. It was very inconvenient for me. So I quit Doordarshan but I continued making documentary films.' She was offered the post of head of department of mass communication in St Anthony's college, a premier institution in Shillong, and she accepted. She registered for a doctorate around the same time. However, her father passed way in 1997. Being the head of the family, it came upon Lyngdoh's mother to choose Marbaniang's political successor. 'Though my brother Robert was a government servant and nowhere connected to politics, my mother decided that he should take over my father's political work. I accepted her decision,' remembers Lyngdoh.

Robert G. Lyngdoh stepped into politics to carry on the family's political legacy. Robert held important portfolios, including home, in the Meghalaya government. Mukhim terms him the best home minister so far as he brought down militancy in the state. In 2006, Robert had a heart stroke and decided to step away from politics the following year. This was just a year before the 2008 assembly elections. Mukhim says Lyngdoh developed political ambitions at this time, which her mother disapproved of. Lyngdoh says as a family they took a big decision to break this chain of legacy. 'In 2008, we distanced ourselves and a candidate was selected by the Congress from my late father's constituency. People were unhappy with the choice of candidate and were determined to get me into politics. It became a big problem as my brother alongwith the Congress block president had decided that we should allow somebody else to contest,' says Lyngdoh. But she showed immense political cunning unexpected of a greenhorn and contested on a ticket of the United Democratic Party (UDP), a regional party.

Out of the twenty-one women who contested the Meghalaya state assembly election in 2008, only Lyngdoh got elected to the assembly. As has been a hallmark of the smaller states in Northeast India, it was a hung house with no political party getting a simple majority. The Congress was short of one MLA. President's Rule was promulgated in the state and the house was kept in suspended animation. Lyngdoh was at the centre of political wrangling and held the key to government formation in Meghalaya. The Congress managers initiated talks with her, and she was won over with the promise of a cabinet berth—a plum incentive for a first-time MLA fighting her maiden election. Lyngdoh resigned from the UDP and her legislative constituency and fought her election on a Congress ticket. Lyngdoh justifies her actions, seen as political opportunism by her family and party workers, with her personal circumstances. 'There were a lot of pulls and pushes. I was not ready for that kind of situation. I started having doubts and I wondered if I should be leaving my valuable job and my family for politics. By then my husband had deserted me and I was a single parent to two young children. I was very nervous.... Congress Party was one short of an MLA and approached me. So I fought my by-election as a Congress candidate. Then the Congress came to power and since then there has been no turning back,' says Lyngdoh. The Congress rewarded her by giving her the education portfolio in the Meghalaya cabinet. Lyngdoh had managed to make a mark with her eventful political debut.

THE REBELLIOUS LEADER

Lyngdoh says women in politics, especially in the Northeast, have it tough. Her marriage failed as soon as she was called out of her family responsibilities. 'It became very difficult for me to rear my children. Fortunately, I had very close relatives and friends who took care of my children in my absence. Sometimes I would be campaigning, and my friends would take my children to stay with them and even took care of their studies during examinations. It was very difficult. This is why my children went to boarding schools at a very young age—class fourth and fifth. Domestic responsibilities of a woman are a big deterrent for a woman to actually get into active politics,' she says adding, 'Whenever a woman becomes the main bread earner of the family, issues crop up. It is not to do with politics but with every other profession. Of course, all this happened in my life too.'

Her first term as a cabinet minister was marred by what is now known as the White Ink Scam. There are few employment opportunities in Meghalaya and government jobs are even fewer. In December 2008, the deputy inspector of schools advertised for the appointment of assistant teachers in lower primary government schools. About 4,928 candidates applied by January 2009 against 857 vacancies. In December 2009, 1,163 were selected in the first list, including a waitlist, issued by the Directorate of Elementary and Mass Education. Several teachers approached the social rights activist Agnes Kharshiing alleging that their score sheets had been tampered with. Activists Kharshiing and Angela Rangad filed applications under the Right to Information (RTI) Act to access original score sheets of the teachers after interview rounds. The RTI replies from the government revealed white ink pens were used to change marks of the teachers. Kharshiing tried to file an FIR against Lyngdoh alleging that she as minister asked her officials to change the marks. It was a decade-long fight which culminated in the Central Bureau of Investigation (CBI) filing a chargesheet against Lyngdoh and two now-retired education department officials in June 2020. The trial is on going in the District Court in Shillong. Lyngdoh has pleaded innocence and maintained that the law will take its course.

The scam has not deterred Lyngdoh from contesting successive elections in 2013 and 2018 and nurturing her constituency of

East Shillong. Mukhim says, 'Ampareen is a good constituency manager—a politician who takes care of the people at the grassroots. Her constituency East Shillong is considered "the brain of Meghalaya". It has the best educational institutions like St Edmund's College, St Anthony's College, and St Mary's College. It is a largely urban constituency with pockets of very poor people. Ampareen takes care of these people. The health infrastructure in Meghalaya is crumbling. The government hospitals do not have good facilities and people are per force dependent on private healthcare. The result is that they run up huge medical bills but do not have the means to pay them. They therefore approach the MLA who helps them in paying up the bills.' Lyngdoh, who started campaigning for the 2023 assembly elections eighteen months in advance, says between constituency work and campaigning she does not have any time left. 'In a twenty-four-hour day I have to create a forty-eight-hour schedule for myself. I don't have the time to even go and get my hair cut. I don't have time to match my shoes or a jacket with trousers,' she says. But it was more difficult when her children were younger. After her first marriage failed, Lyngdoh remarried. Before the 2018 elections, she had her third child—a daughter. 'In the last election in 2018 she was just born. You won't believe how crazy the campaign was. I was running between home and campaign—I would be feeding her and then going back to campaign and then rushing home again every two and a half hours. By then I was really deep into it and I couldn't give it up. Though it was chaotic I managed with a lot of help,' says Lyngdoh.

Lyngdoh has won elections and become the torchbearer of her father's political legacy. Her margin of victory has increased in every election. But it hasn't been an easy ride. Meghalaya politics has been tumultuous with hung assemblies and cut-throat competition and women politicians opting out. 'Women are never encouraged. Sometimes they can't take the toxic atmosphere and just drop out. It is the cut throat competition where men make it tougher for women to survive. Take the case of former Health Minister Roshan Warjri, who was the state's first woman home minister. Suddenly in 2017, she declared she would not fight any more elections. There were many attempts to finish the political career of Deborah Marak, who was Meghalaya's deputy chief minister. Most women politicians do not survive,' she says. A hung house and coalition governments on wafer-thin majority make it tougher for women politicians. 'Whenever we have a hung house, the lobbying begins. Since there are fewer women elected in any House, especially in northeastern states, there are demands from the people to give women ministerial responsibilities. Elected male representatives are so clearly annoyed. They just don't see that women need to be given some encouragement,' says Lyngdoh, who has also held the urban development portfolio.

THE DRIVING FORCE

Just like her father, Lyngdoh believes that nobody—man or woman—can win an election in the northeastern states without the support of women. 'You will be surprised to know that in northeastern region, any man who wins an election wins because of the women who campaign for him. The problem of alcoholism is rampant among men. So they are not dependable campaigners. In fact, I don't even allow men under the influence of alcohol to be involved in my campaign. Women, on the other hand, are the driving force of any election campaign. They are more dedicated and organized,' says Lyngdoh, who is a champion of women's rights.

Meghalaya, which was carved out of the hill districts of Assam in 1972, is dominated by three tribal groups—Khasi, Garo, and Jaintia. Khasi is the dominant tribe accounting for 48 per cent of the state's population, followed by Garos, and then Jaintias. At the time of introduction of panchayati raj system in India, the union government recognized the traditional political systems of the three tribes. Khasis and Jaintias are governed by two-tier traditional institutions similar to village councils called Dorbar Shnongs, Hima, and Doloi. Garos have a single-tier system in which the headman is called nokma. The traditional institutions are run by adult men with women rarely being involved in decision-making. 'In Meghalaya, people have minimal interface with modern institutions of governance. Our main interaction is with the traditional political institutions called Dorbar Shnongs. They are like panchayats in the rest of India. They look after our immediate civic needs such as water, electricity, and even small infrastructure needs at the local grassroots level,' explains Mukhim. 'The reason why states of Meghalaya and Mizoram were kept out of the purview of 73rd and 74th Constitutional Amendment (which introduced women's reservation in local bodies and empowered the panchayats in India) was because the government of India felt that these northeastern states already have a robust traditional political system which should not be disrupted. The policymakers did not understand that these bodies are patriarchal and have minimal participation of women. The general attitude is that women blabber and they cannot ideate. The oft-repeated line is "When the hen crows then doomsday will follow,"' explains the veteran journalist.

Lyngdoh says these traditional village councils have been overtaken by men. 'Even when women are supposed to head village councils their male representatives take over. Take for instance, nokmas, who are the chief of village councils in Garo Hills. I would travel and see only men nokmas. It was only recently that I met three to four women nokmas in some villages. I asked them and they clarified that nokmas are supposed to be women. This is when I started asking men representatives, "Who is the nokma here? Where is she?" They would reply with standard excuses, "My wife doesn't have time. My wife has to take care of children or tend to the herd. But she has empowered me to come." Of all the nokmas, I think about 85–90 per cent are actually the husbands of the nokmas who have taken over councils in Garo Hills,' says Lyngdoh.

For such an outspoken champion of women's rights, Lyngdoh's orthodox stance on the involvement of women in electing heads of Dorbar Shnongs called 'rangbah shnongs' comes as a surprise. Women rights groups in Meghalaya are fighting for allowing women to elect and be elected as rangbah shnongs. There is a raging debate within the state and the matter is now being heard by the Meghalaya High Court. The Khasi Hills Autonomous District Council (KHADC) told the High Court in April 2022 that it will conduct a referendum to see whether people would choose to elect women as rangbah shnongs. Lyngdoh has toed a very careful line on this. To the pointed question of whether women should be elected as rangbah shnong, the legislator said, 'Personally I do not wish to see women elected as rangbah shnong because that would infringe on customs and practices of the prevailing system that has deep cultural roots. I, however, recommend that our traditional institutions should involve women as active participants in these elections and urge all Dorbar to adapt to the changing times,' Ampareen said.[1] Lyngdoh's careful balancing act on this issue is really because her constituency, which is part of East Khasi Hill district, has a huge voter base of Khasis. Dorbar Shnongs are powerful bodies and influence the electorate's vote. Lyngdoh obviously does not want to antagonize this sizeable votebank which is driven by orthodox traditional institutions.

Mukhim says even if there is a raging debate within the state on women being elected as the head of Dorbar Shnongs, women in villages are not even aware of this issue. 'How do you think they will vote when they are asked to participate in this referendum? The systems in place in traditional political institutions relegating women to the background are steeped in patriarchy and unconstitutional. The Constitution of India treats men and women equal. But even today in modern India there are institutions that do not follow this. Traditional political institutions like Dorbar Shnongs can be a natural springboard to state politics. Involvement of women in the working of Dorbar Shnongs can go a long way in increasing the representation of women in the state assembly,' she says.

This could easily pave the way for more women in Meghalaya politics. The statistics on women's electoral participation in Meghalaya are dismal. In the 1998 assembly elections, fifteen

women contested and three got elected as MLAs. This number fell
further in 2003 when fourteen women contested and two made it
to the assembly. In 2018, thirty-two women contested and three
got elected. The assembly has not seen more than four women
as legislators at one time. While the matrilineal society accepts a
woman heading the family, it still does not encourage its women
in politics. She is not seen as somebody who can take decisions
on serious issues. Mukhim says, 'It is not easy for women in
Meghalaya to foray into politics. Tradition is used as a ruse to
bar women from entering into politics. In fact, I have not seen
a single political party in the Northeast which is headed by a
woman politician. Though Meghalaya is a matrilineal society
with women heading households and children taking the name
of their mother's family, the patriarchal attitude is engrained in
the psyche. The traditional saying in Meghalaya is that a man
has twelve strengths but a woman has only one.... Most of the
women in Meghalaya politics are from political families—wives,
sisters, and daughters of politicians. There is very little space for
independent women with no political background to fight the
assembly elections in the state. The most important factors are
family background in politics, muscle, and money power.' Overall
statistics of women's representation in parliament from the eight
Northeastern states remains dismal—three women were elected
in 2019 and two in 2014 parliamentary elections. Nagaland sent
its first woman MP to the Rajya Sabha in 2022—the seventy-
fifth year of Indian Independence.

Lyngdoh feels that reservation for women in state assemblies
and parliament could hold the key to increasing women's
representation. Though political parties have been reserving
a certain percentage of tickets for women, Lyngdoh says the
Congress had initiated it in Uttar Pradesh, where the party's
electoral chances were not bright. 'Congress was at an all-time
low in UP when this formula was tried. It is not the right time to
push the reservation agenda. Though I highly appreciate Madam
Priyanka Gandhi for being brave to suggest this. But it should
not be misconstrued as the only timing available to try a new

formula. When Congress is popular again and then it takes up this agenda that is when I would think it is truly brave. Right now it seems more like reaching out for support of the women votebank rather than truly increasing women's representation and participation in politics,' she says.

Meghalaya's politics is now witnessing a lot of changes. The Congress saw a sudden exodus to the Trinamool Congress, which has been expanding its footprint in the Northeastern states. In December 2021, 12 out of 17 Congress MLAs joined the Trinamool Congress. Lyngdoh and four others remained behind and decided to tacitly support the incumbent government run by Chief Minister Conrad Sangma of National People's Party (NPP). However, the group of five were suspended by the Congress. Lyngdoh's tilt towards the NPP, which was running the government in alliance with the BJP, became obvious over local issues. She and her group of MLAs decided to support the BJP's presidential candidate Droupadi Murmu in June 2022 and not the Opposition's consensus candidate Yashwant Sinha. Another indication of her changing loyalties came when her sister Dr Jasmine Lyngdoh joined the NPP in February 2022 and was declared as the candidate from Nongthymmai assembly constituency. Her brother Robert lost his battle to cancer in July 2022. In December 2022, Lyngdoh joined the NPP and was declared the party's spokesperson and the candidate from her East Shillong constituency. She won the election in March 2023 polling 38.96 per cent of the votes and found a place in Sangma's cabinet for the crucial portfolios of health and family welfare, information and public relations, law and agriculture, and farmers welfare. With Lyngdoh's grasp on the electorate, the party symbol for her has been immaterial—she is the torchbearer in Meghalaya.

EPILOGUE

Mehboob Sayyadlal Pansare greets you outside Jejuri railway station, about 50 kilometres from Pune. It is almost 10 p.m. and Pansare explains in detail why the famous temple town of Maharashtra needs more train stoppages. Then he insists you have tea and meet his wife. Pansare's home, just a few steps away from the railway station, stands out. It is a two-storey house built tastefully. You sit in the opulent living room as he explains the political situation in the Jejuri Nagar Palika and how the Nationalist Congress Party (NCP) and the Congress are placed. His party NCP holds sway in the Nagar Palika, he says. His wife enters with a tray and offers glasses of water. 'My wife—Amina Mehboob. She is Nagar Sevika—the Jejuri councillor,' says Pansare. Amina gently enquires if the journey from Pune was gruelling. She says if more trains stopped at Jejuri station women and elderly people would not be inconvenienced when they came to worship at Khandoba temple. She says a recently-constructed toilet complex has been a blessing. Amina's introduction sums up the common trajectory of an Indian woman politician's career.

Politics is an unusual career choice for an Indian woman. She steps into this field, so far a preserve of men, only if she is a politician's wife, sister, or daughter. It is a rarity to see women with no political family background choosing politics as a career option. If they have done so and carved a niche for themselves, they have never made gender an overarching part of their political identity or rhetoric. Be it Indira Gandhi or Margaret Thatcher, women leaders have made it in a man's world without wearing gender on their sleeve. In his exhaustive biography of Margaret Thatcher, *One of Us*, Hugo Young writes, 'What is certainly not disputable is the reluctance of this controlled and controlling woman to treat women, politically, as any different from men.

She was against this on principle, apparently seeing nothing in her own rise to power which might prompt her to single women out for special attention, or consciously single out herself and her sex and the special effects this might have on her political strategy. Women as a separate category of voters were not of special interest.... A woman whom some fondly expected to give women and their advancement priority in fact did exactly the opposite. Although she had always had a job herself, whether working for Joe Lyons or reading for the Bar or becoming an MP, she led no sort of crusade for others to do the same. Before she got anywhere in politics, she was, as we have seen, strident in her assertion that women were as entitled as men to succeed in public life. She was saying this as early as 1952. When she had reached the top, a change came over the balance of her rhetoric. She became a lot more ready to praise the Conservative model of the housewife and mother. As for positive discrimination or anything which smacked of feminism, she was derisive.'

From the street politics of Mamata Banerjee to the rough and tumble of Mayawati's political journey in Uttar Pradesh— the leaders have been inspirations for younger women but have jostled with men for space and relevance on an even keel. It is beneath them to play the 'helpless woman' card. But at the same time they have struggled against the biases of a patriarchal society. The common refrain is that the easiest way to pull them down is to assassinate their characters, especially by suggesting they have used their looks to fast forward their way up the hierarchy within their political outfit and government.

We expect the parliament and legislative assemblies to be fairer work places. However, women politicians say representative bodies are a reflection of our patriarchal society and cannot be expected to remain indifferent to the biases ingrained over decades. Former Congress MP and India's first woman and child development minister, Renuka Chowdhury, recalls two exchanges in the Rajya Sabha dating back to 2018 to convey what women parliamentarians have to 'grin and bear'—something that their male counterparts never have to. The first one was in February

2018 when Chowdhury was laughing loudly while Prime Minister
Narendra Modi was speaking in the Rajya Sabha. When she
continued even after being ticked off by the Rajya Sabha chairman
and then Vice-president M. Venkaiah Naidu, Modi said he hadn't
got the opportunity to hear such laughs since the time of the
serial *Ramayana* (which aired in the 1980s). In April 2018, in
her farewell speech in the Rajya Sabha, Chowdhury said, 'He
(Naidu) knows me from many kilos before. Sir, many people
worry about my weight but in this job, you need to throw your
weight around.' Naidu replied, 'My simple suggestion is, reduce
your weight and make efforts to increase the weight of your
party.' The two exchanges triggered a debate on the misogynist
comments that women MPs face. 'I did not react then as I did
not want my farewell speech to be about this exchange,' says
Chowdhury. But fellow MP Jaya Bachchan took an exception
to this. She said, 'I don't speak as much in parliament unless
I am very angry. Living with someone who is only angry on
screen, and not otherwise, has worked on me. We hear a lot of
"wonderful" language in the august house that we represent. It
is embarrassing...it is not embarrassing when you hear it, but
it is when you know that men in our country have not been
educated, which is why they use the kind of language that they
do. They don't have the knowledge and they don't know how
to respect women.'[1] Jaya Bachchan was at the receiving end
of such a comment from Naresh Agarwal, who had joined the
BJP and lost out to her. He had said, 'I have been compared
with those who dance and work in films.'

In the same year, then New Zealand Prime Minister Jacinda
Ardern made history as the first world leader to attend the
United Nations General Assembly with her three-month-old
daughter Neve. While she gave her speech at the Nelson Mandela
Peace Summit, her partner held Neve beside her. Though Ardern
had taken just a six-week maternity break for Neve, she had
continued to breastfeed her daughter and had to carry her to
the UNGA. When interviewed for this book, the women leaders
had similar tales to share. Some of them wished they had the

courage shown by Ardern and the acceptance shown towards her by the international community. Such gestures can change women's integration in politics, and the workforce at large. Chowdhury, for instance, carried her three-month-old daughter to party meetings when she was breastfeeding. So, when she was assigned the women and child development ministry she opened a crèche in Shastri Bhawan. 'Once I went for a visit and saw women officers, women police constables, and even workers in Shastri Bhawan bringing their children there. Not everyone has a family support system,' says Chowdhury.

These experiences give women policymakers an advantage over men. While Amina Mehboob Pansare epitomizes the argument against reserving seats for women, her concerns reflected in a ten-minute conversation show why we need more women in decision-making and representative bodies. Women bring a sensitivity to policy-making which is unique. Affirmative action to have more women in parliament and in governance is the need of the hour. There may or may not be more Amina Pansares, but by the second or third election, women will emerge as leaders.

ACKNOWLEDGEMENTS

In the summer of 2020, right after the devastating second wave of Covid-19, my friend and former colleague at the *Economic Times*, M. Rajshekhar, called to check on me. What started as a normal catch-up conversation turned into him nudging me towards book writing. 'Write now,' he said quite convincingly. If there were any doubts, they were settled by my school friend and author Puja Mehra who said, 'You have a book in you.' And that set me on this long and arduous journey of exploring my first book.

The groundwork for the book was done during the Covid-19 outbreak. It was a difficult time to travel and persuade people to meet you. Despite this, women leaders graciously opened their homes and hearts to share their political journey. I am thankful to those who spent hours, sometimes behind the uncomfortable N-95 masks, to share personal anecdotes.

Writing a book requires a lot of patience—not just on the part of the author but more so of the people around them. This journey would not have been possible without the critical insights of my first reader—my husband, Joydeep Roy, who has always believed in me more than I ever can. My sister, Aparajita Sharma, who painstakingly went through the manuscript to introduce Oxford commas and proved how she will always be more meticulous. As I got down to writing, my genial mother-in-law Meena Roy took care of our family. But the surprising cooperation came from my children Agastya and Avni, who gave me the peace and quiet to write.

I remain thankful to my friends Ajay Singh, Ambika Pandit, Anita Joshua, Bhavna Vij Aurora, Dr Geetanjali Nanda, Nitika Verma, Priyanka Chaturvedi, Renuka Puri, Seema Gupta Saksena, Soni Mishra, Urvashi S. Pathak, Utpal Borpujari, and Vasudha Venugopal who became my sounding boards, midnight calls, and unsuspecting guinea pigs. My editors at the *Economic Times*—executive editor Bodhisatva Ganguli and associate executive editor Pranab Dhal Samanta—have been constant sources of support and encouragement. I am grateful to many others who enriched the book with their insights and off-record conversations and have chosen to remain in the shadows.

Much of the book shaped up in the peaceful Nehru Memorial Museum and Library. As I made NMML my home for months, Dr Ajit Kumar and his efficient team ensured a steady and timely flow of books, documents and photocopies.

My heartfelt appreciation for my publisher David Davidar who saw the potential of a political book. This book would not have been possible without the support of my editor, Aienla Ozukum, and members of her team—Vidisha Ghosh and Karishma Koshal.

PHOTO CREDITS

The photographs in this book have been sourced from the following people or organizations:

Indira Gandhi (p. 3): Wikimedia Commons

Sucheta Kripalani (p. 34): Nehru Memorial Museum and Library

Sonia Gandhi (p. 55): Media Department, All India Congress Committee

J. Jayalalithaa (p. 81): Shekhar Yadav/The India Today Group via Getty Images

Vasundhara Raje (p. 99): Vasundhara Raje Archives

Sheila Dikshit (p. 115): Sandeep Dikshit

Mayawati (p. 140): Sonu Mehta/*Hindustan Times* via Getty Images

Pratibha Patil (p. 165): Office of Pratibha Patil

Sushma Swaraj (p. 185): Sushma Swaraj's family

Mamata Banerjee (p. 208): Debajyoti Chakraborty/NurPhoto via Getty Images

Brinda Karat (p. 230): Nidhi Sharma

Ambika Soni (p. 246): Wikimedia Commons

Smriti Z. Irani (p. 269): Prerna Sodhi

Supriya Sule (p. 288): Official website of Supriya Sule

Kavitha Kalvakuntla (p. 305): Office of Kavitha Kalvakuntla

Kanimozhi Karunanidhi (p. 320): Office of Kanimozhi Karunanidhi

Ampareen Lyngdoh (p. 334): Office of Ampareen Lyngdoh

NOTES

INTRODUCTION

1. 'India-Key Indicators', *National Family Health Survey (NFHS-5) 2019-21*, New Delhi: Ministry of Health and Family Welfare.
2. Jawaharlal Nehru, *Letters to Chief Ministers*, Volume 3, New Delhi: Oxford University Press, 1988.
3. Gargi Chakravarty, Supriya Chotani, *Charting A New Path: Early Years of National Federation of Indian Women*, New Delhi: People's Publishing House, 2014, p. 21.
4. *Constituent Assembly Debates*, Volume I, New Delhi: Lok Sabha Secretariat, 2014.
5. Ibid., Volume V.
6. Ibid., Volume I.
7. Ibid., Volume X.
8. The committee included Phulrenu Guha, Maniben Kara, Savitri Shyam, Neera Dogra, Vikram Mahajan, Leela Dube, Sakina A. Hasan, Urmila Haksar, Lotika Sarkar, and Vina Mazumdar. Committee on the Status of Women, 'Towards Equality', New Delhi: Ministry of Education and Social Welfare', 1974.
9. Committee on the Status of Women, 'Towards Equality', New Delhi: Ministry of Education and Social Welfare', 1974, p. 290.
10. Ibid.
11. Ibid., p. 203.
12. Later, a similar recommendation was made by the Ashok Mehta committee in 1978.
13. Interview with T. R. Raghunandan.
14. National Perspective Plan for Women (1988–2000), pp. 164–65.
15. Bhajan Lal held the agriculture portfolio from February 1988 to December 1989.
16. Interview with Mani Shankar Aiyar.
17. Interview with Renuka Chowdhury.
18. Interview with Sanjay Kumar.
19. Study conducted by the Centre for the Study of Developing Societies.

INDIRA GANDHI

1. Pupul Jayakar, *Indira Gandhi: A Biography*, New Delhi: Penguin Books India, 1992, p. 17.
2. Zareer Masani, *Indira Gandhi: A Biography*, London: Hamish Hamilton, 1975, p. 37.

3. *Navjivan*, 30 March 1950.
4. Jayakar, *Indira Gandhi*, p. 36.
5. 'Mrs. Indira Gandhi in conversation with Arnold Michaelis Part 1', April 1966, The Walter J. Brown Media Archives & Peabody Awards Collection.
6. Jayakar, *Indira Gandhi*, p. 137.
7. Masani, *Indira Gandhi*, p. 103.
8. Feroze had risen in the Lok Sabha and directly asked Krishnamachari if the newly-nationalized Life Insurance Corporation had used the premium payments of 5,500,000 life insurance policy shareholders to buy shares at above-market prices in companies controlled by the stock speculator Haridas Mundhra. Krishnamachari had denied it but a judicial inquiry instituted by Nehru had revealed all charges to be true leading to the finance minister's resignation and Mundhra's arrest.
9. Trevor Drieberg, *Indira Gandhi: A Profile in Courage*, New Delhi: Vikas Publications, 1972, p. 38.
10. Ibid.
11. Nayantara Sahgal, *Indira Gandhi: Tryst with Power*, New Delhi: Penguin Books, 2012.
12. Ibid.
13. Drieberg, *Indira Gandhi*, p. 41.
14. Jayakar, *Indira Gandhi*, p. 158.
15. Sahgal, *Indira Gandhi*.
16. Drieberg, *Indira Gandhi*, p. 46.
17. K. A. Abbas, *Indira Gandhi: Return of the Red Rose*, Pune: Popular Prakashan, 1966, p. 13.
18. Interview during Mauritius visit 1976, Prasar Bharati Archives.
19. Inder Malhotra, *Indira Gandhi: A Personal and Political Biography*, London: Hodder & Stoughton, 1989, p. 83.
20. Drieberg, *Indira Gandhi*, p. 55.
21. Abbas, *Indira Gandhi*, pp. 138–39.
22. *The Years of Challenge: Selected Speeches of Indira Gandhi (January 1966– August 1969)*, New Delhi: Publications Division, Ministry of Information and Broadcasting, Government of India, 1971.
23. Malhotra, *Indira Gandhi*, p. 95.
24. Ibid, p. 99.
25. Sahgal, *Indira Gandhi*.
26. Jayakar, *Indira Gandhi*, p. 226.
27. Ibid., p. 237.
28. Ibid., p. 252.
29. Pranab Mukherjee, *The Dramatic Decade: The Indira Gandhi Years*, Rupa Publications, 2015.
30. Ibid.

31. Ibid.
32. Sahgal, *Indira Gandhi*.
33. Ibid.
34. Jayakar, *Indira Gandhi*.
35. Richard M. Weintraub, 'Parliament Expels Grandhi, Orders Her to Delhi Jail Cell', *Washington Post*, 20 December 1978.
36. Kuldip Nayar, *Beyond The Lines: An Autobiography*, New Delhi: Roli Books, 2012, p. 282.
37. *The Years of Challenge: Selected Speeches of Indira Gandhi (January 1966–August 1969)*.
38. Abbas, *Indira Gandhi*, pp. 106–07.

SUCHETA KRIPALANI

1. Sucheta Kripalani, *Sucheta: An Unfinished Autobiography*, Ahmedabad: Navajivan Trust, 1978, p. 7.
2. Ibid., p. 16.
3. Ibid., pp. 20–21
4. Ibid., p. 21.
5. Interview to Uma Shanker, Centre of South Asian Studies at the University of Cambridge, available at: <https://www.s-asian.cam.ac.uk/archive/audio/collection/s-kripalani/>, last accessed on 10 May 2023.
6. Ibid.
7. Ibid.
8. Ibid.
9. Ibid.
10. Ibid.
11. Kripalani, *Sucheta*, pp. 51–52.
12. Interview to Uma Shanker.
13. Acharya Kripalani, 'In Memoriam', in Kripalani, *Sucheta*, pp. 16–17.
14. Interview to Uma Shanker.
15. Interview to Uma Shanker.
16. Acharya Kripalani, 'Chief Ministership Ends', in Kripalani, *Sucheta*, p. 224.
17. Personal papers of Sucheta Kripalani, Nehru Memorial Museum Library, New Delhi.
18. Kripalani, 'Chief Ministership Ends', in Kripalani, *Sucheta*, p. 225.
19. Sucheta Kripalani, 'Women: Past, Present and Future', in Verinder Grover and Ranjana Arora (eds.), *Great Women of Modern India*, New Delhi: Deep & Deep Publications, 1993.
20. Ibid.

SONIA GANDHI

1. Vir Sanghvi, 'Party has right to raise issues: Sonia', *Hindustan Times*, 27 October 2006.
2. K. Natwar Singh, *One Life is Not Enough: An Autobiography*, New Delhi: Rupa Publications, 2014, p. 139.
3. Vaiju Naravane, 'In Maino Country', *Frontline*, 25 April 1998.
4. Rupa Chatterjee, *Sonia Gandhi: The Lady in Shadow*, New Delhi: Butala Publishers, 1999, p. 6.
5. Ibid., p. 9.
6. Shekhar Gupta, 'Walk the Talk: Interview with Sonia Gandhi', *NDTV*, February 2004.
7. Chatterjee, *Sonia Gandhi*, p. 36.
8. Gupta, 'Walk the Talk'.
9. Chatterjee, *Sonia Gandhi*, p. 65.
10. Ibid., pp. 102–03.
11. Singh, *One Life is Not Enough*, p. 288.
12. Shankar Dayal Sharma, who was seventy-three years old then, refused on age and health grounds. He went on to serve as the president of India from 1992 to 1997.
13. Inder Malhotra, 'Rear View: How Sonia took over Congress', *Indian Express*, 21 September 2015.
14. Ibid.
15. Rasheed Kidwai, *Sonia: A Biography*, New Delhi: Penguin Books, 2003.
16. 'Sonia Gandhi steps into Indian politics', *BBC News*, 11 January 1998.
17. Gupta, 'Walk the Talk'.
18. Interview with Aroon Purie at the India Today Conclave 2018.
19. After about eighteen months, Sonia gave way to the low-profile Gujarat politician Ahmed Patel, who became the Congress and later UPA's chief troubleshooter, engaging with difficult allies and bringing the party out of several crises. After Rahul became the Congress president, Gandhi persuaded Patel to take over as party's treasurer, a post he retained till his death in 2020 due to Covid-related complications.
20. Kidwai, *Sonia*, p. 158.
21. Ibid., p. 89.
22. Then BJP president Bangaru Laxman was caught on camera accepting bribe to influence defence deals.
23. UTI scam of 2001 saw a safe public investment instrument called US-64 sinking and UTI refusing to pay its investors.
24. The July 2001 summit between Pakistan's President Pervez Musharraf and Vajpayee was the latter's attempt to solve the Kashmir issue and sign a treaty. The talks broke down, and no agreement could be signed
25. 'BJP Attacks Sonia', *The Tribune*, 8 September 1999.

26. Ibid.
27. Atal Behari Vajpayee, 'Who Started The Fire?', *Outlook*, April 2002.
28. G. Vinayak, 'PM lashes out when he loses "his mental balance": Sonia', *Rediff.in*, 13 April 2002.
29. 'Our tunes can never match: Sonia to PM', *Zee News India*, 16 September 2003.
30. 'Sonia Gandhi's roadshow in Vidarbha', *Zee News India*, 2 April 2004.
31. Deepshika Ghosh, 'Sonia Gandhi On Difference Between PM Modi and Atal Bihari Vajpayee', *NDTV*, 9 March 2018.
32. In its second avatar, NAC's new team included others M. S. Swaminathan, Mihir Shah, and Narendra Jadhav.
33. An independent inquiry had been instituted under Paul A. Volcker to investigate into financial misappropriation in the oil-for-food programme, which was established in 1995. The programme allowed Iraq, which was facing world sanctions, to sell oil in the world market in exchange for essential items, including food and medicines.
34. Shah Bano, a Muslim lady, had taken her husband, a prominent Indore lawyer, to court demanding maintenance for herself and her five children. The husband had contested the claim on the ground that Muslim Personal Law in India required the husband to pay maintenance for the iddat period of ninety days after divorce. The Supreme Court had ruled in favour of Shah Bano, but Rajiv's government brought a law to overturn the verdict.
35. Interview with Mani Shankar Aiyar.
36. Lok Sabha debates, Discussion on the motion of no-confidence in the Council of Ministers, 18 August 2003.
37. PTI, 'My mother cried, she understands power is poison: Rahul', *The Hindu*, 20 January 2013.
38. Manoj C. G., '23 senior Congress leaders stand up, write to Sonia Gandhi calling for sweeping changes', *Indian Express*, 24 August 2020.

J. JAYALALITHAA
1. Aishwarya S. Iyer, 'In 1978, Jayalalithaa Wrote to Clarify the "Truth About her Life"', *The Quint*, 4 December 2017.
2. Vaasanthi, *Amma: Jayalalithaa's Journey from Movie Star to Political Queen*, New Delhi: Juggernaut Books, 2016, pp. 32–33.
3. Bhagwan R. Singh, 'She Writes to Conquer', *The Week*, 22 January 1984.
4. Vaasanthi, *Amma*, 2016.
5. Ibid., pp. 57–58.
6. S. H. Venkatramani and Prabhu Chawla, 'Tamil Nadu: Janaki Government's Foundations Cave in', 15 February 1988.
7. T. S. Subramanian, 'Jayalalithaa's Legacy', *Frontline*, 21 December 2016.

8. G. C. Shekhar, Jayalalithaa's foster son married off amid extravagance and controversy, *India Today*, 30 September 1995.
9. T. S. Subramanian, 'The Return of Jayalalithaa', *Frontline*, 26 May 2001.
10. Karnataka high court acquitted Jayalalithaa and the other three accused in May 2015. In February 2017, two months after Jayalalithaa's death, the Supreme Court overturned the acquittal and convicted all four accused.
11. PTI, 'Jayalalithaa's Ministers Give Away Free Laptops, Fans, Grinders, Mixies', *India TV*, 16 September 2011.
12. A. Mahendran, S. Indrakant, 'How Tamil Nadu's Amma Canteen scheme stood the test of time', *Down to Earth*, 5 July 2021.
13. Ibid.
14. In February 2016, she expanded the scheme to Amma Kudineer Thittam for supplying twenty litres of drinking water per family per day to those who could not afford to buy purified water.
15. Lakshmi Subramania, 'My Life with Jayalalithaa: V K Sasikala', *The Week*, 18 July 2021.
16. Ibid.
17. Ibid.
18. 'Jayalalithaa's death probe | Arumughaswamy Commission indicts Sasikala, Vijayabaskar and two others', *The Hindu*, 22 October 2022.

VASUNDHARA RAJE

1. Vijaya Raje Scindia and Manohar Malgonkar, *Princess: The Autobiography of the Dowager Maharani Gwalior*, New Delhi, Century Publishing, 1985, p. 246.
2. The Economic Policy and Reforms Council transformed into the Chief Minister's Advisory Council in Raje's second term (2013–18). It had sub-groups examining different core areas.
3. Alam Srinivas, 'Rise and fall: In Lalit Modi's never-ending brawls, some wins and many losses', *Scroll.in*, 18 June 2015.
4. Smita Gupta, 'Out of the Premier League', *Outlook*, February 2009.
5. Ibid.
6. Rasheed Kidwai, *The House of Scindias: A Saga of Power, Politics and Intrigue*, New Delhi: Roli Books, 2021, pp. 124–25.
7. Rohit Parihar, 'How Vasundhara Raje's birthday event turned into a show of strength', *India Today*, March 2022.

SHEILA DIKSHIT

1. Sheila Dikshit, *Citizen Delhi: My Times, My Life*, New Delhi: Bloomsbury India, 2018, p. 13.
2. Ibid., p. 17.
3. Interview with Sandeep Dikshit.

4. Dikshit, *Citizen Delhi*, p. 116.
5. Ibid., pp. 126–27.
6. Interview with Shailaja Chandra
7. Interview with Ramesh Chandra.
8. TNN, 'CAG report points out glaring financial GAPS', *Times of India*, 5 August 2004.
9. 'Manufactured Chaos: How the Delhi government evaded the Supreme Court order on CNG to engineer a state of anarchy?', *Down to Earth*, 30 April 2001.
10 Interview with Sindhushree Khullar.
11. Dikshit, *Citizen Delhi*, p. 132.
12. Ibid., p. 142.
13. Ibid., p. 143.
14. Ibid., p. 146.
15 Interview with Haroon Yusuf.
16. Dikshit, *Citizen Delhi*, p. 154.
17. Ibid., p. 155.
18. Ibid., p. 164.
19. Ibid.

MAYAWATI

1. Interview with author.
2. Personal interview with a senior leader.
3. Vidya Subrahmaniam, 'From Emergency to Now: The Wide Arc of a Hack's Ideological Journey', *The Hindu Centre for Public Policy*, 25 July 2015.
4. Shekhar Gupta, 'Witnessing the rise of Kanshi Ram, the man who first created Dalit politics', *The Print*, 7 January 2018.
5. Ajoy Bose, *Behenji: The Rise and Fall of Mayawati*, New Delhi: Penguin Books, 2008, pp. 71–72.
6. Ibid., p. 72.
7. Mayawati, *Mere Sangharshmay Jeevan Evam Bahujan Movement ka Safarnama*, Volume 2, New Delhi: Bahujan Samaj Party, p. 90.
8. Anil Swarup, *Ethical Dilemmas of a Civil Servant*, New Delhi: Unique Publishers, 2020.
9. Kulsum Mustafa, 'Kalyan Good, Mulayam Grounded And Mayawati Greedy Like None...Bureaucrat Of 38 Years Tells All!', *News Agency*,
10. Rahul Shrivastava, 'BSP has never promoted dynastic politics', *NDTV*, 19 May 2007.
11. Vivek Kumar, 'Behind the BSP victory', *Economic & Political Weekly*, 16 June 2007.
12. Shekhar Gupta, 'Walk the Talk: Mayawati', *NDTV*, May 2005.

13. Rahul Shrivastava, 'BSP has never promoted dynastic politics', *NDTV*, 19 May 19, 2007.
14. Venkitesh Ramakrishnan, 'A New Caste Formula', *Frontline*, 1 July 2005.

PRATIBHA PATIL
1. Jayanth Jacob, 'Presidential election: How UPA came up with Pratibha Patil's name in 2007', *Hindustan Times*, 27 June 2017.
2. Ritu Sarin, 'Probe how bank was sold dirt cheap, file criminal case: order came in April', *Indian Express*, 30 June 2007.
3. TNN, 'Pratibha Patil ignites a row over purdah', *Times of India*, 19 June 2007.
4. TNN, 'Know Patil better: BJP puts up website', *Times of India*, 11 July 2007.
5. HT Correspondent, 'Pratibha Patil most merciful Prez in 30 years', 22 February 2012.
6. PTI, 'President Pratibha Patil's foreign trips cost record ₹205 cr', *NDTV*, 25 March 2012.
7. Vinita Deshmukh, 'President Pratibha Patil grabs 2,61,000 sq ft of land meant for soldiers and officers', *Moneylife*, 11 April 2012.
8. TNN, 'Controversial Khadki bungalow turns into institute for soldiers', *Times of India*, 12 August 2017.
9. 'Patil shifted 150 gifts to Amravati museum', *Indian Express*, 4 August 2012.

SUSHMA SWARAJ
1. Interview with author.
2. In conversation with journalists.
3. Ajay Kumar Pandey, 'When Sushma Swaraj kept audience seated the whole night in 1977', 8 August 2019.
4. He mentioned this in conversations with reporters (including me). More recently, his aide Deepak Chopra corroborated the same to me (mentioned later); 'I'm more of a blogger now than political activist, says Advani', *TwoCircles.net*, 12 July 2013.
5. Political resolution, National Executive of the Bharatiya Janata Party, 9–11 June 1989.
6. Swaraj Kaushal was nominated in August 1998 and retired on 1 August 2004.
7. Sumit Pande, 'Remembering Sushma Swaraj, The BJP Leader Who Could Never Say No to Her Party', *News18*, 7 August 2018.
8. *Women Members of Rajya Sabha*, New Delhi, Rajya Sabha Secretariat, 2003, p. 129.
9. PTI, 'Pak decision to release Hamid Nihal Ansari due to pressure from New Delhi: official sources', *Times of India*, 17 December 2018.

10. 'Helped Lalit Modi on humanitarian ground: Sushma Swaraj', *India Today*, 17 June 2015.
11. Utkarsh Anand, 'Sushma Swaraj's daughter part of Lalit Modi's legal team in passport case', *Indian Express*, 15 June 2015.
12. Anita Katyal, 'Everyone in the BJP and RSS turns out to defend Sushma Swaraj – except Arun Jaitley', *Scroll.in*, 15 June 2015.
13. Archis Mohan, 'How Sushma Swaraj helped Modi get his Pak groove back', *Business Standard*, 28 December 2015.
14. Archis Mohan, 'How Sushma Swaraj helped Modi get his groove back', *Business Standard*, 28 December 2015.

MAMATA BANERJEE
1. The interviewee did not wish to be identified.
2. Mamata Banerjee, *My Unforgettable Memories*, translated from Bengali by Nandini Sengupta, New Delhi: Roli Books, 2012, p. 29.
3. Ibid., p. 66.
4. Interview with author.
5. Banerjee, *My Unforgettable Memories*, p. 76.
6. Ibid., p. 64.
7. Ibid., pp. 79–80.
8. Banerjee, *My Unforgettable Memories*, p. 120.
9. Swagata Sen, 'Singur, Nandigram land troubles bring Buddhadeb's West Bengal govt in focus', *India Today*, 22 January 2007.
10. Mahato joined Trinamool Congress in 2020.
11. Sen, 'Singur, Nandigram land troubles bring Buddhadeb's West Bengal govt in focus'.
12. 'Knew Mahato, but no link with Maoists: Mamata', *Indian Express*, 21 June 2009.
13. Monobina Gupta, *Didi: A Political Biography*, New Delhi: HarperCollins India, 2012.

BRINDA KARAT
1. The constitutional validity of the legislation was challenged by Danial Latifi, Shah Bano's lawyer, in a writ petition in 1986. The Supreme Court verdict in 2001 is considered a path-breaking one in which the court has upheld the law while upholding the Muslim women's rights.

AMBIKA SONI
1. The Indian Youth Congress' five-point programme included tree plantation, the educational programme, 'Each One Teach One', family planning to implement the government's 'Hum Do Hamaare Do' campaign, and campaigns against the dowry system and caste system

2. Coomi Kapoor, *The Emergency: A Personal History*, New Delhi: Penguin Random House India, 2015.
3. Ibid.
4. Sunil Sethi, 'Emergency: A traumatic experience that taught India the virtues of democracy', *India Today*, 1 April 1977.
5. Ibid.
6. TNN, 'Antony, Dasmunsi only top Cong leaders to openly criticize Sanjay: US Cables', *India Today*, 10 April 2013.
7. 'Where are all the political superstars and glamour girls of yesterday?', *India Today*, 15 January 1978.
8. Sharad Pawar, *On My Terms: From the Grassroots to the Corridors of Power*, New Delhi: Speaking Tiger Publishing, 2015, p. 155.
9. Ibid.
10. PTI, 'No evidence to prove existence of Ram, Centre to SC', *Rediff.com*, 12 September 2007.

SMRITI Z. IRANI
1. Rohini Mohan, 'Role of a Lifetime: The Unsteady Rise of Smriti Irani', *The Caravan*, 1 November 2016.
2. Barkha Dutt, 'The Buck Stops Here: Smriti Irani', *NDTV*, 26 May 2016.
3. Ritika Chopra, 'Prakash Javadekar does what Smriti Irani didn't: Agrees to free IIMs via new Bill', *Indian Express*, 8 October 2016.
4. Anant Vijay, *Dynasty to Democracy: The Untold Story of Smriti Irani's Triumph*, New Delhi: Westland Books, 2021, p. 57.
5. Ibid., p. 57.
6. Ibid., pp. 78–79.
7. Ibid., p. 46.

SUPRIYA SULE
1. Sharad Pawar, *On My Terms: From the Grassroots to the Corridors of Power*, New Delhi: Speaking Tiger Books, 2015, p. 1.
2. Ibid., p. 4.
3. Ibid., p. 10.
4. 'Marriage ceremony displays Sharad Pawar's strength', *India Today*, 31 March 1991.
5. 'Pawar's daughter fights IPL allegations', *NDTV*, 22 April 2010.
6. Ibid.
7. 'Hill City Lavasa, Sharad Pawar's dream project near Pune, loses special status', *India Today*, 26 June 2017.
8. Ibid.

9. 'HC refuses to interfere in plea against Lavasa hill city citing "gross delay"', *Indian Express*, 26 February 2022.

KAVITHA KALVAKUNTLA

1. There is a demand for a turmeric board, separate from the Spices Board of India, as it could help in production, processing and marketing of turmeric in the region.

KANIMOZHI KARUNANIDHI

1. In 2019, the Tamil Nadu government decided to replace 'Thirunangai' with the term 'Moondram Palanithavar' in all official references, a move which drew flak from transgender community and rights activists.
2. Karunanidhi had a son Muthu with his first wife, three sons M. K. Alagiri, M. K. Stalin, M. K. Tamilarasu, and a daughter, M. K. Selvi, with his second wife Dayalu Ammal.
3. Sandhya Ravishankar, *Karunanidhi: A Life in Politics*, New Delhi: HarperCollins India, 2019, p. 184.
4. Ibid., pp. 184–85.
5. 'DMK leaders recall MK's arrest in 2001, term it unforgettable', *DT Next*, 1 July 2021.
6. In February 2012, the Supreme Court cancelled 122 licences issued to eight companies by A. Raja. Seven of the eight companies could not survive the shock and dissolved.
7. In March 2018, the investigative agencies filed appeals in Delhi high court against the trial court verdict.
8. Karthick S., 'Sharad Yadav's remarks on south Indian women reveal the attitude of several people, Kanimozhi says', *Times of India*, 13 March 2015.

AMPAREEN LYNGDOH

1. 'Reluctance galore on women leading Dorbar Shnong', *Shillong Times*, 25 April 2022.

www.ingramcontent.com/pod-product-compliance
Lightning Source LLC
Chambersburg PA
CBHW030906070526
44654CB00030B/390/J